THE LIVES OF CONN SMYTHE

KELLY McPARLAND

THE LIVES OF
CONN SMYTHE

FENN
M&S

LIBRARY AND ARCHIVES CANADA CATALOGUING IN PUBLICATION

McParland, Kelly
    The lives of Conn Smythe : from the battlefield to Maple Leaf Gardens : a hockey icon's story / Kelly McParland.

ISBN 978-0-7710-5683-3

    1. Smythe, Conn, 1895-1980. 2. Toronto Maple Leafs (Hockey team) – Biography. 3. Hockey team owners – Canada – Biography.
4. Soldiers – Canada – Biography. 5. Hockey – Canada – Biography.
I. Title.

GV848.5.S69M46 2011   796.962092   C2011-905555-4

We acknowledge the financial support of the Government of Canada through the Book Publishing Industry Development Program and that of the Government of Ontario through the Ontario Media Development Corporation's Ontario Book Initiative. We further acknowledge the support of the Canada Council for the Arts and the Ontario Arts Council for our publishing program.

Image on p. ii © Hockey Hall of Fame

Published simultaneously in the United States of America by McClelland & Stewart Ltd., P.O. Box 1030, Plattsburgh, New York 12901

Library of Congress Control Number: 2011935277

Typeset in Stempel Garamond by M&S, Toronto
Printed and bound in the United States of America

FENN/McClelland & Stewart Ltd.
75 Sherbourne Street
Toronto, Ontario
M5A 2P9
www.mcclelland.com

1   2   3   4   5   15   14   13   12   11

For Coleen and Leigh

CONTENTS

FOREWORD

Sportswriters loved Conn Smythe. Even the ones who didn't like him loved him. Reporters love anyone who gives them something interesting to write about, and Smythe always had something newsworthy going on. If you asked a serious question, he'd answer it. Even if he knew his response would upset people, he'd say it anyway. Sometimes he'd say it *because* he knew it would upset people, because controversy put butts in the seats at Maple Leaf Gardens. Not that the Gardens' seats lacked backsides: from the time Smythe finally gained full control in 1947 until he quit his last post with the team two decades later, there hadn't been a single unsold ticket to a Leafs game, and there wouldn't be for many more years to come.

They loved him because of his outsized character, fierce pride and uncompromising devotion to success, which was also useful newspaper fodder. They described him as fiery, stubborn, imperious, explosive, volcanic, "a flinty mixture of heart and head," "an eruption of Mt. Etna," a firebrand, "the Toronto pepperpot," "the Little Pistol," "the Little Corporal," "the little Major."

Trent Frayne wrote that Smythe was a "bombastic, romantic, bigoted, inventive, intimidating, quixotic, terrible-tempered paradox of outlandish proportions."[1] Frayne's wife, June Callwood, portrayed him as "a high-hearted despot, a patriot, a brave, outrageous, generous and honest man" who had learned to simplify the confusion of his childhood "by eliminating the soft baggage of tact, tolerance, forgiveness and sociality by which most people draw closer to one another."[2]

Ralph Allen, who joined Smythe's "sportsmen's battery" in the Second World War, joked he was "as diplomatic as a runaway

Rhinoceros."[3] Ted Reeve, who also signed on to the battery, claimed that when Smythe addressed the men, he sometimes grew so heated his helmet rattled like the lid on a tea kettle.

He was great for profiles. Any magazine with a cover to fill could send someone around to talk to Conn Smythe and come away with something worth reading. They wrote about him in his early days as Leaf boss roaring around the gangway that circled the Gardens, hurling hats and insults at wayward referees or skidding across the ice in his spats as he took his complaint directly to officials. Later, after war wounds reduced his mobility, they described him perched in his redoubt in the green seats, assessing the game from on high, just as fervent as ever as he dispatched runners with mid-game "advice" for the coach behind the bench.

They called him "The Ice Man." They talked about his mix of harshness and sentimentality. They recounted the time Rocket Richard was thrown out of a game after a wild brawl and Smythe countered the resultant pooh-poohing with the remark: "We've got to stamp out this kind of thing or people are going to keep on buying tickets."[4]

He was, more than anything, a contradiction. He valued loyalty above all else but left two of his most devoted allies, Frank Selke and Hap Day, feeling betrayed. He admired Ted Kennedy as one of the greatest Leafs ever, even while excoriating Selke for bringing him to the team. His anti-Catholic rhetoric flowed freely, yet several of the men he regarded most highly were ardent Catholics. He was a fierce proponent of free enterprise who willingly gave away money, just as long as it was requested, not demanded. He advocated a rough, tough, no-nonsense style of hockey, yet two of his favourite players – Syl Apps and Joe Primeau – rarely spent a minute in the penalty box. He blocked Harvey Jackson from the Hall of Fame for years because he drank too much and got into trouble, but happily supported Doug Harvey, who drank just as much.

He was more than simply a hockey manager. Twice he risked his life to go to war for his country and was injured both times, the second set of wounds causing permanent, painful damage. He joined up to fight Hitler when already in his mid-forties, with a wife and four children to care for, and refused numerous offers of safe, high-profile appointments, insisting on a battlefield position. On his return he launched a controversy that almost brought down the government of Mackenzie King, creating turmoil in Ottawa while he lay prone in a hospital bed.

One reason for writing this book is to remind people that Conn Smythe was not only the builder and owner of a hockey team but a fascinating Canadian who for forty years or more contributed enormously to the development of this country's culture and character. He founded the hockey dynasty that, for much of his life, really *was* Canada's team (if you didn't happen to live in Quebec). He built the most famous arena in the country, a building that drew gawking, reverent tourists from across the country. When radio was still a novelty – some said a gimmick – he recognized its power and hired a young announcer named Foster Hewitt to turn his team into national heroes. He battled relentlessly for the ideas he believed in – in sports, politics, and civic responsibility – even after the country turned in a new direction and left him largely preaching to himself. He suffered the death of his oldest son amid a scandal played out on the front pages of the country's newspapers. He lost a mother, son, and daughter to alcohol, which he rarely touched himself.

Another reason to write about Smythe is that many Canadians know little about him despite the important role he played over so many years. You have to be older than fifty to remember the last time the Toronto Maple Leafs won the Stanley Cup. You have to be close to sixty to remember when Conn Smythe ruled the team and to appreciate that no Leafs team has ever won a Stanley Cup when it wasn't run by a man named Smythe. He sold the team to his son, Stafford, in 1961, but the core of the club that hoisted the Cup in 1967 came up through the ranks of the talent machine developed by Conn Smythe.

Today's Leafs teams still profit from that legacy. The legend of the team – the inexplicable fervency and loyalty of fans who have fiercely supported it through four decades of frustration – was nourished, developed, and brought to term by the spectacular successes between the 1930s and the 1960s. The players from that period – Conacher, Clancy, Broda, Apps, Bailey, Kennedy, and Day – still look down from the rafters at the Air Canada Centre, though images of Smythe himself are curiously scarce. The vast money-making machine that is the current Leafs ownership is deeply indebted to the bedrock of devotion created by Smythe, which even Harold Ballard couldn't destroy. The fact that Toronto is still accorded a home game almost every Saturday night – despite justifiable grumbling from rivals – dates from Smythe's success in establishing Saturday as the night Canada gathered around its radios to listen to his team.

Some of the details of his life are hard to authenticate with certainty. Hockey men in the early years of the game loved a good story and weren't overly fussy about details. Players gave different versions of the same events. Foster Hewitt claimed he was eighteen when he made his first hockey broadcast. He was born in 1902 and the broadcast was in 1923; there's no way you can get eighteen from that. Many of the stories that survive from Smythe's time have been retold so often that the original details have long since disappeared into myth and the altered versions are taken as fact. Who is to know who really decked Eddie Shore just before he all but killed Ace Bailey with a check in 1933? King Clancy and Red Horner both claimed credit. The news reports at the time favoured Clancy, but goalie George Hainsworth, who had the best view, said it was Horner. Many accounts of Smythe's experience as a prisoner of war in the First World War insist he tried repeatedly to escape, and succeeded on two occasions, though Smythe, in his autobiography, only laid claim to one attempt. Similarly, many histories of the Leafs report as fact that Smythe bought the Toronto St. Patricks in 1927 with money he won betting on football and hockey. Except Smythe only gained $10,000 from his wagers, and the St. Pats sold for $160,000. Smythe said he used the gambling winnings to pay off the mortgage on his new home, though mortgage records show he didn't. Until 1947, Smythe was never more than a minor shareholder and well-paid employee of the team.

Nonetheless, he was aware that his life represented a great story, and he left much material behind when he died. Between that and numerous other archives and sources it is possible to separate most of the fact from the fiction.

Canadians should know more about their history and that nation-building isn't something solely practised by politicians (who are, in truth, often pretty bad at it). Character and culture come from the combined activities of a population over an extended period of time, not from official pronouncements of legislated activities. Conn Smythe was one of the most fascinating Canadians of the twentieth century and left his mark in ways that had a permanent impact on his country. Hockey is at the core of Canada, and much of hockey as it exists today owes an immense debt to Conn Smythe.

My gratitude goes to a number of people who helped make this biography possible. Hugh Smythe for being generous with his time, and his eagerness to see his father's story told to a new generation. Dick Duff, Bob Baun, Frank Mahovlich, Howie Meeker, Frank Selke Jr., Dick Irvin Jr., Kerry Day, Jim Gregory, and Gaye Stewart (who unfortunately passed away during the writing of the book), for agreeing to be interviewed. Scott Young, Trent Frayne, and Jack Batten for so skilfully chronicalling Smythe's years in earlier works. The helpful people at the Ontario Archives, City of Toronto Archives, Trent University, Library and Archives Canada, Maple Leaf Sports and Entertainment, NHL Players Association, and the Hockey Hall of Fame. Michael Levine for ensuring it saw the light of day. And of course my wife, daughter, and family for not thinking it was a dumb idea.

PART ONE

POOR BOY

On February 1, 1895, the day Conn Smythe was born, the reigning Stanley Cup champions were known somewhat prosaically as the Montreal Hockey Club, or Montreal HC, an amateur team that had captured what was then known as the Dominion Hockey Challenge Cup in 1893 – the first ever awarding of the brand new prize – and hung on to it.

The trophy was a silver bowl sitting on an ebony base purchased in London by an aide to Baron Stanley of Preston, the Governor General, whose sons, Arthur and Algernon, were mad about the game. The Montreal HC wore jerseys with a distinctive crest – a wheel with two wings attached – that would later be appropriated by a grain merchant named James E. Norris, a big fan of the club, for a team he called the Red Wings.[1]

It may be just coincidence that the Cup holders on that day happened to be one of the more disputatious teams ever to serve as champions. When the Cup's custodian arrived for the presentation, he mistakenly delivered it to a representative of the Montreal Amateur Athletic Association (MAAA), believing the club and the association to be intertwined. Turned out he was wrong: the players had a testy relationship with the MAAA and refused to accept the trophy.[2] Conn Smythe, if it hadn't been his first day on earth, might have appreciated a club that was so firm in its convictions it would turn down the Stanley Cup. For five decades he would be among the most irascible men in the game, though he would never have rejected the Stanley Cup.

It's also doubtful either Albert or Polly Smythe, Conn's parents, knew or cared much which hockey team happened to be classed as Canada's best. The Cup was hardly a national symbol yet; not until

1903 – when Ottawa won its first of many – would it belong to a team from somewhere other than Montreal or Winnipeg. Hockey wasn't widely accepted as the national game, or the national passion – though it was making headway – and neither Albert nor Polly were big fans. Even after Conn became famous as the man with the most popular team in the country, Albert didn't go to the games. Smythe's parents had immigrated just six years before his birth. Albert was a gentle, quiet, scholarly man of simple tastes, son of an Irish Protestant choirmaster from Gracehill, a village northwest of Belfast. He was far more interested in Dickens and Tennyson than in the winter sporting activities of his adopted home. He had already published a book of poetry, *Poems Grave and Gay*, and was deeply immersed in theosophy, a mix of spiritualism, philosophy, and the occult created by the splendidly named Helena Petrovna Blavatsky, a Russian wanderer whose death had sparked a power struggle within her church.

Besides, the Smythes had bigger worries than men on skates chasing a puck. It was already evident their union had been a mistake. They met on board the SS *Sarnia* as it headed to Canada in the summer of 1889, travelling separately in cabin class, a step up from steerage. Mary Adelaide Constantine – known as Polly – hailed from the Manchester area and boarded ship in Liverpool. Albert Ernest Stafford Smythe was twenty-eight, and joined the ship in Belfast on its first day out.[3]

The Smythe and Constantine families were acquainted with each other,[4] though whether the two shipmates had previously met is not clear. In any case, Albert was clearly smitten with Polly, who was seven years younger, short, cheerful, and outgoing. According to the *Sarnia*'s manifest, Polly planned to catch the train to Winnipeg when the ship docked in Montreal. But somewhere on the Atlantic her plans changed; Smythe told people his parents were married before they landed August 5, though the match wasn't officially registered until December 19 in Toronto.

It must have seemed logical enough – romantic even – to tie the knot before starting their new life together in their adopted homeland, but it was never a likely match. In adulthood, Conn Smythe developed a habit of comparing people to racehorses and declared he'd been "sired by an Irishman and dammed by an Englishwoman. I've got my father's fight and my mother's good sense."[5] It was an oft-quoted line, but wasn't accurate: Albert Smythe wasn't a fighter and Polly's strong point wasn't her common sense. He was disciplined, studious, not given to displays of affection. He didn't drink or eat meat. Polly liked to have a good time. She drank too much, put on weight, liked to laugh and make friends. Albert, not being the partying type, was ignored and Polly made friends on her own. In Conn's memory they were rarely together. His mother would disappear for long periods, never explained, before turning up again with a cast of new acquaintances. That would be his father's cue to leave.[6] The temperance movement was already a powerful force in 1895, and a woman who drank openly and to excess was about as socially acceptable as the plague. This was especially so in Toronto, a straitlaced, narrow-minded, God-fearing town that considered fun a blasphemous concept invented by heathens, to be avoided at all cost.

Nonetheless, Albert and Polly gave it a go. They settled in Toronto and produced two children, the second of which they named Constantine Falkland Cary Smythe – Constantine after Polly's family name and Cary after Albert's mother's maiden name. Falkland may have derived from a distant tie to the Viscount Falkland, whose family name was Cary. Young Constantine hated the name from the time he was old enough to understand it. He would grow up to be a lot of things, but pretentious wasn't one of them. The first chance he got – which came after Polly's premature death – he shortened it to Conn, after an Irish king known as the "hero of a hundred battles."[7]

Albert was enjoying a temporary bout of prosperity around the time of Conn's birth. His small family was living in a house at 51 McMillan Street, a short walk from Church and Carlton, where Maple Leaf Gardens would later be built. City records identify him as the owner of the property, which was valued at $3,200, pretty average for a middle-class home.* It was a respectable enough neighbourhood, a block west of the northern reaches of Jarvis Street, a far more expensive and desirable address, home to some of the city's most splendid names. Albert listed his occupation as "cement sales," having started up his own company around the same time he moved the family to McMillan. It was a sensible occupation, even if Albert wasn't cut out for it. The city was growing, though not as rapidly as hoped. It was a compact place, not yet two hundred thousand in population, packed along the north shore of Lake Ontario between High Park and the Don River. The most northerly tip was near Yonge and Summerhill. Streets were mostly hard-packed dirt. Heat came from coal, sold by Elias Rogers Co., which had two immense coal mountains on the waterfront. Milk trucks trundled through town with large open vats from which people filled their household containers.[8]

It was a two-tiered town. The upper stratum was High Protestant, rigid, prosperous, grey, dull, and very Victorian. The lower orders were just trying to get by. The approved religion came in three flavours: Church of England, Presbyterian, or Methodist, none of which was known for being the life of the party, or even having attended one.

The best-known families were the Eatons (retail goods), the Masseys (overpriced farm equipment), and the Gooderhams (whose distilleries annually produced enough hooch for a town twice the size). They were all proper, distant, and hidden behind the protective walls of immense mansions. They presided over a town that was overwhelmingly British, loyal to a fault, and closed on Sundays. City politics was a wholly owned subsidiary of the Orange Order of Canada, which disapproved of Catholics, the French, and anything that might threaten the eminence of the British Empire. Toronto's devotion to the Lord's Day dictated that the newly electrified streetcar system must stop for a day of rest, even if that slowed the expansion city council had been advocating.

---

* Conn Smythe maintained that his parents were renting the house he was born in, but the Toronto city directory from that year shows Albert as the owner.

As late as 1912 it was still forbidden to toboggan on the Sabbath.

Soon after arriving, Albert had formed a partnership with two other men, providing contractors' supplies. Nichols, Smythe and Co. operated until some time in 1894 when it was dissolved and Albert set up AES and Co., cement dealers, on the first floor of a building on Bay Street. As a sideline he also established Albert Smythe and Co., publishers, whose main product was *The Torch*, the voice of the Toronto Theosophical Society.

Albert was a man of character and intellect, but he had no business sense. "My father was a tender man, not like me at all," according to his son.[9] He cared little for material things, wasn't good with money, and was easy prey for charlatans. What Albert liked was books, and he had a collection that never ceased to expand no matter how challenged the family circumstances. He hauled them from address to address as the family migrated from one home to another, Conn viewing the library and the effort expended on it as a waste of time.

AES and Co. disappeared from the city directory in 1898, by which time the Smythes had made the first of several moves down the economic ladder. They relocated to North Street, a short residential block stretching from Bloor south to Charles, which later became part of Bay Street, to a dark, inexpensive, badly built home. When Conn was barely two, he put his fist through the wall while raging against being put to bed.[10] In the winter, Albert, Conn, and his older sister, Mary, born in 1890, would huddle around the meagre fire, a screen stationed behind them in the faint hope of trapping the fleeting heat. Polly's whereabouts weren't altogether clear. Her drinking was already a problem. Alcohol was cheap, easily obtained, and considered so damaging a social scourge that the federal government, under pressure from the temperance movement, held a national referendum on Prohibition in 1898. It passed in every province except Quebec, but so few Canadians voted (only men could cast ballots) that the result was ignored and the boozing continued. Polly's frequent and prolonged absences left the children largely to Albert's care.

It was on North Street that Conn began noticing there were different socio-economic levels in society, and he was in the wrong one. Although North Street was barely two blocks long, it touched two distinct worlds. Bloor was a pleasant, narrow, tree-lined route with comfortable homes, churches, and a few shops, bordering the outskirts of town. At the Bloor end of North Street, families had horses, carriages, and servants. There were several barristers, including Frank Arnoldi, a prominent lawyer who owned a pony cart for his children and whose son, nicknamed "Bay," befriended the younger Conn. But the south end was something else, perilously close to the outskirts of the Ward, a notorious downtown slum teeming with saloons, sweatshops, and ramshackle houses lacking water, heat, or indoor plumbing, swarming with immigrants and the unemployed, where children were put to work the moment a job could be found for them.

Although there were laws requiring children to attend school, there was little enforcement. Sometime during the 1890s a society established to prevent cruelty to horses was persuaded to extend its mandate to children, but only as an afterthought.[11] Children could beg, peddle newspapers, or pimp for prostitutes. They could be sent off to jail before age ten for minor crimes. Conn's upbringing was light years ahead of those unlucky urchins. He was sent to school the moment he was old enough, and his home, if chilly in winter and often absent a mother, was safe and relatively secure. But the impression of poverty stuck with him. He would see himself as the kid who'd dragged himself up from nothing, the self-made man who didn't need handouts to get ahead and didn't approve of them for others. He wasn't against privilege, but he felt it should be earned. He couldn't abide people who had things handed to them on a platter, who hadn't worked for the benefits they enjoyed, who didn't chase their goals as diligently as he had.

Albert sent him to kindergarten at a school on the corner of Wellesley and Bay. Though not a hard man, Albert had been raised with all the anti-Catholic prejudices of the Church of Ireland and passed them on to his son. It was common wisdom in the Smythe household that the only people as untrustworthy as Catholics were the French, who were a priest-ridden breed with dubious morals and questionable loyalty, answering to the Pope rather than the Crown. Conn grew up terrified of nuns in their flowing black habits, their pinched faces hidden save for pursed lips and eyes ever on the alert for children to kidnap. His daily route to school required passing St. Michael's College; to survive, he and the other Protestants developed a convoy system, the smallest children in the middle with the bigger boys acting as outriders for protection.

"It was a known fact if anybody straggled that in a very short time a gentleman in a long black robe would come out, you would disappear into those robes and into the big building there, and that would be the last seen of you," Smythe later related in a speech at St. Michael's. "It was a proven fact, because we used to hear, as we passed the place, the cries and yells and screams of some innocent Protestant kids having the other faith pounded into them."[12]

If Catholics were to be feared, they were also to be admired for their fighting abilities. Smythe once watched a running battle between two boys picking on a third. "One fought the other two up a lane and then along street after street, always with his back to the wall or he would never have been able to hang on. It was a lesson I didn't forget: If you looked after your rear, you could keep going. It works in fights, war, business."[13]

Smythe wasn't sure what his father did for money during their tenure on North Street – a national census in 1901 showed his profession as "bookbinder" – but funds quickly ran short. The 1890s were not happy years for the Canadian economy, which was struggling under an ill-conceived tariff regime that was strangling trade. The national railway had been built, but the immigrants hadn't come yet, and Canada was actually losing more people than it gained. It was a difficult time to make a living, and Albert Smythe wasn't able to overcome the hardships. Soon after Conn had finished kindergarten, the Smythe family left North Street for a new home in the distant reaches of Scarborough, an unheated ramshackle house without power, water, and plumbing. There was a one-hole outhouse just beyond the back door and a pump for water. A woodstove in the kitchen provided the only source of heat as well as the means of cooking. The house belonged to a friend of Albert's from the theosophical society, and the price was right: the Smythes paid no rent or taxes and no fees for services because there weren't any to pay for.

Beachell Street was a dead-end dirt road in Scarborough Village, a farm town established at the dusty crossroads of Eglinton Avenue and Markham Road. In many ways it was an idyllic location, a bucolic little community surrounded by farmland well to the east of the city limits, located where the ground begins to rise toward the bluffs along Lake Ontario. A village history described it as "consisting only of a brick schoolhouse, a general store, a blacksmith shop, a building for the sale of farm implements, the Methodist parsonage, less than a dozen dwellings, and a large railway hotel converted to other uses."[14]

The Smythes' house was at the end of the street, which ran into the railway tracks, near the school. Albert's benefactor owned a number of other similar homes nearby, mainly empty. They scrounged for wood for the stove, kept chickens, and grew food in a garden where Conn, a short, slight boy with sandy hair, scratched away at the dirt as part of his chores. In the winter he rose early to heat water on the stove, poured it down the well to melt the overnight ice, then pumped up enough water for the rest of the day. Another task was to fetch his father's daily paper. Albert had a friend on the railway, which ran along the bottom of a hill outside the back door. Each morning Conn raced out the door and down the bank, watching as the train approached around a bend, and chased the paper as Albert's acquaintance flung it from a passing car.[15]*

They lived simply, breakfasting on porridge, which Conn hated. He blamed it on the milk, which they obtained unpasteurized from a

---

* The Smythe house was at 44 Beachell and has since disappeared. In 2010, a two-storey home (with parking for ten cars!) at the same address was for sale with an asking price of $639,000. A new development of townhomes runs west off Beachell, named Conn Smythe Drive in Smythe's honour.

local farmer. Conn thought the milk tasted like turnips, and when his father wasn't looking he'd dump his share in the yard for the chickens. Eventually Mary tattled on him, setting off a row that fed Conn's belief that she was Albert's favourite.

He was self-centred and didn't share well. "I would give something freely, didn't mind giving it, but nobody was going to take it away from me, or just move in and use it." Although Mary was the first-born, Conn felt she intruded on his claim to his father. Their first Christmas in Scarborough, Conn threw an epic tantrum, angry at having to share Albert's attention, flinging things around the room and wrestling with his father and sister.[16]

It was their only Christmas together in the Scarborough home. Shortly after, Mary developed a swelling in her throat that her brother blamed on the turnip-tasting milk. Albert took her to the hospital, where she died in May 1903, at age twelve. The death devastated Albert, but Conn felt freed of the burden of competing for attention. The sense that he hadn't been the favourite stayed with him and may have had much to do with his drive to succeed. Success brought attention and acceptance. Long after Conn Smythe had all the money and attention he could ask for, he continued to fight for what he considered his. He enjoyed the competition, but he especially liked to win.

In 1905, when Conn was ten, Albert obtained a job with the *Toronto World* newspaper, and the Smythes moved out of the shack and into the city, taking a single room in a building where St. Michael's Hospital now stands, at $1.50 a week. Although small and threadbare, the room had one great advantage in that the building's main stovepipe ran through it, keeping it warm in the winter.

The *World* offices were located just around the corner on Yonge Street, a hard-packed road still dominated by horses and carriages, though trolleys ran up its centre and there were a growing number of motor-powered automobiles. Albert had plenty of experience as a writer, both through the theosophical society journal and his work as a poet. Now he found himself employed by one of the most entertaining figures of the day, William Findlay Maclean, a member of Parliament and incorrigible rabble-rouser, who is largely forgotten today, but was a well-known figure in Ottawa for more than thirty years. Maclean was a vibrant, outspoken, independent-minded back-bencher who launched the *World* in 1880 as a mouthpiece for his visionary ideas, which included renaming Hudson's Bay "Canada's Sea" and jettisoning the Governor General for an elected head of state.

He may have been skilled at creating controversy, but he had little business acumen, and *World* staff regularly went weeks, or months, without being paid, adding to the pressure on the Smythe household budget.[17] Nonetheless, Albert was delighted. The *World* allowed him to write about anything and everything that interested him. A devotee of the theatre, he became the theatre critic; Conn said the only time he ever saw his father truly angry was when someone laughed during what was meant to be an emotional moment in a play he was attending. He reviewed books and music and covered the horse races, which was by far the most popular sports pastime of the day. Conn would accompany him to the old Woodbine racetrack on the lakefront east of downtown and hustle the results back to the paper so they could make the morning edition. It was while hanging around the jockeys and touts that he developed his lifelong affection for horses and for the colourful, free-spirited culture of the racing world. He found a special nobility in horses and the men around them. It was a mascu-line world, grounded and no-nonsense, filled, he said, with "honest, real men. They're workers and producers. They give every ounce of stuff they've got. Just like the horses."[18]

Despite his unreliable wages, Albert enrolled Conn in private schools, first St. Alban's Cathedral School on Howland Avenue and later Upper Canada College (UCC), which had recently acquired a sumptuous campus on a woodsy expanse of land north of the city. They made him aware of his poverty, and he disliked them intensely.

"In St. Alban's I was again the poor boy," he wrote, "and by then I was old enough to know it. I think maybe that hating so much to be the poor boy then gave me the urge not to be poor, the sooner the better. I didn't covet what others had, but I hated what I was, that I had to have a handout, that when I had to go somewhere urgently another fellow had to lend me his bicycle, that my clothes weren't as good as the others had."[19]

He often got by on handouts: the parents of wealthier boys sent in sumptuous food packages, which he was allowed to share. The mother of a friend gave him his first pair of decent skates – Albert never bought him sports equipment, "even at Christmas" – which he promptly lost. He filched change from Albert's trousers, knowing his father was indifferent to money, and when a collection plate over-turned during a service at St. Alban's, he tucked some under a rug where he could get it later.

It was worse at UCC, which he entered in mid-year when he was thirteen. "I hated Upper Canada College. I hated the new-boy duties, fagging [running errands, doing odd jobs] for seniors. It seemed an unjust place from the first. They made me serve a full year of the new-boy stuff; I had entered just after Christmas, so I had the rest of that school year and the first half of my second year to be at every senior's beck and call."[20]

UCC made no bones about its ambition to serve as an elite school for the upper crust. The school's board of governors was a who's who of Ontario's great and mighty. To celebrate its seventy-fifth year, it had recently moved to an expansive new campus on high ground north of the city, from which it could look down on the less fortunate. It had its own flag, its own college poem, its own rifle corps, infir-mary, dining hall, library, gymnasium, and prayer hall.[21]

"When I was there," wrote Conn, "two or three other poor kids and I would run together like mice, admiring the moneyed people, practi-cally saluting when we were allowed to share the fantastic food parcels that would come from some boy's mother, delivered by chauffeur."[22]

Scraping together the modest fee was all Albert could manage. Conn would sometimes deliver it a week at a time. Once, stacking coins in little piles on the registrar's desk, he looked up to see tears in the man's eyes. It was an embarrassment he never forgot. "I don't think he cried any when the Heintzmans and others among my rich classmates sent in their fees," he recalled.[23]

Adding to his sense of isolation was the fact he was now mother-less. Polly had died while he was at St. Alban's, and while he'd seen her only occasionally in life, her death left him with the sense of a boy against the world and a deep feeling of guilt over an incident that took place on one of the last occasions he'd seen her alive. During a choir practice at the school she had appeared unexpectedly at the church with a bag of cookies.

"She had on a fat and frowzy looking straw hat and was carrying a paper bag," he recalled. "She looked half stewed. We were all up there in the front of the church when I saw her coming down the aisle. The other boys saw her about the same time I did. You sure couldn't miss her. One of them said: 'Gee, who's this old bird coming?'

"I hadn't thought it out in advance. I just said it, bang. 'It's my nanny.'"

He was still justifying the incident to himself decades later. "It wasn't that I didn't love her – it was something else," he related. "She could make great cookies and the bag was full of them. I shared them around and my friends enjoyed them. It gained me a lot of stature to have a nanny who could bake like that, but if I'd owned up to her being my mother it would have been something very different."[24]

She was just thirty-eight when she died, worn out by drink. The last time he saw her was at the hospital, the same hospital in which his sister had died. He borrowed a bicycle and pedalled over to visit. On the way he stopped and bought her a pack of jujubes; when he presented it to her she burst into tears. "She couldn't help it, she said. I was her little boy and was so kind, bringing her jujubes. I don't remember seeing her after that. She died."

Albert's aloofness made the loss that much worse. As a boarder at school, he saw his father only when absence from school was approved.

Once, he skipped Sunday school and went to visit Albert instead. When he was caught, the housemaster called him to his office, where there was a row of hockey sticks. He invited Conn, who weighed just 112 pounds, to pick one out. When he did, the master hit him with it, "a hell of a blow," adding another item to his list of grievances.

When he did see his father, he felt unable to measure up. Albert would have preferred a more scholarly son who shared his literary interests; instead, Conn was boisterous, competitive, and increasingly involved in athletics. Albert didn't begrudge him his love of games and sports, but he didn't encourage it either. He was busy with his books, his poetry, and his ever-deepening involvement in his religion. Once Polly was gone, he also developed new friendships with women, which left Conn once again feeling he was in the way.

"I had got used to the idea that with him, sometimes I came second to somebody else. We loved one another, but he had his life and I had mine, part of mine being that I was so attracted to sports."[25]

In place of a family life he discovered sports. He was drawn to the competition and the camaraderie, the levelling effect that sports had on social barriers, and the degree to which determination and effort could make up for variations in raw talent. Despite his size he was named captain of the UCC junior hockey team, which played ten games and lost just two. The college had its own covered arena, a long wooden building with a sloping roof, large enough to contain a sheet of ice but not much more. He was one of the smallest boys on the team and certainly the poorest. His teammates included two scions of the Heintzman family – Howard and G. Bradford – heirs of the wealthy piano manufacturer. But money had no effect on the ability to score goals or prevent opponents from scoring them, and once the boys were on skates, family background became unimportant. Perhaps best of all he discovered a productive outlet for his natural bossiness and organizational skills. Most players just wanted to skate around and shoot the puck; if he was willing to take on additional tasks, they were happy to let him.

"There were extra duties in being captain that others didn't want to be bothered with, but I loved. It meant being in charge, telling the others we had to practise at such and such a time, you play right wing and I play centre, and so on."[26]

He liked to give instructions. He liked people to do what he said. He liked the fact that, poor kid or no, as captain even the Heintzmans had to listen to him.

After a year and a half at UCC he convinced Albert to let him quit and transfer to Jarvis Collegiate, a less ostentatious school where he buried himself in games. He and his new friend Harvey Aggett – nicknamed "Wreck" – joined everything in sight. Hockey, football, rugby, basketball – if there had been a tiddlywinks team, they'd have been on it. At five-foot-seven, Smythe was again the shortest member on any team he joined; the 1912 basketball team photo shows the boys ranked by height, with Smythe at the bottom of a sloping hill, the runt of the litter, a little blond boy wearing a serious expression and an enormous *J* on his jersey. Not much good at dribbling or defence, he spent hours practising his shot and learned to stand around the net looking inconspicuous until one of the taller boys could get the ball to him. He had the same approach to hockey, positioning himself at the goal and shovelling loose pucks past the netminder.

The *World* was a morning paper and Albert worked late, so home was often empty. Conn spent most of his time on the rink, the field, the basketball court, or killing time with Wreck, whose father was a plumber prosperous enough to own a Cadillac he occasionally lent to the boys. Never enthused about school, as the end of grade twelve approached, Smythe decided he'd learned enough and determined to quit school and make his fortune as a homesteader in northern Ontario. The provincial government was advertising great opportunities for enterprising men and women willing to put up with difficult conditions in a remote setting.

The Great Clay Belt was an area stretching from the recently established town of Hearst to the Quebec border, with horrific winters and bug-infested summers. The government was eager to build up the population and promised rosy prospects to anyone willing to give it a try. "Twenty million acres of virgin soil await the farmer's plow . . . Where men with determination, good health and strength need have no fear of failure," it advertised. The Temiskaming and Northern Railway would get them there, but homesteaders were otherwise left on their own to clear the land and try to make something of the hard, wet clay.[27]

Albert objected to his plan, but Conn, at seventeen, wouldn't listen. In March 1912, he headed north to Clute Township, closer to James Bay than to Lake Superior, where he bought 150 acres and spent the summer laboriously constructing a rough log home for himself. His notebook carefully tallied his costs: $75 in dues at 50 cents an acre, $9.90 in interest on same, $63.78 to clear two acres, $23.35 for logs for his house, 500 feet of lumber for $7.50, $12.25 for roofing, $1.15 for nails, 45 cents for hinges, $3 for windows . . . [28]

It was backbreaking work. At the end of the day he was too tired to eat. In midsummer, with the log house complete, he visited Toronto, where he was watching a horse race when he learned fires had swept the area – the result of homesteaders burning bush – and destroyed his house. He informed Albert he would not return, and they had another row, this time because Albert wouldn't abide a quitter in the family. Neither would give ground, and when Conn enrolled in civil engineering at the University of Toronto that fall, Albert wouldn't give him the tuition. So Conn, Wreck, and a group of friends hit on a scheme to win the money at the track by picking a mediocre horse and bribing other jockeys to let the nag win. The plan almost worked until a mix-up prevented them from getting their bets in on time. Although the bribed jockeys kept their end of the bargain, the boys barely made enough to cover their expenses. All in all Smythe's plans weren't unfolding as he'd planned. But the disappointments were bearable thanks to the presence of Irene.*

---

* Although he wasn't naive about what went on at racetracks, Smythe said that was the one and only time he became involved in a fixed race. There were too many imponderables that could upset even the most carefully laid plans.

CHAPTER 2

Conn Smythe met Irene Sands after a disastrous football game against Parkdale Collegiate. Jarvis was a football powerhouse and the players were so certain of victory in the championship that Smythe joined others in a celebratory parade before the game even began. He bungled the first punt, though, and dropped the second as well, allowing Parkdale to score. After that, it was all downhill.

Afterwards there was a dance, and Irene was one of a group of Parkdale friends who called themselves the Nights of Gladness and specialized in getting involved in things that were fun. Smythe had noticed her before, but hadn't managed an introduction. He finally arranged one that night, and she became his first and only girlfriend. "They say there is no such thing as love at first sight, not love that lasts, but there was for me."[1]

He was almost seventeen, she was two years younger. "It just seemed that from the moment we met we talked the same language," he recalled. She was pretty, dark-haired, friendly, and kind. Her father, like Polly Smythe, drank too much.

"Her mother was one of those quietly typical English wives, a slave to her husband, who treated her like a dog."[2] Both feared the other might come from a wealthier family and avoided revealing their own background. When Irene finally invited Conn home and led him up some stairs to a small apartment above a store, he was overwhelmed with relief, as was Irene when she discovered he was no better off.

Although Albert had been at the *World* for seven years, his financial situation hadn't improved. He and Conn shifted from one rented address to another, rarely more than a room or two, each move feeding his sense of aggrievement. There was a place above a bank on Simcoe Street, another on Jarvis Street he remembered only because "the bedbugs were so big, they almost carried me off," a building called the Ellington Apartments on Gerrard Street, and finally a two-storey gabled building on Bleeker Street, the first one big enough for Albert to store his books in a room of their own. Smythe remembered Bleeker Street as "a street of sex maniacs and murderers. I was ashamed and disgusted that we lived there."[3]

His interest in Irene was a big reason he abandoned his homestead. When he made the Varsity hockey team at the university – Albert having cooled down and agreed to pay the tuition – Irene came to all his games. They took in football matches as well, plus theatre and movies and vaudeville shows. A diary he kept for several months in the winter of 1912–13 shows days split between schoolwork and evenings with Wreck and Irene. On February 1, his eighteenth birthday, he wrote:

Up at 830. Very cold. Went to [Varsity]. Drafted . . . Got ready and met I. Went to dance at Foresters Hall. About 50 couples there. Had great time. Evy and Wreck were there. Had dances with I. Shady Thompson. Home bed 1.00 [*Note:* Spelling as in original]

Feb. 3: Another dance at Hunt Club. Had great time. I and I had 5 [dances]. Good place. [Irene] had sore feet. Home bed. Wreck was there but Evy wouldn't go."

Feb. 5: Up 9.30. Cold. Went downtown got books . . . Went to nickel shows. Wreck came down bought sweater coat. Made $1.00. Home. Went to I's. All went out.[4]

In his second year at university he was named captain of the junior team, which dressed in the blue and white colours he would later appropriate for the Maple Leafs. He noted proudly they'd played fifteen games, lost just three, and he'd scored thirty-three goals. Varsity made it to the semifinal round of the Ontario championship, where they came up against a team from the farm town of Berlin – later

20

renamed Kitchener – managed by a tiny young man of serious demeanour and short-cropped hair named Frank J. Selke.

Barely two inches over five feet, Selke, twenty, came from a world as uncertain as Smythe's own. Passionate about hockey, he realized at age thirteen he lacked both the size and the skill to succeed as a player and had considered himself a "manager" ever since. His father, a labourer who immigrated from German-controlled Poland when his wife was pregnant with their fourth child, had recently died, leaving Selke as head of the family. By day he worked at the Waterloo Furniture Manufacturing Co., making five cents an hour as a bandsaw apprentice. Nights he spent at an abandoned brickyard, where ice rinks formed in the craters left behind when clay was scooped out to make bricks. The ponds were crowded with hockey players, and Selke had put together a squad for the Berlin city league that did well enough to gain admittance to the Ontario Hockey Association (OHA).

As its name suggested, Berlin was largely populated by German immigrants, who suffered increasing hostility as Europe approached war. Eager to reassure fans of their loyalty, Selke's team was named the Union Jacks and sported elaborately patriotic jerseys in red, white, and blue, with crossed flags on the chest, the Union Jack on one side, and the Canadian Red Ensign on the other. The show of fervour did little good. The taunting was merciless. One Union Jack – a youth name Bialkowski – was so viciously treated he began playing under the alias Albert White.[5]

The fact that the Union Jacks had survived long enough to make the playoffs was something of an economic miracle. Selke and a friend financed the team themselves – Selke contributing his share from his nickel-an-hour job and some money he'd borrowed from his widowed mother. They quickly ran through their budget, though, and were more than $400 in debt at one point, rescued when a kindly supporter volunteered $72 to tide them through.[6]

Varsity was too much for them, winning the two-game contest by scores of 3–1 and 5–2. Smythe's team went on to the finals, defeating

Orillia 4–3 in the first game – all four goals scored by Smythe – before being crushed 10–3 in the second game and losing the series on total goals. A year later, Berlin was back for a rematch, this time when both teams made the finals. Canada by then was six months into the war in Europe, and the fans' abuse of the Berlin team had escalated dramatically. The Union Jacks had to fight their way in and out of arenas, where fans serenaded them with calls of "Krauts," "flatheads," and "babykillers." Berlin fans responded in kind, aiming streams of tobacco juice at opposing players. Smythe claimed he was hit by so much juice his sandy hair was streaked brown.

The first of the two-game series, in Berlin, ended in a tie. The all-important second match took place at Toronto's Arena Gardens – often known simply as the Arena or the Mutual Street arena because it was the city's premier rink – where a crowd of almost five thousand packed the stands for a contest hailed as one of the best of the year.

Hockey in 1915 was still played with seven men aside and no substitutes; in addition to the forward line and two defencemen, a "rover" lined up behind the centreman and did pretty much what the name implies. Players were on for the full sixty minutes. If someone was hurt and had to leave the ice, the other team dropped a player as well. If a goaltender got a penalty, he served it himself and the team made do without him.

Once again Varsity prevailed, but this time the game turned on a crucial moment that ended with Selke feeling foolish. A Berlin player named Irvin Erb had broken a blade and left the ice. Smythe, winded from a recent check, took himself off to even the sides. His absence gave Berlin a boost – though far from the best player, he was the driving force of the Toronto team, and without him Selke's team fought back to a one-goal lead.

Although he had been warned to keep Smythe off the ice, Selke left the bench in the third period to keep an eye on the timekeeper – hometown officials being notorious for letting games "accidentally" run long when the local team was trailing. While he was away, a

Toronto partisan produced a new pair of skates for Erb, who leapt back onto the ice. That allowed Smythe to follow. Varsity scored five goals in twelve minutes, two by Smythe, and won the crown.

The game was covered by Lou Marsh, a *Toronto Star* reporter who doubled as a referee and would track much of Smythe's progress over the next twenty years. In this case he singled out the young captain for praise: "Conny Smythe, the Varsity centre, is a game lad. Even though his physical advantages are not as great as those of the majority of his opponents, he has them all faded when it comes to courage and daring," he wrote. "In the Berlin final Smythe actually took a flying dive along the ice trying to prevent a Berlin shot. It was a regular football dive, and it must have almost caved Smythe's 'slate.'"[7]

Smythe informed Irene after the game that he intended to enlist in the army and hoped to be sent to Europe. The players had been discussing it for months; they had agreed to sign up as a group, and on the Monday following their hockey triumph nine of them presented themselves at a recruiting office, putting in their names for a pair of artillery units. It was the Ides of March 1915, and Smythe, who had just turned twenty, came home as a gunner in the 25th Battery, Canadian Field Artillery.*

His determination to enlist couldn't have come as a surprise. Toronto, like much of the country, was awash in war fever, not yet sobered by the crushing death tolls that were still some months away. He had tried to sign up just weeks after Canada entered the war in August 1914, but had been turned away by a recruiter who suggested he come back when he was old enough to grow facial hair.

Like most of the male population of English Canada, Smythe took for granted that defending the Empire was a matter of duty. For a young man of his background and beliefs, it would have been inconceivable to be anything but desperate to get in on the fighting. He was

---

* Although Smythe insisted he and the other players signed up the Monday after their victory, his papers are dated March 16, 1915, a Tuesday.

a Canadian citizen and a British subject, and the two were inseparable in Canadian eyes. As Sir Wilfrid Laurier had declared: "When Britain was at war, Canada is at war, there is no difference at all."[8]

Although free to make its own laws, Canada remained "a self-governing Dominion" under the umbrella of the British Empire. London, England, not Ottawa, controlled the country's foreign affairs.[9] Legal matters that couldn't be settled in Canada went to a higher authority in London. Governor Generals all came from England and would for another two generations. Even Canada's flag was the British flag, though the Red Ensign was widely used. Canadian schools taught British history; British heroes were Canadian heroes; Canadian politicians looked to England for guidance and direction.

Outside Quebec, Canadians couldn't wait to back the British against the Germans. Support for the war in Toronto, Selke recalled, was "almost fanatic."[10] Britain was the world's greatest power, and English Canadians were immensely proud of their place in it. Probably nowhere was the British connection more revered than in loyalist, Tory Toronto. More than 85 per cent of the population gave their ethnic origin as British; almost 75 per cent gave their religious affiliation as Church of England, Church of Scotland, Methodist, or Presbyterian.[11] To demonstrate Canada's eagerness to contribute, Prime Minister Robert Borden had offered to spend $35 million building three warships to be handed over to Britain, to use as it saw fit.[12]

Smythe was as fervent a Canadian patriot as existed, but his devotion to the Crown, and the country's British roots, ran equally deep. He wanted to belong, and he wanted to win, and Great Britain was the world's surest bet at the time. He saw his country and its heritage as one and the same thing.

Even if he hadn't been so inclined, it would have been difficult to resist the pressure to enlist that swept the city. Canadian men figured they'd be in Europe a few months, kill some Germans, and be home to bask in the glory of victory before anyone noticed they were gone. If he was like thousands of other recruits, Smythe's worst fear was that the fighting might end before he could get to it. The country's mood of blind optimism was bolstered by the swagger of the generals and a press eager to cheer them on. Far from a young country embarking on a journey for which it had little training, Canada was represented in the papers as if it was part of a military juggernaut rolling to an inevitable victory. On the day Smythe signed up, the *Globe's* front page gave the impression the end was already at hand: "GREAT BRITISH VICTORY: SMASH GERMAN ARMY," "TEN THOUSAND GERMANS ARE LOST IN THE BRITISH FIGHT FOR LILLE," "BRITISH GIVE SMASHING REPULSE TO THE GERMANS; RUSSIA STEMS FOES ADVANCE IN POLAND," "GERMAN ATTACK FAILS NORTH OF PRZASNYSZ." A British vice-admiral in the Dardanelles offered assurances that the Turks would be easily handled at Gallipoli and the Allied troops would "hammer their way through" within three weeks. What could possibly go wrong?

Enlistees were signing up faster than they could be trained. Troops paraded through the streets accompanied by marching bands. Men in brand new uniforms stood on corners making fiery speeches and exhorting others to join in the fun. At the time he added his name to the list, Smythe said, the University of Toronto grounds "looked like an Army camp, with tents on the campus, marching bands, recruiting speeches almost every day." It didn't take much to win him over – he was dying to fight.[13]

Wreck Aggett had signed up too, as did another friend, George Walker, nicknamed "Squib" and even smaller than Smythe. Walker, who would become chief scout for the Maple Leafs, was nearly blind without his glasses. To sneak him through the eye exam Smythe and the others hid someone behind a door to hiss out answers as the doctor pointed at an eye chart. They were sent off to Ottawa for preliminary training, then on to Valcartier in Quebec, where Sir Sam Hughes, the mercurial minister of defence, had quixotically decided to concentrate his troops even though better facilities existed at Petawawa in Ontario. Valcartier had been built from scratch in three weeks and was jammed with eager young soldiers-to-be. Smythe soon grew disconsolate; at five-foot-seven he wasn't viewed as officer material and found himself in the hospital after a horse stepped on his foot. While he recuperated, his friends were shipped overseas. He was "despondent, bored, upset and angry" and wrote a letter to Albert complaining about the injustice of it all. Albert got in touch with Smythe's friend from North Street, Bay Arnoldi, whose uncle had some influence in Ottawa. Shortly after, Smythe was ordered to Kingston for officer training.

In Kingston, Smythe ran across Gordon Southam, son of William Southam, founder of a national newspaper chain. Southam was twenty-nine, a well-known athlete who played tennis, football, hockey, and cricket, and was recruiting his own battery to take overseas, filled with sports-minded young men like himself. Smythe leapt at the chance to join not only because it might get him to Europe, but also because Southam was assembling a hockey team while awaiting orders. Smythe recognized enough of the players to know it would be a competitive squad and got himself put in charge of organizing and managing it. Although he wouldn't play, once again he could be the boss.

From Kingston, Southam's 40th Battery was moved to Toronto, where they joined three other teams in the OHA senior division. They quickly got involved in a heated series with a team named the Argonauts, which attracted considerable fan interest and money for the team. By the time they met for their third confrontation, both ticket sales and betting had taken off. Just before the game was to take place, Southam got word the troop would be heading overseas. He and Smythe kept the secret to themselves, but when they were approached by a man wanting to place a wager, Southam turned to Smythe and asked for the entire season's receipts – which amounted to $2,800 – and they bet the whole thing.

When told of the bet, and the fact it would be their last match, the 40th came out like a house on fire, scoring four goals in the first nine minutes. It was a cakewalk: 8–3, and the team ended up with $7,000 in winnings, an enormous sum that was used to buy Christmas dinners for the entire battery – about two hundred men – throughout the duration of the war.[14]

It wasn't the first time Smythe had bet on himself, but it was the biggest so far. He would take similar gambles again and again in the future, exhibiting a nonchalance toward the possibility of loss that both startled and impressed friends and colleagues. "All my life I have marvelled at Conn Smythe's willingness to bet against seemingly insurmountable odds," Selke confessed after years of watching Smythe take risks the cautious Selke would never have contemplated.[15]

The battery shipped out four days later, but not before Smythe asked Irene to marry him. She agreed. Smythe was turning twenty-one, and neither had any experience with sex, but they decided to postpone the ceremony and the consummation until after the war, a bit of chivalry that saved Irene from giving herself up to a man who might not come home. That Sunday Conn had dinner with his father, who was unaware of Irene's existence even though his son had been seeing her for four years. After Polly's death Albert had remarried, a woman named Jane Henderson, an Irish immigrant like himself. Conn resented her for the same reason he'd resented his sister – she was another rival for his father's affections, an intrusion into the two-man household they'd shared since his mother had died a decade earlier.

Jane was understanding enough to leave father and son alone so they could talk, and two days later, to his surprise, Smythe received a letter from his father that poured out the warmth and affection he had never been able to express in person. Albert Smythe wrote thousands of letters in his life and kept almost all of them. But Conn's files hold only two of them: one is an inconsequential note mailed near the end of Albert's life, and the other is the letter he received that day as he waited for the train to take him off to war.

My dear boy, I suppose you find it hard to think of yourself twenty-one years ago, but the dear little chap who used to love me so much and put his arms around my neck, and climb up on my knee, and play ball and do all the other little things which you won't think anything of til you have children of your own, are all in my mind. Well dearie, you are a man now, and your own master, as I have always tried to have you be. I may not have done as well by you as I had hoped, but you are all I could wish in the main things, clean, truthful, honest, brave and generous. I think you will have enough regard for the old days to keep these things in your heart all your life.

I do not know anything about the girl you were talking about Sunday night, but try and be all, in all things, that you can think she would wish you to be. If she is worth anything she will wish the best and highest for you.

You know I do not set much store by worldly possessions. Those who work hardest do not always get the greatest rewards. But no reward worth having or that will afford real satisfaction is to be had without hard work. I am looking forward to a life of great success for you, but success is only to be had on the old hard terms. You are not a shirker and I feel sure you will face the conditions and win the success.

. . . The war has interfered with many plans I had for you. You are going to England but not as I expected. I do not know what another year may bring, but we are all in the hands of the Eternal. I hope you won't think this is a sermon or a screed. It is just a loving word from your old Daddy to wish you all the best things in the world and to kiss you goodbye as you go away and leave all the old times behind forever. Don't forget, no one will ever love you better than I do. It makes me all the sorrier that I have such a poor way of showing it.

God bless you dear, now and always. . . . Love, my dear boy. Your loving Daddy.[16]

———

When Smythe set off for England he was entering a crucible that would help forge both Canada's future and his own. Both would mature considerably over the next four years. Canada would emerge still proud of its British heritage, but less deferential and more independent-minded and demanding of the recognition due a country that had sacrificed the lives of sixty thousand of its sons and daughters.

Smythe would fight at four of the most storied battles of the conflagration, survive them all, and return home a man equipped with the confidence and drive to pursue the ambition he already felt.

Canada entered the contest as a junior member of Britain's forces, there to supply men and money and take orders. But as the years passed, and the human price grew steeper, attitudes changed. With a quarter-million men in the field, Prime Minister Borden began demanding a say in their deployment. Initially given the brush-off, he persisted and by 1917 – after Ypres and the Somme and Vimy Ridge – he was a member of the Imperial War Cabinet and a driving force in the reorganization of postwar relations between the dominions and His Majesty's government.

Smythe would go through an equally transformative experience, watching men die, killing some himself, and establishing the principles and beliefs by which he would live.

As a young lieutenant, his mind was chiefly on the glory he could attain. But Canada went into the war ill prepared and ill equipped, stumbling through the early months by dealing with each crisis as it arose. In those days men were plentiful and Ottawa raised its commitment to five hundred thousand troops. But by the time Smythe landed at Plymouth in February 1916, the horrors of the initial battles at Ypres had sunk in and enlistment was falling off dramatically. Not only were the realities of war making themselves apparent, but the government's massive wartime spending had fired up the economy and made it far more attractive to skip the fighting and stay home to earn money.[17]

Once in Britain, Major Southam's battery marched around country lanes for a few months, then headed to Salisbury Plain – the great forging ground for Britain's imperial forces – and practised shooting their big guns. On July 1, they were inspected by the King himself, giving off a little extra sparkle thanks to nickel-plated stirrups Southam had acquired for their horses. Two weeks later they left for France, landing at Le Havre, where all their fancy stirrups were stolen on the first night.

They left immediately for Belgium, occupied by the Germans, save for an arc around the ancient city of Ypres. There had already been two costly battles as the Germans sought to seize the town and continue toward the sea. Although little if anything was gained, the casualties were horrific. In the second battle, in April and May of 1915, the Germans used poison gas for the first time, unleashing green clouds of chlorine gas into the French lines on April 22 that killed thousands of men within minutes. Two days later they sent a second cloud drifting toward Canadian troops near the village of St. Julien. When Smythe arrived near the southern end of the arc in July 1916, fighting had settled down into a humdrum routine: the Germans on the higher ground rained down shells during the day; the Canadians would fire back at night. Stagnation had set in and trenches criss-crossed the broken, barren landscape. For a time Smythe's "bed" consisted of a ledge on a bunker wall, where rats would land on him in the middle of slumber. "They didn't bother me," he said. "They got so much to eat from the dead that they left the living alone." After a couple of months, Smythe concluded he was an expert at war and got into a shouting match with Major Southam, who he felt could learn a few lessons. "I wanted to get promoted and the war seemed very slow and I told him he wasn't running the battery right." He challenged Southam to a punch-up, but was pulled away by another man before the much stronger Southam could take him up on it.[18]

In October, he got his wish for greater excitement. The battery was withdrawn from Ypres and sent on a hundred-kilometre march to the Somme, where a bloodbath of unprecedented proportions had been under way for three months. When the slaughter finally ended around Christmas, more than 250,000 men would be killed between the two armies. The 40th Battery arrived October 7 near the town of Courcelette, about fifty kilometres from Amiens near the Belgian border, which had been seized by the Canadian Corps in mid-September, one of the first times tanks had been used.[19] Canadian officers were trying a new approach to cut down on losses: they would send a "creeping barrage" of shells at the enemy, advancing behind the moving wall of fire ninety metres at a time across no man's land as the enemy sheltered from the fusillade. The attack worked so well the Canadians, who had only been meant to capture the remnants of a sugar factory nearby, overran the entire ruined village.

A few days after arrival the battery set up its guns and began aiming a steady fire at the German lines. The soil was chalky and easily spotted from afar, and the battery's shelling went on so long the German gunners were able to pinpoint their location and began sending return fire directly at the Canadian guns. Southam ordered the gunners to take cover and began shepherding them into bunkers, Smythe close behind, when someone grabbed him and dragged him into another dugout. Inside were three corpses, all Canadian, that had been mouldering since the initial attack several weeks earlier. One of the bodies was still upright, wrapped around a stovepipe where it had fallen. Despite the overwhelming smell, the men huddled from the bombardment until a sergeant came along and abruptly informed Smythe he was now the acting head of the unit.

Both Southam and the sergeant major who had been with him had been killed by a direct hit while getting men into the bunkers; Smythe was convinced he would have been killed too if he hadn't been hauled into the dugout with the three corpses. He remained in charge briefly until a senior officer could be sent to replace him, then faced the task of removing the battery's twelve guns to a new location without getting killed by the withering German fire. "I was never so scared in my life," he confessed, describing how the guns – each of which was hauled by six horses – had to be moved at night down the only available road, a fact of which the Germans were well aware, subjecting the road to constant shelling. Although he survived that ordeal, a short time later he was shifting the guns to yet another location when a gunner, a talented hockey player from Regina, was hit by a shell and lay – still alive – in a water-filled shell hole with his insides spread around him. Smythe was shocked at the sight and the agonized moaning of the man; a sergeant sent Smythe away for a few moments while he pulled out his service revolver and ended the man's suffering.[20]

In another close call, Smythe found himself isolated near a series of trenches that had traded sides several times. He had been sent to an observation post to watch as shells landed on the German lines, calling back by telephone to provide direction to the gunners. When the phone went dead he was trapped for hours as the Germans once again laid down a heavy bombardment. Intensive shelling usually signalled an attack was coming and, terrified, Smythe began collecting guns and ammunition from corpses in bomb craters and shell holes around him, watching as shadows began to move toward him in the smoke and fog.

"That's when I knew I could be as scared as anyone living. I was shaking so much I could hardly put a cartridge in a gun at all. The firing got worse and worse and all of a sudden out of the fog I could see men crouched over moving toward me and I thought, my God, here goes the last of the Smythes and nobody's ever going to know what happened to me."[21] When one of the men suddenly stood up, Smythe could see he was Canadian. Although relieved, he sat for some time in his battered post wondering whether he would have had the nerve to kill if the troops had proved to be German. He would find out soon enough.

After two months at the Somme the 40th Battery was transferred out and given some leave time. No sooner did they return to duty than they were sent to the battle that would cement Canada's new status among the top rank of fighting men, at Vimy Ridge.

Vimy would be the first time all four divisions of the Canadian expeditionary force – almost one hundred thousand men – fought together as one.[22] They were grouped into the Canadian Corps, assisted by a British division and led by a British commander, Lt.-Gen. Sir Julian Byng, who would later serve as Canada's Governor General and whose wife would donate the Lady Byng Trophy, awarded, ironically enough, to the NHL's most gentlemanly player. It was a meticulously planned operation, including a scale model built so the men would understand the overall plan and their part in it. The task was to seize a strategic slope that had been captured by the Germans in 1914, fortified heavily and held against earlier assaults by the British and French. The Canadians would have to attack over open ground against German artillery and machine-gun fire, against three defensive lines protected by trenches, tunnels, gun embankments, and immense coils of barbed wire.

In the weeks leading up to the assault, Smythe volunteered for an experimental approach to guiding artillery. Rather than wait back near the guns, he would accompany the infantry as they attacked the enemy, tracking the effectiveness of the shelling from up close and sending back reports. As they approached the German trenches he advised the gunners to shorten their range, thinking they were overshooting the target. Soon after, he saw puffs of smoke nearby and feared that the range had been shortened *too* much and Canadians were being killed by their own artillery. Thinking it might be his fault, he rushed to join the infantry troops and found himself in a pitched battle. Grenades, gunfire, and artillery exploded all around. Diving into a trench, he quickly shot two German soldiers and rounded a corner to see another on a parapet. "He just had time to look at me when I jammed my revolver in his stomach and pulled the trigger. He slid down into the trench, cursing me in German all the way. I don't know German, but I know what he thought of me."[23] Smythe met up with some of the men from his unit and together they helped an injured officer and two prisoners back to Canadian lines. Not until later did he realize the bullet he'd fired into the German's stomach had been his last. If he'd run into any more of the enemy, he'd have been finished.

His bravery won him the Military Cross. On his official war record back in Ottawa, it was noted dryly: "17/4/17: Awarded the Military

Cross for conspicuous gallantry and devotion to duty. He organized some men and led them forward with great dash, thereby dispersing an enemy party at a critical time. He himself accounted for three of the enemy with his revolver. He has previously done fine work."[24]

The attack on Vimy was preceded by twenty days of constant shelling, varying in intensity to prevent the Germans from guessing when the main assault would begin. On the morning of the attack, the battery began a barrage at 5:30, laying down cover for the men to proceed behind. One of Byng's tactics had been to dig tunnels enabling the troops to break through unexpectedly, close to the German lines. It worked spectacularly and the Canadians made rapid progress, often seizing prisoners and territory at a faster pace than expected. Smythe and his gunners worked feverishly. The morning had been freezing, but as the fighting went on it began to sleet and snow, turning the battlefield into a quagmire and rendering a plank road – set up to move men, guns, and ammunition – useless. Horses were slipping and sliding, wagons were tipping. The gunners fired all day and slept with the rats at night. They moved forward methodically – advancing, setting the guns, firing, and reloading. The attack began April 9; on April 15, Smythe and his battery reached the ridge itself. He could look down the far side and see Canadian troops in the town of Vimy, surrounded by rubble and wreckage, still under fire. The next day he moved his own guns down to join them and spent several dangerous days shuttling back and forth to ammunition dumps, picking up shells, and ferrying them down the ridge to the town square where the battery was dug in.

Twelve days before the attack, the 40th had been amalgamated with another gun crew and a new commander. Smythe liked the old boss, Capt. Bill Wilson, and took an instant dislike to his replacement, a Major Syre. His attitude hardened once fighting began and Syre spent too much time, in Smythe's view, hunkered in the safety of his bunker rather than out with the men. One morning after the battery had reached Vimy, Smythe was picking up more ammunition when he learned two of his fellow lieutenants had been hit by German shells and seriously wounded. He hustled back, raced into Syre's dugout, and demanded to know how they were, only to be told they were still out on the square where they had been hit.

Smythe exploded. "You mean to say that they've been out there wounded all this time, and you're still sitting down in this dugout?"[25]

He ran out to the square, where both men were lying, one dead, the other moaning in pain. He was fishing for the wallet of the dead man to send home to his family when the man's leg fell off. He got some help and they picked up the second man, who was calling for his mother, and carried him to safety, where he died soon after. Smythe, unable to control himself, confronted Syre, who he felt had left the men to die when they could have been saved. He shouted that he would no longer serve in a battery run by a man like him and demanded a transfer. It was a mistake: the major was soon replaced and Bill Wilson – now also a major – reinstated. But it was too late for Smythe, whose transfer came through, and he was forced to leave his old unit and the men to whom he had become so close. He realized the error he'd made soon after when his life was saved by a batterymate who'd come looking for him during a nighttime gas attack, found him sleeping in an abandoned house, and put a gas mask on him.

Smythe's transfer to the Royal Flying Corps meant a summer in Britain training to observe artillery from the air and obtaining his own wings. One of his instructors was Lt.-Col. W.G. Barker – "Billy" Barker – a hero of the first order who was the main challenge to Billy Bishop's status as Canada's greatest wartime flying ace. Barker would survive an epic airborne battle against a German squadron, in which he fainted twice from injuries before managing to crash land his plane. But he wasn't happy in his job training rookies like Smythe and succeeded in getting out of it after buzzing the airfield and flying his plane in one end of a hangar and out the other, sending senior officers scrambling for their lives. Smythe admired his daring and would remember Barker when he began building his hockey empire a decade later. His own stay in England proved to be an idyll that ended when he was shipped back to Belgium as an artillery spotter in the sodden, grinding, corpse-strewn effort to capture the village of Passchendaele.

The ground around Passchendaele was marshy at the best of times, and that summer had been cold and wet. It had been fought over for three years by then, the combatants pummelling one another relentlessly with neither side able to move the other more than a few kilometres at a time. The battlefield was a morass of shattered trees, shell holes, empty villages, and broken ground – one great long sea of muck that could, and did, swallow tanks and their crews, who sometimes drowned before they could escape. Smythe flew above it in his RE8, a rickety two-seater biplane with a single propeller, watching artillery and radioing back instructions. He and an observer named Andrew Ward manned the plane, which had a maximum speed of just over one hundred miles an hour and usually came equipped with one gun in the front and one or two more in the rear cockpit. The RE8 had only recently been introduced and was designed for speed and stability, but quickly became known as a death trap, prone to bursting into flame or spinning out of control, especially when flown by inexperienced pilots like Smythe. There were so many fatalities in the first few months of service that pilots began exchanging them for the earlier model, which it had been intended to replace.[26]

On October 14, he and Ward took off into a grey sky with low-hanging cloud – too low for effective reconnaissance. Instead of returning to the airfield Smythe flew down below the cloud, making himself an easy target. While zigzagging between German observer balloons they took a hit in the rudder and began to spin. He put the nose down and shut off the engine. It was, he said, like a leaf falling to the ground in the autumn, drifting downward in widening circles as he tried to steer away from some shattered trees pointed upward like the spikes on an iron fence. As he looked for a place to land, Ward – a Roman Catholic – tapped him on the shoulder "very coolly" and asked, "What's going to happen now?"

"We've done a lot of arguing about religion, Wardsy," Smythe responded. "In about five seconds we're going to find out who's right."[27]

They hit ground in the middle of no man's land, the plane skidding through the mud until it dropped into a shell hole and turned on its nose. Smythe had been hit twice by rifle fire, in the leg and in the calf, neither shot striking bone. They climbed from the plane and dodged from crater to crater, heading for a man who was waving at them, ducking bullets as they went. When they finally reached the man, Smythe realized with a shock that he was German. He'd been leading them directly to his gun placement. Irrational and upset, Smythe erupted in anger, cursing until the German pulled out his revolver and fired twice at his chest, from just inches away. Somehow, miraculously, the bullets missed, one passing through his flying jacket on the left, the other on the right. Before his aim could improve the German was halted by a comrade who preferred dealing with live prisoners rather than corpses.

A few days later a notice appeared in the pages of the *Toronto World*.

Reported Missing: Mr. A.E.S. Smythe, of *The World* editorial staff, received word this morning from Ottawa that his son, Lieutenant 'Conny' Smythe, who left with the Flying Corps last May, has been missing since the 14th. The young aviator was well known in sporting circles, having been captain of the Varsity Hockey Club, winners of the Junior OHA championship in 1915. He also played with the 40th Battery team in the senior series.

In the school photograph used with the item Smythe looked about ten years old.

At some point in the next several weeks, Albert was told his son had been killed. He presumably shared the information with Irene. It wasn't until almost a month later that they learned he was alive and being held in a prisoner of war camp, at which point another notice was printed in the *World* sharing the happy news: "His many friends in Toronto will be pleased to learn that the previous news received was unfounded, and the best wishes of all will go out to this youthful and gallant member of the brave air service."[28]

If Albert was relieved, Conn was miserable. Immediately after being captured he was taken to a lice-ridden hospital just beyond the German lines, filled with wounded enemy troops and under constant bombardment. The German doctors ignored him, and three weeks after arriving he was unable to walk. Moved to another hospital, his wounds were finally treated and he spent four months recuperating "amid fair comfort."[29] From there he was moved to Karlsruhe, a town on the eastern side of the Rhine. A few weeks later he was moved again, heading north this time to Magdeburg, where he ended up in solitary confinement after running afoul of the censors who scrutinized prisoners' mail. Once his status as a prisoner had been confirmed he was able to send and receive letters and parcels. Irene kept him supplied with biscuits and other food he liked, and they kept in touch regularly throughout his ordeal.

He was only in Magdeburg a few weeks before being moved to Halle, near Leipzig, and a week after that to Blankenburg, where he learned his friend Wreck Aggett had been killed at Passchendaele. It was at Blankenburg that Smythe and another flyer named Seaton Broughall made an escape attempt, deciding they could catch the guards by surprise if they made a run for it in broad daylight. They planned to clamber over two barbed-wire fences with the help of some accomplices and blankets to cover the barbs, then outrun any bullets directed their way. "Even if we got shot at, the guards by 1918 were oldtimers, we didn't think they could hit us if we moved fast enough."[30] They got over the fences, but Broughall tore most of his pants off in the process and they raced across a field with guards firing as they ran. Near a river they hid in some bushes and took a moment to repair Broughall's pants. They were busy at the repair job when a guard with a dog tracked them down.

Smythe's reward was a trip farther east to Poland, where he was returned to solitary at a tougher camp at Schweidnitz, a town in Silesia near the border with today's Czech Republic. He arrived in April 1918 and remained there until the end of the war, passing the time by trying to teach himself the harmonica until a guard levelled a rifle at him to indicate he'd heard enough. Although conditions in the camp were bearable, Smythe was a witness one day when a group of fifty British men returned from forced labour in a local mine. "They bore every evidence of starvation and rough treatment," he said. "We gave them all we could lay hands on and pretty soon they picked up splendidly and were becoming really strong and healthy when the commandant of the camp sent them back to the mines. When they were sent back another batch of fifty men was returned from these same mines to the camp, and in just as unfit a condition."[31]

When the war ended in November, the Canadian prisoners were taken to a port and put on a boat to England, landing on Christmas Eve to discover British repatriation officials had gone home. They commandeered a locomotive in a nearby rail yard and drove it to town, where Smythe caught a train to Manchester to spend the holiday with his mother's relatives. The immense crowds of returning soldiers in England created a backlog that delayed his return to Canada for two months; he finally arrived in Toronto in February, and Irene and Albert met him at the station. He stayed that night with Irene, watched over closely by her father "as if there might be something going on between us."[32]

There wasn't. "We'd waited that long and we weren't going to make any mistakes." If Smythe was anything, he was a man of discipline.

CHAPTER 3

Aprisoner camp offered much time to ponder the future. When he stepped off the platform in Toronto, Conn Smythe was twenty-four years old and had just given four of them for his country. He had been present at four of the greatest battles of the war – Ypres, Vimy, the Somme, and Passchendaele – confrontations that had changed the very nature of Canada and how it thought of itself, that had left tens of thousands of young Canadians dead and many more grievously wounded. He had survived them all. It had been a time of maturing for him, and he emerged largely set in the views that would guide his future.

Army life had made an immense impression on him. Young men can be utterly alienated by the experience: the rigid discipline, the fixed lines of authority, the expectation of unquestioning obedience. Smythe embraced it. He was attracted by the certainty, the security, the straightforward, no-nonsense approach, and the emphasis on team effort. He would defend it fervently ever after. Sixty years later he would tell an interviewer: "Of a hundred men in the army, you could trust maybe 95 of them. From a hundred people in civilian life today, you would be lucky to get five you trust."[1]

It struck him as self-evident that you needed a boss in life, and it must be clear to everyone who that boss was. The job of the boss was to make decisions and give direction; the role of everyone else was to follow instructions. If the boss was no good, you got rid of him; if you wanted to be a boss yourself, you had to win the trust and support of the people you hoped to lead. Once you were the boss, you didn't suffer fools or challengers lightly.

The qualities he admired most were "guts" and loyalty, and he had his own definition of what these entailed. "Guts" meant not being "yellow," not backing down before a fight, not letting yourself be pushed around. The army had confirmed his observations from the sidewalks of Toronto: keep your back covered and be prepared to defend yourself at all times. People who turned the other cheek were likely to get walloped on that cheek too. His most famous quote became, "If you can't beat 'em in the alley, you can't beat 'em on the ice." He was criticized by people who thought he was encouraging aggression, but his meaning was misunderstood. It was more than just a remark about hockey, it was a philosophy on life.

"It means if you can be bullied anywhere, you will be bullied everywhere. It applies to every person and it applies to every nation. It is a phrase that should be repeated when you are young, and remembered when you are old."[2]

His notion of loyalty was noble enough in conception but could be self-serving in practice. During the war his life had been saved a number of times by fellow soldiers willing to risk their own skin to save his. It struck him that there was nothing more honourable or admirable and that civilian life had nothing to match it. For all the challenges presented in the peacetime world, none equated with the everyday realities of war, when each step might be your last, and giving a few moments' thought to the safety of a friend might prove critical to keeping him alive. Outside the military, Smythe would cite lack of loyalty numerous times as justification for breaking off a relationship, although to others his definition of the word often seemed to equate with a failure to adhere to his wishes, to share an opinion he held, or to back a cause he supported.

He believed deeply in his own luck. He had come to view himself as "chronically lucky."[3] It showed in his supreme self-confidence – or abrasive cockiness, depending on your point of view – which in his early years struck many as unjustified in someone just starting his adult life. Risks didn't scare Smythe; he welcomed challenges and loved emerging on top. Having faced death, very few more mundane things frightened him, and lacking fear gave him a big advantage on competitors. The war had cemented his faith in his good fortune; he calculated there had been at least five instances in which his chances of dying were better than 50 per cent, but each time he'd emerged alive. "Each time it was luck, not guts or planning or intelligence on my part. I simply believed in the existence of The Man Upstairs."[4]

The Man Upstairs was one of the few select teachings of theosophy he had adopted from his father. He was still uncertain in his religion. On his original enlistment papers in March 1915 he identified himself as a Presbyterian; seven months later when he signed on with Major Southam the enlisting officer typed "Theosophist." Albert Smythe thought his beliefs had failed to take root with his son, but Conn picked and chose among them and adopted a few that suited him. Above all he believed in the maxim "As ye sow, so shall ye reap," which was hardly exclusive to theosophy. It was similar in nature to the notion, taught by the despised Catholics among others, that one should "do unto others as you would have others do unto you." Smythe often proclaimed his adherence to this view, despite the harsh treatment he meted out to others. He was aware of his reputation as arbitrary and unforgiving but found a way to justify it to himself: yes, he was hard on people, but he was motivated by a desire to improve them. "I've been rude to people, blasted people, but I always did so only when I believed it was for their eventual good."[5] When Foster Hewitt once told him he was impossible to satisfy, he took it as a compliment.

Theosophy wasn't so much a religion as a grab bag of ideas borrowed from better-known faiths – in particular, Hindu and Buddhist teachings. Albert Smythe came upon it during a trip to the United States several years before he immigrated to Canada. He was smitten and became an immediate convert, helping form a Toronto lodge soon after arriving in his new home.

Theosophy holds that all religions derive from one original philosophy – "branches of the parent tree." It taught that the dead eventually return to life via reincarnation, gaining wisdom with each return. The body is simply a vessel to occupy while accumulating learning for the next reappearance.[6]

Conn didn't buy into all of that, but he did believe in The Silent Watcher – which he called "The Man Upstairs" – a godlike entity that kept an eye on earth-bound individuals and decreed who got the breaks and who didn't. He credited his good fortune in surviving the war to The Man Upstairs, as he did many of the breaks he would receive in life.

He had been raised by Albert to distrust Catholics, and he did. He considered the religion a racket: sin all day, head to the confessional, say a few prayers, and all was forgiven. "It's the opposite of 'as ye sow, so shall ye reap,'" he argued. "I *know* that there is no such thing as being forgiven."[7] He thought priests just got in the way, telling an interviewer once that "A Protestant is worth two Catholics because we can talk direct to God, and they have to go through a phone system."[8] In another interview he noted, "Those who do the most praying don't necessarily do the most giving."[9]

He lumped people into categories of race, religion, and nationality, and made no effort to hide it. Although there's little evidence he treated people differently based on their beliefs or ethnicity, he could speak in the most casual terms using the most bigoted terminology. His biases were not unusual for the time: during his life Canada banned Chinese immigrants, locked up Japanese Canadians, assigned women to secondary status, and subjected Aboriginals to government-sponsored persecution. It wasn't until he was well into his sixties that Canadian society's inherent biases came into widespread question. Smythe stood out because he made less effort than others to hide his views. Foster Hewitt, according to his biographer, Scott Young, despised French Canadians and embarrassed his friends with his prejudice toward blacks.[10] Mackenzie King willingly overpaid for his home at Kingsmere because it was important "to prevent Jews or other undesireable people getting in."[11] Even the most enlightened of men balked at the notion that women were their equals. But Hewitt and King were both wary of their public image and knew when to veil their bigotry. Smythe felt people should take him as he was.

In 1919, he was a young man in a hurry. He re-enrolled at the University of Toronto to complete his engineering degree. Thanks to the army he had a bit of money: while he was in captivity the government deposited forty dollars a month in his Bank of Montreal account,[12] and when he was formally released a friendly officer made sure he was paid off at the rate due a flyer, which was higher than a battery officer. He spent as little time as possible in class, too busy chasing opportunities to make money. When writing tests he would answer only as many questions as required to pass, then get up and leave. While working for York Township north of Toronto he noticed how difficult it was to get sand and gravel for construction projects. The city was growing, the streets were filling with cars, and roadways had to be extended, widened, and paved. One day a man named Frank Angotti arrived with some construction estimates. Angotti owned one truck and a nascent paving business; Smythe told him his estimates were wrong and he needed a partner – a partner like Smythe, who just happened to be available.[13]

The team of Smythe and Angotti lasted a short time until Angotti decided he preferred paving to hauling gravel. Smythe split the business with him, then bought his own truck and his own pit, a big chunk of farmland on Scarlett Road just below Eglinton Avenue on what was then the city's fringes. Today the land has been reclaimed and turned into a park – named after Smythe – but the outlines remain evident: a steep dive in the landscape where Smythe's equipment chewed into the ground and dumped it into trucks painted a distinctive blue and white. He called the company C. Smythe for Sand, a gag he enjoyed.[14]

The business was an immediate success, riding the back of an expansion that began soon after the war. Toronto's population, just over two hundred thousand at the turn of the century, was more than half a million twenty years later. The long-promised immigration boom had filled the prairies and fuelled demand for manufactured goods shipped from the east. An explosion in technological innovation had produced entire new industries based on the telephone, radio, and especially automobiles, creating a consumer culture like none that had previously existed. Cities were electrified, people went to movies, and builders erected suburbs where there used to be fields. The more there was to do, the more people needed a car to get it done. It was a great time if you were in the construction business, and Smythe, his luck holding, found himself in a growing industry in a booming city.

Despite his hurry, he and Irene had elected to put off their wedding until a year after his return. Given his traditional values, it's likely he felt unwilling to take on a bride until he felt capable of supporting her in their own home. They were finally married in March 1920, a year after his army discharge. Both still had no experience with sex; Smythe was not only unskilled but innocent. His father's only advice, when Conn asked him about the embarrassing surges of testosterone that struck him as a teen, had been to take cold showers.[15] In London once with Wreck, when both were on leave during the war, they picked up a couple of girls and Smythe was bewildered when Wreck and his girl disappeared behind a closed door, from which grunting sounds soon emerged. Smythe naively asked his friend later for an explanation.[16] He quickly mastered the practical details, however, and their first son, Stafford, was born a year after the wedding, in March 1921.

Stafford's birth finally gave Smythe the family he'd yearned for and the sense of being needed he'd craved. Stafford was followed by a daughter, Miriam, in 1923. Irene helped with the business in the early days and happily looked after the home and family. Smythe was the first to admit he liked to be the centre of attention, the fulcrum around which the family revolved, and his wife and children provided all he had sought but rarely received from his father. He wasn't yet wealthy, but was no longer poor and proved to have a facility for making money, running his business, as he would his hockey teams, along military lines, with him giving the orders. Irene was warm and accepted his role as the boss in the way she no doubt knew he needed. He understood his good fortune and appreciated it in his gruff manner. Smythe quickly made strong connections in the construction industry and formed friendships with men like himself who were making their own way in the world, shared his opinions, and were happy to send business his way.

The days started early. The Smythes rented a house near the pit, and the phone began ringing with orders at 5:00 a.m. The long days were made longer by Smythe's hockey activities, which began soon after he arrived back in Canada. His playing days were over, but he liked issuing directives as coach and manager as much as he had as captain and was soon involved with the Varsity teams he'd once played on. The university hockey season was short but intense – the first ads for players appeared in *The Varsity* in mid-November; the first practice was a week or two later and the first game a week after that. January and February were the peak of the season, with a game or practice every few nights and road trips added into the mix. Smythe added to the intensity by taking on more than one team at a time. In the 1923–24 season he started as coach of the junior team, added an intermediate team, and midway through the season began coaching the seniors as well. The University of Toronto hockey program, in effect, consisted of teams coached by Conn Smythe.

When he wasn't at the pit or on the road hustling business, he was at the rink. On some days the teams played "double-headers," a match in the afternoon followed by another the same evening. He often faced scheduling conflicts, with the seniors and juniors playing on the same day, but in different arenas or one team playing out of town while the other was at home. One year "the big shots in Hart House" argued he should choose one team and stick with it, but he kicked up such a fuss they left him alone.[17] He also scouted regularly for new prospects, coached an all-star team from a "prep league" that included St. Michael's, University of Toronto Schools, and UCC, and occasionally even refereed. In addition to intercollegiate matches, the junior and senior teams both competed in the OHA, which brought Smythe into contact – and conflict – with people and players who would play larger roles down the road. Frank Selke had left Kitchener for a job as an electrician at the U of T and was managing a team for the Catholic parish of St. Mary's that played in the same division as Smythe's senior squad. He also came to know a bland young man named Foster Hewitt, who started making radio broadcasts from a glass box near the penalty box at Arena Gardens in March 1923. Hewitt's father, W.A. Hewitt, was among the most powerful men in amateur hockey, as long-time secretary of the OHA and sports editor of the *Toronto Star*. Smythe also came to know a promising player from Owen Sound named Clarence "Happy" Day, who was studying at the university and wanted to be a pharmacist. Smythe wooed him vigorously, but Day needed money to continue his studies and accepted an offer from the Toronto St. Patricks to turn pro and play in the National Hockey League instead.

Audacious as it may seem for a university coach to be seriously pursuing an NHL-level talent, Smythe's timing – he would have called it luck – had landed him in the right place at just the right time. While professional hockey had been struggling to build a following for a decade, it was very much in its infancy. The years between the end of the war and the late 1920s were a high point for Canadian amateur hockey, especially in Toronto, where resistance to the incursions of the pro game was unusually strong.

There were good reasons for that. Pro hockey had little to commend it to fans. There were many rival leagues, which came, went, raided one another, signed up teams and players, and then disappeared. Although the Stanley Cup grew steadily in prestige, it was for years a challenge cup that could be claimed by any team able to defeat the current holder. Among the first fifty challenges, only one winner – the Kenora Thistles in 1907 – wasn't from Montreal, Ottawa, or Winnipeg. When Toronto finally managed to put together a competitive team, it couldn't seem to hang on to a name or an owner for more than a few years. The 1914

Toronto Blueshirts became the 1918 Toronto Arenas, who gave way to the 1922 Toronto St. Patricks, all Cup winners and all linked in one way or another to a contentious, quarrelsome, astonishingly litigious man named Eddie Livingstone, a local sports entrepreneur who more than any single person was responsible for the formation of the NHL in 1917, which his fellow team owners created out of an overwhelming desire to get rid of him. The NHL was in every major element identical to its predecessor, the National Hockey Association, except that Eddie Livingstone wasn't invited to join.

Even without Livingstone the NHL's early years were a struggle. The league bumbled through much of its first decade, expanding and contracting as teams came and went. The Quebec Bulldogs appeared, disappeared, then reappeared. A team was placed in Hamilton, but when the players demanded extra money to compensate for an expanded schedule, NHL president Frank Calder suspended the entire lineup. At one point the league was down to just three teams.

Compared to the confusion and unreliability of the NHA/NHL, Ontario had a wealth of skilled amateur teams with strong roots in their communities. The connection only increased after the war, when thousands of veterans streamed home and once again took up the game they loved. Toronto was particularly rich in amateur leagues offering competitive teams. When the *Globe*'s sports section reported scores, the "pro league" (as it called the NHL) was just one among many that included the OHA (which had myriad levels of play), the Northern Ontario Hockey League, the intercollegiate league, interprovincial league, the prep school league, the Toronto league, the Mercantile league, a Beach league, and a bunch of church leagues, the Catholics being devilishly prolific at churning out God-fearing goal scorers.

The University of Toronto – which referred to all its teams as Varsity, making headlines in the school paper, also called *The Varsity*, some-what repetitive – traditionally iced a strong team. The senior squad had made the finals for the Allan Cup in 1920 and 1921, winning in 1921. The cup was the symbol of Canada's top amateur team and in those years rivalled the Stanley Cup both for prestige and the level of excitement generated. Smythe continued the school's tradition, pumping out intercollegiate champions and teams that regularly vied for top spot in their OHA divisions. The senior Varsity squad made a trip every year to New England, playing teams from Harvard, Yale, Boston College, and other Ivy League schools, generally winning handily while drawing big crowds and much newspaper attention. During the 1925 circuit Smythe announced a plan to launch an international intercollegiate league, which would pit four teams from Canada – Varsity, Queens, McGill, and Montreal – against four from the United States. That same year he took the seniors all the way to the Allan Cup final in Winnipeg, where they lost to a formidable team from Port Arthur anchored by a tall, laconic goalie named Lorne Chabot.

Smythe's shooters simply could not beat Chabot, who produced a 4–0 victory in the first game of the best-of-three playoff. In the second game, the teams were tied until Port Arthur scored the winner with just fifteen seconds left. Newspapers of the day tended toward floridity at the best of times, and the sports reporters often lost all control as they sought to convey the excitement of the moment. According to the *Globe* correspondent, the last period of the final game in Winnipeg witnessed "a finish that transformed a band of meek individuals into 5,000 raving maniacs. The Goddess of Fortune was swaying its pendulum to and fro in such rapid fashion that the fans hardly knew what it was all about."[18]

That was nothing, however, compared to the rematch a year later, when a more mature Varsity team once again faced Chabot in a series of games that had Toronto in a tizzy. The rivals were to meet in another best-of-three playoff, starting in Montreal before moving to Toronto. The first two games took place at the recently built Forum, alternating nights with the Stanley Cup semifinals between the Montreal Maroons and Pittsburgh Pirates, promising what the *Globe* called "the greatest hockey feast ever known in the history of the winter game."[19] Port Arthur was considered so strong, its players were rumoured to have been offered $5,000 apiece to quit en masse and turn professional. The reports were dismissed, only to be replaced by firm assurances from unknown sources that the entire team planned to turn pro and enter the NHL the next season.[20]

Unfortunately, the greatest hockey feast ever began as a disappointment. Montreal fans weren't nearly as thrilled about watching two Ontario teams as the organizers had hoped. Amid much grumbling about poor crowds – only 3,500 showed up for the first game, in an arena built to house three times that many – Chabot again blanked Varsity, winning 1–0. Toronto goalie Joe Sullivan was knocked unconscious by a puck that caught him in the face, inspiring suggestions that goalies really should consider wearing masks. On the day of the second game all of Quebec went into mourning when it was announced Georges Vezina, the legendary goaltender, had died in Chicoutimi. The *Star* reported he was just thirty-eight and had twenty-two children; the *Globe* said he was forty-four and had seventeen.[21] The Hockey Hall of Fame maintains he was thirty-nine and had twenty-four children, of which only two survived. A recent history of the Montreal Canadiens says he had two children, and the tales of more were a myth created for gullible Anglo reporters.[22] While tributes flowed for Vezina, Varsity finally got some pucks past Chabot, winning 3–1.

If Montreal fans had been unenthused, Toronto fans were beside themselves. A line for the third game began to form well before dawn and stretched for blocks by the time tickets finally went on sale at 9:00 a.m. They sold out immediately, the first in line being two enthusiastic youths who said they'd been paid five dollars to wait up all night. There were fears the match might be cancelled – coaches had a say in choosing referees, and for obscure reasons Smythe had refused to accept any officials from Ontario. In the end the game went ahead as planned, though Smythe might have wished it hadn't. His team raced out to a quick three-goal lead and then watched Port Arthur whittle it away, tying the game in the third period. Three ten-minute overtime periods couldn't produce another goal, so an unprecedented

fourth game was announced, to be played two days later. The *Star*'s
Lou Marsh, whose prose was flamboyant even for the day, produced
a highly critical report in which he accused Smythe's team of throwing
the Cup away:

> Jumping Tuna! Wotta nerve-wracker last night's Allan Cup deadlock
> was!
>
> It would have made a Chinese Buddhist uncross his legs and yell like
> a Comanche Indian.
>
> Ninety minutes, a 3-3 tie.
>
> Yep! Three for Port Arthur and three for Varsity.[23]

Marsh was aghast that the "skull-improvers" (i.e., students) had
failed to hold on to their lead, blaming it – without naming names – on
Smythe. The players, he said, "need more schooling on tactics and
strategy." At times his writing could be difficult to decipher, such as
his description of an early Varsity goal:

> Chabot was Morphousing when Plaxton won the washer on the initial
> saw-off, took a couple of strides and let her go. The armoured armadillo
> from back beyond the big lake did not even see the flying gutty. He simply
> stared in consternation when the port light flashed above his head.[24]

Marsh's displeasure only increased during the next game. It was
played amid a massive windstorm, which blew over trees, knocked
down poles, and cut off communications for much of the province.
The *Star* had advertised that its radio station CFCA would broadcast
the game live, but the storm disrupted things to such an extent that
reports had to be hurried by train to Guelph where they could be
relayed to news-starved fans in Port Arthur.[25] Marsh's report the next
day began, "Howling dog fish!" and accused Varsity of playing "brain-
less hockey." Sullivan, he recorded, faced eighty-two shots. "How he
kept them out is the eighth wonder of the world."

The game went into two overtime periods before Port Arthur scored the winning goal. Smythe was unapologetic. Two days after the game he told Marsh – who would remain forever one of his least favourite sportswriters – that his players had simply been overwhelmed by their opponent's aggressive four- and five-man rushes. "They were in on top of our goal like wolves and our boys did not know how to get out," he said. "When they tried to stick-handle their way out the Port boys poke-checked them to death, and when they tried to lift or bang it out they unfortunately fed the puck right to enemy sticks. The boys tried all they knew, but they were just too good for us. This Port Arthur team surely has been a nightmare to me."[26]

PART TWO

BUILDER

CHAPTER 4

A few weeks before Varsity's disappointing loss, something happened that would change the future of hockey in Canada. Smythe received a message from Col. John S. Hammond of the newly created New York Rangers, who was looking for a general manager. Hammond worked for Tex Rickard, the larger-than-life Manhattan impresario and boxing promoter who had bought Madison Square Garden and moved it to a new location well away from Madison Square, presiding over the formal opening just a few months earlier.

Rickard had a team and a building, but lacked players and a manager who knew the game. He and Hammond had both been persuaded that hockey would draw well in New York, providing the Garden with a regular revenue stream between the boxing matches that were Rickard's bread and butter, but neither had more than a passing acquaintance with the game. They needed someone who did, and Smythe had been recommended by Charles F. Adams, the grocery magnate who owned the Boston Bruins. Adams had watched Smythe's Varsity squads regularly beat up on local college teams and was impressed. Smythe was young, cocky, energetic and already well into a feud with Boston's equally thick-skinned coach, Art Ross, but he seemed to have a facility for building winners. Adams suggested the Rangers give him a try.

Hammond duly offered a contract, and Smythe signed on March 25, 1926, accepting $5,000 his first year and $7,500 for each of the next three, plus 5 per cent of the Rangers' net profits, with a $2,500 minimum guaranteed for the first year. Either side could back out with appropriate notice, with Smythe guaranteed his salary plus $5,000 if he was fired before March 1927. The details would prove to be important.

Smythe's entry into professional hockey was the first step down a road that would lead to the creation of the Toronto Maple Leafs, the construction of Maple Leaf Gardens, and the establishment of a dynasty that would last forty years and win eleven Stanley Cups. Along the way it would create a pantheon of Canadian hockey heroes – too many to begin to list – and a handful of national icons. It would make Smythe one of the best-known figures in the country, see his arena become a national sports shrine, and turn Saturday night into a near-religious experience as Canadians from one coast to the other gathered around the radio to listen to Foster Hewitt describe the latest exploits of Canada's favourite team. It would also alter the fortunes of the NHL, which Smythe helped transform from just another pro league into the dominant sports organization in the land, and the only league allowed to compete for the Stanley Cup. By the time Smythe retired, he would have built a prosperous enterprise so unshakably healthy it would withstand recession, depression, war, scandal, and an entire generation of perilously awful management.

For the moment, though, Smythe's opportunity presented a problem on the home front. While he was understandably elated, it was a move that alarmed Irene. She was a young mother with two children, living in a small house near her husband's gravel business. She was accustomed to her husband being absent in the hockey season, but the prospect of the whole family – Stafford was five and Miriam three – moving to New York wasn't part of her long-term plans. Toronto was growing rapidly enough, but New York was ten times the size and a world away in terms of its pace, intensity, and sophistication. Everything about it was bigger, faster, and more demanding. It was far away from everyone she knew, and she could expect to see even less of her husband.

To reassure her, Smythe promised they would make their permanent home in Toronto while he commuted. He set out to find her a bigger house, scouted neighbourhoods, and quickly settled on a pleasant new area named Baby Point on the western reaches of the city overlooking the Humber River. It had a solid and comfortable feel, dotted with large, stone-fronted, English-style manor houses with mullioned windows and flagstone walks, many of them backing on to deep ravines with mature trees. It was also just down Jane Street from the pit. Smythe bought a ravine lot and paid an architect $15,000 to erect a large, comfortable home, big enough for their growing brood, but not the sort of ostentatious monster home a self-made man eager to show off his success might build today. He and Irene would live there the rest of their lives, adding other properties along the way but always with Baby Point as the place to which they came home.

The new job meant Smythe would be spending six months a year in New York, dropping in to see his family when the Rangers played in Toronto, and the other six running his gravel business. It wasn't a perfect arrangement, but to Irene it was preferable to uprooting the clan and shipping them to a big, strange city away from their friends and families. Nine months after they moved into the new house, their third child, Hugh, was born.

That spring was a propitious moment in the life of the NHL and hockey in general. Just as Smythe had returned from the war at the moment amateur hockey was entering its golden age, so he was getting out as it was about to be eclipsed forever by the professional game.

A decade after its formation, the NHL was finally seeing some success. From three teams in 1918 it had grown to ten for the 1926–27 season, and interest was building in the U.S. northeast. As usual, American involvement stirred mixed feelings in Canada. The three latest additions to the league, in New York, Chicago, and Detroit, shifted the balance significantly. Instead of a seven-team league with four clubs in Canada, the NHL was now a ten-team league with six in the United States.

At the same time, the NHL's most serious rivals disappeared. For years the league had vied with western competitors for players and prestige. The main threat was the British Columbia–based Pacific Coast Hockey Association, owned and operated by the Patrick brothers, Lester and Frank. Another western-based league, the Western Canada

Hockey League, had teams in Calgary, Edmonton, Regina, and Saskatoon/Moose Jaw. The western teams had plenty of talent, including Eddie Shore, Cyclone Taylor, Dick Irvin, and the Patricks themselves, but western Canada didn't yet have the population to support a league of its own, much less two, and both leagues had died out by the end of the 1926 season.*

For the NHL, the timing was perfect. The east had both money and population and plenty of interest in hockey. The NHL quickly granted franchises to Chicago and Detroit and approved a second team in Manhattan, where the New York Americans had already begun play. The Chicago team was owned by Maj. Frederic McLaughlin, who named it the Black Hawks after his First World War machine-gun battalion, and let his wife design an Indian-head crest for the jerseys. The newly named Hawks had spent the previous year as the Portland Rosebuds, led by Dick Irvin, a serious-minded centre from Regina who had scored thirty goals in thirty games. McLaughlin bought the Rosebuds to stock his team – spending somewhere between $100,000 and $200,000 depending on which report you believe. In Detroit, the new owners bought up Lester Patrick's Victoria Cougars, who had won the 1925 Stanley Cup, the last non-NHL team to do so.[1]

The new owners were just what professional hockey needed: wealthy men in large markets who could build big arenas and sell the game to an American audience. So many U.S. teams were signing up that NHL governors reluctantly agreed to split into two divisions, with a U.S. division comprising New York, Boston, Chicago, Detroit, and Pittsburgh,† and a Canadian division including Toronto,

* Lester Patrick owned and played for the Victoria club in the PCHA. When the league folded, he was the last owner/player until Mario Lemieux in Pittsburgh more than seventy years later.

† Bruce Kidd, *The Struggle for Canadian Sport* (Toronto: University of Toronto Press, 1996), 207. This book gives 1926 census figures as New York (5.9 million), Boston (787,000), Chicago (3 million), Detroit (1.3 million), and Pittsburgh (637,000).

Ottawa, the Maroons and Canadiens from Montreal, and, incongruously, the New York Americans. Like Rickard, though, most of the new owners had little more than a passing understanding of the game itself.

There are two distinct versions of how Tex Rickard came to own a hockey team. Personally, he wasn't much interested in the sport. He'd built his name as a boxing promoter, turning his friendship with heavyweight champion Jack Dempsey into a spectacularly successful run of record-setting fight promotions, sometimes building an entire stadium just for one fight, then tearing it down afterwards. The Garden had been built for boxing, which was wildly popular, but not enough to keep the lights on every night. Rickard needed something to fill the gap.

Frank Boucher, who knew Hammond and spent his career with the Rangers as player, coach and manager, said Hammond convinced his his friend and business partner that hockey was the answer to their problem. Hammond had been to Montreal, where he took in a few games at the old Mount Royal arena, which he complained was "cold as Greenland" and so crowded he couldn't get out of his seat to warm himself between periods. But he was impressed by the enthusiasm of the patrons and the excitement of the game, and he figured people in New York would be just as enthusiastic. [2]

A second version maintains that it was Rickard who was lured to Montreal for a Canadiens game, where he took one look at Howie Morenz and pledged that if Morenz would play in New York he'd agree to buy a franchise.[3]

Both Rickard and Hammond were characters it would be difficult to invent. Rickard was one of the best-known men in New York at a time when it was stuffed with celebrity competition, from Babe Ruth and Lou Gehrig to Duke Ellington and George Gershwin. There were reputed to be twenty thousand illegal drinking establishments in Manhattan alone, despite Prohibition, and mobsters by the carload to keep them all supplied.

Rickard came to the Big City by way of the Wild West and the Klondike gold rush. He was born in Missouri, one farm down from the James family. His mother claimed she missed his first cry because a posse happened to be passing, chasing Jesse and Frank. He made it to the end of the third grade before quitting to spend a decade herding cattle and riding the range on ranches around Kansas. When his young wife and newborn died, he lit out for gold country, making and losing several fortunes in the Klondike and Nome gold rushes, mostly running a series of saloons and gambling joints he anointed with the same name, The Northern. Eventually he headed south to Nevada, where he opened a new Northern in the town of Goldfield and got into the boxing business as a way of attracting customers to the fly-blown desert location. He prospered as a promoter and took out a ten-year lease on Madison Square Garden in 1920 when it was losing $25,000 a year. Five years later he built a new version twenty-five blocks away, on top of what had been the city streetcar barns.

Hammond was born to a family with deep roots in the military and iron manufacturing. He trained at West Point, where he starred as a sprinter, competing in the 1904 Olympic Games. He also took up polo, and was working as a military attaché in South America when he met Rickard, who had taken a sabbatical from digging gold and hustling fights to start up a cattle business. Hammond quit the army and the two teamed up in a number of oil and cattle ventures. When Rickard moved to New York, Hammond went with him and was put in charge of overseeing new ventures.

Whether it was Rickard or Hammond who first hit on the notion of a hockey team for the Garden, they initially agreed it would be better if someone else owned the team. They found their man in a well-known bootlegger named Big Bill Dwyer. Dwyer lived in a suite at the Forrest Hotel, which featured an open bar and plenty of women of easy virtue.

He liked the idea of being a hockey impresario. Frank Calder, the NHL president, was less enthused. When Smythe and Ottawa

Senators owner Frank Ahearn once accompanied Dwyer to a lunch meeting, Calder was appalled: "Don't you fellows know he got a bullet through the overcoat last week?" he demanded.[4] Hammond arranged for Dwyer to acquire a franchise and some players, and the New York Americans were born. They debuted at the Garden in 1925 and were such a hit Rickard and Hammond quickly decided they needed their own team, instantly dooming the Americans to also-ran status.*

It was probably preordained that Smythe would clash with the polo-playing, aristocratic Hammond, who had exactly the sort of pedigree Smythe resented. Colonel Hammond had learned his military skills at soldier school; Lieutenant Smythe picked his up while getting shot at in Europe. The colonel wrote a handbook on artillery; Smythe studied artillery by firing it at Germans. Smythe was confident of his ability, having spent years producing winning teams in Toronto. "I knew every hockey player in the world right then," he would brag.[5] Hammond, on the other hand, knew what it took to pack the Garden and excite a New York crowd. Smythe might have been a superior hockey man with a strong record and plenty of chutzpah, but on Broadway he was still just a little guy from Toronto whom nobody had ever heard of.

He set out to build the Rangers a team, armed with a short list of players. The collapse of the two western leagues had flooded the market with talent, but there was also plenty of competition and he knew he had to move quickly. One of his first stops was Port Arthur in pursuit of Lorne Chabot, the big, sad-eyed goalie who had twice stymied his bid for the Allan Cup. Chabot was a large man, an inch over six feet, in an era of small goalies. It was commonly accepted that small, quick men were better in net because they moved faster. Chabot didn't move quickly. Sometimes he barely seemed to move at

---

* Bill Dwyer didn't get to see his team's first game in 1925, having been arrested for bootlegging a few days earlier.

all. When not busy, he liked to lounge on the crossbar "like a mantle-piece" according to one observer, chewing gum and rarely saying a word. He was superstitious and a bit vain, always shaving before a game because he thought stitches showed up less on a clean-shaven face. When under fire he would flop around the crease in a style that left more than one coach unimpressed. But he had a decided facility for stopping pucks, which was all that Smythe cared about.

From Port Arthur Smythe went to Minnesota to watch Ching Johnson and Taffy Abel, who played as a defensive pairing for the Minneapolis Millers in the U.S. amateur league. Johnson was 210 pounds and solid muscle; Abel outweighed him by 15 pounds, most of it flab. Johnson, big, balding, and cheerful, loved body contact and appeared to be grinning while he played, especially after hitting somebody. When you ran into Johnson, teammates said, it was like slamming into a wall. Hitting Taffy, on the other hand, was like falling into a pillow.

Still, at a time when restrictions on forward passing forced players to try to carry the puck past the defence, getting by Taffy and Ching was a formidable task. They moved quickly for big men and had the ability to smother the play of attacking players. Ching, whose real first name was Ivan and whose nickname came from his habit of acting as cook during summer camping trips – a job usually reserved for Chinese hired hands – was careful with his money and gave Smythe a hard time during bargaining, constantly walking out to "phone his wife," like a car salesman pretending to check with the manager.* Abel was even worse. On the day Smythe was leaving town, he still didn't have a deal and asked Abel to meet him on the train. When the train lurched into motion he blocked Abel's exit. "'Taffy,' I said, "the money's good, you won't do better, and the next stop is two hundred and fifty miles away.

---

* Ching's nickname was perfectly acceptable by the standards of the time, which didn't share today's greater social and ethnic sensibilities. While possibly just inside the bounds of acceptability by modern standards, the chant fans put up when he was on the ice – "Ching, Ching, Chinaman!" – would be considered beyond the pale.

If you don't sign, you won't be getting off this train until then.'" Abel signed and leapt off the moving train.[6] *

Smythe intercepted Bill and Bun Cook in Winnipeg while they were on their way to see a man from the Montreal Maroons. The Cooks had been playing for Saskatoon in the WCHL, with Bill usually leading the league in scoring. Smythe badly wanted both brothers, though Bill was the star of the two. Bill Cook was a serious, intense man who had spent four years in Europe during the First World War, then signed up for two extra years fighting Bolsheviks in Russia. He loved to shoot the puck, but wasn't much for passing. "When I want that puck, I'll yell for it, and you get that damn puck to me," he'd say.[7] Frank Boucher, who would centre the brothers, said Cook's on-ice cry "was the most amazing half-grunt, half-moan, half-yell I ever heard. He'd let this weird sound out of him, which meant he was in the clear."[8] Smythe signed them both, for an eminently reasonable bonus of $5,000, the greater share going to Bill. The Cooks in turn recommended he sign Boucher, who Smythe had never seen. Taking them at their word he sent a cable to Hammond, who obediently bought Boucher's rights.

Frank Boucher would spend three decades in the NHL as player, coach, or manager, and never come to like Conn Smythe. The trouble started right off the bat, at their first meeting on a train platform in Ottawa, where Boucher had been summoned to meet his new boss. Boucher had spent a miserable summer caring for his wife, who'd been ill since giving birth to their first child, and he'd lost a lot of weight. He thought his rights belonged to Boston and hadn't realized he'd been traded to New York until that morning, when Ahearn called and told him Connie Smythe was in town and wanted to meet him. Boucher later related the conversation in his memoirs:[9]

---

* Although he liked the Johnson/Abel defensive tandem, Smythe almost didn't sign Abel. When Smythe turned up to scout the team, he noticed Abel was playing with a ragged old stick and decided he wasn't the sort of player for the Rangers. He changed his mind after Abel explained that someone had stolen all the team's sticks the night before, forcing him to scrounge whatever replacement he could find.

"Connie who?" I asked.

"Smythe. S-m-y-t-h-e."

"Well, who is he and what's he want to see me for?"

"I'm not sure, Frankie, but I assume he wants to talk about your contract. He's recruiting players for the Rangers, you know."

"The Rangers? But I'm going to Boston."

"Good God Frankie," Ahearn shouted. "Where have you been? You were sold to the Rangers a month ago."

The meeting at the train station didn't go well. Author Trent Frayne, who co-wrote Boucher's memoirs, recounted that when Smythe was peeved his bright blue eyes turned into "round dimes of ice." Smythe was less than impressed when he sized up his scrawny new centreman, and Boucher got the ten-cent eyeball treatment.

"What do you weigh?" he demanded.

"Around a hundred and thirty five," I said.

"I paid fifteen thousand dollars for *you*?' Smythe grunted. "Bill Cook must be crazy."[10]

Adding Boucher meant the Rangers were all but complete. Teams consisted of one main forward line and a pair of defencemen, with a handful of spares. The forwards played up to forty-five minutes a game, the defence up to sixty minutes or more, if there was overtime. Goalies often had no backups – if one was hurt during a game, everyone waited while he got stitched up.

Smythe's no-nonsense approach to negotiations had secured the entire new Rangers team, eleven players in all, for $32,000. It was a remarkable feat, even for the time. The winner's purse for a single Dempsey-Tunney match in 1927 was $990,000. Babe Ruth was earning $70,000 a year, double the entire Rangers payroll. In a few short weeks, Smythe had managed to put together a strong squad willing to play for what amounted, in New York terms, to peanuts.

Training was set to open October 18 at the Ravina Gardens, a rink in the west end of Toronto near High Park. Pre-season fitness wasn't taken too seriously by most teams. The schedule was just forty-four games, recently raised from thirty-six. Players turned up in November and played themselves into shape in the opening weeks. Smythe, though, was a stickler for conditioning and intended to put the players through an extended training program, with roadwork in the mornings and skating in the afternoons. He immediately got into a quarrel with Boucher, who objected when Smythe informed him he'd be paid the same $3,500 he'd earned the year before. Boucher argued that Toronto was a lot more expensive than Vancouver and demanded a raise. They got into a shouting match before Smythe relented and agreed to a $1,500 increase.[11]

The rookie manager wasn't in any better odour with Hammond, who had developed serious doubts about the opinionated little man from Toronto. Their temperaments were similar: each considered himself the boss of any enterprise of which he was part. Hammond wanted a team he could sell on Broadway. That meant big names, colourful characters, and outsized personalities. New Yorkers didn't care about quiet, gum-chewing goaltenders from Port Arthur, even if they had won two Allan Cups. Hammond and Rickard were accustomed to dealing in large figures; the colonel would happily have doubled the $32,000 payroll if Smythe had delivered even one big-name player.

Hammond urged Smythe to make a bid for Babe Dye, an all-round athlete who had played halfback for the Toronto Argonauts football club and been offered $25,000 to play baseball in Philadelphia. Dye had averaged more than a goal a game over the previous six years with the Toronto St. Patricks. Although easily the team's best player, he was being offered at a reasonable price because the St. Pats needed money. Hammond was eager to make a bid. Smythe refused. He considered Dye too much of a one-man band. Smythe emphasized team play and felt a big star on an otherwise nondescript team upset the balance. He noted the St. Pats had a lousy record despite Dye's scoring prowess. When word came through that Dye had been sold to the Black Hawks, Hammond was irate. He intercepted Smythe, who had been at the theatre with Irene, and informed him Dye had gone to Chicago for $15,000. Smythe shrugged it off. "I wouldn't want Dye on my team, no matter what the price," he told Hammond. "He wouldn't help this team one day."*

Soon after, Lester Patrick got a telegram in Victoria, B.C., inquiring whether he was interested in managing the Rangers. The next day Hammond called to confirm the offer, and Patrick accepted. He was just forty-two, but already had the stature of a grand old man of hockey. He and his brother had built the first artificial ice rinks in Canada and had launched the Pacific Coast League to ensure there were teams to play in them. They'd introduced a dozen or more changes to the game, regularly altering rules and introducing innovations. Lester was the more regal of the two, tall, stately, and grey-haired, looking more like a Victorian gentleman than a confirmed rink rat. If anyone had the mix of gravitas and showmanship to suit New Yorkers, it was Lester Patrick.[12]

A few days later Smythe got a call to meet Hammond at Union Station. When he got there, Patrick was with Hammond. "I knew without being told that I no longer was coach of the New York Rangers," Smythe said.[13] Hammond told him Patrick would be taking over immediately. He offered $7,500 to buy out Smythe's contract instead of the $10,000 he had been promised. Too upset to argue, Smythe agreed.

With Smythe's co-operation, Hammond put on a song and dance for the local papers to explain the sudden change. He called a press conference at the King Edward Hotel October 25 and declared that everyone was parting as friends. Smythe was leaving, he said, because the Rangers had decided they needed a year-round coach, and Smythe

---

* Babe Dye had a strong first season with the Black Hawks, leading the team in goals with twenty-five and placing second in scoring to Dick Irvin. However, at training camp the next year he broke his leg and never regained his previous level of skill. He scored just one goal over the next three seasons before retiring in 1931.

had decided he couldn't abandon his sand and gravel business in Toronto and move to Manhattan.

"I am sorry to lose Smythe," Hammond told the *Star*'s Lou Marsh. "He has done exceptionally valuable work for us in getting together this team and I am certainly sorry to lose him. He is a bright young man of exceptional executive and business ability, and we could use him to advantage if we could only pay him enough to induce him to drop his business here." Any suggestion that the Rangers were dumping Smythe to go with the more experienced Patrick was "sour," he said.

Marsh accepted the explanation without challenge, reporting that Hammond was "a superior type of man" who "inspires loyalty."

"Smythe and the Rangers part with the friendliest of feeling," he reported.[14]

It was all balderdash. Smythe was crushed and Hammond was happy to be rid of him. Over the next few days Smythe grew increasingly irritated at being stiffed out of his extra $2,500. He felt Hammond and Rickard didn't know enough about hockey to appreciate the quality of the team he'd assembled. Rickard tried to soften the blow, inviting him to the Rangers opening game and promising tickets to several Broadway shows, at the Garden's expense. Smythe tossed the invitation aside, but Irene retrieved the letter and insisted they go. It turned out to be a lucky thing for her husband that she did.

CHAPTER 5

A time would come when Smythe would concede that the Rangers made the right decision in firing him.

"Patrick did a better job than I ever could have," he said. "I've seen what happens to other men who go to New York and can't handle all the wine, women and song. What the hell was I – 32? – right down in New York with all the girls you wanted and nothing to do . . . In time I came to see that Col. Hammond had done me a favour."[1]

Frank Boucher couldn't have been happier: Smythe's demanding style would never have produced the "comradeship" and "maturity" the Rangers developed under Patrick, he argued. "Smythe ruled by the sword; Lester had discipline, but he was one of us, too."[2] Murray Murdoch, one of the substitutes he had signed for the Rangers, didn't dislike Smythe as Boucher did, but conceded the players weren't upset to see him go. "Conn and Lester were totally different personalities," he said. Smythe set high standards, expected them to be met, and singled out anyone who failed. Patrick was quieter and less given to outbursts and face-to-face confrontation, though in the end his message was just as stark. At one of his first team meetings, he warned the players: "When we start playing in the National Hockey League you're going to win some games and you're going to lose some. I just want to stress this: If you lose more than you win, you won't be around."[3]

Even his critics conceded it was Smythe's lineup that produced the success the Rangers would enjoy over most of the next decade. Boucher and the Cook brothers, backed by Abel and Johnson, with Chabot in goal, won the 1928 Stanley Cup. Boucher, the Cooks, and Johnson remained the heart of the team when it won again in 1933. Of the six starters hired by Smythe that summer, four would make the Hall of Fame, with pudgy Taffy Abel and, oddly, Lorne Chabot being the only exceptions. Bill Cook was already thirty when he signed but would score more goals than any player in the league over the next seven years. Boucher won the Lady Byng Trophy so often – seven times in eight years – the league told him to keep it and introduced a new one for everybody else to compete over. Even Murray Murdoch proved his worth, turning into the league's iron man by playing in 508 straight games over eleven years.

All that was in the future, though. Smythe was still grumbling about his lost $2,500 as he and Irene chugged to New York in November 1926 for the opening game. It wasn't the money itself that was important. Smythe made plenty of money from his sand and gravel business and would have been wealthy even if he'd stuck to Varsity hockey. It was getting cheated out of something he felt he was owed that rankled. It also annoyed him that no one in New York seemed to appreciate what he'd done for them. Since the Rangers hadn't cost much, and few had even played in the NHL before, New Yorkers assumed they couldn't be much good. Even the press jumped to the conclusion the no-name manager had assembled a no-hope squad. The morning of the first game, against the Stanley Cup champion Maroons, a headline in New York read: "WORLD'S BEST MEET WORLD'S WORST TONIGHT IN GARDEN." Rickard had obviously been reading the papers and believed what he read: when the Smythes arrived at the Garden that night and were seated in Rickard's box, he came by to say hello and asked Smythe: "Well Connie, do you think we can hold the score to single digits?"[4]

That only added to Smythe's irritation. "Keep your eyes open and you'll see your team win," he replied.[5]

Frank Boucher left behind a vivid portrait of the first Rangers game ever played, which took place before a packed house on November 16, the women in evening dress and furs, their men in tuxedos. The heat from the crowd – reported as eighteen thousand – was so intense that little puddles formed on the ice, sending patches of mist rising from the surface. Even before the puck was dropped the rafters were fading into a haze of smoke.[6] The referee was Lou Marsh, who moonlighted as a referee, enabling him to officiate the game and still cover it for the *Star*. Marsh was an old-school referee who used a school bell in place of a whistle, having experienced temperatures so frigid that whistles would stick to the lips.

The Rangers started Hal Winkler in net, who would last just a few games before Chabot took over the job. The Rangers' publicity man, Johnny Bruno, had hit on a scheme to attract fans from the city's substantial population of Italians and Jews. When Chabot played in New York, he was listed in the program under the name Chabotsky. He would be Jewish for home games only; Bruno figured he was too well known in Canada to fool anyone. Similarly, a backup winger named Oliver Reinikka, a Canadian of Finnish descent, was listed as Ollie Rocco, to attract New York's Italians. Bruno had proposed another stunt to stir up local interest. He wanted to arrange for the kidnapping of Bill Cook, which would guarantee headlines for days, until Cook was fortuitously rescued just in time for the first faceoff. But Patrick vetoed the plan.[7]

From the beginning, pro hockey's popularity in the United States was related directly to the amount of violence that could be expected. Paul Gallico, a much-respected columnist with the *New York Daily News*, wrote that the game's immediate success was due to the fact that "it is a fast, body-contact game played by men with clubs in their hands and knives lashed to their feet, since the skates are razor sharp, and before the evening is over it is almost a certainty that someone will be hurt and will fleck the ice with a generous contribution of gore, before he is led away to be hem-stitched together again."[8]

The Rangers gave the crowd what they wanted, as the match quickly developed into a three-period brawl. The Maroons were the toughest team of the era, a take-no-prisoners squad that played to an English crowd in Montreal while the Canadiens played to the French.

Like everyone else they assumed the inexperienced Rangers would fold fast, and when Bill Cook scored the game's first goal, and they were unable to put an equalizer into the Ranger net, they grew surly and violent. Ching Johnson took a stick over the eye and left the ice trailing blood, returning with five stitches and a white patch on his brow. Cook was slashed across the arm, then cross-checked in the head. With no such thing as a flood between periods – the Zamboni was still just a glint in some inventor's eye – the ice quickly deteriorated, slowing play. Boucher recalled the players struggling along like a group of heavyweights late in a fight "who'd pounded each other through all the early rounds and now were leg-weary and arm-weary though still mean and game."[9] The *New York Times* reported that the game had been "savagely" played and set a new indoor record for penalties. Things got so rough, as the Maroons sought to avoid an upset, that Boucher was goaded into the one and only fight of his career, twice knocking down a player named Bill Phillips and getting knocked down himself once in return.[10]

In the end Cook's goal stood as the only one of the match, and Smythe's prediction of victory was vindicated. With the crowd in a frenzy, it dawned on Rickard that Hammond may have been hasty in dumping Smythe. Rickard asked him to come by his office in the morning for a chat.

As Smythe told it, he returned to the Garden as requested, was offered a position as vice-president of hockey operations, and turned it down flat. "I wouldn't work for you bunch of cheapskates if you gave me the franchise," he replied.[11]

Rickard was taken aback. He took pride in his reputation for honesty. During his days as a saloonkeeper in the North, many a prospector had trusted him to hold a stash of gold for safekeeping. As a promoter he could raise huge sums of money on his good name alone. He may have done a steady trade with mobsters, hoods, bootleggers, and bent politicians, but he didn't cheat them.

"What do you mean, cheapskates?" he demanded.

Smythe told his story, and Rickard sought out Hammond for an explanation. Hammond said he'd expected Smythe to move to New York and since he hadn't, his expenses were lower than anticipated. Rickard waved off the excuse. "Pay this young man what we owe him."[12]

Smythe took the cheque and headed home with Irene, travelling by way of Montreal. Never one to hide his accomplishments, he shared news of his victory with several gentlemen of the press. A photo shows Smythe, immaculately dressed as usual, surrounded by sports-writers in a crowded room in Montreal's Mount Royal Hotel, "being congratulated upon receiving cheque . . . from New York Rangers hockey club." Smythe is clutching a bottle – possibly champagne – and showing something to Marsh, who had switched back to being a reporter. The boys were obviously whooping it up: there are at least nine packed into the photo, one of whom appears to be sprinkling something on Smythe's head.[13]

With his penchant for timely risk-taking, he bet the extra $2,500 on a McGill football game, and won. He took the $5,000 payoff and wagered it on the Rangers' second game, in Toronto against the St. Patricks. Everyone thought the Rangers' opening-night victory was a fluke, but they won easily and Smythe doubled his money again. In four days he had turned $2,500 into $10,000.

It was a silver lining to his clouded experience with the Rangers, who sent him an engraved loving cup to show there were no hard feel-ings. Over the remainder of the winter he experienced another run of success, reclaiming his coaching position at the University of Toronto and taking two teams – the Varsity club and the Grads – to champion-ships. The teams were so successful he found himself in the uncomfort-able position of coaching both clubs as they headed into a showdown for the right to play for the Allan Cup and represent Canada at the 1928 Olympics.

The Grads that year were one of the great squads of the era. Made up largely of the players he'd coached to the Allan Cup finals the year before, they rolled over opponents without a defeat all winter. On

February 14 they overwhelmed the Toronto Canoe Club at Arena Gardens by a score of 14–1. "The losers were completely outclassed and they could do nothing against the superior ability of the club under the tuition of 'Conny' Smythe," the *Star* reported.*

They won a tough game against a team from London, but were held to a surprise tie by Quebec's provincial champions, the St. Francois Nationals. The ubiquitous Lou Marsh opened his report on the game in his usual overcarbonated style: "Hot hamburger, what a nice dash of vinegar this St. Francois team . . . tossed into the Olympic cocktail of Varsity Grads here last night."

Marsh suggested the Grads were overrated, putting himself deeper into Smythe's bad books. The Nationals, he wrote, were playing their fourth game in four days and "had their back up against the wall so hard they looked like wallpaper." Yet they'd managed to hold the Grads to a 1–1 tie.

His lack of faith annoyed Smythe, who treated doubts about his team as doubts about himself. He promised the Grads would win the rematch by at least three goals and backed it up with a convincing 7–1 victory. Marsh had to eat his words: "It would have taken a team of supermen to have overshadowed Varsity Grads at the Arena last night," he reported.[14]

While the Grads were cutting through opponents, Varsity had played its way to the top of the intercollegiate circuit. On the night the Grads played their second game against the Nationals, Smythe was in Ottawa with Varsity for a game against New Edinburgh that resulted in chaos and farce before a crowd of eight thousand fans.

It was to be the deciding match of a three-game series, but ended in a 3–3 tie. According to the rules, the teams should have continued into overtime, but a telegram arrived from league president Dr. Frank Sandercock ordering an extra game to be held in Kingston. Varsity

---

* Before the Second World War, Smythe was usually identified as Connie or Conny by the newspapers, the reporters picking whichever spelling appealed to them.

headed to the dressing room, but New Edinburgh insisted on playing on, milling around the ice as the referee debated what to do.

Strenuous efforts were made to contact Sandercock, who proved to know nothing of the situation. The first telegram had actually been sent by W.A. Hewitt, the *Star* sports editor and OHA secretary, who had the authority to issue rulings in Sandercock's name. Working in the dark, Sandercock finally cabled back that the ruling was up to the referee, who ordered the game completed in overtime. When Smythe refused to put his boys back on the ice, New Edinburgh lined up, the referee dropped the puck, and a New Edinburgh player fired it into the empty net. Game over.

Smythe, predictably, was livid, denouncing the show of amateurism among league officials. The game took place on Thursday; on Saturday the papers announced that an emergency session of the OHA had settled on a compromise. The Grads would play New Edinburgh in a two-game series beginning Monday, the winner of which would play an additional match against Varsity. New Edinburgh foolishly predicted an easy victory and declared they wouldn't show up for the added game against Varsity.

As it turned out, they didn't get the chance. They were humiliated 10–0 in the first game and 7–1 in the second. Reports the next day suggested Smythe's team could have run up the score higher but were in "a charitable mood."

Smythe's Grads were now supposed to play his Varsity team to decide who went to Vancouver for the Allan Cup. He escaped the conflict when several Varsity players, with exams imminent, agreed to cede the championship to the Grads, who were the stronger squad in any case. In return, Smythe promised to add two of the Varsity players to the Grad team if it qualified for the Olympics.

On April 2, the *Globe* ran a picture of Smythe and his team, stretching across the entire front page of the paper. It was taken as they prepared for the three-day train ride to Vancouver, where they would meet Fort William for the championship. W.A. Hewitt would be travelling with the team to cover the contest for the *Star* (where he was referee/sportswriter Lou Marsh's boss) while providing reports for his son Foster to broadcast.[15]

The confrontation in Vancouver wasn't decided until the second overtime of the fourth and final game. The first game had ended in a tie, Fort William had won the second game, and the Grads had won the third. The final match drew a crowd of ten thousand and ended when the Grads finally broke a 1–1 tie with just three minutes left in the second overtime period. After the victory Hewitt wrote of Smythe: "A great deal of the team's success is due to his untiring efforts and uncanny ability to handle the players. He has coached the Varsity teams for a number of years and has been in the Dominion finals with them for the past three years."[16]

Smythe was so elated he not only allowed the players to celebrate with a booze-up but joined in and got drunk for the first and only time in his life. "I got pretty high and then I got sick," he remembered. "Just got over to the basin in the hotel room before I let go. I had never felt so rough. I said, if that's what drinking is, it isn't for me."[17] Although he would never be completely teetotal, from then on he drank rarely and usually just at celebrations, generally limiting himself to sips of champagne.

As Allan Cup champions, the Grads qualified for the Winter Olympics, to be held the next winter in Switzerland. They would win easily, so overpowering that the other countries elected to play off against one another first, with only the best teams challenging the Canadians. In the end Canada took the gold, winning its three games by a combined score of 38–0. But Smythe wouldn't be with them; instead the team was coached by the multi-talented W.A. Hewitt, assisted by the young Harold Ballard. (Smythe's coaching position with the Varsity intercollegiate team had passed to another up-and-comer named Lester Pearson).

Although Smythe was occupied with other business by the time the Games came around, his refusal to travel to St. Moritz was a matter of principle based on his promise to add two Varsity players to the Olympic squad. As the Games approached, a pair of Grad players blocked his pledge, unwilling to see their own teammates miss the trip. Smythe insisted, but was overruled. If the Varsity players didn't go, he said, he wouldn't either. And he didn't. He also didn't forgive the two Grad players, goalie Joe Sullivan and forward Hugh Plaxton, both of whom later went into politics, Plaxton as a Liberal MP and Sullivan as a Progressive Conservative senator. Sullivan had a distinguished career as a surgeon and air force captain in the Second World War, but to Smythe he was always the guy who "queered" his promise to a couple of decent hockey players.

"He is just a rotten Roman Catholic mick," he complained years later. "He's a skunk, and no good."[18]

CHAPTER 6

With an Allan Cup championship, his coaching positions at the university, a new baby on the way, and his increasingly profitable gravel business to run, it wasn't like Smythe was desperate for something to fill his time in the winter of 1927. But he was rarely satisfied juggling just one or two careers, and his treatment by the Rangers still grated on him.

Immediately after being fired he had approached John Paris Bickell, senior member of the partnership that owned the Toronto St. Patricks. He told Bickell the club was badly run and he was the man to fix it. The St. Pats were looking for new leadership, and Bickell considered the brash young man and his proposal, but decided instead to hire Mike Rodden, a sportswriter and NHL referee. Smythe told Bickell that Rodden would be a disaster – he was never subtle about these things and had already concluded that sportswriters' only talent was for telling other people how to do their jobs. He was quickly proven correct. A few weeks later, as the St. Pats floundered, Bickell got in touch and asked if he was still interested.

He was, but his terms had changed. Now he wanted a share of the club. A group of buyers in Philadelphia was offering $200,000, but Smythe convinced Bickell he had a duty to keep the team in Toronto. This meant selling to him, even though he couldn't match the Philadelphia offer.

Smythe developed immense respect for J.P. Bickell over the years. He was a self-made man of great integrity and presence who had opened his own brokerage firm at age twenty-three and later made a fortune in the mining business, developing the McIntyre Porcupine gold mine in northern Ontario, one of the most important gold strikes in Canadian history. He was just forty-three when Smythe met him, but carried an influence beyond his years. More than once it would be Bickell who provided the money, influence, or faith in Smythe that enabled him to achieve goals that might otherwise have proven beyond his grasp. He started by agreeing to keep the St. Pats in Toronto and by holding on to his $40,000 share if Smythe could raise $160,000 to pay off the other investors. Smythe put down $10,000 and spent a few weeks hustling around the city in search of backers. On St. Valentine's Day 1927, they bought the club for $75,000 down, with another $75,000 to be paid within thirty days.[1] *

It was a fair price. The Montreal Canadiens had changed hands for just $11,000 less than six years earlier, but the NHL was growing and new NHL franchises, stocked with players, were selling for $100,000 to $200,000. Smythe got an established team in the middle of that price range.[2] †

The deal wasn't big news. It merited a one-column item on page ten of the *Star* and brief mentions in the sports pages, where OHA games still generally received more attention than professional leagues. A *Globe* report headlined "GOOD-BYE ST. PATS! HOWDY MAPLE LEAFS" incorrectly reported that the new sweaters would be red and white. Stockbroker Ed Bickle, one of Smythe's investors, said

---

* Over the years, many a writer attested that Conn Smythe took the $10,000 he'd won from wagering his Rangers payoff and used it to buy a hockey team. In his memoirs, when he was eighty-five, Smythe said the money "just about paid for our new house." (*If You Can't Beat 'em in the Alley*, 85). Both were correct to a degree, though not quite true. The money would have been enough to retire what he owed on the Baby Point property, if he'd chosen to use it for that. But his financial records show he held a $10,000 mortgage at 6 per cent in October 1926, the month he was fired by the Rangers. Seven years later a note from his mortgage company reminded him he still owed $4,100. He'd also purchased a house on a new housing estate near Lawrence and Yonge as an income property in 1926 and a cottage at Orchard Beach on Lake Simcoe the next year. It seems most likely he used the $10,000 in winnings to make the down payment on the St. Pats.

† When Detroit and Chicago joined the NHL in 1926, they paid more than $100,000 each to buy players, on top of the franchise fee. The New York Rangers bargain roster proved to be an exception, thanks to Smythe's shrewd bargaining.

there had been higher bids not only from Philadelphia but also from Montreal, which already had two teams. *Globe* sports editor Frederick Wilson suggested the name change, from St. Patricks to Maple Leafs, was the end of efforts to lure Toronto's large Irish community away from its traditional devotion to the St. Michael's junior team.[3]

Most attention focused on the club's new image. As early as December 1926 an item in the *Sault Daily Star* had hinted at a sale and argued the name St. Patricks "signifies nothing" and might be changed to Maple Leafs with an appropriately patriotic crest, the better to impress "the uninitiated hockey fans of the American cities."[4] On February 4, W.A. Hewitt reported that a reader named J.M. McCormack was suggesting a suitable new sweater would have "a red background covered with maple leaves, red, white and blue collar and cuffs, with a Union Jack on each arm and across the breast." McCormack thought that would be a good way of showing up the New York Americans with their gaudy stars-and-stripes outfits, which plainly offended his Canadian sensibilities. On February 9, Hewitt wrote that a second reader had proposed "a large maple leaf representing Canada on a white background representing 'The Lady of the Snows.' This to be surrounded by nine red, white and blue smaller maple leaves (in contrast to the starry banner) and the Union Jack to appear on the collar and sleeves [sic]."*

Smythe's involvement drew little notice. His name did not appear in the news stories and wasn't among the club's new list of directors. His low profile reflected the moderate size of his ownership stake, a situation that would persist for the next twenty years. Although Smythe would quickly become the public face of the team, and his authority in hockey matters would never seriously be challenged, he was not the all-powerful impresario he was taken to be as the team

---

* After the St. Pats changed hands, someone suggested the players might be able to declare themselves free agents and demand more money on the basis that the old team had ceased to exist. To avoid this, Smythe added the old name *St Pats* in small letters on the front of the new jerseys until the end of the season.

grew into a national institution. He had bosses and plenty of them. Right from the beginning his ability to wheel and deal was restricted by financial constraints, a situation that brought out his best instincts as a canny trader of hockey flesh. But the restraints were real and only increased with the onset of the Depression and the costs of erecting Maple Leaf Gardens.

Nonetheless, he was unquestionably the driving force behind the new team and the tenets that guided its development. This started with the character of the men he'd recruited as its directors, a list that read like a roll call of prominent First World War veterans. Most exalted was the team's new president, Lt.-Col. W.G. Barker, the same heroic Billy Barker whom Smythe had encountered while learning to fly in 1917.

The new uniform, the Maple Leaf chosen as the team's emblem, the military background of the new directors – it was all part and parcel of Conn Smythe's view of the world, his place in it, and the kind of hockey team he wanted the Leafs to be. He was fiercely proud of his country and its traditions, as devoted to its heritage, history, and British background as he was to its emergence as a growing nation developing a character of its own, and he intended the Leafs to be a reflection of that.

"The Maple Leaf, to us, was the badge of courage, the badge that meant home," he said. "It was the badge that reminded us of all our exploits and the different difficulties we got into, and the different accomplishments that we made. It was a badge that meant more to us than any other badge that we could think of, so we chose it, hoping that the possession of this badge would mean something to the team that wore it, and when they skated out on the ice with this badge on their chest, they would wear it with honour and pride and courage, the way it had been worn by the soldiers of the first Great War in the Canadian Army."[5]

Hockey, to Smythe, was "total war,"[6] and a good team required the same qualities that went into a sound fighting unit: strong leadership, teamwork, discipline, and a willingness to engage in hand-to-hand combat. "Nobody pops someone on this team without getting popped back," he once declared. "I'm not interested in hockey players who don't play to win. You can take penalties, but you gotta play to win."[7] He would preach that doctrine throughout his career. It was behind his preference for hard-working, self-effacing, team-oriented players over high-scoring, high-maintenance stars, whom he generally viewed as more trouble than they were worth. It was the reason he'd refused to buy Babe Dye for the Rangers. He valued pugnacity and would willingly kill a few penalties for a player who put the fear of the Lord in the opposition.

His best teams would consist of hard-nosed warriors, as skilled with their elbows as they were with the puck. A hockey team, he insisted, should attack on all fronts at all times. If a Toronto Maple Leaf happened to win a scoring title he could expect scant praise from Smythe, who like as not would use it as evidence he wasn't spending enough time in the corners.

The St. Patricks had few of these attributes. They played in a cold, undersized rink before rowdy crowds in a largely undeveloped market. There had been hints Toronto might be squeezed right out of the NHL as U.S. cities began Americanizing the league. They were an exhausted team in the middle of a woeful season, their second in a row. They had lost nineteen of the thirty-one games they'd played so far and were dead last in their division. After Dye was peddled to Chicago, the remaining roster had few bright lights other than two young players – Hap Day and rookie winger Irvine Bailey, not yet nicknamed "Ace," who was in his first year as a pro.

The last match under the old regime served as a metaphor for the state of the franchise – out of gas, out of ambition, and almost out of time. It took place against the Detroit Cougars, played in Windsor because the Olympia, the new Detroit arena, wasn't completed yet. Even though they were playing to small crowds in a second-tier rink, Cougar management had elected to charge premium prices so they wouldn't have to raise them when they moved in to the Olympia.[8]

The papers reported barely 150 people had watched the "home team" Cougars skate to a 5–1 victory over the sad-sack St. Pats. It was a sorry end, and the tide seemed to change with the next game – the first under the new name – as the Toronto Maple Leafs beat the New York Americans 4–1.

"Last night's game was one of the best, if not the best, of the season," the *Star*'s Bob Hayes enthused, adding that without the old green uniforms they "looked like a lot of galloping ghosts in white." They closed out the season winning six of their remaining twelve under interim coach Alex Romeril, who would guide them until Smythe completed his hockey obligations to the University of Toronto and could take over in the fall.

The challenges facing Smythe were daunting. Although the St. Pats had won the Cup a few years earlier, it wasn't a team with a lot of history or tradition on which to fall back. It existed mainly due to the determination of the NHL to rid itself of Eddie Livingstone, who nonetheless found ways to hound the new league as persistently as he'd hounded the old one. The first Toronto team in the NHL had been named the Arenas (because that's where they played). They were closed down and renamed the St. Patricks to avoid legal action from Livingstone.

Both versions of the club were run by Charlie Querrie, a well-known local lacrosse player who switched to hockey teams when public enthusiasm for lacrosse began to die out. Querrie was a man of many interests. Apart from his lacrosse and hockey ventures, he wrote a newspaper column and served as manager of hockey operations at the Arena Gardens.

This sort of arrangement was not unusual: In addition to his many newspaper and hockey activities, W.A. Hewitt organized day trips to regional racetracks for thoroughbred fans and booked local theatres to stage dramatized presentations during the World Series. Querrie was tired of the uncertainties of big-league hockey, however, and happy to bequest the team to Smythe.

Apart from the quality of the team Querrie left him, Smythe had to contend with the state of its home rink. The Arena Gardens had been among Canada's leading facilities when it opened in 1912. It was the third in Canada to boast artificial indoor ice; the first two were built by the Patricks in Victoria and Vancouver. The Gardens had housed both the Arenas and St. Pats, but by 1927 it was looking decidedly dowdy. The wealthy new U.S. teams either had spanking new rinks or were in the process of acquiring them. Madison Square Garden could easily hold more than twice the Mutual Street facility's capacity – officially listed as 7,150 though normally closer to 8,000. Rinks in Boston, Chicago and Detroit could all pack in 13,000 or more, and showed a mysterious ability to host crowds even larger than their official maximum. Montreal's Forum, opened in 1924 as home to the Maroons, proved so popular the Canadiens broke their contract with the Mount Royal arena and moved there as well.[9] Only Ottawa had a rink as small as Toronto's, a fact the club would ultimately pay for with its life.

In addition to its size limits, the Arena Gardens lacked a lot in the comfort department. The best seats were little more than wooden benches and the building wasn't heated, so the temperature inside depended on the temperature outside. The condition of the ice varied accordingly – it could be hard and fast on cold nights or wet and slushy when the weather turned warm.

Frank "King" Clancy, who played nine years with the Senators before joining the Leafs in 1930, claimed that visiting the Toronto rink in midwinter was more than he could endure. Even though he'd grown up playing shinny on Ottawa's frozen rivers on frigid winter nights – when bouts of frostbite were taken for granted – he found the cold in the Arena Gardens oppressive, and retreated to the dressing room when he wasn't on the ice. Smythe wasn't happy with the rink situation, but for the moment had little alternative. He signed a new five-year lease binding the Leafs to play all their home games there. Pro hockey was so low on the priority list of Toronto fans that Smythe was allowed just two Saturday night games a month and minimal practice time.[10]

He also didn't have an immediate solution for the behaviour of the fans who frequented the games. Hockey wasn't for the faint of heart, either on the ice or in the crowd. It was often brutal and attracted men who liked their competition raw. They also liked to get directly involved. The Toronto rink, like most others, had little in the way of barriers between fans and players. There was a screen behind the net, but otherwise the ice was wide open to whatever devilment the crowd – almost exclusively male – could get up to. Fans sat beside, behind, or right next to both benches. It was easy to reach over the sideboards and grab a passing sweater or toss programs or opinions at players and officials. Brawls were common-place, especially among fans who took the trouble to insulate them-selves from the cold by getting plastered before the game. Drink was a serious problem. When Charlie Querrie ran the St. Pats, he would make the rounds of bootleggers before game time to gather up his squad.[11] Players drank before the game and sometimes during, a con-dition not limited to Toronto by any means. When playing with the Montreal Maroons, Mervyn "Red" Dutton sat next to defence partner Reg Noble in the dressing room. "He'd drink a case of beer the day of a game," Dutton complained. "His breath would knock you down."[12]

Lou Marsh once quit his referee duties in disgust at the abuse he took in Toronto.[13] Montreal-born defenceman Sprague Cleghorn was so violent he was once suspended after a playoff game by his *own* manager. Querrie was seated on the players' bench one night when a monkey wrench went sailing past his head; he retrieved it and had it silver plated and decorated with a small clock.[14]

Referee Jerry Laflamme and Boston's Billy Coutu were involved in a celebrated confrontation, which was raised at the first NHL board of governors meeting Smythe attended. It was held in Montreal and the main agenda item was the "famous Ottawa riot" following the last game of the 1927 Stanley Cup final, which Boston lost to Ottawa. Both officials – Laflamme of Toronto and Billy Bell of Montreal – were assaulted by Boston players in "an unprovoked and apparently pre-meditated assault."

The attack was instigated by Art Ross, who was upset at Laflamme and told the players, "the first man who gets that referee gets a $500 bonus."[15] Coutu led a mob of Bruins who jumped Laflamme, knocking him down and roughing him up, with Ross and even owner Charlie Adams reportedly getting involved.[16] NHL president Frank Calder, who was at the game, banned Coutu for life, but took no action against Ross, already notorious for his complaints about the inconsistency of refereeing. Rather than punish the Bruin boss, NHL governors agreed to hire a referee-in-chief to supervise officials and "keep them up to a standard and strict interpretation of the rules."*

At the time of the Montreal meeting, Smythe had already started what would become a legendary feud with Ross, who shared his short temper and capacity for confrontation. Ross "was the most devious man I ever met," Smythe claimed.[17] "Arthur was a man of the old school, and if there was some direct way of doing something, it was against his common sense to do it."[18] Selke, who tried to get along with everybody, made an exception for Ross: "Art Ross writes the rules, and then lies awake at night thinking of ways to circumvent them," he complained.[19]

While neither was shy of controversy, there was a qualitative difference between the two men. Smythe was more than ready to make a spectacle of himself and would be the most publicized sports figure in Canada over the next thirty-five years, but his escapades were rarely accidental. He recognized the value of publicity in drawing fans and upsetting opponents. He became renowned for flinging hats, or leaping over the boards and skidding off across the ice in pursuit of some

---

* Coutu was ejected again the next year, this time from the Canadian-American Professional Hockey League, where he was playing for New Haven. This time the suspension was for the rest of the season (*Toronto Star*, January 26, 1928).

official who wasn't living up to his expectations. It amused the crowd, excited the reporters, and made his point, all in one neat package.

Ross wasn't that subtle. His background read like Hollywood's notion of a typical Canadian upbringing. He was the twelfth of thirteen children born to the chief factor of a Hudson's Bay trading post in the northern Ontario community of Naughton, a few miles west of Sudbury. He grew up speaking fluent Ojibwa and playing hockey on the frozen surface of Whitefish Bay, wearing blades that strapped to the bottom of his boots. When the Rosses moved to Montreal, young Arthur – his middle name was Howey and usually misspelled – made friends with a pair of neighbourhood kids who were as hockey-mad as he was, Lester and Frank Patrick. They remained close, though the fact you were Ross's friend didn't mean he wouldn't try to club you during a hockey game. Frank Patrick liked to recount how, during a game on a frigid night in the Ontario mining town of Haileybury, Ross was playing with a pair of fur gloves and a woollen toque pulled down over his face with holes cut for his eyes. "He looked the very devil himself, and he played as mean as he looked," Frank said. Just to stay warm, Ross picked a fight with Lester, bashing him over the head with his stick. When Lester retaliated, Ross pulled off his gloves and stood ready for battle. Except that, after a few seconds, the unearthly cold began to bite at his bare skin and he dove for his gloves. That was the end of the fight, "called on account of cold," recounted Frank.[20]

Smythe initiated the Ross feud on one of his tours of the Boston area while coaching the Varsity team. Toronto typically made short work of the local teams while playing before large crowds. Ross had been named vice-president, general manager, and head coach of the new Boston NHL team and was struggling through the first dismal year, during which the Bruins won just six of thirty games. When a local paper asked whether his college players could defeat the Bruins, Smythe boasted he'd "play them for any amount of money, and murder them any time they wanted to play."[21] Ross didn't forget the slight.

As a coach and manager Ross was no slouch. When the Patricks shut down their western league and made the players available to the NHL, Ross got some of the best. Of the seven players he acquired, the most valuable was Eddie Shore, who spent the next decade terrorizing opponents. Smythe could have used a few acquisitions like Shore. Early in his first season as Leafs boss he realized his moderate expectations of the players he'd acquired had been optimistic. They were "a lousy team, $40,000 in debt." The shareholders gave themselves "no better than a 50-50 chance of ever getting their money back, let alone a profit."[22]

He had the young, promising Bailey, who placed fifth in the scoring race in his first NHL season, and he had Hap Day, a natural leader and solid defenceman. Moody little John Ross Roach, the goalie, was serviceable enough, and while centre Bill Carson had a scoring touch, Smythe had doubts about his resiliency. The rest of the lineup had combined for just thirty-six goals the year he renamed the team, only two more than Bill Cook had scored for the Rangers.

Smythe would have liked to set out on another tour of the hinterlands, but for the threadbare Leafs that wasn't an option. The team didn't have the money, for one thing, and his financial backers had a tight grip on the purse strings. Even if he'd been able to afford it, there was no guarantee he could have pulled off a similar coup. The Rangers' success had alerted other teams that the feisty Torontonian was more than just a moderately capable junior leaguer, and they were keeping an eye on him.

Budgets would be a problem for Smythe for some time. Anything that cost money had to be justified, and expenses were rising. New teams in Detroit, Chicago, and New York meant additional travel. The players, too, were increasingly aware of their value. While still commonly treated like serfs who could be exiled to the minors or shipped off in a trade at the manager's whim, they wanted to be compensated for it. Ottawa's Tommy Gorman was scandalized when two players had the temerity to hire a lawyer to assess their contracts, rather than meekly accepting the standard NHL document offered them.[23] As Foster Hewitt noted, "In the life of most sports there comes a time when players stop their play, look at the immense crowd of spectators, work a little problem in mental arithmetic, then exclaim to one another: 'Who gets all this money, anyway?'"[24]

One of Smythe's first innovations was his emphasis on fitness. When the players dispersed for the summer of 1927 he instructed them to reappear the next fall in fighting shape. When they began to gather again in October it was obvious some had taken his instructions more seriously than others. Defenceman Bert McCaffrey, the *Star* noted, "went back to the farm and between pitching hay, ploughing and chasing the cows got rid of all his surplus and came back into town last weekend looking like a million dollars." But Day had passed the summer working at a drugstore, and Roach had divided his attention between the chickens at his Port Perry farm and a horse track near Toronto.

Smythe put them up in a hotel and ran them through a daily regimen of calisthenics and other conditioning practices. It was the closest thing to boot camp he could organize on a tight budget and produced no end of wailing from the players. After the morning workout, they played golf or baseball in the afternoon, followed by a brisk walk accompanied by much hilarity as players tried to wave down passing cars for a lift.

The workouts, which would follow a similar regimen over the next several decades, galvanized the local press, who had never seen anything like it. The coverage drew reporters away from other events and produced unaccustomed attention for the team. "Our team practically eliminated senior and junior amateur hockey gossip from the sports pages. Everybody suddenly became Leaf-conscious," wrote Frank Selke.[25] At five-foot-two, Selke would trot along with the others, struggling to keep up with the six-foot Day. On November 3, the team held an open practice, inviting fans to attend, and drew a respectable crowd of fifteen hundred. Smythe divided the squad into a blue team and a white team and set them against each other. "The whole club looks mighty good, they have faith in each other and there is a lot of harmony and good feeling among the boys," one paper reported the next day. Smythe gave the players one day off for Thanksgiving, but "it will be their last holiday for a long time. Today at noon they will get down to the hardest week's practice they have had, and Conny Smythe will drive them at a rapid pace to get them into shape to step into the New York Rangers and their galaxy of stars on the opening night."[26]

He had tinkered considerably with the lineup. He invited rookies Carl Voss and Joe Primeau to camp, and they played so well they "sent manager Conny Smythe home happy enough to eat wieners and think he had chicken patties."[27]

Primeau drew rave reviews. "He is without a doubt a real find. His work is better every time he steps out on the ice, and he should be one of the most valuable relief players the Leafs have," the *Star* reported. Primeau had signed with the Rangers, but Smythe bought his contract when he left. "I bought it with my own money and for one summer Joe Primeau and I constituted an organization with no franchise, no place to play, a manager and one player."[28] At five-foot-eleven and just 150 pounds, he was a stringbean of a player but had speed and puck sense and an ability to put a pass exactly where it needed to be.

Smythe had also obtained Art Duncan from the Detroit Cougars, a veteran defenceman who had played eight years in Vancouver before moving to the new Detroit team. Before playing a single game, Duncan tested Smythe's patience by demanding a $1,000 pay increase. When he refused, and Duncan held out, he referred the issue to Calder, who suspended Duncan. When rumours spread that the Pittsburgh Pirates were interested in him, Smythe retorted, "Let the Pirates give enough for him and they can have him."

In late October, Duncan declared he'd organized his own trade to Pittsburgh. Smythe had had enough. He bought Ed Gorman, another experienced defenceman, from the Senators and claimed to be impressed with his play. Duncan eventually reported, and became one of the team's most reliable defenders. He missed just one game all season, while Gorman was used sparingly and eventually sent down to the Leafs' farm team.

In an excellent bit of irony, Smythe's first game at the helm of his new team was against the Rangers, giving him a chance to avenge his firing. He did his best to turn the game into a major civic event, complete with the 48th Highlanders and a ceremonial faceoff, with the first puck dropped by Ontario's lieutenant-governor. Cooper J. Smeaton, the new referee-in-chief, was on hand to measure the goaltenders' pads and ensure officials adhered strictly to the rule book, even if it meant building bigger penalty boxes. "The clean hard honest hockey player is to be protected from rough-neck types and the player who persistently fouls to save a goal is going to find himself warming a bench quite frequently," he warned.[29]

Unfortunately the game didn't match the build-up. Thanks to warm weather, the ice was blanketed with a fog that made it impossible to see either net from centre ice. Fans struggled to follow the action as players swooped in and out of the cloud bank. Both teams circled the ice between periods to dispel the mist, but the results were unsatisfactory. The Rangers also refused to co-operate, winning 4–2 in a game that was over well before the final whistle. Bill Cook scored the first goal just over a minute into the game. Toronto got it back, but Ching Johnson scored two more, added an assist, and put on a defensive display that consistently discouraged the Toronto forwards and showed, according to W.A. Hewitt, that "they need a lot more conditioning yet." Johnson's second goal came three minutes into the third period on a shot that caromed off Bill Carson's skate. Thirty seconds after that Frank Boucher scored the final goal, crushing Leaf hopes.

The Rangers, wrote Hewitt, were "a smart, clever team from the goal out" and deserved the victory. Reviews of Smythe's team were mixed. The forwards needed more practice around the net, where they wasted opportunities. They were inconsistent, playing hard in spurts, and then disappearing as the Rangers took over.

"The fans agree [Smythe] has plenty of good material to work with, but that team play as yet is a minus quality," wrote Hewitt. "The Leafs have plenty of speed on the forward line and against a weaker defense than the Rangers might show to much advantage."[30]

The biggest setback for the Rangers came when tubby Taffy Abel broke his arm in the first period, forcing him to spend several days in a Toronto hospital. Feeling bad about the accident, Hap Day took up a collection in the dressing room and sent him a basket of fruit and flowers. "The local players feel sorry for the Rangers defense player and they are going to try and make his enforced stay in the city as pleasant as possible," he explained.[31]

CHAPTER 7

The loss to New York was a harbinger of a year that would be filled with more disappointments than triumphs. Smythe insisted he considered the season "fairly respectable,"[1] but it was mostly an opportunity to learn through failure. Toronto missed the playoffs for the third year in a row. Of the NHL's ten teams, only two produced fewer points. Ace Bailey couldn't match his strong rookie season and fell off drastically in scoring. The two players who impressed Smythe most were Art Duncan, the reluctant defenceman, and Joe Primeau, who made it into only two games but showed promise.

The next few weeks established a pattern that would hold through the season: they beat Chicago, lost to Boston, won two games, went four games without a victory, won a game, lost a game, won another game, lost the next one. By Christmas they had five wins, six losses, and three ties. They seemed to play better on the road than at home, a failing Smythe noted in a sarcastic monologue he delivered to the papers, suggesting that Toronto "is certainly a wonderful hockey town," since the fans kept turning up to see such poor hockey. "It's a wonder to me that the Leafs get any crowd at all after the insults [we] have heaped on the Toronto public."[2]

They lacked offensive power, rarely scoring more than two goals in a game, so in late December he agreed to pay $17,500 to buy centreman Jimmy Herberts from the Bruins. Herberts, known as "Sailor" because he spent summers working on Great Lakes freighters, had been potting goals at a torrid pace his first three seasons. He didn't like to pass much – he averaged six assists a year – but that wasn't unusual; many of the top scorers were puck hogs. Bill Cook won the

1927 scoring championship with thirty-three goals and just four assists; Howie Morenz had seven, Babe Dye just five.

Herberts came highly recommended by Art Ross, which should have been a warning sign. Ross almost sold him to Ottawa, until the Senators balked at the asking price. Smythe offered $15,000, then raised it to $17,500, "the last cent we had in the treasury." The papers weren't convinced Herberts was worth the money. The *Evening Telegram* was outraged that anyone would spend so much on a hockey player when families were going hungry at Christmas.

The deal was a disaster from the word *go*. Smythe knew there would be trouble when Herberts showed up at his King Street office "all perfumed and smelled-up beautifully." He'd brought along his wife, "a showy woman who wore very short skirts, which got shorter every time she moved around in her chair." Ed Bickle, who was on hand, was too distracted by Mrs. Herberts to pay attention to the discussion, which centred on Herberts' reluctance to play for the Leafs. His wife didn't like Toronto and didn't want to live there.[3]

Things didn't improve when Herberts strode onto the ice for his first game, caught his foot on the gate, and fell flat on his face. Picking himself up, he skated to the wrong side of centre ice and lined up with the visiting Black Hawks, standing in his blue-and-white uniform among a pack of players in black and red while the crowd hooted in derision.[4]

Fortunately for Herberts, the Leafs got hot soon after his arrival. They won seven of their next nine, including a 6–1 victory over the Rangers that W.A. Hewitt called their best performance of the season. They beat New York again a few nights later, this time in Manhattan, and were still playing well in February when disaster struck. In a game against the Canadiens, Day was badly injured when a skate blade sliced through the back of his leg, cutting into his Achilles tendon.

"If 'Happy' Day is not a cripple for life as a result of his accident... on Thursday night he is a mighty lucky boy," Hewitt reported. "It looked at first as if the tendon had been completely severed, for the gash was so deep that the bone was exposed... In the dressing room the trainers poured pure iodine right into the gash – a rough but excellent emergency treatment – and he was hustled right across the park to the hospital. Next day 'Happy' was handed a sniff of something that made him forget whether he was a hockey player or a lily white angel and the surgeons went exploring. To their delight they found a shred of the tendon still intact."[5]

It was an enormous setback. Day was both the captain and the unquestioned leader. Doctors suggested he might be able to play the next season, but "if there is infection serious enough to ruin the shred of tendon which remains unsevered, 'Happy' Day will never again don a skate and he would drag his foot for the rest of his days."[6]

It would, in fact, be eight months before Day was able to resume skating, a period of painful rehabilitation that raised him even higher in Smythe's regard. He valued Day so much he offered to sell him a chunk of his sand and gravel company, handing over 16 per cent of the profitable firm he'd built himself and that was his main source of income. It was his own idea and an extraordinary gesture. He talked Day into the partnership, he said, because "I wanted him with me summer as well as winter for a long time, which turned out to be one of my best decisions. He was one of the best men I ever met."[7]

Day's departure put added pressure on Duncan, who at age thirty-three was forced to play up to sixty minutes a game, despite an injured shoulder. A new catastrophe struck when their top scorer, Bill Carson, fell backwards during a game with Detroit and was carried off unconscious.

As their fortunes declined, so did attendance and the attention of the newspapers. The *Telegram*, suspicious of pro sports, barely mentioned the team unless it was to complain about the NHL's chronic lack of scoring. The *Globe* offered perfunctory coverage, while the *Star*'s Hewitt had sailed off to the Winter Olympics with Smythe's former Grads team.

It must have grated on Smythe that, while the Leafs were playing to sparse crowds, his old team had become the toast of the nation. On March 8, when the Leafs could claim just one victory in their past eight games, the papers heralded the Grads' imminent return from

Europe after vanquishing all comers. "Homeward bound the Varsity Grads, Canada's ambassadors of sport, sail today for the land of the maple leaf, bearing on their brows the coveted Olympic laurel," proclaimed the *Star*. "They are known in every country as the world's greatest amateur team. Not bad for an organization that three years ago didn't exist. The rise of the Grads has been meteoric." It managed not to mention Smythe, or the fact that the man who had created the team and produced its "meteoric" rise was even then scratching to get fans to watch his latest project.

As the season dragged to an end, almost any team seemed to galvanize interest more than the Leafs. On March 12, the *Globe* gave just two paragraphs to a preview of that night's game, while devoting the better part of two columns to a playoff between Port Colborne and South Porcupine in the OHA's intermediate division. The Toronto Marlboros were in the midst of a race for the OHA championship, with a team that included two rising young stars, hard-shooting Charlie Conacher and harder-hitting Reginald "Red" Horner. It had suddenly become easy to get tickets for the pro team, which had lots of empty seats, while everyone was scrambling to see the juniors. Even Toronto's industrial league got more attention: Ravina Gardens was stuffed with five thousand fans to watch a team from the stock yards – led by "young and dashing leftwinger" Harvey Jackson – win the crown in the Big Six Mercantile League.[8] There was plainly an audience for hockey in Toronto, it just wasn't interested in the Leafs yet. When they were finally eliminated from any hope of making the playoffs on March 14, it was barely mentioned.

At the end of the previous season Smythe had overhauled the team, adding nine new players. Now he overhauled it again, adding ten more. He unloaded Sailor Herberts on the unsuspecting Detroit Cougars, hustling to cash the cheque after the Detroit owner tipped him that they were on the edge of insolvency. Smythe had quietly instructed players to feed Herberts the puck at every opportunity, padding his statistics so he'd be easier to sell.[9]

He bought Harold "Baldy" Cotton from Pittsburgh for $8,000 and acquired Andy Blair, a centre from Winnipeg, to play between Ace Bailey and Cotton. He swapped netminders with the Rangers, sending them John Ross Roach in return for Chabot, who had just finished winning the Stanley Cup. Lester Patrick didn't like Chabot's floppy style, and suspected his vision had suffered permanent damage when he was hit in the eye during the Cup finals. Chabot's injury led to one of the NHL's most legendary moments, when the forty-four-year-old Patrick donned the goalie pads to personally rescue his team in a moment of crisis. Smythe played a bit part in the story, which was not nearly as celebrated at the time as it became later. He happened to be at the game and raced to the Ranger dressing room when Chabot was knocked out of the play. In his usual take-charge fashion he offered to play goal himself, but got his words confused in the excitement and kept demanding, "Hang the nets on me and I'll go in there."[10]

By the next fall, only four regular players remained from the team Smythe had purchased eighteen months earlier. In addition to Cotton and Chabot, he'd added Horner from the Marlboros, a polite, deferential young man off the ice who played like an avenging angel once on skates and who quickly became a Smythe favourite. He came to the Leafs via Frank Selke, who had revived the Marlboros franchise in mid-decade and was managing the team when Horner, a seventeen-year-old kid who delivered groceries to the Selke household, asked if he might try out.[11] Two years later he was playing in two leagues simultaneously and had just finished his second game in a little over twelve hours when Smythe appeared in the dressing room and suggested he drop "the amateur stuff" and join the Leafs. As in right now. The Leafs were playing Pittsburgh that night and Smythe wanted Horner in the lineup. Horner told Smythe he'd have to talk to his parents first, so Smythe stopped by the Horner home on the way to the game, met the parents, and drove his new defenceman to the rink.[12]

Despite the changes, the second season wasn't much better than the first. Toronto placed third, moving up one spot, but mainly because the Maroons and Senators got worse rather than because the Leafs got better. Chabot cut their goals-against total sharply – suggesting Smythe had won the goalie duel with Patrick – but Toronto ended with just three more points than the previous year. They did make the playoffs, which pleased Leaf directors so much they bought Smythe a new car. And Ace Bailey won the NHL scoring race, though with just twenty-two goals, the lowest total ever to top the league.

League governors knew they had to do something about the low scoring. It resulted from strict limits on forward passes, which made offence difficult and delighted goalies. In all, the ten NHL goalies had racked up 120 shutouts on the season, including 22 in forty-four games by the Canadiens' George Hainsworth, who ended the year allowing an average of less than a goal a game.

The governors had fiddled several times with the passing rules to generate more scoring, and in 1929 they finally got it right, legalizing forward passes anywhere on the ice as long as the puck crossed the defenders' blue line before any of the attacking players.[13] The impact was immediate. Offensive statistics exploded. In 1928–29, only two players had scored more than twenty goals; in 1929, three players scored more than forty. Smythe continued to juggle his roster, adding Charlie Conacher and Harvey Jackson – quickly nicknamed "Busher" – to a club that already included Horner, Bailey, and Primeau. It gave him a promising flock of talented young players, though the payoff was slow in coming. In the 1929–30 season, the Leafs slid back to seventh among the ten NHL teams with just forty points, worse than both the previous two seasons. After three full years as an NHL manager Smythe had yet to prove he was anything more than a tough-talking and often abrasive figure, running an underperforming team in one of the league's least populous markets.

Yet, uninspiring as Leaf fortunes may have looked, the elements that would alter the future were not far from hand. Just before the 1929 season he hired Frank Selke as his assistant, paying him out of his own pocket after Leafs directors refused to approve the expense. They had

known each other ever since the 1914 playoff in which Selke's Union
Jacks had gone down in defeat to Smythe's Varsity team. They met
again after the war when Selke took a job at the University of Toronto
as an electrician at sixty cents an hour, supporting a growing brood of
children that then numbered five and would soon expand to seven. Like
Smythe, Selke spent his nights coaching, scouting, or watching hockey
games. After moving from Kitchener he had taken positions with a
series of local clubs, beginning with the University of Toronto Schools
and later handling teams affiliated with a pair of Catholic parishes,
St. Cecilia's and St. Mary's (where he coached Harold Ballard). Travelling
around the province, shivering at frigid indoor arenas and even colder
outdoor ones, Frank and Mary Selke often came across Conn and Irene
Smythe huddled against the cold, as both men hunted talent.[14]

His schooling was limited; he had quit at age thirteen and worked
at a series of furniture plants to help out family finances. A compact
man, he weighed just 115 pounds on the day he married a woman
named Mary Schmidt, who weighed just 85.[15] He was already familiar
with Smythe's cantankerous reputation – "As coach at Varsity, Conn
came into conflict with all of us," he said –[16], but he admired both his
commitment and his passion for winning, which he shared.

When Smythe signed with the Rangers, he appointed Selke a scout
in Toronto. When Smythe was fired, Selke quit too. It may have been
Selke who tipped off Smythe that the St. Patricks were for sale, and
once the team had changed hands Selke was hired to operate a short-
lived farm team. But his main hockey activity, before being hired by the
Leafs, was the Toronto Marlboros, which he had revived in mid-decade
and built into one of the strongest amateur teams in the province.[17]

It was Selke's Marlboros that attracted much of the press attention
and filled the seats at Arena Gardens when the Leafs were struggling
through their early years. They won the Memorial Cup as Canada's
junior champions in their fifth year of existence and began funnelling
a regular supply of prospects to Smythe's NHL club. As early as 1927,
Selke tried to convince Smythe his junior stars were the answer to the

Leafs' woes, though Smythe at first was reluctant to bite. "There are times when I think there's something wrong with your head," he responded the first time Selke raised the subject.[18]

But he persevered and produced much of the talent that would thrill Canadian hockey fans over the next decade. In addition to Conacher, Primeau, and Jackson, his defence included Red Horner, Alex Levinsky, and Ellis Pringle, all of whom would play in the NHL, though Pringle only briefly, and forward Eddie Convey, who would play parts of three seasons with the New York Americans.

He didn't so much discover Jackson as fail to get rid of him. Jackson grew up in a three-storey home on Quebec Avenue, not far from High Park. He learned to skate on an outdoor surface the kids called Poverty Pond on nearby Keele Street, wearing a pair of girls' skates he'd "borrowed" from a cousin. Once his father got him a pair of boys' skates, he played constantly – on Poverty Pond, on Grenadier Pond, or on the frozen edges of the Humber River.[19] The Jackson household was a short walk from Ravina Gardens, where he eventually pestered the rink manager into making a deal: Jackson could skate all he wanted as long as he also shovelled the ice. When the Marlies arrived for a practice one day, Jackson was on the ice and wouldn't get off. A smooth, graceful, effortless skater, he swooped in and out as the players milled around, trying without success to get the puck away from him.[20] He also had an impressive shot that caught Selke's attention. Cornering the kid, Selke asked whether he had signed with a team.

"Haven't signed and don't want to sign," Jackson responded. That wasn't exactly true – Jackson was usually on two or three teams at a time, but he wasn't playing for a direct competitor of the Marlboros, and when Selke persisted he signed on.[21]

Selke stumbled on Charlie Conacher in a similar manner. Conacher came from a hard-up family of ten kids – five of each – who lived in a rough neighbourhood on Toronto's Davenport Road. His father spent winters cutting ice in the lagoons off Toronto Island, waking at five and walking to the lake, cutting and storing ice for summer use until nightfall, then trudging back home, all for $7.50 a week.[22] The Conacher boys – three of whom, Lionel, Roy and Charlie, would star in the NHL – played shinny twelve months a year, using pucks, tennis balls, or anything else that could be hit with a stick. Before starting they'd line up at attention while a friend played "God Save the King" on his mouth organ, just like in the big leagues.[23]

Conacher was such a poor skater the other kids stuck him in goal, the traditional place to exile slow-pokes, but he advanced enough by age seventeen to try out for Selke's Marlboros team. He didn't make the cut and spent the winter playing at the Ravina rink, lugging his equipment by streetcar as far as he could and walking the final mile. By chance he got into a game against the Varsity Grads; Selke was there and noticed his improvement, inviting him afterwards to try again with the Marlies. This time he made it.

Selke was hired by Smythe to deal with public relations and some scouting, but quickly became the indispensable agent who got things done, jollied up the press, and smoothed feathers when Smythe had ruffled them.

"Frank Selke is a little fellow not even as tall as his boss, Mr. Smythe, but with a pleasing disposition that makes friends wherever he goes," attested Charlie Querrie. "He listens to all the complaints of twelve to fourteen hockey players, arranges all the transportation and hotels for the out-of-town trips, does all the newspaper advertising and tries to keep the newspaper boys satisfied with tickets etc., and when a game is on he is assistant to everybody. He runs messages for the manager, helps carry the spare sticks, looks for a doctor if anyone is injured, and is generally the handyman of the whole affair."[24]

In the summer of 1930 one of the jobs Smythe assigned him was to travel to Ottawa to meet the Senators' star defenceman, King Clancy. Smythe had the nucleus of a winner, but it needed a spark to elevate it from a team of talented youngsters into a cohesive unit with the leadership to excel. Smythe hoped Clancy was the man. He was an undersized defenceman with oversized spirit who had already been in the league nine years. He was born and raised in Ottawa and had never played anywhere else, but the Senators were increasingly desperate for cash and Clancy, their most valuable asset, was for sale.

After Boston's Eddie Shore, he was considered the NHL's best defender. He had a low, hard shot and could skate forever at top speed. He never gave in, and had an optimistic, infectious, enthusiastic personality that inspired teammates and fired up a team. Smythe told a Toronto magazine his "ideal player" would be "a big little man about five feet 10 inches high, around 175 pounds. He is a man who [learned] the game from the ground up when he was very young. He has legs and heart and head. Above everything, he's a fighter, and a good sportsman. Heart is the big thing, more important than either strength or head work."[25]

Clancy had all those attributes, other than size – he was 150 pounds soaking wet. The deal to bring him to Toronto was among the most important Smythe ever made and came at the end of a typically convoluted set of events that depended as much on luck and brazenness as on managerial aptitude.

Smythe had loved horses since the days when he accompanied his father to Woodbine racetrack. In the late 1920s, he bought a few of his own, putting the Leafs' blue and white crest and colours on his racing silks. He'd never won a race, or even owned a decent horse until shortly before the 1930 season, when he paid $250 for a filly named Rare Jewel.

Rare Jewel was available because her owner, a Mrs. Livingstone, had abandoned racing after being humiliated one day at Woodbine. She owned another horse, named The Monkey. When it was withdrawn from a race at the last minute, a track announcer walked through the stands calling, "Scratch Mrs. Livingstone's Monkey! Scratch Mrs. Livingstone's Monkey!" The crowd picked up the call and started chanting along. Shortly after she sold her entire stable and gave up the sport.[26]

Even at $250, Rare Jewel wasn't much of a bargain. She ran last so often that Smythe finally bet a friend she would come last during a race in Montreal.[27] Rare Jewel came second last, spoiling even that bet. Nonetheless, Smythe entered her in the Coronation Stakes, an important annual event for two-year-olds at Woodbine with a purse of almost $4,000. Although reluctant, he was persuaded at the last moment by jockey Dude Foden, who thought she'd been showing improvement. Just before the race, Rare Jewel's trainer and a betting pal of Smythe both surreptitiously snuck into her stall and fed her half a flask of brandy to provide a bit of extra pep, neither aware the other had also done so.

At first Smythe made just a token bet, but as the odds lengthened he upped his wager. Still, he had so little faith he decided to offset the risk by putting money on the favourite, a horse name Frothblower. He was standing in line with his $30 in hand when the Leafs' former doctor happened by. Smythe had just fired him for misdiagnosing an injury – the doctor hadn't noticed the player's leg was broken – and the doctor started ribbing him for betting against his own horse. Quickly boiling over, Smythe put the money on Rare Jewel instead, then headed to the stands expecting to lose it all – along with $7 Irene had added to the pot. Instead, the brandy kicked in, and Foden – who had also bet on Frothblower – brought her home in first place. The payoff was $9,372 plus the purse. It was a monumental amount, enough to make the front pages of the papers the next day. Smythe gave the purse to Foden and the two men with the brandy flasks. He had already decided to use the rest to buy King Clancy.[28]

There were still some problems to overcome. Chief among them was uncertainty over whether Clancy would agree to play for the Leafs. The Senators were an established team, oldest in the league, and had been competing at the highest level since the turn of the century. The Leafs were newcomers, the latest variation on a team that couldn't seem to hold on to its name or owners for more than a few years at a time. Ottawa had four Stanley Cups since formation of the NHL, and many more before that; the Leafs couldn't seem to get out of fourth place.

Clancy made a good living in Ottawa: the Senators paid him $7,200 a year, plus $500 as captain. He also held down a job at the Customs Department that brought in $1,800 a year, for a total of $9,500, and at twenty-eight he still lived at home with his parents, where, he noted, "I don't have any board to pay unless I feel like it."[29]

There was also the matter of Clancy's apparent hostility to the Leafs. Nothing seemed to give him more pleasure than whipping the Toronto team. The only conversation Clancy could recollect having had with Smythe was over a disputed goal, when Clancy told him: "Kiss my ass." Clancy's battles with Hap Day were so fierce and frequent, Smythe seriously wondered whether the Senator would be willing to wear the same uniform.[30]

But Selke discovered that Clancy off the ice was an altogether different creature than Clancy on skates. God-fearing, devoted to his family, and a man who seemed incapable of disliking even the most dislikable people, he professed surprise that Toronto was even interested in him.[31]

Selke reported back that Clancy was willing. That prompted a meeting with Smythe, where they quickly came to terms. As Clancy remembered it, he asked for $10,000. Smythe couldn't afford it but offered $8,500 and $1,500 later. Clancy accepted.[32]

Reassured that Clancy would turn up, Smythe entered the bidding war for his services. With the onset of the Depression and the increasing costs of the expanded NHL, the Senators were a team in trouble. They had the lowest ticket prices in the league, charging just $2 for the best seats. In the 1929–30 season, when the NHL average gate per game had been more than $11,000, Ottawa averaged just $4,200. Even the Detroit team, forever teetering on insolvency, had averaged more than $7,000, and Toronto, in a rink similar in size to Ottawa's, averaged more than $8,000.[33]

On September 1, the Montreal *Gazette* reported that Clancy had been sold to the Maroons for $35,000. Toronto's *Globe* claimed both Clancy and goalie Alex Connell were part of the deal, "but for reasons best known to themselves, neither the Ottawa nor the Montreal club wishes to make an announcement at present."

The report proved to be premature. New York and Detroit were also said to be interested. The *Star* reported on October 7 that the "scrappy manager of the Toronto Maple Leafs . . . breezed into town on Monday and went into a huddle with officials of the Ottawa hockey association" to talk turkey. When he emerged with a deal for Clancy it was treated as a triumph, except once again Smythe's shallow-pocketed directors were balking.

The price he'd agreed to was $35,000 plus two players. After he put in his winnings from Rare Jewel, the club would owe $25,000. That was enough to pay four or five players at normal rates, and Smythe's bosses weren't convinced Clancy deserved it. To turn up the pressure, Smythe ran an ad in the Toronto papers: "Fans – The Directors of the Toronto Maple Leaf Hockey Club will make their decision on Friday regarding the purchase of Frank 'King' Clancy from the Ottawa Senators. What do you think of this deal? Write the hockey club's office, 11 King St. West. Signed C. Smythe."[34]

The response was immediate. More than two thousand letters poured in urging the club to complete the deal, on top of telegrams and telephone calls. Some fans stopped by Smythe's office personally to lobby him. The directors, cornered, had little choice but to give their okay.

Everyone agreed it was a brilliant coup. The *Star* called Clancy the "most spectacular and useful player in professional hockey." The *Globe* noted that "even in these days of frequent substitutions, he rarely rests, going at top speed all the time he is on the ice. A brilliant rusher and deadly shot, Clancy is also an invaluable player on the defensive side of the game."

W.A. Hewitt wrote that the pairing of Clancy and Day "should make one of the greatest defences in hockey. With another speed merchant like Clancy working alongside of him, Day should rise to great heights and become one of the outstanding players of the game."

Neither of the players Smythe sent Ottawa amounted to much. Eric Pettinger played twelve games without scoring a point and then disappeared to the International Hockey League. Art Smith played one season, gaining six points. Nonetheless, adding them to the trade raised the price of obtaining Clancy to $50,000, a figure that astounded people. No one had ever paid anything near that for a single hockey player before. Not long before the deal, a Toronto paper carried an advertisement for a "beautiful residence in the best part of Rosedale" on a seventy by two-hundred-foot lot, with twelve rooms including a billiard room, library, six bedrooms, twenty-seven-foot living room with heated sunroom, overlooking a wooded ravine and adjoining tennis court. Asking price: $23,000, less than half the Clancy price tag.

Attendance at Leafs games shot up, not only at home but on the road. "Around the league, people wanted to see what kind of hockey player was worth $50,000," Smythe said. Tim Daly, the gruff, hard-to-impress trainer Smythe had inherited from the St. Pats was enthused despite himself.

"Before Clancy's purchase they sold booster tickets at half price and such. But that ended when Clancy came. What hockey player could be good enough to cost $35,000, people asked. They were curious to see for themselves and it paid off. From then on there were no more booster tickets."[35]

Clancy also had the hoped-for impact on the rest of the roster. Toronto finished the 1931 season in third spot among the ten teams. Conacher, Bailey, and Primeau all made the top-ten scoring list and Conacher led the league in goals. Clancy's arrival had Smythe feeling so buoyant he went out and ordered a fancy new car for Irene as a Christmas present – a Franklin Transcontinent sedan, an enormous car with a running board and big, protruding headlights. At $2,395 it was the cheapest model Franklin made, introduced in a futile effort to stave off the ravages the Depression was having on the luxury car market. Having spent his Rare Jewel winnings, Smythe couldn't really afford it. He just felt good about the future and was increasingly excited about another big project he had in mind, a new home for the Maple Leafs that he intended to be the best hockey arena on the continent.

CHAPTER 8

Scholars have written entire theses on the decision to build an ambitious new hockey rink in Toronto in the middle of the Great Depression. Was Conn Smythe a civic-minded citizen with a strong sense of duty who sought to lift the spirits of a demoralized city while providing badly needed jobs or a cynical capitalist out to exploit the misery of the unemployed?

Was he a visionary who saw the future of professional hockey long before others or a self-centred martinet unconcerned with anything but having his own way? Was he inspired by (and jealous of) Tex Rickard's Madison Square Garden or a local yokel with a swollen ego who wanted to build a gaudy monument to his own pride?

It depends on your point of view. Smythe would have scoffed at the deep thinkers and their analysis of his motives. In his mind, if you owned a hockey team and wanted to attract fans, you needed a place for them to watch the game. The more attractive the arena, the more tickets you'd sell. He also wanted to elevate the status of the game he loved, away from dingy surroundings and drunken, rowdy fans. He wanted a place where men could bring their wives or girlfriends and where ladies wouldn't object to being taken. To achieve that he needed an arena swish enough that women could justify wearing their best shoes and evening clothes and could sit in comfort without shivering from the cold.

He also wanted to make money, though getting rich wasn't the driving force behind Maple Leaf Gardens. The Gardens was heavily mortgaged and Smythe ran it as a hockey venue first and entertainment centre a distant second; under his direction it never approached the money-spinning heights achieved after his departure. Foster

Hewitt, calling the plays from his gondola, grew far richer, far faster than Smythe did.

In the end the Gardens proved to be a bigger success than anyone anticipated. The city got a building and a team in which it took inordinate pride, and still does. But none of that was evident when the notion came to Smythe to spend more than $1 million on a hockey rink just as the stock market was crashing and the economy was grinding to a halt. Most people in 1930 just thought he was nuts.

Putting finances to one side, it wasn't hard to understand his drive for a better place to play. The five-year agreement he'd signed with the Arena Gardens in 1927 had been a poor deal. The Leafs had the rights to just two Saturday night games a month, the other nights being reserved for senior amateur teams. They had access just an hour a day between 10 a.m. and 4 p.m. for practices, with no practising allowed on Sunday. The arena, not the club, controlled concession licences for refreshments, and the sale and pricing of tickets. The Leafs got a cut of the gate, but the arena collected the money and only later handed over the team's share. Arena Gardens management also got forty free tickets a game and a free box for the use of directors. The agreement awarded the owners 30 per cent of gross receipts up to the first $80,000 a year and 35 per cent thereafter.

Smythe couldn't be blamed for feeling his team was playing for the benefit of the rink owners rather than the club itself. To address the problem of limited seating, arena management agreed to consider adding galleries at one end to squeeze in an additional eight hundred to sixteen hundred fans, but only if the Leafs produced at least five sold-out games a season and gross receipts of at least $150,000. And if they did hit those targets, the rink's share of the gate would increase to as high as 35 per cent, and the lease would be extended by an additional ten years. Toronto would be stuck in a building that could accommodate nine thousand or ten thousand at most – and then only if the fire marshall wasn't looking – in a league where U.S. teams could accommodate seventeen thousand or more.[1]

Smythe wouldn't have signed a deal like that if he'd had an alternative, but he didn't. In 1927, Arena Gardens was the best available, followed by the much smaller Ravina Gardens in the west end. The Leafs played at the Arena or they didn't play at all.

By 1930, though, things were changing. The Leafs were a better and more exciting team. Tickets were increasingly difficult to come by. Smythe had engineered a complete makeover and could now ice a team of future stars that included Conacher, Primeau, and Jackson – soon to be united in the dominating "Kid Line" – high-scoring Ace Bailey and left winger Baldy Cotton, with reliable Hap Day and the twenty-one-year-old bonecrusher known as Red Horner on defence. With the addition of Clancy, Smythe knew he had a team able to compete with the best in the league.

Increased attendance reflected the growing hold the Leafs had on Toronto. About half the games were sellouts, and fans sometimes filled not only all the seats and available standing room, but crowded the aisles and the passageways as well. Revenue increased sharply every year from 1927 on, from $83,000 in Smythe's first year to $123,000 two years later.[2]

The days when pro hockey was buried deep in a corner of the sports pages were also fading; the Leafs were news from the start of training camp until their last game of the season. Smythe was increasingly recognized as the face and the voice of the team, appearing as regularly in the sports pages as he felt inclined.

It was all heading in the right direction, but Smythe could see trouble ahead. It was fine to win $10,000 in a horse race and use it to buy a player, but he couldn't be counted on to repeat that miracle every year. (Tragically, Rare Jewel died of pneumonia barely six weeks after the race of her life.[3]) The limited seating capacity at Arena Gardens was a de facto salary cap on Smythe's ability to recruit big names or to pay players the amounts they could command elsewhere. Clancy might have been satisfied with $8,500 and the promise of a raise if he performed well, but he wasn't the best-paid player in the league and it might enter his head at some point that he should be.

Smythe understood instinctively a truth that still stands: owning an NHL team without control of the arena is a lesson in frustration. Black Hawks owner Frederic McLaughlin learned that the hard way when, after three seasons in the dilapidated five-thousand-seat Coliseum, he signed a long-term lease at the seventeen-thousand-seat Chicago Stadium and spent the rest of his days being squeezed mercilessly by "Big Jim" Norris, who controlled the building and hoped to hound McLaughlin into selling him the team.

Even at his most prosperous Smythe would never match Norris's bottomless millions, but without a bigger rink he might not even manage to stay in the league. Montreal, Detroit, Boston, and the New York teams all played in larger, newer homes. If he wanted the Leafs to have a future, he needed one too.

The problem was in the timing. There couldn't be a less promising moment to take the sort of risk Smythe had in mind. "Awful" doesn't begin to describe the state of the Canadian economy at the start of that most depressing of decades. Calamitous, appalling, unnerving . . . it was all of those. Even the most pessimistic of forecasters couldn't have imagined the depths the Depression would reach and the years it would drag on.

On the day the market crashed in October 1929, the Leafs were just wrapping up training camp in Port Elgin, where they'd engaged in their by-now traditional routine of calisthenics, roadwork, baseball, soccer, and golf. Smythe was being hailed for the wisdom of acquiring centre Andy Blair from Colonel Hammond for a no-name college player. There was talk that Lou Marsh, while hanging on to his job as a newspaper columnist, was pondering retirement as a referee.[4]

The next morning, everyone awoke to headlines that signalled ten years of misery ahead. "STOCK PRICES CRASH EARLY, SLIGHT RALLY LATER," "RUSH TO 'GET OUT,'" "MARKET FLOODED IN WORST CRASH IN TORONTO'S HISTORY," wailed the *Star*. "UTTER COLLAPSE IN STOCK MARKET NARROWLY AVERTED," "STRENUOUS EFFORTS OF

GREAT BANKS TURN STAMPEDE OF FRANTIC SELLERS DURING RECORD DAY ON WALL STREET," reported the *Globe*. There was a sense that Armageddon was upon the land and a real sense of fear, though as the weeks went on and life appeared to be unfolding as normal, the fright temporarily faded. Optimistic reports suggested the worst was already over, and there were signs of recovery. Occasional rallies came along to reassure investors that sanity would prevail. Investors persuaded themselves the crash was just a short break for the market to catch its breath before easy money returned.

There was no evidence of panic in the sports pages, where Leaf prospects were also being looked on with optimism. After making the playoffs the previous year, great things were expected from the speedy young team. CFCA Radio announced it would broadcast the team's games, with popular young Foster Hewitt at the microphone "as usual." Broadcasts would start at 9:00 p.m. and end about 10:15 p.m. "Between periods J. Wilson Jardine and his Orchestra will provide an excellent dance program from the Palais Royale."[5]

More than two thousand fans turned out just to watch a practice. Red Horner wowed the crowd – a "brilliant defence player" with a "wicked" shot, said the *Star*. The papers were also agog at a remarkable new tactic Smythe introduced early in November, just a few days after the stock market debacle. In a pre-season game he began using "two full teams" – i.e., two forward lines – changing them in "rapid fire" shifts every five minutes. Musing on the innovation, Charlie Querrie remarked in the *Star* that it wasn't entirely new. Eddie Livingstone had tried something similar back in the old days, he recalled. But this time it looked like it would catch on: Querrie reported that Art Ross was planning to use *three* complete forward lines when the season opened. That would mean players making $6,000 to $8,000 a year would only have to play twenty minutes a game. Querrie reminded his readers that old-timers like Sprague Cleghorn and Newsy Lalonde "played every minute and every game for somewhere around one thousand smackers for the season."[6]

Inevitably, though, the reality of the times became evident. The Ottawa Senators – suffering poor attendance even for their small arena – announced they would play five "home" games outside Ottawa: two in Detroit, one in Boston, and two in Atlantic City, in an attempt to "at least meet operating expenses."[7]

In Pittsburgh it was evident the Pirates were not long for this world. They were in the middle of an abysmal campaign, their arena needed upgrading so badly the team left town in February and finished out the season on the road, and the steel industry on which Pittsburgh depended was crumbling beneath the weight of the Depression. Pirates owners announced the team would spend the next season in Philadelphia, where they played a single, final season as the Quakers.

In Detroit, too, the Cougars were in trouble. The owners were tight-fisted and ham-handed, the club was a perennial also-ran, and playing in a pint-sized arena in Windsor hadn't helped. Manager Jack Adams had slowly improved the quality of the club, but support was so fragile the team let local newspapers hold a contest in 1930 to pick a new name, The Falcons. At one point Adams traded standing room seats to an exhibition game for five bags of potatoes.[8]

Even as determined an optimist as Smythe could hardly miss the accumulating signs. By mid-1930 construction in Toronto was plummeting, unemployment was soaring, calls for relief were multiplying, and the politicians were fighting over whose fault it was. William Lyon Mackenzie King was ousted as prime minister that summer when it became evident he had no solution to the crisis – he continued to insist, in fact, that there *was* no crisis. Before the election he argued it would be madness to call a national conference to debate the growing ranks of the jobless because it would only serve to draw attention to the problem, which was bound to go away on its own if just given time.

The seriousness of the situation was no secret to the growing crowd of men who, lacking jobs and anywhere better to stay, had taken to sleeping in and around a brick factory in the Don Valley, establishing a "hobo jungle" of tents, huts, and claptrap lean-tos of scavenged bits of wood and plastic. Managers of the brick works had taken pity on the men, letting some of them sleep inside on the warm bricks on cool nights.

Smythe wasn't immune to the sense of desperation, but he wasn't intimidated by it either. He'd been working on plans for a new arena since at least June 1929, when he and his friend Larkin Maloney played golf with a young advertising executive named Jack MacLaren at a course near Smythe's cottage. During the round he agreed to sell MacLaren the rights to find a sponsor for Hewitt's radio broadcasts for an arena with no investors that still existed only in his own mind.[9] Hewitt himself wasn't aware of the arena plan, much less that he was expected to broadcast from it. Smythe brought him into the picture a few months later and they agreed Hewitt would form Foster Hewitt Productions, which would not only broadcast Leafs games but have authority over other broadcasts from the new building and commercial rights to sell advertising.[10] At that point Smythe planned to have the rink built in time for the 1930–31 season, a deadline the onset of the Depression rendered impossible. He was already working up his promotional pitch: Maple Leafs Gardens, he insisted, would be the biggest and best in Canada. It would seat twelve thousand and change hockey into an evening's entertainment suitable for the best sort of people. He'd get rid of the dinginess, the drunkenness, and the rowdiness that tainted hockey's image. Going to the Gardens would be equivalent to a night at the theatre. People would dress up.

It would also be a credit to the community. He took immense pride in his hometown and wanted a facility that reflected its rising glory. The Gardens, he told prospective investors, was a civic betterment project, a means of projecting the pride Toronto increasingly felt in its status and stature. It was something Torontonians should get behind. When Smythe organized the purchase of the Toronto St. Patricks in 1927, he'd convinced J.P. Bickell to accept his bid even though it was lower than other offers, on the basis of civic pride. As a corporate titan and community figure, Smythe insisted, Bickell had a responsibility to keep the team from leaving town. Now he used the same argument to sell investors on the merits of backing a piece of his dream.

It was still not an easy sell. Smythe and Maloney put together a lunch meeting at the King Edward Hotel with Ed Bickle and Bill MacBrien, both Leafs directors who they hoped would help bring in investors. Bickle was a stockbroker, MacBrien an insurance executive. Neither was as enthused as Smythe had hoped. MacBrien was lukewarm; Bickle was against the whole idea, arguing it was the wrong time to be risking $1 million. Maloney and Smythe were both annoyed; Maloney was particularly upset that the two men seemed to think he and Smythe were in over their heads. Maloney, like Smythe, wasn't afraid of risk; they'd bought their first horse together, and Smythe trusted him.

They kept up their search even as the fallout from the crash spread. In September, bricklayers agreed to a three-day week and a cut in pay from $55 a week to $27.50 so jobs could be shared around.[11] Ottawa proposed spending $20 million on construction projects to relieve unemployment, and the *Star* launched a new campaign – "Give a man a Job" – in which readers were invited to fill out a coupon and send it in, listing odd jobs that needed doing around the house. The paper would then dispatch an unemployed person to the scene.[12] In the midst of this Smythe decided he was too busy looking for investors to continue handling his coaching duties, so four days after Leaf directors approved the trade for Clancy, he announced that Art Duncan would serve as coach.

As he did his rounds of potential backers, it occurred to Smythe that a show of public enthusiasm might help bring investors on board. It was similar to the tactic he'd used to pressure Leafs directors into approving the money he needed to buy Clancy. This time he asked Selke to prepare a program extolling the benefits of a bigger and better arena and then pressed Hewitt to plug it over the radio during his next Leafs broadcast. Hewitt agreed, even though he'd be extolling the merits of a new rink from the rafters of the old one, whose owners were sure to be hurt if Smythe succeeded.

Selke readied the program, which included photos of all the Leafs directors, a shot of Rare Jewel crossing the finish line, a second shot of the tote board showing the winning payoff of $214 on a $2 bet, and a third shot of Smythe posing proudly with his horse and its Maple Leafs colours. The case for a new arena was written by Nutsy Fagan, a character invented by the *Telegram*'s Ted Reeve:

> Now that they have brought the matter up, I will tell you all why we need a bigger Arena in case you think we are building one just because some of the players are putting on weight.
>
> Civic pride demands it, that's what. Have we not in this grand and glorious hamlet the Canadian National Exhibition, the tallest skyscrapers in the British Empire, the most beautiful race track in North America (Woodbine not Dufferin), government control, the University of Toronto, and the Balmy Beach Canoe Club? The answer is, 'Yes, we have the Canadian National Exhibition, the tallest skyscrapers in the British Empire the etc.' We have all these and many more remarkable and prepossessing public institutions, and why, then should we be curtailed to a theatre of thump that will only hold eight thousand people with one foot in the aisle?

Selke contributed his own testimonial, in the guise of Abner Tiffen, another invented character, who he'd dreamed up one summer while working at a hotel in Muskoka. Abner was a rube who had a high opinion of his hockey skills and continually pestered the Leafs for a tryout.

> I seen in the Daily Star that the Leafs are selling shares in Maple Leafs Gardens Arena. I don't see why you should have a garden by the Arena when the farmers have lots of stuff to sell but city folks are queere and I guess you know best.
>
> I want to buy some shares in the rink. Kate and I have been saving our money and she wants ten shares and I want twenty. Sell us Preffered shares cause I cant be bothered with no common stock.[13]

Smythe had hoped to sell thirty-two thousand programs with the help of Hewitt's on-air endorsement. Instead, requests poured in for three times that number. To boost interest, Smythe had priced it at just ten cents, less than the cost of production. But the loss was well worth it as far as he was concerned, giving a shot of adrenalin to his fundraising drive. Until that moment his plans had remained under the radar of most Torontonians, as Smythe had avoided a grand announcement until he was sure he could deliver. In the weeks after the printing of Selke's brochure, however, more frequent reports began to turn up in the newspapers. He still didn't have the financing he needed, and he didn't have a site to build on. But the bags of mail that poured into his office expressing excitement and impatience for a new arena renewed his faith in the proposal and fed the urgency he felt to get it under way.

He had begun looking at potential sites months earlier and had whittled the possibilities down to three: a piece of land owned by the Toronto Harbour Commission on the Toronto waterfront, the site of the old Knox Divinity College in the Spadina Circle just north of College Street, and a parcel owned by the T. Eaton Company on Carlton Street east of Yonge. On January 7, the *Mail and Empire* broke the news that a business group was planning a rink at the Spadina location, then being used as an armoury. It would be called Spadina Gardens and cost $1.5 million, seat sixteen thousand for hockey and up to twenty thousand for wrestling and other sports, and include the novelty of underground parking for one thousand cars. The announcement indicated construction would start soon, and the builders "expected to house the professional hockey games next winter."

The announcement caused a small uproar. Alderman Nathan Phillips and two local clergymen – the Rev. Dr. John Gibson Inkster of Knox Presbyterian Church and Dr. Salem Bland, a well-known Methodist preacher – declared their opposition. The Rev. Dr. Inkster, described as a "pillar of Presbyterianism and Calvinist theology," declared he wasn't against sport, just professionals. "These people who follow professional sport do it for the sake of blood. It would be a crime to permit the building of an arena where thugs could gather and infest the neighbourhood."[14]

Despite the claims of its backers, the project had nothing to do with the Leafs. Smythe confessed he was mystified. Although he had investigated the same site, he said, he had dismissed it due to objections from local businessmen. Still, it gave him another excuse to press Leafs directors to quit stalling. Accordingly, a week after details of the Spadina plan were released, Smythe put out a statement of his own indicating that Maple Leafs directors had gathered that day and "unanimously decided that they will sponsor and build an arena themselves."[15]

He told reporters it had been evident for three or four years that the Mutual Street rink wasn't adequate. There had been discussions about a new arena since early 1929, just two years after he had signed the five-year deal with the Arena Gardens. "Unforeseen delays" had stalled plans but now, at last, it was time to forge ahead. Although the site was still not finalized, the *Star* related, "it is practically assured the magnificent new hockey arena . . . will be located within four minutes walk of King and Yonge streets, at the corner of Yonge and new Fleet St."[16] Smythe admitted he was keen on the Fleet Street site, on newly reclaimed land on the east side of Yonge, a block east of today's Air Canada Centre. Plans for a lakefront boulevard meant it would have easy auto access, and it was close to trolley lines on Bay, Front, and Yonge.

While pursuing the waterfront site, Smythe and Ed Bickle had also been in negotiations with Eaton's. On March 4, 1930, Eaton's director James Elliott sent a memo to secretary-treasurer J.J. Vaughan noting that he'd had an inquiry from a real estate broker about a lot fronting Church Street and stretching from Wood to Alexander. Elliott wasn't sure, but he thought the broker, J.A. Gibson of Gibson Bros., was working for someone who wanted to build a hotel. The structure, whatever it was, would cost no less than $500,000, Elliott reported.[17]

Two days later Elliott wrote to Vaughan again informing him the interested parties "are those who own or control the present Mutual Street Arena." They wanted to build a new rink with at least double the seating "with probably stores around the front of it on three sides. . . . They also intend to have Bowling Alleys and any other sports which might possibly be included."

Elliott noted that Eaton's had paid $200,000 for the site and would likely need $350,000 to break even, but would probably have to take less, given the market. Vaughan was willing to sell, but the deal ran into an immediate problem in the form of Charles G. Carmichael, owner of 60 Wood Street, the only lot on the property Eaton's didn't own. Carmichael's lot was crucial to the plan, but, Elliott noted, he wanted "the ridiculous price of $75,000" for a lot worth closer to $10,000.

Talks between Elliott and Gibson dragged on all spring. When the problem of Carmichael's greed couldn't be overcome, Gibson asked about land farther south, fronting Carlton. Like the Wood Street lot, it actually belonged to International Realty Co., a firm owned by the estate of Sir John Craig Eaton. It was a better site, with direct access to the Carlton streetcar, but Vaughan was a lot less enthusiastic about selling it, and Elliott wasn't sure the hockey men could afford it – he'd heard they were having difficulty raising money. Eaton's suggested they might be happier with an "inside lot," either on Wood Street, or Carlton, but without frontage on Church. Smythe wasn't interested: he wanted fans to be able to step off the trolley and directly into an entrance on one of those two streets.

The issue for Eaton's came down to more than just price; Vaughan and the other executives assumed they'd lose money on the sale of either site. They were more concerned about the sort of people who attended hockey games. Like Inkster and Bland, they weren't against sport per se, they just didn't want a professional hockey team nearby. The company had just opened Eaton's College Street department store, an art deco showpiece on the corner of Yonge and College. Eaton's planned it to be the first leg in a massive business and retail complex to rival Rockefeller Centre in New York, with a soaring office tower and developments to the west and south.[18] The store included its own world-class concert hall, approached by a grand foyer on the seventh floor. It was intended to be the latest word in haute shopping, aimed unapologetically at an upper-class clientele, and the firm's executives weren't convinced the patrons of a professional hockey team were the sort of folks they wanted in the neighbourhood.

Gibson promised his clients would erect "a building of a handsome appearance with first class modern store fronts to produce the maximum amount of rental and give the best possible appearance," and would pay as much as $350,000. But Vaughan refused. "Therefore, unless the Arena people wish to negotiate with respect to an inside block the matter is closed," Elliott wrote in May.

And it was – at least for six months. But late in November Gibson was back, this time bypassing Vaughan and appealing to vice-president Harry McGee. The Leafs, he said, were willing to pay $250,000 for 350 feet of frontage on Carlton – less than he had offered in the spring. The proposal was submitted at a directors meeting and rejected. Eaton president J.A. Livingstone noted the arena would be empty most of the day and instructed Gibson to "Keep it off" either Church or Carlton.

For the next two months letters flew back and forth weekly, and sometimes daily. Eaton's was determined to pawn off a lesser lot on the buyers; Smythe and Bickle, through Gibson, were determined not to take it. Numerous variations were proposed: an inside lot with passageways to Carlton and Church; a rink on Wood to the west of the troublesome Mr. Carmichael; a rink on Church north of Wood that would require paying Carmichael his bounty. The price rose and fell: Eaton's variously calculated the value of the preferred Carlton Street site anywhere from $211,000 to $600,000. Gibson raised the offer back to $350,000 and insisted it was more than generous. Just after Christmas Bickle pointed out the proposed building would serve as a much-needed convention site in addition to hockey, that there would be motor shows, circuses, bicycle races, track and field, and possibly a large pool, and even offered to name the building "Eatonia Gardens," a suggestion he can only have made without Smythe's knowledge.

The logjam finally broke at the end of January. Smythe and Bickle visited J.J. Vaughan personally to lay out their position and somehow managed to win his support. Until then Vaughan had been the biggest obstacle in their path. While Smythe might still have preferred the Fleet Street location, he balked when someone involved in the sale demanded a $100,000 kickback, leaving Carlton Street as the last best hope. The meeting with Vaughan took place just two weeks after Smythe had told the papers he'd have a new rink built for the next hockey season. At that point he had nothing to back up his promise, and if construction was to begin in time he needed something soon.

He got it from Vaughan. After insisting for the better part of a year that Smythe's people would just have to make do with a lesser lot, he suddenly changed his tune. Three days after the meeting, Elliott informed other Eaton's directors the firm would sell the Maple Leafs organization a site on Church extending from Carlton to Wood for $375,000 (later lowered to $350,000) and the right to approve the exterior of the building. The arena group would have to build stores on Church and Carlton – which Eaton's would approve – and meet set construction dates. Eaton's also reversed its refusal to invest in the project, agreeing to purchase $50,000 in preferred shares or bonds.[19]

In his memoirs, Selke suggested Vaughan's change of mind resulted from inroads Smythe was finally making with investors. Alfred Rogers, a coal and cement baron, had agreed to buy in. Perhaps more significantly, Maloney and Smythe had recently returned from a trip to Montreal where they had finally hooked a big fish: the Sun Life insurance company, with some prodding from their Toronto directors and the powerful architecture firm of Ross and Macdonald, had agreed to invest $500,000.[20]

Ross and Macdonald had designed the Château Laurier in Ottawa, Toronto's Royal York hotel, the new Union Station – and, crucially, Eaton's College Street store. At Gibson's urging, the firm contacted Eaton's and voiced support for the arena plan, declaring, "We are familiar with the property mentioned and are of the opinion that the location is admirably suited for the project in mind."[21] Elliott forwarded the letter to R.Y. Eaton, who had been running the firm since the death of his cousin Sir John Craig Eaton in 1922.

As Smythe made his rounds of wealthy Torontonians, his new-look Maple Leafs were playing just the way he'd hoped they would. They lost their first game of the season, but played solidly from then on, and by mid-January were challenging for the league lead. The trade for King Clancy was making Smythe look like a genius. Clancy's high-octane blend of skill and enthusiasm helped push the team from its traditional spot in third or fourth place straight into the top rank. Howie Morenz, everyone's choice as the league's biggest star, volunteered in mid-season that Clancy was the best all-round player he'd ever faced. He was, as Smythe once marvelled, the most "amateur" player in the league: he played for the sheer love of the game and the desire to shove the puck – and maybe his stick and fist as well – straight down his opponent's throat. His will to win was infectious, and the Leafs became a club that refused to give in, refused to surrender, refused to acknowledge the possibility of defeat until the final bell had rung.

Added to Clancy's verve was Hap Day's leadership and defensive skills and the puppy-like joy with which the litter of talented young new Leafs played the game. Coach Duncan was able to ice an entire line – Conacher, Primeau, and Jackson up front, with Red Horner and Alex Levinsky on defence – consisting entirely of recent graduates of Selke's Toronto Marlboros. Primeau, the oldest of the five, was all of twenty-three. (Levinsky, one of the first Jewish players in the NHL, was known as "Mine Boy," allegedly after his proud father's boast, "That's mine boy!") After a comparatively fallow season, Ace Bailey was back among the league's scoring leaders, bracketed by Conacher and Primeau, with Jackson not far behind.

Even more satisfying to Smythe was his team's pugnacity. They played with a constant edge, with Conacher, Jackson, and Horner surpassing even the ever-belligerent Clancy in racking up penalty minutes. Jackson led the team overall, but Smythe was impressed by the emerging nastiness of the twenty-one-year-old Horner, which would only increase as he grew in confidence. The fans responded with enthusiasm. For a Saturday night game against Montreal, Smythe received twenty-five thousand ticket requests, more than three times what the rink could accommodate. In another game that month, Lou Marsh claimed Foster Hewitt got so excited "they had to shackle him to his perch" in the rafters. Both games paled, though, next to a classic confrontation with the Canadiens in which the Leafs pulled off a "double comeback," spotting the Habs a two-goal lead in regulation time and another in overtime, yet storming back each time for a tie. (Overtime periods lasted a full ten minutes, no matter how many goals were scored.)

It was a wild, brawl-filled night during which the teams took turns making the other look ill prepared. A movie camera had been set up to capture the action – the first indoor hockey game ever to be filmed, according to the papers – and the players and fans alike responded with appropriate lashings of drama. Someone in the crowd threw a knife at referee Bert Corbeau – it was a "heavy, horn-handled knife," according to Marsh. Corbeau said it was the second time he'd had a knife flung his way and he intended to keep it as a souvenir, to go with the frozen turnips once directed at him during a game in Ottawa. The game's other official, Vic Wagner, also had an object aimed at him, but in his case it was a watch and he kindly returned it to the abusive fan.

Partway through the third period, with the Leafs down two goals, Conacher ran Canadiens' defenceman Marty Burke into the boards and was sent to the penalty box. On the next play Burke cross-checked Jackson, and Jackson responded "with a clean-cut right that dropped Burke on his back." Burke popped back up and they started swinging at each other, until Corbeau escorted them off the ice and warned them against trying to mix it up in the box, which served for players of both clubs. Burke and Jackson ignored him, leaping on one another right away, joined by Conacher, who "suddenly turned and whipped a series of rights into Burke's face as he was struggling with Jackson." A policeman gamely tried to separate the players, but was dragged into the brawl as the bench turned over and all four tumbled to the ground, still swinging.

Suddenly, reported Marsh, Conacher rose up from the jumble and swung at the cop, catching him in the eye. The officer swung back with "some more plunks and a couple of blams, and Conacher was left with a blinker from an official fist."

Jackson and Burke were ejected from the game, but Conacher was back on the ice after serving his two minutes, slugging a cop not being a violation of any known NHL rules. Buoyed by the battle, the Leafs scored twice in the dying moments to send the game to overtime, then just as quickly gave up two goals before finally fighting back again for another tie, with Conacher putting the last puck past goalie George Hainsworth with just forty seconds left.

"Wotta night brother, wotta night," marvelled Marsh, calling it "the greatest hockey hoedown Toronto fans ever saw." After the game, he noted, Conacher "apologized to the cop he hit. Said he was a little off when he let his right go. He probably intended to hit someone in China."[22]

Smythe could have used more nights like that. The fans gobbled it up, the papers were excited, and Smythe could legitimately claim that despite the Depression his team was doing better than ever. Revenue was up for the fourth year in a row; one January game raked in the biggest one-game total in team history. Six times that season – usually against teams from Montreal – the gate had surpassed $10,000, more than the previous three seasons combined.[23]

Now that they were investors, even Eaton's started to get excited. James Elliott spent part of one day idly listing possible names for the new rink on a lined sheet of paper. Eatonia Gardens, thankfully, had died an unlamented death, perhaps because Eaton's already sold a six-ply tire with that name – "guaranteed for 15,000 miles!" Other possibilities that struck Elliott included the Sports Gardens, Maple Leaf Arena, College Gardens, the Midtown Arena, Hub Arena, the Metropolitan, and the Palace. He wrote to contacts in New York and

Montreal seeking information on the impact of Madison Square Garden and the Forum on their surrounding neighbourhoods. He even sent someone to count the cars around Arena Gardens during a Saturday night Leaf game to get an idea of the traffic. Total: 2,698.[24]

Maple Leaf Gardens Ltd. was incorporated February 24.[25] Smythe hadn't been able to recruit enough of Toronto's aristocracy yet and was still relentlessly pushing stock. "Five shares would make you as enthusiastic a fan as the wealthiest subscriber," the prospectus promised. "You would assure yourself of a moderate annual dividend and help complete the erection of America's finest Sports Palace." Shares also made good gifts or the seed for a trust "for a growing boy or girl." There were plenty of gags, and appeals to feminine fans. "The Maple Leaf management particularly encourage The Ladies to take up small holdings in the company," it said, under a cartoon of thoroughly modern female fans casting admiring eyes at Busher and Charlie, while complaining that, "It's a shame the wonderful team hasn't a better home."

Design details promised unobstructed views from everywhere in the rink. "Unlike Madison Square Garden," Toronto's would be built by people "who grew up hand-in-hand with the game of hockey." At Montreal's Forum or Chicago's Stadium, "the rooters in the back rows are so far away that they carry opera glasses." Not in Toronto, where seating would be in two tiers to keep fans close to the action, with an elevated gallery to ensure a clear view even in lower-priced seats.

The board of directors read like an all-star team of Toronto business interests. In addition to Bickell, Bickle, and Alfred Rogers, there were representatives from Eaton's and Simpson's, Canada Life, the CNR, the Bank of Commerce, the William Wrigley Co., Algoma Steel, the British-American Oil Co., the Bank of Nova Scotia, and Sun Life. Sun Life would hold the mortgage, though at one point late in the game it got cold feet and tried to back out.[26] The Gardens would buy the hockey club, valued at $350,000, for a mix of common and preferred shares. "They will thus own the only Professional Hockey franchise in Toronto and no other organized professional hockey can be played in Toronto without their consent." It revealed that the OHA had signed a five-year deal to play its games in the new arena, and that "Maple Leaf Gardens have also been fortunate in inducing Mr. W.A. Hewitt, sports editor of the *Toronto Star*, to become general manager in charge of all other attractions." So while Foster was calling the action, his father would be booking boxers and lion acts, while continuing to run the OHA on the side.

In April, Hewitt reported that demolition had begun on site but that "radical changes" had been made to the design, eliminating the gallery seats and turning the ice surface to face north and south, with the bulk of seating along the sides. The gallery had to go because the architects concluded they could not provide a clear view of the ice from every seat. But they had made a "close inspection" of other NHL cities and pledged the Gardens "will be the last word in arena construction."[27] The article was accompanied by an illustration depicting the yellow-brick, domed box that would soon become a city landmark.

One last crucial date remained: Thursday, May 28, when tenders would be opened on contractors' bids for the job.[28] The meeting was held across the street from Smythe's office at 11 King Street West, in the office of Sir John Aird, president of the Bank of Commerce and one of the Gardens' most important backers.[29] Smythe, with his engineering background, had estimated the cost of the job between $500,000 and $800,000. With the price of the Eaton's lot, architect fees, and other charges he hoped the total would not surpass $1.2 million to $1.3 million, roughly the amount he had raised. But sitting in Sir John's office as the bids were opened he grew increasingly downcast, as one after another came in far above expectations. The lowest of the ten was from the Toronto firm of Thomson Brothers at $989,297, not including steelwork estimated at $100,000. With other costs – including $25,000 to get out of the Arena Gardens' contract – the price would reach about $1.6 million,[30] maybe $300,000 more than Smythe had or could hope to raise. Aird suggested putting off the whole idea until conditions improved, which was the last thing on earth Smythe wanted to hear.

All the buildings on the Carlton Street site had already been knocked down – Smythe had paid Eaton's $85,000 to start demolition before the deal formally closed. He even ordered Selke to hire a watchman to keep an eye on things, though Selke joked that "only a lunatic would have tried to make off with the crumpled pile of bricks" that remained.[31] Steam shovels were booked to begin digging at midnight Sunday – just three days away. Work would have to continue day and night to make the November 12 opening of the Leafs' season. Money was so tight Smythe had cut all pay at his sand and gravel company by 10 to 20 per cent, reducing his own salary to twenty-five dollars a week. And with all that in motion, Aird was suggesting he call the whole thing off, possibly triggering a clause in his deal with Eaton's that would have nullified the sale.

During a break he wandered disconsolately into the hall and slumped down beside Selke, who was waiting to hear the result.

"It's no go," he told Selke. "They want to hold off for a year or two."[32]

Selke, with six kids to feed, had mortgaged his house to buy $4,500 of Gardens stock.[33] Smythe had also borrowed to buy 3,880 shares.[34] They pondered the hopelessness of the situation. "We had tapped everybody who had any money, not once but two or three times," said Smythe.[35] "There was no going back to them, and nowhere else to go."

It was Selke who suggested cutting costs, a proposal Smythe barked at, having pared every cent possible. But Selke had a novel idea: he was still a member of the electricians' union, and there was a weekly meeting of the Allied Building Trades Council going on nearby. The unions were being crushed by the Depression. Tens of thousands were jobless in Toronto, and the government couldn't hope to meet the demands for relief. The number of men sleeping in the camp by the Don Valley Brick Works was swelling; Ottawa was preparing to deport more than two thousand British men who had come to Canada with government help in better times.[36] Such was the despair that radical talk was spreading, and police had begun laying charges against communist pamphleteers.

It struck Selke, reasonably enough, that construction workers might be happy to have a job at less than their normal pay, rather than joining the swelling army of despair. Hurrying from the bank building, he jogged to the labour hall and asked to address the assembly. He laid out the argument: here was a company willing to press ahead with a major building project in a city where large-scale construction had ground to a halt. Now it was all in danger of being cancelled for lack of funds.

The union bosses were unimpressed. Why should they care if a bunch of businessmen couldn't put up their building? None of them would go hungry, unlike many of the unions' members.

Selke worked his little frame into a lather. He pointed out that cancelling the Gardens would have a devastating effect on what was left of the industry. If the richest men in Toronto couldn't scrape together the wherewithal for a new arena, what hope was there for anyone else? The papers had been full of stories about the plan for months, and people were excited. Amid all the desperation and despair, hockey was something that offered a momentary diversion – Foster Hewitt's broadcasts were becoming such an attraction that the *Star* sometimes noted on the front page when he would be calling a game. Take away that hope and Toronto would sink deeper into the quagmire of despondency that was threatening to swallow it.

Selke's emotional address had its effect, though the practical-minded men in front of him were still wondering what it had to do with them. Then he unveiled his idea: the Gardens project might still go ahead if union members would agree to take four-fifths of their usual pay, with the rest in stock shares. The paper wouldn't be worth much now, but would likely increase in value as the years passed, and would give the men a stake in the success of the venture. His pitch didn't go down well – union men, Selke discovered, thought anything to do with stock shares was related to "big business," and they were opposed to big business on general principles. If the stock was worth having, they assumed, the greedy capitalists would have kept it to themselves.

Only when Selke told them he'd bet his own house on the project did they start to come around. He was making sixty dollars a week as Smythe's assistant general manager, and still moonlighted as an electrician to pay the bills. He'd borrowed $3,500 and kicked in his savings as well to buy his shares. He couldn't afford to be making investments of that sort, but he believed enough in the project to take the kind of leap he'd never taken before in his life.[37]

His plea brought them around enough to offer tentative support, on the condition he present the plan individually to all twenty-four member unions and win the approval of each. It was hardly carte blanche, but it was enough. Selke raced back to the meeting at Aird's office and shared the news. Smythe could barely believe it. When he passed on the message, it had a profound impact, Aird and the others being as suspicious of wage earners as the unions were of them. If the trade unions were willing to make that sacrifice, Aird said, the Bank of Commerce would pick up whatever difference remained.

Smythe recalled it as both the worst and the best day of his life. "I have always been given the main credit for building Maple Leaf Gardens in the depths of the Depression," he wrote in his memoirs. "I didn't even know what a Depression was, so I just kept pushing. But to my mind the final decision, the final laying to rest of the feeling among some people that it was a crazy idea, came when the union men came in and Sir John Aird said, for the Bank of Commerce, 'We'll pick up the rest.'"[38]

CHAPTER 9

Even with the plan in hand and financing in place, Maple Leaf Gardens remained a project under pressure. Money issues remained: Thomson Brothers, who took part of their fee in shares, failed to make a profit. There was a fistfight at the construction site one day over the decision to give the builders a break on wages. An official with the electrical union, who favoured the deal, won the battle as other workers cheered the two on.[1] As costs mounted, Eaton's agreed to a second mortgage that would delay repayment on $100,000 of the money they were owed.[2]

Mostly, though, the challenge was one of time. Thomson's crews had just over five months to erect the immense structure. The steam shovels started at midnight Sunday, May 31, and worked day and night through the summer. As Smythe had hoped, the project quickly became a matter of civic pride. "It will be a credit to the city and the province, an arena of unequaled facilities and an imposing building that will be an ornament to Toronto's latest retail district," wrote Hewitt. "The project is strictly a Toronto concern in every respect, designed, financed, built and controlled, and will be a matter of pride for all good citizens. To Connie Smythe's determination and vision goes the lion's share of the credit for putting the project over, although everybody interested has put his shoulder to the wheel – and soon their dreams will be realized."

Smythe virtually lived at the site, as did Allan Thomson, one of the four brothers who, with their father, made up Thomson Brothers. Smythe marvelled at Thomson's composure – not once did he lose his temper "regardless of the provocation."[3] People stopped to watch from the sidewalk as the skeleton took shape, then as the vast web of steel that would support the dome was put in place.

Impressive numbers were quoted and details shared: the Gardens consumed 13,500 cubic yards of concrete, 600 tons of reinforcing steel, 760 tons of structural steel, and 1.5 million bricks and tile. The dome, 207 by 225 feet, rose 150 feet above street level. The ice pad consisted of four inches of concrete, topped by four inches of cork, which was in turn covered with zinc. Ten miles of cooling pipes from Stelco were laid on top, covered with another inch and a quarter of concrete. A local engineering review devoted sixteen pages to describing the project, most of them filled with ads from suppliers boasting of the parts, equipment, walls, or wiring they had provided.[4] Pits for column footings and retaining walls were dug by hand by some of the thirteen hundred men on site. Two concrete mixers were installed, one at the east end and one at the west, so the centre could be kept open for the steel contractors. To achieve the promised sightlines the rink was designed with no supporting pillars, which required girders so weighty they had to be made on the spot.* Although C. Smythe Ltd. provided some of the building material, Smythe limited the business he gave himself to avoid criticism.[5]

Foster Hewitt was impressed by the icemaking operation, which he described in some detail: 16,000 gallons of brine was pumped through 68,000 feet of pipe at a temperature as low as minus 28 degrees Fahrenheit. As the concrete cooled, a thin layer of water was sprayed on top. In all it took sixteen layers of water to produce half an inch of ice.[6] Harold Ballard, decades later, would also be intrigued by the brine system, though for different reasons – he suggested filling it with pickles to sell to Gardens patrons.[7]

For most of June the site was an enormous hole in the ground with men scurrying about, building support walls, pouring cement, and creating the substructure. By mid-July the pit began to disappear and signs of walls appeared. By early August the first evidence of support for seating areas was evident, and an enormous tower had sprouted to

---

* The figures for steel, bricks, etc., come from Contract Record and Engineering Review November 11, 1931. Other numbers have been quoted elsewhere, including in Foster Hewitt's book *Hockey Night in Canada: The Maple Leafs' Story* (p. 97).

enable the steelwork for the roofing. By September the exterior walls were recognizable along Carlton, with elongated windows and protruding brickwork to disguise its size and prevent the finished building from looking like a big yellow box. The laying of the cornerstone on September 22 was presided over by Lt.-Gov. W.D. Ross, with a dedicatory prayer by none other than the Rev. John G. Inkster of the Knox Presbyterian Church, who had evidently lost his aversion to professional sports once they moved far enough away from his pulpit on Spadina Avenue. "Grant, O Lord, that it may contribute to wholesome entertainment, healthful recreation and good fellowship. Keep everything connected with this arena clean, pure and honest," he intoned.[8]

By mid-October – with just weeks to go – the Gardens was at last enclosed, with exposed beams, a cement floor, and seating areas. Ticket sales had started in an office across the street, and demand was healthy. Smythe and Selke stopped by one day to watch appreciatively, drinking in the scene as eager fans stood in line waiting their turn. One family wanted to ensure they'd get a good look at Horner, their favourite Leaf, finally deciding on seats by the penalty box where he spent so much of his time. Smythe objected to a complaint that prices had been increased. No such thing, he responded. Tickets could be had at all prices, he had simply added plusher padded seats for those willing to pay more.[9]

Icemaking began in early November, with the Leafs able to practise in their new home a week before opening night. Busher Jackson turned up with his arm in a sling after he "tried to make his car do a trapeze act on a hydro tower," according to Marsh. "Where the Busher and his car landed there were no nets."[10] Charlie Conacher provided a second shock when he demanded a big raise. Rumour had it that Conacher, after just two seasons, wanted $10,000, the kind of money paid superstars like Morenz and Eddie Shore. Shortly afterwards the papers revealed that Conacher had been quietly wed over the summer and felt he needed more money as a result.[11]

Jackson's arm healed in time and Conacher signed for a raise – though not as big a boost as he wanted. And on the evening of November 12,

Maple Leaf Gardens opened exactly on time, with all the pomp and circumstance Smythe could muster. As the players skated out for the first time, the 48th Highlanders and the Royal Grenadiers, lined up at the north end, played "Happy Days Are Here Again," a signal that it was okay, at least for one night, to ignore the gloomy tide of events that had become too commonplace in the world. That very day a Toronto court had sentenced seven "communist leaders" to seven-year prison terms for "being parties to a seditious conspiracy." Sir Arthur Currie, in a speech at the Military Institute, warned that Japan was deliberately trying to provoke a war to soak up its two million unemployed men. Russia was reported to be on the brink of collapse, and eight officials in York Township were sent to jail for corruption.

But for one evening none of that mattered, as Torontonians were allowed to forget, and marvel at the wondrous new sports palace their city had gained.

"With its row upon row of eager-eyed enthusiasts rising up and up from the red leather cushions of the box and rail seats, where society was well represented by patrons in evening dress, through section after section of bright blue seats to the green and grey of the top tier, the spectacle presented was magnificent," wrote the *Globe*'s Bert Perry. "The immensity of this hippodrome of hockey, claimed to be the last word in buildings of its kind, was impressed upon the spectator, and those present fully agreed that Toronto had at last blossomed forth into major league ranks to the fullest extent."

The *Telegram* pointed out that the top row of seats at one end was a full city block from the top row at the other and heaped praise on the ventilation system, which kept the air in "a pleasant state" for three hours despite a sold-out crowd of 13,542.

Smythe loved a ceremony, but had laid it on a bit thick. After the bands played, the Leafs lined up and were presented with floral horseshoes on behalf of the city. J.P. Bickell, fortified with a few advance libations, talked too long, determinedly finishing his speech despite cries of "Play hockey!"[12] from the crowd. He was followed by

Ontario premier George Stewart Henry, who gave way to Chicago Black Hawks' Marvin Wentworth, who surrendered the microphone to the Leafs' Hap Day, who said a few words and turned it over to Mayor W.J. Stewart. By this time, the *Telegram* reported, the crowd had had more than enough. "It must be reported, one fears, that the crowd was a little bit rude, and that they made it pretty clear that they had come to see a hockey game and didn't care much about speeches."[13]

Finally, Mayor Stewart dropped the first puck and the game got under way. It was, everyone agreed later, a disappointment. The Leafs, perhaps overwhelmed by the glitz and glamour, looked sluggish and disorganized. They outshot Chicago 51–35, but displayed little of the speed and teamwork they were purported to possess. Conacher lit up the crowd when he fired one of his patented rockets past the Hawks' Charlie Gardiner, but it was the only goal the Leafs could manage. Conacher aided the cause again by crashing into Gardiner and sending him to the dressing room for a lengthy delay, the crowd forced to sit and wait again as Chicago had no spare. Unfortunately for the Leafs, on his return he was just as effective and Chicago put the night to bed with a 2–1 victory.

It barely mattered. There would be plenty of hockey games to come. "It was a night that will live long in the memories of the fans, even if the home team lost," summed up W.A. Hewitt.

The accolades were not out of place. There was simply nothing else like Maple Leaf Gardens anywhere in Canada. As a hockey rink, and as a venue for concerts, circuses, or conventions, it was in a class of its own. It was more than just a step-up on the old, cramped, badly ventilated Arena Gardens; it was a generation or more ahead of any other building in the country. It was clean, comfortable, and welcoming. It had conveniences no one had imagined for a hockey arena. Smoking in the seating areas was strictly forbidden, a risky idea for a sport favoured by men with cigars. Everyone smoked in those days. Even the players smoked, though the Leafs had to sneak butts between periods while hiding in the toilets because Smythe had banned booze and tobacco in the dressing room. Hallways were wide and there were lounges for congregating between periods. A reporter marvelled that the building could be cleared in a matter of minutes without a sense of being crushed by the crowd. Smythe was a stickler for cleanliness and took particular pride in keeping the toilets clean. Years later, when he got into a battle with the Detroit Red Wings' ownership, he repeatedly made disparaging remarks about the women's washrooms at the Olympia until someone shut him up by asking why he was so interested in women's washrooms. Paint was applied so frequently that, even decades later, the building had the feel of newness. To keep the place running smoothly, Smythe had hired away the Arena Gardens' manager, Andy Taylor, and paid him well enough that Taylor was able to buy himself a new home in the ritzy Forest Hill neighbourhood.

Seat prices were reasonable. The cheapest seats could be had for a dollar and sometimes less – on slow nights the Gardens would occasionally discount tickets to boost the crowd – within the range of anyone lucky enough to be employed. Despite its exalted status the Gardens was never out of reach of the average Canadian. The best seats went for three dollars.[14] As with the theatre or other cultured forms of entertainment – which Smythe wanted to emulate – higher prices bought greater comfort. At the Arena Gardens, other than a few box seats, even the best locations were little more than plank benches. In Smythe's new rink the seats in the greys, the least expensive section, were little better, but comfort increased as you descended toward ice level, culminating in the top-priced reds, which were wider and better padded and served by usherettes in cute little uniforms in Maple Leafs blue.

Patrons in the reds were expected to dress for the occasion. Men wore suits and ladies came in stoles and heals. The emphasis on proper attire had a self-perpetuating effect: well-dressed women weren't about to arrive with poorly dressed men, and if every other man in the section had on a tie, any man who turned up without one would stick out. Everyone – absolutely everyone – wore hats, of course, and flung them on the ice when they got excited or angry. Even in the Depression, people typically dressed more formally than they do now in any case. Men wore ties to work or when dining out; even lowly paid sports reporters wore decent suits. Foster Hewitt was always immaculately dressed in suit and tie to sit in his little wooden gondola, dangling from the rafters fifty-six feet above the ice where no one could see him.

Hewitt was fearless when it came to heights. As a young broadcaster he would sometimes climb to the roof of football stadiums to get an unobstructed view. Once, covering a game in a hail storm, he became frozen to a tin roof and could only be dislodged – minus the seat of his pants – by repeated yanking on his safety rope.

The catwalk that led to his gondola was a full ninety feet above the ground, just eighteen inches wide, and in the early days lacked a railing to help maintain balance. Smythe, Selke, and Hewitt's own father never went there, too intimated by the dangers involved.[15]

Hewitt's broadcasts from the Gardens made him a national celebrity. The self-contained, moon-faced young man was already well known in Toronto, where he was the radio voice for everything from football games to marathon swims. His name appeared in the paper almost as much as his father's, and when he covered an out-of-town college game it would sometimes be broadcast back to the Arena Gardens, where management piped it out over loudspeakers. But this was an entirely different business. As Smythe discovered when Hewitt agreed to plug his special Leafs program, people listened to Foster. He became a part of their family – not just a disembodied voice on the radio, but someone they felt they knew. The first broadcast from the Gardens was carried on just three stations, but within a year a rudimentary national network of twenty stations had been set up, carrying his voice across the country.[16] Canada had a population of just over ten million in 1931; one survey calculated that one in ten were tuned in to Hewitt when a game was on.[17] Within a year his audience had grown to an estimated three-quarters of everyone listening to the radio on Saturday night.[18]

While French Canada remained loyal to the Canadiens and English Quebec to the Maroons, thanks to Hewitt's broadcasts the rest of the country went over wholesale to the Leafs. On post-season "barn-storming" tours with other NHL teams, fans would wait at distant railway stations, ignoring stars from Detroit or Montreal while crowding around Leafs players for autographs and demanding, "Where's Foster?"[19] Smythe realized that a growing percentage of ticket sales were going to out-of-towners, so the more famous Hewitt became, the better for the team. For the most part he left him alone, though he did suggest he find a phrase besides "He shoots, he scores!" every time there was a goal. Smythe thought it was unoriginal and repetitive. Hewitt, wisely, ignored him.[20]

They were an odd pair in many ways, but alike in others. Hewitt was cool, aloof, and self-contained; Smythe was bold, outspoken, and prone to explosions. Hewitt had made his first broadcast at age twenty, though he told people he'd been eighteen, an odd bit of vanity from a man who normally disliked attention.[21] He fell into the job largely as a way to stay out of his father's shadow: W.A. got him a position at the *Star*, but eager to establish his own identity, Foster stayed away from the sports department.

He had been broadcasting for several years before Smythe bought the St. Patricks, delivering his first play-by-play into a telephone receiver from inside a glass box at rinkside, which fogged up for lack of air holes. He had been warned that Smythe had "a dominant personality" and dealt with him cautiously. "I made a practice through the years of discussing only matters of importance."[22] For his part, Smythe found Hewitt difficult to sort out. "He's a hard man to get to know and, like me, he paddles his own canoe," he said, adding, "He and I were friends without being married to one another."[23]

Despite their differences Smythe and Hewitt were both ambitious, determined men. Smythe was impressed by his surprising toughness, which poked through the bland exterior any time he was challenged. Hewitt lacked his father's engaging personality, but had inherited his knack for making money; while Smythe drew a paycheque at the Gardens, Hewitt worked for himself and built extensive interests in broadcasting, advertising, mining, and oil, which made him a millionaire many times over.*

Hewitt sometimes wondered what would have happened if the Leafs hadn't been such an exciting team in the 1930s. The Gardens made a profit of $40,535 its first season and, despite some dips, made money all through the Depression, doubling net income to $87,000 by 1938.[24] It might have been a different story if they hadn't quickly become Stanley Cup champions and a fixture in the finals every spring, if they hadn't had the Kid Line and Clancy and Horner, and, later, Syl Apps, and the unflappable goalie, Turk Broda. No matter how impressive the building, it would have been harder to excite listeners over a last-place club stuffed with also-rans; if "He shoots, He scores" had constantly referred to the visiting teams.

After that first game in the Gardens it looked like that might be the case. The Leafs immediately went on a losing streak: in their first five games they managed only two ties. Smythe thought they looked flabby and uninterested. He decided he'd made a mistake in hiring Art Duncan, who was so disinterested that he only attended games he had to coach.[25]

Two weeks into the season he sent a telegram to Dick Irvin, another former player he admired, who had retired after fracturing his skull in a game. He spent the 1930–31 season coaching the Black Hawks for the irascible – and frequently irrational – Major McLaughlin. Perennial underachievers, the Hawks nonetheless responded to Irvin and came within a game of winning the Stanley Cup, blowing their chance after a handful of Hawks went out and got drunk the night before the final game.[26] McLaughlin waited through the summer before sending Irvin a brusque telegram informing him he was no longer employed. Two months later the offer from Smythe arrived. Duncan was out; Smythe

* When Smythe died, his estate was valued at about $2 million, which grew to about $3 million after his stable of horses was sold. (Hugh Smythe interview, Feb 20, 2010) Hewitt's holdings from his investment in CFTO-TV alone were worth about $25 million, according to John Bassett, and when he sold CKFH, the Toronto radio station that carried his initials, estimates put the price at about $4 million (*Hello Canada! The Life and Times of Foster Hewitt*, pp. 149, 186).

gave the job to Irvin, who arrived in Toronto three days later in time for a game against the Boston Bruins.

With the Leafs in last place, Smythe decided he should give the new coach a chance to get to know the team before taking over; he declared he would coach that night while Irvin could sit nearby and observe. Smythe had the Leafs up by three goals when Boston rallied and tied it up. Smythe turned to Irvin and said, "You take over, Dick," and walked away.[27]

Irvin won that game, then proceeded to turn the Leafs into champions. Smythe had many reasons to admire him: he was a veteran who had been wounded in the war and still occasionally felt the after-effects. He'd been a fine player and tough competitor, and was a skilled and innovative coach. Like Smythe, Selke, and Day, he didn't drink or smoke, giving the Leafs a uniquely temperance-minded leadership. That included Clancy, who maintained he'd never had a drop of alcohol in his life, though he joined other Leafs in sneaking smokes behind Smythe's back. In addition to his skills as a coach, Irvin mastered the difficult art of getting along with Smythe while remaining his own man. Selke recalled that on the day Irvin arrived in Toronto, showing up hours early for his appointment at the Gardens, he inquired what Smythe was like. Selke replied that the Leafs manager was the boss with a capital *B*. Smythe called the shots and brooked no challengers. At the same time, he didn't like yes men. The trick was knowing when to stand your ground.

Irvin passed that first test, getting into a heated debate during his interview with Smythe over the correct way to check opposing forwards. When they emerged, said Selke, Smythe was shaking his head and muttering about Irvin's stubborn streak. In one of Irvin's first games as coach, the Leafs were manhandled 8–2 by the Maroons, but by Christmas they were out of the basement and above .500. Irvin had quickly spotted the problem: Art Duncan's coaching philosophy hadn't included excessive concern over conditioning, and the Leafs had grown flabby. They started well enough, but ran out of gas partway through the game.

Smythe concluded a few weeks into Irvin's tenure that he finally had a winner on his hands. There was a new intensity, a hunger not just to succeed but to conquer. Even when they'd defeated one opponent, the team would come off the ice snarling for more. Chabot was suspended for a game for trying to punch a goal judge over a disputed call. In another game, in Boston, Smythe became so incensed at the referee he reached out and grabbed him as he skated past the bench. When the referee ejected him, he refused to leave, sparking a standoff – with players, ushers, and police all involved – until the Bruins owner negotiated a truce.[28] Toronto ended the season with the league's third-best record and three players – Jackson, Primeau, and Conacher – among the top four scorers, with Jackson leading the league. They beat Chicago in the quarter-finals and eliminated the Maroons in a two-game total-goal contest in the semifinals.

The victory sent Toronto into the finals for the first time in ten years, facing the New York Rangers – still coached by Lester Patrick and led by the players Smythe had recruited six years earlier. As if Smythe needed any extra motivation, Patrick had declared that Montreal was the class of the league and the Leafs of no real concern. Colonel Hammond added to the bad blood when he suggested his Rangers had been sitting around too long between series and demanded the winner of the Maroons-Leafs contest hustle immediately to New York for the finals.

If they were trying to intimidate the young Leafs squad, it didn't work. Toronto enjoyed a three-day rest before opening the series in New York. CFCA announced that Foster Hewitt would call all the games in full, travelling with the team so fans wouldn't miss a minute of action. And action there was: Toronto roared into a 5–1 lead, with Jackson scoring three goals in three minutes in the middle period.[29] But the Rangers stormed back, scoring three goals and hemming the Leafs in their own end, where they spent most of the third period desperately icing the puck. They were saved, wrote Lou Marsh, by a little quick thinking by Clancy and Chabot – "the solemn-faced habitant from Trois-Rivières." After a sustained barrage by the Rangers,

Chabot suddenly threw himself to the ice. While Clancy distracted the referee with an invented dispute over an offside call, Chabot managed to unbuckle one of his pads. Then he took his time fixing it, despite the spirited heckling of Rangers fans.

When Chabot was finally ready, the team was rested and reorganized. Horner potted another goal to widen the margin to two. Nonetheless, "an hour after the game was over, Conny Smythe was still fanning himself with his derby" at the narrowness of the escape.[30]

In the second game, wrote Marsh, the Leafs made New York "look like a $4 bankroll in a Broadway speakeasy,"[31] spotting them a two-goal lead before scoring six times in succession. The victory set up a third, and possibly final, game in Toronto, igniting a hockey frenzy like none the city had seen before. W.A. Hewitt said the Gardens had received eighty thousand ticket requests. A rumour spread that Smythe intended to throw the third game to ensure at least one more gate at the Gardens. When Smythe heard it, Clancy related, he delivered one of his patented pre-game motivational addresses, demanding they "go out there and prove to the people of the world that hockey is played on a high plane, that it's strictly on the up-and-up . . . If you lose, sure it's more money in the till for me, but I'm telling you I won't tolerate a loss tonight."[32]

The team responded, opening up a three-goal lead and holding off a late comeback for a 6–4 victory, winning their first Stanley Cup. "What a lacing the Leafs gave Colonel Hammond's Hussars in their emphatic answer to the murderous attack upon the integrity of professional hockey," exulted Marsh. More than fourteen thousand fans were squeezed in to see the game, which dominated front pages the next day, even crowding out the search for the kidnapped Lindbergh baby. Mayor Stewart, invited to make an address after the game, only got as far as "Ladies and gentlemen" before he was chased away as fans demanded to hear from Clancy.[33] Smythe acknowledged he couldn't have written a better ending if he'd tried. He'd beaten Lester Patrick three games in a row, putting six goals in each game past former Leaf John Ross Roach. He'd shown up Colonel Hammond, who hadn't believed he could run an NHL club. He'd built his arena against overwhelming odds and filled it with fans who couldn't get enough of his team. And now he'd brought them a championship.*

* Smythe celebrated his first Cup victory by naming three of his horses in its honour: Stanley Cup, Six to Four, and Three Straight.

CHAPTER 10

n the ordinary way of things, Smythe's dramatic rise should have been matched by an equally dizzying fall, as hubris, foolishness, or life's way of balancing credits with debits caught up with him. But the fall didn't happen. While much of the country struggled to get by, and the NHL was whittled down team by team, Smythe and his Leafs prospered. His players grew to be idolized by a generation of fans. Both his businesses flourished. He established himself as a leading figure – perhaps *the* leading figure – in the NHL. He used the position to shape a team that represented his view of hockey as both a sport and template for life.

From the beginning the Gardens wasn't just about hockey. Too many "dark days" – when there was no hockey or other major event scheduled – would do serious damage to the bottom line. W.A. Hewitt was in charge of booking, and the variety of events he found to fill the building underlined its utility as a major entertainment facility beyond its role as home of the Leafs.*

Just a few weeks after the opening game it was jammed with a Sunday afternoon religious service that almost started a riot. W.A. had arranged an appearance by Denton Massey and his York Bible Class. Foster, in addition to his announcing duties, was responsible for technical arrangements for all public speakers. The Hewitts expected a moderate crowd and were overwhelmed when forty thousand

---

* The construction of Maple Leaf Gardens instantly doomed the arena on Mutual Street. It struggled on, hosting big-band concerts, tennis matches, and bicycle races. In 1962, it was renamed The Terrace and turned into a three-level parking garage, curling rink, and roller-skating arena. It was demolished in 1989 and replaced with condominiums (*Globe and Mail*, April 22, 1989).

believers tried to cram themselves inside. Two hours before the service was to begin, police on horseback struggled to control the crowd. Traffic was paralyzed and W.A. hesitated to open the doors for fear someone would get crushed.[1]

Winston Churchill, long before he took on the Nazis, visited Toronto and took on Foster over the appropriate microphone to use in addressing a packed house. Churchill insisted on a lapel microphone and dismissed Hewitt's warnings that it wouldn't be adequate in the huge building: "When I want your advice, young man, I'll ask for it." Foster was right, but Churchill bellowed on anyways, microphone be damned.[2]

There were wrestling matches, including a charity contest between Hap Day and Red Horner for which admission was a bundle of wearable clothing. There were six-day bicycle races, rodeos, motor shows, and concerts, including one by a group known as Phil Spitalny and His All-Girl Orchestra.[3] There were prize fights as well, although Smythe distrusted the notoriously corrupt boxing industry and wanted little to do with it.

But the Maple Leafs were the main attraction. They dominated sports sections, covered by a growing army of reporters, from the opening day of camp to the final game of the playoffs. After their 1932 triumph, Toronto made the Stanley Cup finals seven times in the next ten years. Fans came to take it for granted, the way New Year follows Christmas.

As the Depression went from bad to worse – the prairie soil drying up and blowing away, hobo jungles swelling, desperation growing, politicians wringing their hands at their inability to cope – fans found the money, year after year, to fill the Gardens. Regular-season games averaged around ten thousand paid fans for every one of the twenty-four home games. The Gardens made a profit of $40,000 its first year, $48,000 the next, and, after a dip in 1934, worked its way up to more than $87,000 by 1938. The subscriber list grew as well, so that by 1940 almost half the seats were sold before the season opened.[4]

Fans couldn't get enough of their new heroes. There was always plenty of drama. Ace Bailey's near death after being pulverized by a check from Boston's Eddie Shore in December 1933 had the city on edge for weeks. There was the team's mysterious inability to repeat its 1932 Cup triumph, beset by so many close calls the papers started debating the Maple Leaf "jinx." There were regular soap operas as Conacher and Jackson staged salary holdouts, or Smythe went to war with one of the other owners.

Toronto was still a compact city in the 1930s, and NHL rosters were smaller than they are now. Only fourteen players on the 1932–33 team played more than twenty games. They were mostly kids, just in their twenties, and good-looking local kids at that. Jackson was twenty-one, Conacher twenty-two, Horner twenty-three, and Primeau twenty-six. All grew up not far away. The Conacher brood went to Jesse Ketchum Public School on Davenport Road. Primeau was from Lindsay, Ontario, but played his hockey at St. Michael's College, where the Roman Catholic priests seemed to have a licence from God to churn out NHL players. Jackson lived a short walk from the Ravina rink, where Frank Selke first ran into him. Horner worked his way up through the Toronto Hockey League from the time he was a bantam and was delivering groceries for his half-brother's shop on Spadina.

Selke knew every Toronto team that ever won the Stanley Cup – and led Montreal to a half-dozen more – and maintained there were more "truly great players" in the league from 1927 to 1934 than at any other period.[5] For five years the Kid Line was the toast of the city and the scourge of other teams. It aggravated Lester Patrick that while his own top line – the one recruited by Smythe – was considered the best in the league, it was the Kid Line people wanted to see.[6] It seemed deliberately assembled to mesh the personalities and playing styles of its three members: Primeau the calculating, self-effacing centre, who assessed opposing weaknesses and ruthlessly exploited them. Jackson, the slick, elegant speedster, with moves so smooth they disguised just how artful he was. Selke considered Jackson the personification of style – an effortless, fluid, natural skater "with the profile of a movie star, the physique of a champion wrestler, and the poise of a ballet dancer."[7] And Conacher, the big, charging, elemental right wing, whose modus operandi was to bull straight at the net – going over opponents if necessary – before unleashing the most feared shot in the league.

It wasn't really assembled that way, of course. It came together the same way as most other lines: trial and error, by a coach sticking players together to see what happens. In the case of the Kid Line, magic happened, the result proving so effective and popular that in later years, when Smythe wanted to break it up, he shrank from doing so for fear of the outcry.

Primeau may have been the brains of the operation, but Conacher gave it its impact. In a 1932 interview for *The Canadian* magazine, Selke observed: "Conacher is a hunter. His interest lies solely in the kill. From the moment he takes the ice until he returns to the bench the boy is thinking in terms of goals. Nothing else occurs to him as of any interest whatsoever." He was a large man in an era of small players. Most NHLers ranged around 150 or 160 pounds, with some even less. At 200 pounds Conacher was among the biggest, with an impressive build and a natural authority that gave opponents pause, often enabling him to avoid mayhem simply by making clear his readiness to engage in it. He quickly became King Clancy's personal policeman, protecting the small but excitable defenceman, who rarely won a fight, but never quit trying. "I'd get into a fight with somebody and the first thing you know [Conacher] would knock the poor fellow down and push me down on top of him," Clancy remembered. "He'd say, 'King, you won that one.'" Once, Conacher and Jackson hauled Clancy out from under an opponent, carefully placed him on top, and skated away pleased with themselves, turning around to find Clancy back on the bottom.[8]

Conacher had honed his shot through endless repetition, firing pucks, Indian rubber balls, or whatever else was available all through the winter and summer, strengthening his wrists and his accuracy. Once, he amused himself by standing at the blue line and targeting pucks at the clock on the end wall of the Gardens, shattering it on the second try. In 1931, he led the league in goals, and for the next five years dominated the upper reaches of scoring leaders, twice topping the list. Foster Hewitt loved to watch Conacher bull his way up his wing and unload his howitzer at the opposing goalie. The two became friends and remained so long after Conacher's career was over. Clancy deeply admired him and Turk Broda, when he joined the Leafs halfway through the decade, followed Conacher around like a little brother.

When he came to write his memoirs, Smythe claimed Conacher and Jackson were both overrated and depended too much on Primeau to set them up. He thought they relied too heavily on natural ability and didn't take care of themselves, "too busy driving their new cars and chasing women."[9] But that was later, when he'd built up a lifetime of resentments. In a 1947 address outlining the attributes of a good sportsman and good citizen, he picked Conacher and Syl Apps among the best six players of the previous decade. His criteria did not depend on performance alone: "If you do not live right in any other profession it is often still possible to continue and make a success. But in sport if you do something that is against the good of the sport you blacklist yourself immediately and are through."[10]

Conacher was just about everything Smythe demanded in a player: dedicated, hard-working, able to score goals by the bushel, but more than willing to use his fists when required. If anything, the big right winger pushed himself too hard, abusing his body when less intensity might have considerably prolonged his career.

Smythe had more of a case against Jackson, who took his fleeting good fortune for granted. Although his personal troubles became more pronounced when his career had ended, the signs were evident early on. He was a big, boyish kid who liked hunting, fishing, golf, the great outdoors, women, and alcohol. He treated his talent the way he treated money, spreading it around until it was gone. He was just eighteen when he broke in with the Leafs and could have served as the prototype for generations of similarly ill-starred hockey greats to follow, young men who were handed their dream when they were too young and inexperienced to keep it from sliding into tragedy. Jackson's approach to responsibility was to avoid it; his attitude to temptation was to give in.

Smythe saw hockey in broad terms, as a demonstration of attitude and personality that reflected the fundamental character of a person. "In picking hockey players, it is as important to pick a man off the ice as on the ice," he said. "Those players who can live right off the ice, think right, control themselves off the ice, are the best on the ice." He repeated the sentiment many times to different audiences, and enforced it on his teams.[11]

He expected them to comport themselves properly at all times. Players were representatives of the team, their community, and their country, and they were to demonstrate proper manners and solid citizenship. They wore shirts and ties in public and were clean-shaven. They behaved themselves on the road as well as at home.

When the Leafs were travelling by train there were jokes and card games, but no alcohol and certainly no women. The same went for the dressing room: the strongest drink available was ginger ale, Smythe's preferred beverage.

Smoking was also forbidden in the change room. During a crucial playoff series with Boston, Toronto was being manhandled by the Bruins until Clancy and Conacher hatched a comeback plot while huddled in a cubicle in the toilet, sneaking a smoke.[12] And Smythe couldn't always control outside visitors. Billy Barker, the First World War ace he'd named as Leafs president, was due once to deliver a pep talk. Barker, though, had a drinking problem and crashed his car on the way to the arena, turning up muddied and bloodied and smelling of booze (though still able to deliver a passable speech).[13]

Smythe also made an exception on almost all his rules for Tim Daly, the team trainer he inherited from the St. Patricks. Smythe had a soft spot for Daly no one could explain, allowing him to violate almost every creed Smythe set down. Daly gave Busher Jackson his nickname, calling him a "fresh young busher" when the cocky rookie refused to help carry some sticks. Daly smoked and drank and got into trouble. Once, Smythe had to retrieve him after he drunkenly tried to register at a YWCA. His actual name was Thomas, but he was nicknamed "Tim" and had been a boxer in his youth. He talked like he still had a few teeth loose; sportswriters loved trying to decode his unique interpretation of the English language and puzzled endlessly over why he got special dispensation from the usually inviolable code of conduct. Smythe denied Daly received preferred treatment, but insisted he was willing to make allowances "for people that are worth making them for." Daly, he insisted, "was a good man, a good trainer. He did his job, part of his job, absolutely perfect. Never lost a stick or a bit of equipment."[14]

Yet another Smythe code outlawed fraternization with players on other teams. Even a passing remark during a pre-game skate could result in a fine or banishment. If teams happened to find themselves on the same train, there was no mingling, no conversations, little eye contact, and no sharing tables in the dining car. Players who got too friendly might not dislike one another enough for the rugged type of game Smythe preferred. The other teams had the same attitude; though there was no official rule against fraternization, the league encouraged the sense of mutual hostility that predominated.

He favoured slogans that reflected his views. One – "Defeat does not rest lightly on their shoulders" – would be painted in the Leafs dressing room. Gardens stationary was inscribed with "The heart of the nation's sporting life." A Leafs publication recounting the team's history was headlined "FOR THE GOOD OF THE PEOPLE."

It was one of his core contradictions that he advocated total war on the ice while simultaneously lecturing on the importance of sportsmanship, clean living, and traditional values. Someone gave him a copy of "The Sportsman's Prayer," which he kept, and which included the plea: "Help me always to play on the square, no matter what the other players do. Help me to come clean. Help me to see that often the best part of the game is helping the other guy."

If asked, he would probably have insisted the prayer accurately reflected his view. Yet one of his most favoured players – a man he insisted was grossly underappreciated – was Red Horner, who for eight consecutive years beginning in 1933 topped the NHL in penalty minutes, even surpassing Eddie Shore for the all-time single-season record in 1936, which would stand for another twenty years. Rather than curbing Horner's aggressive instincts, Smythe made him captain and later made sure he entered the Hall of Fame.

He would have argued that Horner was just doing his job and refusing to be bullied. His value was in his ability to draw attention from opposing forwards. When Horner went to the penalty bench, Smythe told people, he usually took a player of equal or greater value with him. Opponents were so busy trying to flatten him, he'd add, they gave Conacher and others the room they needed to score goals.

Joe Primeau was the opposite of Horner, but stood equally high in Smythe's regard. Primeau averaged less than sixteen minutes in penalties per season over his seven-year career. His life off the ice was just as ordered and gentlemanly. He and Clancy were both staunch Catholics and sometimes met to attend mass together.

For all his promise, Primeau had trouble breaking the Leafs lineup. For two years he was up and down for tryouts, never quite sticking. In a game against the Maroons, Smythe let him onto the ice for a single shift, late in the third period, to take a faceoff against Nels Stewart with strict instructions to ensure Stewart didn't get the puck. The puck dropped, Stewart grabbed it, stepped past Primeau, and scored. Elapsed time, maybe three seconds. Primeau headed back to the bench and straight back to the minors.[15] But once he made it, Smythe viewed him as the key to the Kid Line, the skilled passer who got the puck to his linemates at just the right time, even if he had to absorb considerable punishment to do it. In one game, when an opposing player knocked out two of his teeth, Primeau wiped away the blood and kept playing. He rarely had anything to say to reporters that wasn't about teamwork or his devotion to the game, and Smythe was convinced that without him Conacher and Jackson would be far less effective.

Despite the ascetic conditions Smythe favoured, the spirits of a dozen youthful hockey players were too much to contain.[16] Conacher, Clancy, and Hap Day were among the worst offenders. Smythe never understood how an otherwise sober, disciplined, straitlaced man like Day could be such a chronic practitioner of practical jokes.

Day once dove into a hotel pool in his best suit for a twenty-five-dollar bet.[17] Another time, he and Conacher stole into Clancy's room while he was having a pre-game nap, removed all the lights bulbs, closed the curtains, and covered him with black ink, racing from the room to leave him groping in the dark.[18] When Baldy Cotton complained too much about another of their gags, Conacher dangled him by the legs out a hotel window, demanding, "Do you think you could shut up if I let you back in?"[19]

Smythe prized Clancy as much for his spirit as for his skills. He managed somehow to be fiercely competitive, yet popular even with the most bitter rivals. He was friends with everyone, even counting Eddie Shore as a pal despite innumerable clashes. Shore was easy to bait, and Clancy was a champion baiter.[20] In one game, finding Shore on his knees, Clancy took the opportunity to give him a shot to the head. When Shore dared him to try it again, Clancy said sure, "get back down on your knees."

Clancy was a devout Catholic and liked to tell how, having been sucker-punched by the much-feared Sprague Cleghorn, he awoke to find himself looking into the face of a priest and assumed he was being given the last rites.[21]

Everything the Leafs did took on larger-than-life importance as the team grew to dominate winter sports. It was no longer enough for newspapers to simply report the outcome of a game; fans wanted news on anything to do with their heroes. The *Toronto Star* had as many as four columnists covering the team by mid-decade, competing with one another for descriptions of the team's magnificence. An April 1933 game took precedence on the *Globe*'s front page over news that Hitler had put the notorious Jew-hater Alfred Rosenberg in charge of his foreign office.[22] Imperial Oil began a tradition of picking a game's best players as a means of selling its "three-star" brand of gasoline. The choices, selected by Charlie Querrie, ran in the next day's paper and didn't skimp on the praise. In a game against the Canadiens, he wrote, Busher Jackson, "the Boy Phenom," was "going by his checks so fast he put braids in their legs."[23]

Smythe was more than willing to play his part in feeding the frenzy. The writers wanted material and he gave it to them, encouraging Selke and Irvin to dream up angles as well. Reporters poked fun at his temper, creating the popular image of red-faced, pepper-pot Connie Smythe, the "little corporal" or "little dictator" who was always on the edge of erupting at something or other, who kept a supply of hats (light grey with a black band) in his office so he could fling them at referees, who baited and berated opponents, coaches, and officials alike. Smythe became notorious for tearing off around the rink, circling the galleyway fronting the box seats, as he chased players and officials like a hound after a rabbit, waving his arms and shouting instructions and insults. His official perch was near the end of the bench, but he was often absent, preferring to follow the play wherever it took him.

He was no less reluctant to leap the boards and skitter across the ice, if he felt his concerns were falling on deaf ears. One December an official turned around to find Smythe standing behind him on the ice and demanded to know what he was doing there. "I just came out to wish you a Merry Christmas," Smythe deadpanned.[24] Far from being embarrassed about his behaviour, he was happy to feed the image, once posing for a series of photographs in an empty arena, shaking his fist through the wire mesh screen at an imaginary referee, so the papers could get a decent shot. He developed a much-publicized taste for spats, a fashion that covered the shoe and buttoned up over the ankle.

A magazine ran a photo of a player and two officials trying to lift Smythe off the ice, where he'd gone "to throttle one of the referees" only to end up flat on his back. Smythe isn't visible in the photo, but is identifiable by "his spatted ankle."[25]

Andy Lytle, a *Star* columnist who began covering the team in the mid-1930s, termed him "a deliberate scene-stealer." "No man in sport is more alertly aware of publicity's value than Smythe . . . He is that rare thing in sports writers' lives, a man constantly alert to story potentialities."[26]

Feuds were a staple source of free publicity, and Smythe had almost as many as there were teams. He bickered with managers, coaches, owners, players – whoever was available. It reflected his will to win and his view of all opponents as enemies, but there was more than simple choleric at play. He felt any action that disrupted an opponent's equilibrium was a weapon to be used. He did his best to distract competitors and shatter their focus. If opposing players were busy griping about Smythe, they couldn't be giving their full attention to the game.

It was a tactic that worked better with some than others. Despite his resentment at being fired by New York, it was hard to provoke an eruption from the patrician Lester Patrick. He had much more luck with short-fused warriors like Jack Adams in Detroit and Art Ross in Boston, both of whom were rough-edged former players who'd gotten into coaching or managing as a way to stay in the game.

All three were caustic and autocratic. Smythe earned Adams's ire by unloading the fast-declining Sailor Herberts on his struggling team, after Ross had unloaded Herberts on *him*.* Adams got even by tricking Smythe into revealing he had an eye on a promising defence-man named Wilfred "Bucko" McDonald, then snapping up McDonald before Smythe could.[27]

* Smythe was quick to get even with Ross for selling him Herberts, talking up the qualities of centre Bill Carson and then selling him to Ross at an exorbitant price just as Carson's skills went into swift decline (www.bobbyorrhalloffame.com/inductee-corner/2003/inductee/3/bill-carson/).

His rivalry with Ross was a case of mutual detestation that kept newspapermen scribbling joyously for years. Ross had constructed the Bruins from the ground up, creating a strong, successful franchise that won Stanley Cups in 1929 and 1939. When Toronto arrived in Boston for the 1933 semifinals, they hadn't won a game there in four years. Many in the league complained that Ross and Bruins owner Charles Adams fostered an intimidating atmosphere that made a trip to the Garden a low point on most schedules. Referees hated officiating there and opposing players weren't much happier. The visitors' dressing room was tiny, dirty, smelly, and cramped.[28] To get to the ice, visiting teams had to run a gauntlet of loud-mouthed fans who specialized in heaping abuse with braying Boston accents.

Boston's constant carping about the quality of refereeing got on everyone's nerves. When Ross claimed once that league officials were biased in favour of Canadians, Frank Calder reminded him that all the players on U.S. clubs were Canadian too.[29] Mocking Boston's defensive style, Smythe once placed an ad in a Boston paper inviting people to watch "a real hockey team, the Toronto Maple Leafs."[30] When he heard Ross was having hemorrhoid problems he sent a dozen roses across the ice, with a note – written in Latin – indicating where he should shove the flowers.[31]

The Boston coach's approach to the rivalry was more heavy-handed than Smythe's, which tended toward needling and mockery. Smythe and Frank Selke had several run-ins with thugs they charged were encouraged by Ross. A group of longshoremen spent an entire game behind the Leafs bench trying to goad Smythe into a fight. During another game two men, apparently mistaking Selke for Smythe, provoked him repeatedly until a policeman intervened, warning Selke that one of the men was a well-known local killer.[32] On yet another occasion a pair of heavies threatened Smythe on his way to the dressing room as Ross watched. The diminutive Selke dove at Ross and knocked him down; as the Leafs duo made a quick exit, Smythe called back that he wouldn't waste his time on "anybody that a man as small as Selke can lick."[33]

Ross's eagerness to pick a fight culminated in a spectacular beating administered to the Boston manager at a gathering of league governors late in the decade. According to Smythe, Ross spent the evening insulting Red Dutton, a hard-nosed former defenceman who was managing the New York Americans. Dutton had carved out a successful NHL career despite being so badly injured in a 1917 blast of shrapnel that doctors had almost cut off his leg. Dutton ignored Ross until the Boston manager threw a punch, and then broke his nose, his cheekbone, and knocked out several teeth. "I never saw a man take such a beating and say nothing," said Smythe. "Couldn't have happened to a more deserving recipient."[34]

The most storied clash between the two took place after Eddie Shore levelled Ace Bailey in the second period of a game on December 12, 1933, with a hit that ended Bailey's career and very nearly his life. Bailey had no idea Shore was coming, and Shore claimed he had no idea Bailey was there. The hit happened behind the play, so most of the crowd was looking the other way when it took place.

The game, as usual, had been chippy. There had already been a number of clashes involving Shore. Boston's all-star defenceman was a walking explosive device: anything could set him off at any given moment. He was said to have collected nine hundred stitches during his playing career and once famously played every minute of a game in Montreal after missing the team train in Boston and driving all night and all day through a blinding snow storm, his hands frozen to the wheel. Not only did he play, he scored the only goal.[35]

He wasn't having a good night, though. With the game tied and two Leafs in the penalty box, Smythe sent out Bailey to kill time, backed by Clancy and Horner. Bailey managed to rag the puck for at least a minute, killing off half the penalty by himself. After a whistle he got the puck again and used up more valuable seconds. Finally, tiring, he shot it into the Boston end and coasted to his own blue line for a rest.

Shore picked up the puck and lugged it toward the Leafs net, but was met by Horner and Clancy, both of whom later took credit for dumping him. Clancy said he gave Shore a knee, Horner said he slammed him into the boards. Half the papers next day sided with Clancy, the other half – and goalie George Hainsworth, who had the clearest view – backed the Horner version. In any case, Shore went down and skidded into the faceoff zone to the side of Hainsworth.

Clancy grabbed the puck and skated away.

For Shore it was just one more frustration. He paused and glared at the referee, then got to his feet and skated away wearily, heading for a gap between Horner and Bailey on the blue line. Bailey was hunched over with his stick on his knees, still catching his breath, when Shore suddenly changed directions, picked up speed, and smashed into him with such force Bailey was launched into the air and landed on his head with a loud crack.

He lay on the ice, his legs twitching, his head bent as if his neck had been broken. The crowd howled, then quieted as they realized Bailey was hurt. Horner – who sixty years later was still wondering if Shore's hit had been meant for him[36] – went straight for Shore, spoke to him briefly, then punched him so hard Shore went backwards and cracked his own head open, a pool of blood spreading across the ice. The arena went berserk. The Bruins bench emptied as they set out after Horner, who found himself alone until Conacher arrived and the two raised their sticks to do battle against the legion of Bruins. Fortunately, the showdown ended without additional injuries, and the players divided to carry off their wounded, the Bruins hoisting Shore onto their shoulders while the Leafs gingerly moved Bailey to a small room used by a Boston minor-league team.

Selke had been watching the game from the press box and hurried down just as a local doctor made a quick examination of Bailey and said ominously, "If this boy is a Roman Catholic, we should call a priest right away."[37] Smythe, meanwhile, had run into a mob of Boston fans outside the dressing room. One man, named Leonard Kenworthy, yelled that Bailey was faking it. As the next day's paper reported, "Kenworthy said Smythe told him he would 'knock his block off' and

Kenworthy told him to try it. Smythe did, Kenworthy claimed, and in striking him broke his glasses and cut Kenworthy's face to such an extent three stitches were taken to close the wound."[38]

Clancy and a Leafs spare named Charlie Sands heard the commotion and came to help out. "They parted the crowd, punching as they went along. The King opened a pathway wide as a door and got to Connie's side and pulled him away while he and Sands held the belligerent crowd at bay."[39] Kenworthy reported Smythe to the police, who arrested him and bundled him off to jail, where he was held until well after midnight and released on a promise to appear next time the Leafs were in Boston.

Shore, who had been stitched up and fitted with a bandage, appeared in the tiny room where Bailey was lying, along with Ross. Shore stuck out his hand to apologize; when Bailey sat up to grasp it his face turned a sickly grey and he was pushed down again. First reports on Bailey's condition said it was "serious but not critical." The next day it had worsened to a skull fracture and cerebral hemorrhaging. Doctors were fighting to save his life. Smythe was indignant at the lack of cooperation from Boston officials, complaining he'd been pestered by police when he should have been with the injured player.

After doctors performed emergency surgery on Bailey's skull they realized he had suffered a double concussion and would need a second operation, which he was in no condition to endure. For a week he teetered between life and death, the papers obsessively covering every development. Smythe, convinced Bailey couldn't survive, phoned Selke and instructed him to begin arrangements to ship his body home.[40] Selke refused, instead telephoning radio stations and asking them to urge listeners to pray. On December 20, Bailey was finally declared out of danger; two days later it was reported he could move his arms and legs and feed himself. It wasn't until a month after the hit that he was judged well enough to go home.

Ross and Smythe spent that time in a high-wire contest that carried dangerous implications. Ross was convinced Canadian teams – which meant Smythe – held too much sway with Calder. Ross's boyhood friend, Frank Patrick, had recently been appointed NHL managing director, largely as a means of remedying the balance. Calder disliked Patrick and didn't trust him. They travelled separately and stayed in different hotels, even when attending the same league event.

As the Leafs lined up behind Bailey and the Bruins behind Shore, their duel threatened the cohesion of the league. There were suggestions the Smythe-Ross conflict could prompt the U.S.–based teams to break away from the NHL.[41]

Smythe, who stayed at Bailey's side throughout the ordeal, launched sulphurous blasts at Boston management. Like Bailey, he didn't blame Shore, whom he called "one of the finest sportsmen I ever met."[42] Instead he blamed Ross and Adams for overworking him, leaving him in a near stupor.

"The owners have made a million dollars out of the Bruins in the past three years, and now they won't spend a dime on the team. They are letting Shore and Tiny Thompson [the Bruin goalie] bear the brunt of the game. Shore has been used so much I doubt he fully realized what he was doing when he knocked Bailey down."[43] At the same time, he demanded Shore be suspended for the rest of the season as a lesson to the team and wanted Boston to share Bailey's medical expenses.

Ross responded in kind, blasting Smythe for "giving to the newspapers interviews which I regard as the wildest kind of ballyhoo, calculated to pack them in when the Bruins play in Toronto. It seems a shame that Smythe takes this time to wash his dirty linen and cause new feuds. I feel, personally, that the Boston fans, every single one of them, regret, as we do, this unfortunate accident to a very fine chap. They are even more disgusted with the ranting from one supposed to be representing the city of Toronto, while our players and our entire organization are praying that this lad's life may be spared."[44]

Toronto newspapers questioned the sincerity of Ross's distress. Shore had been bundled off to Bermuda to escape the spotlight, but was suffering "mental anguish," a phrase Ross repeated so often that fans started mocking him with it and Ottawa owner Frank Ahearn told reporters Ross should shut up. "Many people wish that Art Ross would quit talking about Shore's mental agony. All this talk will not make people forget about poor Bailey lying in hospital with two holes sawn into both sides of his skull. No one will forget the real mental agony of Mrs. Bailey and Bailey's family."[45]

In the end, perhaps the only two people who emerged with their reputations intact were Shore and Bailey. The Boston defenceman was suspended for six weeks, but the incident actually seemed to increase his popularity. Bailey publicly absolved him, he was treated like a hero in his first game back in the Bruins lineup, and fans in other arenas didn't boo him as lustily as they used to.[46] Toronto newspapers went overboard in assuring readers that beneath his crusty exterior, Shore was just a good old Canadian farmboy. Oddly, it was Horner who was suddenly cast as a villain for having belted Shore after the fact. He began receiving death threats and was warned before a game in Chicago that someone in the crowd might take a shot at him. When a light bulb fell to the ice and exploded, he thought the threat had been fulfilled.[47]

Bailey returned home January 19, stepping off a train at Sunnyside Station near High Park to be greeted by Smythe, Primeau, and Jackson. Coincidentally the Leafs were to play Boston at the Gardens that night, and, though Shore was still serving his suspension, no one was taking any chances. One fan counted forty-two policemen protecting the player benches and dressing rooms. The Bruins wore new leather headgear designed by Ross. Toronto won easily, 6–2, but it was a rough affair that left half a dozen Leafs bruised or battered.

Shore and Bailey met again on the night of St. Valentine's Day at an all-star game – the first ever – played in Bailey's honour. Ross said Shore wouldn't play – he didn't want anyone making money off his star's new notoriety – but Shore did suit up, accepting a commemorative medal and souvenir sweater from Bailey. The wounded Leaf wore an overcoat and glasses, the long thin scars on his skull plainly visible beneath cropped hair. They shook hands and briefly embraced.

The crowd roared. Fans were in a forgiving mood that night: they cheered when Shore first appeared, cheered again when he clasped Bailey's hand, cheered almost every time he got the puck. The previous day Bailey had explained his philosophy to a reporter visiting his home: "If Shore meant to slough me, in the fullness of time something will happen to him. If he didn't, if it was just one of those things that occur when men clash in the heat of physical combat, then everything will be all right with him. I believe it will all work itself out."[48]

Smythe told the crowd of fourteen thousand that Bailey's sweater No. 6 would never be worn by another Leaf, the first major professional sports team to retire a number. The game produced $20,909.40 for Bailey. On top of $6,000 he'd received from the Bruins, it amounted to about four years' pay. He never played again, though he coached the University of Toronto to several championships and worked at the Gardens as a timekeeper until fired, as an old man, by Harold Ballard when Smythe was safely dead. Smythe continued to help with the Baileys' finances for more than forty years after that 1934 benefit, working with NHL president Clarence Campbell to increase payments from the Bailey trust in 1962 and again in 1974.[49]

CHAPTER 11

The success of his various ventures meant Smythe could afford to live well, even while much of the country was flat on its back. His salary as managing director was $12,500 through the end of the 1936–37 season, when it jumped to $15,000. In addition, he had his income from C. Smythe Ltd., which he deliberately kept to a minimum, plus income and dividends from other investments. Although it didn't provide immediate cash, the equity value of his shareholdings in the Gardens and his sand and gravel business increased steadily despite the Depression. It was an enormous amount of money at a time when a family could live comfortably enough on $50 a week. Smythe's hockey salary was more than double what most players made, a sharp contrast to the current NHL norm in which even the best-paid general managers make the equivalent of a fourth-line checker or spare defenceman. He wasn't a millionaire yet, but he was a wealthy man at a time when people had very little. The mortgage on the Baby Point home was easily managed (Smythe claimed he had no mortgage, but his financial documents from the period indicate otherwise), he owned a cottage and at least one rental property, and could indulge his taste for cars: in addition to Irene's lumbering Franklin sedan, he had a McLaughlin Buick convertible with big white sidewall tires and a rumble seat, just like the ones driven by his two young hotshots, Conacher and Jackson. He liked convertibles and drove them despite the Toronto winter, sticking one of the kids in the front seat and someone else in the rumble seat and tooling down the Lakeshore into the city. He was personally acquainted with Col. Samuel McLaughlin, the Canadian entrepreneur who had established the McLaughlin Motor Car Co. in 1907 and later sold it to General Motors, and took great pride in owning what he considered an all-Canadian car.

The Smythe children lived pampered lives. They attended expensive private schools – Stafford and later Hugh enrolled at Upper Canada College while Miriam attended Branksome Hall in Rosedale. There was no showing up at school clutching term fees in a little paper bag or scrounging leftovers from the food parcels of richer friends for the Smythe children, though Stafford, like his father, disliked UCC and left to attend a public school closer to home. If they wanted something, they got it. Even as a young man Stafford had a convertible of his own. Moira Davis, Conn's sister from his father's second marriage, visited occasionally, but felt "like a poor country mouse" around Miriam and Stafford, who she thought had too much money and looked down on her.[1] Stafford, forced to deal with the challenges facing the oldest son of a wealthy, well-known man and domineering father, was in regular trouble. If there was a choice to be made between two potential friends, Smythe said, Stafford would pick the wrong one every time.[2] Miriam was high-spirited and popular and often similarly in trouble at school, to the point that Conn and Irene moved her from Branksome Hall to Alma College in the southwest Ontario town of St. Thomas, where they hoped distance would reduce the temptations of city life. Hugh, the younger son, had none of his brother's demons and had inherited his mother's gentle and friendly nature. Hugh didn't share Stafford's need to compete with their father; he looked up to him frankly and admiringly and would enjoy his company in a way Stafford never could.

Irene, accustomed to her husband's frequent absences, developed a wide circle of friends and interests of her own. She was partial to golf and played often – at one point the Smythes were members at four clubs, in Toronto, Mississauga, and at the cottage on Lake Simcoe. In 1935, they sailed to England for the silver jubilee of King George V and afterwards toured Europe, where Smythe formed a poor opinion of preparations for the war that was already in the wind. When they returned – he was forty-one and Irene in her late thirties – she discovered she was pregnant again. They named the little girl Constance Patricia and for the short time she had on earth Smythe doted on her.

His wife, according to Conn, was not a disciplinarian, and much of that was left to Jessie Watson, a young Toronto woman who had come to work for the family after the birth of Hugh and stayed to the end of Conn's life. He grew deeply attached to Jessie, as did all the family; in his last years she was his main source of domestic care and comfort. Smythe seemed to be aware of the dangers of indulging his children, but did it anyway. He was a self-made man and proud of it. He dressed well, he lived well, he owned expensive cars, and he was more than generous with his children. It was all a proclamation to the world that a kid who'd started with nothing could now afford the best and didn't care who knew it. He knew his drive to succeed derived from his early poverty and his determination to escape it. If he worried he might rob his children of that same motivation, he didn't show it.

From early on he was determined Stafford should succeed him at the helm of his businesses and steered him toward that end. Stafford resisted for a time, but to no effect. It was difficult for even the strongest of personalities to divert Smythe from a course he was set on and even harder for his son. Eventually, Stafford bowed to the inevitable: he would be groomed to run the Toronto Maple Leafs when the time came, and he might as well accept it.

Smythe's outsized personality meant that even when he was away from home, he was a dominant presence. Life centred around him, his hockey team, and his schedule. Irene regularly attended the games, while both Stafford and Hugh served as stick boy in their turn, blessed with the privilege of hanging around the Gardens, meeting the men who were legends to most Canadian boys their age. On Sundays, when the Gardens was unused, the Smythes, Selkes, Irvins, Hewitts, and others would gather with their children for family skates – though even then Foster Hewitt tended to glide off on his own, a little separated from everyone else.[3]

With Conn's help Hugh organized a team composed largely of friends, known as the Leaf Imps, which competed in a local league. Even for them Conn set high standards and expected them to be met. Frank Selke Jr. played goal for the team, his skinny legs protected by cricket pads while he clutched a sawed-off regulation stick in place of the goalie's larger and wider version. Even standing up straight his head didn't touch the crossbar, and he was on the ice one day when a photographer from a local magazine arrived at Smythe's behest to shoot some pictures. Selke was in the net, doing his eight-year-old best to guard its vast expanse, when Smythe appeared in the stands, surveyed the scene, and spotted something that didn't please him. Hustling down through the seats to ice level, he reached the boards, fixed Selke with a glare, leaned out over the ice, and barked, "Get yourself a goddamn goal stick!"[4]

A magazine writer, telling a story from around the same time, recounted a similar example of Smythe's implacable determination to have the world follow his rules. Standing alone at centre ice one day, spraying water over the frozen surface, a Gardens worker puffed contentedly at his pipe. The big building was quiet and seemingly empty, but as he worked he became aware he was being watched. Looking around, he spotted Smythe in the stands, following his progress. He called out a greeting. Smythe, at first, ignored him. Eventually, though, he raised a finger, pointed at a No Smoking sign, and snapped, "Can't you read?"[5]

If he allowed little leeway to eight-year-olds and hourly workers, he wasn't about to offer it to anyone else. He believed people, like horses, could be judged by their "bloodlines," and some lines were just flat out better than others. Most of the players he favoured over the years had premium bloodlines, in his view. It was certainly true for Hap Day, Joe Primeau, and King Clancy and would later be true for Syl Apps, Ted Kennedy, and George Armstrong.

Good bloodlines didn't necessarily mean they came from wealthy, prominent, or important families. It was more a reflection of upbringing, character, and work ethic. They were the "right sort." They were stoic, dependable. They didn't have to be told what to do or supervised while they did it. A first-rate horse gave you everything it had, without complaint, and could be counted on when money was at stake. People, he suggested once, could be handicapped "just like horses."

Syl Apps was an example. "He was the stake horse. When he was out there, his opposing centreman was busy. Very busy. Apps put weight on all the opposing clubs. They had to use their best lines just to keep track of Apps. Take Apps out and all the other centres in the league are carrying that much less weight."[6]

His love of horses had grown during the war, when he commanded teams of them to haul his heavy artillery guns through the mud and mayhem, working themselves to death if pushed to do so, rarely balking at the demands made of them. He spoke of them with deep admiration, as if they possessed something that was hard to find in men – the unswerving loyalty and perseverance he demanded but felt he too seldom received. They were strong, dependable, stoical, and enduring.

He shared his passion with his friend, Larkin Maloney. Before the rise of professional football and basketball, horse racing was the biggest competitor to hockey as Canada's most popular sports activity. When he wasn't at the office or the arena, he was often at one of the numerous tracks sprinkled around the city, where he and Maloney and other cronies would happily spend hours assessing the passing horses and laying down wagers. He took Irene to the Kentucky Derby most years, and they made an annual pilgrimage to Saratoga Springs in New York, leaving Jessie to look after the kids.

He enjoyed gambling and wasn't afraid to bet heavily, a habit that had earned many a lecture from his father. Late in the 1930s, he and Maloney calculated his losses for the decade and came to a figure of $30,000. They set out to recoup it in a series of bets and only managed to make back about half.[7] Such setbacks didn't bother him. If he'd lost similar amounts on the Maple Leafs it would have left him desolated, but he viewed the pleasures of horse racing as rewards in themselves.

An ugly court battle in the summer of 1933 revealed some of the details of his gambling and other less-than-salubrious goings-on in the hockey world. The case centred on a claim for wrongful dismissal brought by Gardens manager Andy Taylor, whom Smythe had hired away from the Mutual Street rink in the fall of 1931 and fired less than a year later.

Smythe claimed Taylor had authorized another man named William D'Alesandro to cash thousands of dollars in cheques without his authority.[8] Taylor insisted Smythe was aware of his dealings, but was using it as an excuse because he was under pressure to cut costs at the Gardens.

Taylor won the case, and Smythe's personal reputation took several knocks in the process. Testimony showed Smythe was not only familiar with D'Alesandro but was partners with him in running the Marlboros junior team, along with Selke. Smythe had bought a share of the club on behalf of the Gardens, but hadn't notified the directors, and had also involved the Gardens in an ill-advised investment in professional lacrosse. When the lacrosse team ran short of cash, Smythe sought to make it up by withdrawing seven hundred dollars from the Marlboros' trust account and betting it on a horse.

He'd made similar wagers before, of course, the best known being the bets that let him buy a share of the St. Pats and bring King Clancy to Toronto. This time was different, though – he wasn't betting his own money, and the horse he placed it on strolled to the finish line in eleventh place.[9]

The case galvanized the press. As an amateur team, the Marlboros weren't supposed to earn a profit – extra cash was to be pumped back into the trust that financed operations. The seven hundred dollars, the judge suggested, looked a lot like it was Smythe's share of the surplus, being surreptitiously skimmed off in violation of the rules. Smythe objected strenuously to the suggestion, but the judge was unmoved, especially after he discovered Smythe, to hide his link with the Marlies, had destroyed his copy of an ownership agreement on the day the court case opened. He was even more upset when he learned that D'Alesandro's chief function – the reason he'd been busy cashing cheques – was to lure "amateur" players to sign with the Marlies in return for illicit payments.

The judge, Mr. Justice McEvoy, denounced it as "shamateurism" and suggested people like Smythe were destroying the high-minded ideals of amateur sports. He added to the public shaming when he announced that, in his opinion, Smythe had only hired Taylor to learn the business of arena management, then discarded him once he'd "squeezed the sponge pretty dry."[10]

The prosperity that clung to Smythe and his ventures stood out not only against the gloom that gripped the economy but the fortunes of the NHL as well. The short-lived expansion to ten teams had gone bust with the stock market, and clubs were withering and dying like crops on the Prairies. Toronto with its reliable fans and stable bottom line was the exception to the rule. Everywhere else teams were struggling.

The Philadelphia Quakers had disappeared after one miserable season. While the Quakers' demise was not a surprise, the collapse of the Ottawa Senators was cause for alarm. Ottawa had iced strong teams since before the Stanley Cup was created, but was hobbled by its small rink and limited population. Desperate to survive, the team approached Smythe about playing games at the Gardens, but the cost was too high. In 1931, the Senators took a year off, renting out its players to the remaining teams, then returned for two more seasons and finally, in an act of desperation, moved to St. Louis for a year as the Eagles. In 1935, the franchise fell into a slumber that would last almost sixty years.

Next to go were the Montreal Maroons, the pride of English Quebec. One of the great teams of the era, a rough, tough, no-nonsense gang that dominated the Leafs and won two Stanley Cups, they nonetheless played before empty seats in the increasingly shabby Forum. Montreal just wasn't big enough for two teams, and the 1937–38 season was the Maroons' last.

The demise of the Quakers, Senators, and Maroons left behind seven teams in varying stages of financial health. Toronto was at the top of the heap. The club made a profit every year, though in 1933 money was so tight Smythe had to ask his Stanley Cup champions to take a pay cut. On the day the Gardens opened it was almost $2 million in debt[11] and the directors had installed a financial watchdog named George Cottrelle[12] to keep track of the money. Frank Selke called him "the most cold-blooded businessman I ever met."[13] One of his first acts was to cut wages. Smythe regularly butted heads with Cottrelle, protesting when he was directed to prepare a budget for the team that he'd do so as soon as Cottrelle could predict how many playoff games they would play in.[14]

Even with Cottrelle squeezing the purse strings, the Leafs were head and shoulders ahead of their floundering competitors. The New York Americans struggled from paycheque to paycheque, doomed since the end of Prohibition brought a close to Big Bill Dwyer's bootlegging riches. Dwyer became increasingly dependent on "loans" from manager Red Dutton, who only managed to pay the wages at one training camp thanks to a fortuitous crap game.[15] Eventually the league took over the club and ran it as a charity case.

Other teams would almost certainly have folded if not for the clandestine intervention of Chicago grain magnate James Norris. Norris bought the Detroit Falcons for next to nothing in 1932, saved them from bankruptcy, and renamed them the Red Wings. He quietly loaned money to Boston's Charles F. Adams to keep the Bruins afloat and just as quietly bought a major piece of Madison Square Garden.[16] He badly wanted a team in Chicago too, and tried to buy and relocate the Ottawa Senators, but when that plan was foiled he invested in the new Chicago Stadium, making him landlord of the Black Hawks and putting him in a position to torment Maj. Frederic McLaughlin, their eccentric owner.[17]

McLaughlin was a dapper, polo-playing, Harvard-educated millionaire with a clipped moustache who had a habit of firing his coach almost every year, no matter how well the club was performing. He knew the other owners looked down on him and, in turn, considered them a collection of ill-bred parvenus, mailing off caustic letters to Calder complaining about the lack of respect he received. It was McLaughlin who'd blocked Norris's bid to buy the Senators.[18] Norris got even by raising McLaughlin's rent and starting a rival team and rival league to compete with the Hawks.

Norris was a big, bluff, overweight man who could easily have bought and sold anyone else in the NHL several times over. The NHL's shoddy bylaws allowed him to operate via false fronts, decoy managers, and dummy companies, so it was years before anyone realized how much he had come to control the league. He shunned the spotlight to avoid drawing attention to his extensive involvement in professional boxing, as crooked a racket as existed at the time. As late as the early 1950s, Smythe would have to spark an interleague showdown to get an honest answer as to the extent of Norris's holdings in the league. His reticence, coupled with the other owners' financial problems, let Smythe hog the limelight more than was strictly his due. The last thing "Big Jim" Norris wanted was to talk to a bunch of reporters or have his picture in the newspaper; Conn Smythe, in comparison, was not only willing but often eager.

Press coverage was good for seat sales. Although Smythe had a fairly low opinion of the press – for fifty dollars they'd write whatever he wanted – it was part of the business and Smythe was a realist. He learned to control his message the way he did everything else, and to a degree that wouldn't become commonplace in the sport until decades later. In the thirty years starting in 1931, the name *Smythe* appeared in the sports pages of the *Toronto Star* more than seven thousand times, or almost 250 times a year. If only a third of those referred to the Leafs owner – an extremely conservative assumption – it still works out to more than once a week, every week over three decades. And that's only one paper in a city that had three or four throughout that time.

The *Star* was the quickest to seize on the Smythe phenomenon. Although they were poles apart on politics, the conservative Smythe and liberal Joseph Atkinson, the *Star*'s publisher, shared a mutual respect and an affinity for the wonders of marketing. They understood the benefits to be had from the drawing power of the Leafs. Hockey fans read newspapers, and newspapers helped attract more hockey fans. While the *Globe* and *Telegram* were slow on the uptake – usually sending a lone reporter to provide standard goal-by-goal coverage of the game – the *Star* assigned three and sometimes four writers and columnists, offering not only the score and the play-by-play, but colour, analysis, opinion, gossip, and personalities as well. Eventually Smythe began to demand higher standards from the low-paid men – and occasional woman – who haunted the Gardens looking for stories. Complaining that too many had their hands out (in addition to the free meals and travel that were customary), he went to Atkinson and agreed to buy a regular quota of advertising if the publisher would increase their wages. One time, he assigned Selke to mimic the writing style of the *Star*'s Andy Lytle for several days when the columnist went on a bender that would have cost him his job had the abstemious Atkinson found out.[19]

It didn't make the reporters like him, but they did appreciate the regular material his team provided. He was always willing to be quoted – unlike Hap Day, who believed reporters should be seen and not trusted. Smythe didn't mince words, he didn't retract statements, and he didn't deny anything he'd said. When the Leafs travelled to other arenas, there was always a crowd of local reporters jostling for a few words from the Leafs boss. His frequent appearances in the press added another layer to the caricature of a hot-headed, scrappy little terror who hustled around his rink in perpetual pursuit of recalcitrant referees. He was also recognized as a superior judge of talent and master of the game.

Most newspapers at the time openly supported the hometown team, and Toronto was no different. Lytle called the players "the boys," or "your Leafs," or "the Smythians." The *Star*'s Gordon Sinclair, in his column "Hook Line and Sinclair," called them the "Lambasting

Leaferinos." Smythe, said Lytle, "doesn't masquerade to deceive as so many sports characters like to do. He may employ the humour of pretending despair about his team or he may be curt to the point of insolence if he thinks you are prying into affairs that aren't your concern. But he'll either be frank with you or he won't discuss it. What he tells you, when he does talk, is the truth, though he may embellish it or slant it in a Leaf direction. It's up to the individual what he does with what he's given."[20]

Hugh Smythe maintains his father's public performances were usually just that – an act. Even when he went into his "Herr Hitler routine," waving his fists while his eyes popped from their sockets, it was a calculated display intended to produce a specific effect, he argues, whether to unsettle an opponent, energize his team, divert attention, or sell even more tickets.[21]

Soon Smythe was being treated as the league's dominant figure, smartest operator, and quickest thinker. If that was an exaggeration, he wasn't about to tell anyone. He was easily the best known, most quoted, and highest profile sports figure in Canada, not as celestial as Foster Hewitt, perhaps, but held in equal awe. It was taken for granted by fans across the country that Conn Smythe called the shots at Maple Leaf Gardens and to a large degree within the NHL as well. Smythe exulted in the image, which he took as his due. A visitor coming across the league for the first time could have been forgiven for believing the NHL consisted of some struggling teams in the United States, a struggling team in Montreal, and the Toronto Maple Leafs.

PART THREE

WARRIOR

CHAPTER 12

The life of the Kid Line was an exhilarating but brief five years, ending in the summer of 1936 when quiet "Gentleman" Joe Primeau sent Smythe a polite letter confirming his plans to quit hockey to concentrate on his concrete block business. His departure was like the fall of the first domino, which set others tumbling in turn. Before the final one landed, Clancy and Conacher would both be retired, Hainsworth out of the picture, and Day playing out the string as a New York American.

Smythe didn't see it coming. Day was thirty-five, Clancy thirty-three, but both seemed to have several seasons still in them. Primeau, the senior member of the Kid Line, was just twenty-nine. It was clear the Leafs would need a replacement for Hainsworth, who had been acquired from Montreal for Chabot and was ancient at age forty-one. But Smythe had someone in mind for that.

Conacher's decline was the most disheartening. Entering camp in 1936, he was examined by the team doctor and judged to be in the best shape of his career. When he was slashed hard on the wrist in a pre-season game by Detroit rookie Johnny Sherf,[1] he expected to shake it off quickly. But his recovery lagged and in November he was still not right. "Every time I try to shoot, the pain shoots from wrist to finger tips," he complained.[2] He lacked his old power, a situation opponents quickly seized on. Despite repeated rests and specially designed casts, the problem persisted all season, limiting him to just three goals in fifteen games.

He was injured again the next fall, this time in the shoulder. He spent frustrating weeks recovering, his arm strapped to his side, his forearm folded across his chest. When he was finally judged healthy again he struggled on the ice. Something just wasn't right. In January he skated angrily off the ice after a practice, briefly consulted the team doctor, and announced he'd had enough. He was hanging up his skates at age twenty-eight.*

Clancy's departure was less of a surprise. He was a small man who'd been in the league sixteen years and thrown himself into every game without restraint. During training camp he noticed he was losing weight at an alarming rate. Six games into the season, in a match against Detroit, he couldn't keep up with his check. It was his second game in two nights, and it was too much for him. After brooding about it for a day, he informed Smythe, Selke, and Irvin he was through. Then he went and woke up Andy Lytle to ask him to keep it out of the papers until he'd talked to his wife and wired his father. Lytle obediently waited a few days before sharing the moment with his readers.

"His fighting chin was out and his voice didn't quaver as he told me it was goodbye to a playing career that began when he was seventeen and ended Sunday night in Detroit," Lytle wrote. "'I know I've lost that old speed, that mythical half yard athletes talk about,'" Clancy told him. "'I saw it very clearly in Detroit. I knew I was supposed to take a certain player out of it, yet I stood as though rooted and let him score.'"[3]

Smythe promised to pay him through the end of the season and keep him on as an "ambassador" for the team. Clancy tried to address his teammates, but couldn't find his voice and left the locker room in tears.

As the 1937 season opened, only Horner and Jackson remained from the team that had christened Maple Leaf Gardens six years earlier. There were prospects in the pipeline, but Smythe hadn't expected he'd have to press them into action quite so soon. Still, his luck held. He solved his goaltending problem when he went to scout a Detroit goaltender named Earl Robertson and stumbled instead on a pudgy, little-known kid from Brandon, Manitoba, named Walter Broda. Primeau's

---

* Conacher attempted a comeback, playing a year in Detroit and two with the New York Americans, but never approached his level of play with the Leafs.

departure was offset by the arrival of Sylvanus Apps, signed by Smythe after he took Irene to a football game and watched Apps run rings around the opposition. Apps was so good he turned right winger Gordie Drillon into a scoring star, much as Primeau had stoked the skills of Conacher and Jackson. Add in Nick Metz, a twenty-three-year-old left winger from Wilcox, Saskatchewan, and – after dipping to fifth place for a season – the Leafs were back on top of the league, and with much younger legs. Horner, at twenty-eight, was suddenly the oldest man on the team. It was possible to argue that, in losing Conacher, Primeau, and Hainsworth while gaining Apps and Broda, they were even stronger as a team.

Apps was an all-round athlete from Paris, Ontario, who qualified fully for Smythe's idea of a hockey player with great "bloodlines." He didn't drink, he didn't smoke, he didn't curse. He was so morally upright he'd been pondering a career as a Baptist minister, and so firm in his convictions he kept Smythe waiting two years before acceding to his pleas to join the Leafs. First he intended to compete in the 1936 Olympics, where he placed sixth in the pole vault. He didn't play a single hockey game in the minors; he went straight from little-known amateur to NHL star, so steeped in natural ability he led the team in scoring his first season, beating out Busher Jackson by five points and coming within a point of tying Dave "Sweeney" Schriner as the league's leading scorer.*

He was, said Smythe, "the epitome of the kind of player I wanted," a particularly telling accolade given that Apps was missing an ingredient his boss never tired of stressing – he didn't take penalties. Horner, who Smythe had named captain on Conacher's retirement, averaged more than one hundred minutes a year in infractions. Apps, in his *entire career*, would spend just fifty-six minutes in the box and go one full season without a single penalty. It didn't matter: Apps, like

---

* Schriner was born in Russia, but moved to Calgary as a baby. His nickname, seldom explained, came from his childhood adulation of a semi-pro baseball player, Bill Sweeney.

Primeau, managed to be tough but clean at the same time and made everyone around him better. He won the Calder Trophy as rookie of the year, contributed to a resurgence in Busher Jackson's career, and was viewed as largely responsible for Drillon scoring at a rate of almost a point a game. One year, when he broke his leg and missed much of the season, he tried to return part of his paycheque to Smythe.

Broda's talents were as camouflaged as Apps's were obvious. He was unemotional and unsophisticated, fresh off the Prairies and not skilled enough to hide it. On his first trip to Manhattan he stared up at the skyscrapers and observed innocently, "It ain't much like Brandon, is it?"[4] When Conacher mischievously told him he could be thrown in jail for sneaking a few souvenirs across the border, he panicked and eagerly handed them over to Conacher instead. He had a grade school education – barely – and was known as Turk because he had freckles like a turkey's egg.[5] He and Hainsworth were supposed to play alternate games, but after Hainsworth allowed four quick goals in a 5–1 loss to New York just seven games into the season, Smythe abruptly gave him his release. Except for the war years, when he was in uniform, Broda would miss precisely one game over the next eleven years.

Broda didn't qualify as a man with top bloodlines but earned Smythe's next greatest accolade: he was "decent and loyal as a man can be."[6] Bob Davidson, who joined the Leafs the year before Broda, was similarly favoured because he was "loyal."[7] Loyalty meant staying put. Elmer Lach and Doug Bentley, on the other hand, weren't loyal because both had tryouts with the Leafs but ended up starring elsewhere. Lach and Bentley were a couple of Saskatchewan boys spotted by a Leafs scout in 1937 and invited to a tryout. Neither weighed more than 130 pounds, according to Lach, and were sitting on the bench looking tiny when Smythe happened by and wondered out loud what those two "peanuts" were doing in Leafs uniforms. When Selke gave them five hundred dollars a few days later to visit Niagara Falls, they headed straight back to Saskatchewan instead. Fifteen years later, when

Lach was considering retirement, Smythe reminded him: "You still owe me five hundred dollars."[8]

Being loyal and having good bloodlines were separate attributes. Bloodlines were about leadership ability and character. Players with good bloodlines tended to abstain from alcohol and tobacco and qualified in Smythe's mind as suitable to serve as the team's captain. Being loyal implied devotion to the team and Smythe's way of doing things, and a willingness to obey instructions. You had to be loyal to have good bloodlines, but loyalty alone didn't signify good bloodlines. Both measures were part of the ranking system he applied to all his players. There were "plus" players, "neutral" players, and "minus" players. "You have to have plus players to win hockey games . . . A plus man is a man who can do more than his own job. In other words, he can hold his own man, can play his own position and out-do the other man. A neutral man, if you cannot get plus men, is effective, but minus men are no good."[9]

Toronto's rapid revival in the late stages of the decade was fortuitous, as Smythe's attention was increasingly drawn to the imminence of war in Europe. He was determined, once again, to play his part. The fact he was in his mid-forties, had a wife and four children, and had more than fulfilled his duty to his country was of no consequence. When Irene and military authorities did all they could to dissuade him it only hardened his resolve. He was going to fight, and that was that.

Irene, understandably, couldn't comprehend his insistence on enlisting. She had waited for him once, for four long years, agonizing when he was shot down, reported dead, then carted off to POW camp. There had been much less at stake then – just the two of them, pledged to each other, but not married yet and young enough to start again if necessary. Now everything was different, except his attitude. Adding to her bewilderment was Smythe's resistance to any position away from the front lines. He wanted to get out there where the bullets were flying. He wanted to risk his life.

He was straightforward in his reasoning. In a 1941 interview he explained:

I'm the kind of a fellow that when we come back from New York or Chicago and get off at Sunnyside, I take a big breath and am glad this is my country. I've got a wife and family – four little kids, and I have always had one old enough to be proud of and one young enough to make me a big shot. A long while ago I started as a barefoot boy, and through a lot of generous acts and through a lot of gracious people I got where I am today. If a man like me won't fight for my country, I'd just like to know who would.[10]

He also felt he had little choice. For years he had been teaching hockey in military terms: teamwork, selflessness, bravery. "When war came I had to face that. Had I been talking fiction or fact? Was I a fraud or did I live up to my own principles?"[11]

He saw the battlefield and hockey rink as symbiotic: both depended for success on shared habits and attitudes. Hockey players needed to play as a team, be constantly vigilant, but ready to attack on all fronts. "A good way of life would be a combination of the army way and the sports life," he said. "In the army faithful dogged perseverance will get a man ahead, and he will be looked after in the line of social services – have his clothes and living and medical care. If that could be combined with sports, where the individual can, on his ability, hurdle the requirements of seniority and red tape, you can have a good way of life."[12]

Barely a week after Germany invaded Poland in September 1939, Smythe and other NHL governors met to discuss implications for the league. As soon as the federal government passed the National Resources Mobilization Act (NRMA) enabling Ottawa to requisition men for military duty, Smythe urged Leaf players to join up promptly: "It is my advice . . . no matter what your age or your position as a family man is, that you sign up immediately with some non-permanent militia unit and get your military training in as soon as possible. The advantages of this move are obvious. In case you are honoured by a call to the Canadian Army . . . you will be ready. [In any case] you will have complied with the regulations and be free to play hockey until called on."[13]

He followed up with individual memos, requiring each player to identify which unit he'd registered with. A 1940 report on enlistments among the seven NHL teams showed Toronto led with twenty-five. Players resident in Toronto had mostly joined the Toronto Scottish regiment while those elsewhere had signed on to local outfits. Even Foster Hewitt had registered, with the 45th Field Battery.

Even before a shot was fired Smythe found himself at odds with Prime Minister William Lyon Mackenzie King's handling of the conflict. He complained the thirty-day training period specified in the NRMA was unrealistic – you couldn't build an army on men with just four weeks' training. He won that argument – the training period was later extended indefinitely – but it was just the first of many differences he would have with King's war policies. The prime minister, opaque and evasive as ever, was far from enthusiastic about preparing for war. They were at opposite ends of the ideological pole: Smythe still an unapologetic Empire loyalist, King worried about preserving the fortunes of the Liberal party and holding together a country split between English speakers who felt the tug of duty and French speakers who saw no need to fight another of Europe's wars.

Before he could begin telling Ottawa what to do, however, he had to get the army to accept him and organize his hockey team to do without him. The second task was easier than the first.

With Apps and Broda as its backbone, and the subsequent addition of Sweeney Schriner (in a trade for Busher Jackson), Lorne Carr, Wally Stanowski, and diminutive centre Billy Taylor, he felt he was leaving the team well stocked. But he had concluded that after nine years at the helm, it was time to replace Dick Irvin. Irvin had taken the club to the finals seven times, but for all Toronto's dominance of the regular season, it still had just one Stanley Cup. Somehow, something always seemed to get in the way of victory: in 1933, Toronto was so worn out by its semifinal victory over Boston – the last game of which went to six overtime periods – that it had little energy left for New York. A few years later against Chicago, Smythe outsmarted himself when he forced the Black Hawks to replace their injured goalie with a little-known minor leaguer named Alfie Moore, who was so upset at his poor reception – even the Chicago players treated him like a no-hoper – that he stoned the Leafs and shifted the momentum to Chicago's side long enough for them to win the series.

Smythe had decided Irvin had a fatal weakness. He wasn't "tough enough." He fell in love with players and put the same ones on the ice whether they were performing well or not. Smythe wanted someone more hard-nosed, who could "fire people, bench them, live always on what a man could do today, not what he had done a few years ago." He wanted Hap Day.[14]

Irvin may not have agreed with Smythe's assessment of his strengths and weaknesses, but concurred about it being time to move on. Before the 1939–40 season ended, he and Smythe had reached a gentlemen's agreement, and Smythe had quietly offered his services to the Montreal Canadiens, arguing that Irvin could help save the club.

Montreal's survival was a serious concern. It had changed hands twice in five years, at one point almost suffering the indiginity of being moved to Cleveland.[15] Dick Irvin Jr. recalled that attendance in Montreal for his father's last game as Leafs coach was "about 1,500."[16] The team was dead last, and the Forum, though just fifteen years old, seemed old and run down. Sending Irvin to Montreal served Smythe's own interests by strengthening the team and ensuring the league remained viable. Organizing his own departure, however, was running into some troubling undercurrents.

In 1941, he prepared a document specifying lines of authority for Leafs executives in his absence and the duties that went with them. Day would have full responsibility for the hockey team, Selke would handle scouting with assistance from Smythe's old friend, Squib Walker, while Ed Bickle and W.A.H. MacBrien would liaise with the league office.

Day was delegated authority for any trades or acquisitions. Initially Smythe marked in Selke as well, but scratched out his name and stipulated that Day would make decisions in consultation with himself, when possible, and the executive committee. It would prove to be a crucial alteration.

Under "Policy" he stipulated that the Leafs should at "all times stress offensive tactics and players," Gardens attractions should maintain high standards to avoid reducing prices, and public relations – another Selke duty – should involve "truth and nothing but." In another decision that would provoke criticism, he stipulated it was "very important" that there should be no free passes, including to men and women in uniform.[17]

He called a meeting to explain his directives and was upset at the perceived eagerness of some directors to see the back of him. Even before he'd completed his remarks, he related, Selke, MacBrien, and Bickle left the room to begin discussing plans. "I never saw anybody so anxious to get rid of a man as those three were to get rid of me," he complained.[18] The sense of being hurried toward the exit would only intensify as events unfolded.

His lessened duties came with a 50 per cent cut in pay. He also began selling off the stable of horses he had accumulated, at "sacrifice prices."[19]

Despite his eagerness to answer the call to duty, Canada's army was far from certain it wanted to place the call. The reason was obvious. He turned forty-five in 1940, twice the age of the recruits being sought. The army wanted eager young men in their teens and twenties who could be easily moulded physically and mentally for the ordeal they would face, not middle-aged men with reluctant bodies and fixed ideas about how wars should be fought. No one could quite understand why a wealthy family man with a business to run would insist on a combat position when there were plenty of useful things he could have done on the home front. The army brass felt he would be more useful as part of the cheering section, assisting in recruitment and public relations chores.

Smythe, naturally, thought otherwise. Fighting for his country meant just that – pointing guns at the enemy and pulling the trigger. It didn't mean giving speeches or flying around as a jumped-up ambassador while others were doing the dying. He began calling anyone who had some clout and might help. He pestered Frank Ahearn, the former Ottawa Senators owner, who had been elected as a Liberal MP. He wrote directly to the defence minister, James Ralston, and to C.D. Howe, the minister for munitions. He signed on for drilling practice in Toronto, and when that was cancelled for the winter he wrote Ahearn in frustration: "Surely there must be some way a man could prepare himself at least, if he is not actually able to fight for his country."[20]

He appealed to his old friend from North Street, Bay Arnoldi, who had helped him in 1915 and was a colonel in Canada's militia. Arnoldi came through again, sending him to refresher courses and putting him in charge of training at Toronto's Armouries on University Avenue, where the main law courts now stand. He took a refresher course to renew his qualifications as a pilot, even though he'd disliked flying since getting shot down.[21]

The NRMA stipulated that men could be required to serve at home, but would be sent overseas only if they volunteered. Smythe was volunteering his heart out, but no one was listening. Finally, he hit on forming his own battery, just as Gordon Southam had done twenty-five years earlier. He figured if he offered a prepackaged unit, all trained and equipped and ready to go, the army could hardly say no.

It improved his morale and gave him something to do, but 1941 was not 1915 and Canadian military thinking had come some distance since then. In the first war, even the top soldiers had been little better than enthusiastic amateurs, happy to embrace well-meaning civilians with the means to organize their own outfits. But the ensuing slaughter had buried such thinking, and superior levels of professionalism had been adopted in the interim. Unlike 1915, no one thought this war would be a jolly lark in which they'd deliver a sound thrashing to the Huns and send them on their way. Europe's still-scarred battlegrounds remained as testament to the savagery to come. Hitler wasn't the Kaiser, and this wasn't a family dispute among members of the European aristocracy.

Canadians might not have appreciated yet the full madness of the Nazis, but they understood that Germany presented an enemy that would not be easily subdued.

Smythe didn't let that stop him from tracking down volunteers for his battery, signing up lacrosse players, a golfer, two sportswriters, and members of his staff from the Gardens and the sand pit. The two writers were Ralph Allen, a talented, overweight columnist from the *Globe and Mail* who Smythe judged "the most slovenly soldier who ever lived,"[22] and Ted Reeve of the *Telegram*, a much-admired former athlete who was seven years younger than Smythe and afflicted with injuries from a lifetime of competition. "He had flat feet, bashed up knees, arthritis in every joint, dislocated shoulders. You name an athletic injury and Reeve had it."[23] Smythe considered him a hero just for turning up.

Although he did nothing to advertise it, Smythe's meticulous tracking of NHL enlistments uncovered an embarrassing situation that would dog the league throughout the war. Players were signing up to do their training, but very few took the next step and volunteered for service overseas. Along with his list of Leaf players and the units they'd joined, he had a second account of Gardens staff who had signed on, and it was this second roll, of lower-paid and less-glorified men, who were going to Europe. Smythe knew the name, rank, location, and serial number of almost a dozen men who by 1941 were either already in Europe or on their way. They were ushers, drivers, cleaners, and painters. There was a night watchman and a couple of doormen. While they had put their families and humdrum jobs aside to serve overseas, not a single one of the two dozen men on the roster of players and top Leafs prospects was willing to match them. It would remain that way to the end of the war, a period many top NHLers spent playing to packed arenas on military-sponsored teams in Canada. Smythe defended the situation at the time, but later admitted it had troubled him. He argued it wasn't the players' fault if the government failed to order them to the front. The men had obeyed the rules and completed their training; it was Ottawa's job to institute conscription and send them where they were needed. More than one observer noted the paradox between Smythe's own willingness to put his life on the line while refusing to criticize much-younger hockey players who weren't as bold. The suggestion that he was happy to keep them out of harm's way so they could keep playing hockey didn't hold up, since Apps, Broda, and others spent long periods in camps around the country that kept them away from the NHL in any event.

He *was* careful to ensure fans knew the Leafs were doing their duty, pumping out programs and promotional material with photos of Privates Broda and Davidson of the Toronto Scottish, Privates Nick and Don Metz of the Regina Rifles, and Private Wally Stanowski of the Winnipeg Rifles. Privately, he kept up an active correspondence with the stable-hands, ushers, drivers, and other men in England, sending them regular care packages of cigarettes and other goodies from home. They sent back hand-scribbled letters filled with appreciation, bits of news, and evidence of their homesickness. "I'd very much like to be at the stable this spring painting," wrote Jim Williamson, who was in England with a unit of drivers. "I'd get a kick out of painting a new cottage too. Maybe I could give Hughie some more pointers bass fishing."[24] Lou Pollock, a member of the Gardens cleaning staff who had joined the 48th Highlanders, assured him "the boys" enjoyed listening to rebroadcasts of Leafs games carried by the BBC.[25] They were put together by Foster Hewitt, who worked into the early morning hours reducing his broadcasts to an extended package of highlights that were transmitted to Britain.

Even as Smythe pestered the government for a job, he grew bolder in offering it unsolicited advice. He became deeply involved in a campaign to pressure Ottawa into appointing Andrew McNaughton supreme commander of the Canadian Forces, berating Mackenzie King when he failed to pay heed.

McNaughton was a former chief of defence staff who had entered the first war at the head of the 4th Battery and ended it as commander of all Canadian Corps artillery. He was a man of many talents, both soldier and scientist, and had invented a forerunner of radar, which he sold to the government for one dollar and which dramatically increased Canadian success in knocking out German guns. After the war he joined the regular army, helped establish a network of camps that put unemployed men to work during the Depression, and became head of the National Research Council.[26]

McNaughton returned to the military in 1939 as commander of the 1st Canadian Infantry Division and was sent to Britain as senior Canadian officer as the steady flow of recruits grew into an army. His reputation was so high that a campaign grew up to assign him virtually unlimited power over the war effort. It struck a chord with veterans like Smythe who mistrusted the government and doubted its willingness to prosecute the war as they saw necessary.

In 1940, Smythe wrote a series of letters harshly criticizing the prime minister. In response to a King speech in June, he sent a telegram couched in his usual uncompromising tone:

> Two weeks ago you said on the air that you and your government would welcome constructive criticism. Here is mine – You and your government to stop asking the people to have faith in their leaders but rather for you and your government to have faith in the people. Put in effect immediately conscription of new money and industry. To harness the power thus obtained recall McNaughton at once . . . [Give him] full power to build Canada's war machine not only to protect Canada but to take part when needed for England.[27]

When King's secretary responded with a bland reply, Smythe fired back that the war effort was "to say the least, poorly organized" and bemoaning that King refused to meet him so he could put forward his views "man to man." He warned he was about to publish an open letter to the prime minister, which appeared soon after in a veterans' magazine.

It was even more critical than his previous letter had been. Canada, he suggested, was "at the bottom of the league" in readiness and King was "out of touch with the opinions of the public." He concluded with another warning: "Persons who don't listen to public opinion have a great deal of difficulty holding their jobs."[28]

In his records Smythe left a chart illustrating what he had in mind for McNaughton. It showed the general as the centre of a web of resources that included infantry, artillery, and air power but also "capital," "womanhood," "labour," the "middle class," and "factories." There was no explanation of how it fit together, but Smythe was clearly thinking in sweeping terms.

His politics were straightforward and a bit naive. His dislike of Mackenzie King was intense, but he recognized the Conservatives had no one better. Like King and many others, he had grossly underestimated Hitler. After the German dictator invaded Czechoslovakia and justified it as necessary to provide Germans with *liebensraum*, or living space, Smythe wrote Hitler a letter on Gardens stationary suggesting he cut a deal with Britain, handing over his tanks for safekeeping in return for land Germany had lost in the first war. If Germany needed the tanks for defensive reasons, he reasoned, Britain could always send them back.[29]

His involvement in trying to draft McNaughton petered out as he became more deeply involved with his battery. But he found other ways to agitate. In the winter of 1941–42, he began a course at Petawawa, outside Ottawa, to qualify as a major and came to the conclusion troops were being inadequately trained: "I was astounded to find out that because of dental parades and medical parades and clothing parades and inspections and bath parades and a million other things, and guard duty and so on, that my men were training seventeen hours a week to become a soldier, and that, of course, was not seventeen hours in succession."[30]

He considered it a scandal and contacted Joseph Atkinson at the *Star*. Atkinson frankly admitted he didn't believe the story, but assigned Greg Clark, a respected reporter, to investigate. Shortly afterwards Smythe received a note from Atkinson attesting that he had Clark's report. "It is of such a nature that I don't know what to think or do about it," Atkinson admitted. "The view expressed by you to me is fully substantiated and there is much more."[31]

Smythe met with Atkinson and was told Clark had discovered recruits received even less training than Smythe had calculated. He was unwilling to publish the discovery, however, since the *Star* supported the government and its policies and was unwilling to endanger public backing for either. Some time later Smythe ran into Clark at a train station and upbraided him for his lack of backbone. Knowing what he knew, Smythe said, why didn't he take the story and print it elsewhere under his own name, as Smythe's father had once done? They had a furious argument, followed soon after by a letter from Clark.

Dear Conn,
After due thought on your remarks at the station platform the other night I have reached this point: you go peddle your peanuts and I'll go peddle my papers.
    Yours for Victory,
    Greg Clark[32]

Clark refused to speak to Smythe again for the next twenty years.

Smythe was still at Petawawa when the Leafs staged what was, to that point, the greatest comeback in NHL playoff history, rebounding from a three-game deficit to win four in a row against Detroit and finally capture their second Stanley Cup. It was something of a mixed blessing: Smythe was ecstatic to finally nail down another Cup, but it came in a season when he spent less time with the club than in any previous year and was only sporadically involved in its management. He would have vehemently disputed any suggestion he was not directly responsible for its success, having chosen the players, appointed the coach, and assigned the duties. But it was hard to miss the fact that Hap Day had finally succeeded in bringing glory back to the club in the one year that its micromanaging boss wasn't around to get in his hair.

No one had picked the Leafs to dominate that season. Boston seemed the strongest team, but New York surprised everyone by finishing first, three points ahead of Toronto and four up on the Bruins. Detroit, after finishing fifth, nonetheless hustled its way into the finals, setting up what was expected to be an easy victory for the Leafs.

Once again, though, the Red Wings proved tougher than expected. They won the first two games at the Gardens and the third at the Olympia, all but guaranteeing Toronto would prolong its decade of disappointment. No team had ever rebounded from three games down, and almost no one believed it was possible.

The Leafs comeback began in the second period of the fourth game when, down by two goals, Bob Davidson scored, followed quickly by Lorne Carr. Day had astonished everyone by benching Gordie Drillon and Bucko McDonald, removing his top scorer and one of his toughest defencemen. He replaced Drillon with Don Metz, and it was Metz who scored to put Toronto ahead 4–3. They were still up by one when, late in the game, Detroit suddenly came unglued. It started when Detroit's Eddie Wares earned a ten-minute misconduct for a dispute with referee Mel Harwood. When Wares finally went to the box the Wings sent seven men onto the ice, earning another penalty. Centre Don Grosso, named to serve the penalty, got into his own battle with Harwood and ended with another misconduct. When the final whistle mercifully ended Detroit's misery, manager Jack Adams leapt onto the ice and went straight for Harwood.

"Bedlam broke with the first exchange of punches," the papers reported.[33] "Harwood stood his ground and swapped sock for sock with Adams. Grosso joined in the slugging. Spectators added their punches."

Harwood was removed under police escort, but the crowd converged on a linesman left behind and started a new free-for-all. A reporter noted that during one brawl a female spectator removed her shoe and threw it on the ice. "It wasn't a particularly good shoe," he added. "The sole was worn almost through." Frank Calder was spotted by the crowd and required police help to leave the building. Although Detroit was still up three games to one, Wares – who had started it all – proved prescient when he told a reporter: "You know what's going to happen. It's going to go seven games."[34]

He was exactly right. Adams was suspended for the rest of the series and the betting line immediately shifted in the Leafs' direction. "Sure we're worried," the Wings' chief scout responded sarcastically when questioned. "Why, the Leafs only have to win three games and we need to win one. Boy, are we worried."[35]

That night Toronto overwhelmed the Wings 9–3, and two days later tied the series behind a 3–0 Broda shutout. The teams would return to Toronto for the last game.

Smythe hustled down from Petawawa to be there. Everyone wanted to know whether Drillon would still be on the bench, despite having scored more Stanley Cup points than any previous Leaf. "I won't know myself until Saturday afternoon how we will line up," Day said.[36] Hostility remained high on both sides. Adams was caught by a photographer talking on a Gardens phone. "Get away, you goon," he roared, "or I'll smash that machine to pieces."[37] A record crowd squeezed into every nook and cranny, 16,218 in all.

In the end, Drillon didn't play. Detroit scored in the second period, but Toronto replied with three in the third. Adams spent the game pacing restlessly in the Wings dressing room, listening to Foster Hewitt on the radio. With two minutes left and the Leafs up by two goals, he appeared unexpectedly at the Toronto bench, tapped Day on the shoulder, shook his hand, and returned to the dressing room.[38] The game ended with Toronto up 3–1. The jinx was broken and Smythe, so giddy he could barely talk, grabbed Calder's hat and waved it at the crowd as the league president was in the midst of handing over the Cup.

What hadn't been noticed was the test of wills going on between Smythe and Ed Bickle. George Cottrelle, the Gardens' president, had been named controller of oil for the duration of the war. That left Bickle in charge, and before the game he'd banned Smythe from entering the Leafs dressing room. Smythe, wearing his major's uniform, was uncharacteristically uncertain what to do. Toronto had made the finals without him and staged a miraculous comeback from a three-game deficit. If he defied Bickle and went marching into the room and the Leafs lost, his intervention could be held up to blame. And despite the common assumption that Connie Smythe answered only to himself, Bickle was his boss, and, technically speaking, he was no more than a half-pay former manager who was away on an extended leave.

His dilemma was settled when Day insisted he light a fire under the team at the end of the second period, when they were down by a goal. The strain was showing, and both teams were tiring. Smythe cornered Schriner, Carr, and Taylor, two veterans and a rookie, and delivered one of his patented dressing-downs, designed to annoy them to the point they'd score a goal just to teach him a lesson. Schriner, not exactly taking the bait, grinned at him and pledged, "What ya worrying about, boss? We'll get you a couple of goals."[39] Six minutes into the third period he scored the tying goal, assisted by Carr and Taylor. Ten minutes later he scored again – from Carr and Taylor – to put it away.

Smythe returned quickly to Petawawa, but the dispute with Bickle went with him. He'd been welcomed, he said, like "a skunk at a garden party."[40] It didn't help when, two days after the game, the *Star* ran a column extolling the quiet brilliance of Frank Selke in bringing about the triumph.

Five months after the Cup victory, as Smythe was finally preparing his battery for embarkation to England, he received another unsubtle communication from Bickle, suggesting by telegram that he step down from the Gardens' executive committee. It was supposed to be temporary, but would require a shareholders' vote to return him to his seat later on. "Do not relish being left off executive after twelve years," he wired back. "However if majority of executive in favour of it will make it unanimous." He didn't hear back.[41]

With that simmering in the background, the 30th battery, Royal Canadian Artillery, set sail for England in October 1942. Just weeks before its departure he had received a distraught call from Irene, alerting him that Stafford – who had enlisted in the Navy – was due home on leave soon and planned to marry his girlfriend, Dorothea Gaudette, a Catholic. Unable to get away, he insisted the wedding be postponed, but Stafford went ahead with the ceremony – two ceremonies in fact, one Catholic and one Protestant. Both he and Dorothea wrote him letters explaining their decision, which they'd discussed at length. Dorothea's mother was as staunchly opposed to her marrying a Protestant as Smythe was to his son marrying a Catholic. Dorothea's letter reveals how intense the religious divide remained and how much the young couple feared Smythe's reaction.

Referring to their plan to be married by a priest, she wrote, "I know that is against your wishes but until the end of the war I have to live at home and that is impossible if I get married any other way, as I would be a total disgrace in the eyes of some people."

She begged him not to blame Stafford. "Please don't hold anything against him. He has always considered you first before, but I am taking the blame for this. I want you to take it out on me and not him. He thinks the world of you and always will." She vowed their children would never be put in the same position. "It may be years before the war is over and we can set up housekeeping but when that time comes we will have to go away from Toronto to live so that we won't be hounded by people who think they are doing the right thing."[42]

Irene was in similar agony but for different reasons. "I am sorry about mother but I am afraid she has gone off the deep end about me," Stafford wrote to his father. "I wish you could convince her that I can never forget how much she has loved me all my life and what she's done for me. Tell her for me that no one can ever take over the place in my heart which she has always had, because I think that that is the real trouble."[43]

Although not entirely mollified, Smythe met the newly married Stafford in Halifax on the way to Europe and they had a warm visit, the older man proud of his son's eagerness for action. Besides, it would be almost three years before he was back in Canada to do anything about it, and by then life had changed.

CHAPTER 13

Great Britain in October 1942 was a nation hanging on for all it was worth. The war was three years old and there was little to justify optimism. Hitler, in total control of Europe, commanded a territory that stretched from Scandinavia to North Africa, from the Atlantic coast to the edges of Asia. England, almost alone, had managed to hold out against the Nazi war machine, but was far from sanguine about its ability to continue doing so.

When Smythe's battery arrived that month, Britons had survived the Battle of Britain and the Blitz, the heroic disaster at Dunkirk, and any number of military disappointments. Smythe loved the country and its people, with their stoicism and determination to maintain the shards of everyday life even as it was being demolished around them. London was pockmarked with the evidence of the Luftwaffe's raids, which had failed to produce the hoped-for collapse in morale but had succeeded in decimating entire neighbourhoods and turning the great capital into a world of sandbags, blackened windows, and underground shelters. England being England, life went on as usual, of course, but first-time visitors couldn't help being awed by the extent of the devastation and the determination of the population to endure.

France had been overrun more than two years earlier. The United States had been in the war less than a year. Churchill, desperate for a victory on any front, was facing a vote of confidence in the House of Commons. Just weeks before Smythe's arrival, Hitler's armies had arrived on the outskirts of Stalingrad and were engaged in one of the most brutal and decisive battles of the war. At almost the same moment, Britain had sent six thousand men – of which five thousand were Canadians – on a raid of Dieppe to test German defences and the ability of the Allied forces to penetrate the Atlantic wall.

The raid had been eagerly supported by General McNaughton, who hadn't achieved the near-dictatorial status Smythe had hoped for, but was nonetheless commanding the Canadian Army and hoped to quell complaints that Canadian troops had yet to take part in a major engagement. It was an overwhelming disaster. Nine hundred Canadians were killed and almost nineteen hundred were taken prisoner.[1] Although it was defended as a valuable learning tool for the Normandy invasion that would come later, for Smythe's men it was a sobering introduction to the realities of the conflict they were entering.

They were quickly deployed along the south coast as defence against German air raids. Despite the ugly omen of Dieppe, the war was at a turning point that would soon see the beginning of the Nazi decline. As Smythe was unloading his guns, an army of British, Australian, New Zealand, and other Empire troops were defeating Gen. Irwin Rommel at el-Alamein, giving Churchill the victory he badly needed. Three months later the Nazis would be humbled at Stalingrad and the myth of the unbeatable Wehrmacht broken.

Of course there was no way Smythe's men, strung out at three locations on the English coast, could appreciate the immensity of the changes coming. Smythe's headquarters were at Eastbourne, halfway between Hastings and Brighton, on a point of land jutting into the English Channel across from Dieppe. It had been designated by Hitler as a key landing area for his planned invasion of Britain, which had been put on hold after the failure of the Luftwaffe to seize the skies. When the gunners looked out over the channel they were facing a coastline bristling with weaponry and massed troops, waiting to be used. If an assault was to come, the 30th Battery would be directly in its path.

Smythe spent his days shuttling between the three locations, inspecting, assessing, delivering instructions, and ensuring his high standards were being met. Far from home, surrounded by men half his age,

Smythe developed a friendship with Ted Reeve, based on their similarities in age and their love of sports. Reeve had been a star at lacrosse and football, twice winning the Grey Cup. He proved as adept at coaching and organizing as he did at playing and had a natural writing talent and gentle humour that established him as one of the best-liked and most-admired writers of the day. The crusty major enjoyed the opportunity to let down his guard, if only slightly, and share stories with a kindred spirit.

"Reeve is the story of the war," Smythe later told a reporter. "When he gets up in the morning he tapes his feet to keep his arches from collapsing. Then he slips on two elastic knee braces, after which he puts some kind of contraption on his left shoulder, and then he puts on his uniform." Reeve had only managed to stay with the unit because Smythe forged the signature on his medical tests.[2] Twice, Smythe noted, Reeve turned down promotions that would have elevated him from the lower orders of the battery.[3]

Even though Smythe had made it to Europe, the army hadn't abandoned efforts to replace him with a younger man. Before his departure, they'd dangled a promotion if he would accept a position running sports programs. Now they subjected him to repeated physicals, determined to prove he wasn't in any shape to take his men into battle. He passed them all with ease, but grew increasingly impatient at the efforts to displace him.

He also began getting news from home that reinforced his fear of being squeezed out of the Leafs hierarchy. Throughout 1943 he received a series of letters from George "Squib" Walker, complaining of ill-treatment at the hands of Bickle, MacBrien, and Selke. Walker was among his oldest friends, dating back to his high school years and their adventures with Wreck Aggett. It was Walker whom Smythe and Aggett had conspired to smuggle into the army despite his near-crippling eyesight problems. When Aggett was killed, Walker became an even more important link to Smythe's boyhood. Smythe rarely entertained people in his home, but Walker was an exception and was welcome to spend hours talking hockey and old memories over the dinner table.

He was employed as a scout, but Smythe's directions had put Selke in charge of scouting operations, and Walker didn't feel he was getting the attention he deserved. He wanted more money and to be put on staff full-time, identifying Selke as the main obstacle. If Smythe had been in Toronto, the conflict would have been easily resolved, but under the circumstances it took on an importance greater than it deserved. His responses were filled with the frustrations he felt. He'd been preparing for war for four years now without actually facing the enemy. He'd had to battle military bureaucracy just to enlist and now was busy marching around England while the real fighting was raging just across the channel. The notion the orders he'd left behind were being ignored added to his sense of helplessness and isolation, especially when he found himself unable to help out an old and trusted friend.

At first he urged Walker to remain patient. "Sorry to hear the old firm is not so good," he wrote in March 1943. "Also did not relish your treatment by FJS [Frank J. Selke]. I have not said anything about it but when I get back you can be sure they will do right by our George or else. FJS is not the strongest friend in the world when the chips get right down as is probably due to the R.C. [Roman Catholicism] in him. However he means well and with strong handling will do."[4]

That same month he wrote again, after Walker raised a contract issue. "I had heard from Frank but thought he understood all things were to stay as is till I got back. However, he has not the power probably to right things and maybe there were other reasons. . . . However wait till the old boy gets back and if they don't want to make it up for you I will see you get placed where your talents will be paid for as well as appreciated."[5]

Day wrote Smythe defending Selke and downplaying Walker's complaints, but as the letters continued to arrive Smythe's mood darkened, especially after he learned of a trade engineered by Selke and Day, sending a young defensive prospect named Frank Eddolls to

Montreal for a little-known teenager named Ted Kennedy. Smythe had extravagant expectations of Eddolls and was livid when he learned of the deal. "There isn't a defenceman of [Eddolls'] age around for many a mile," he wrote Walker. "He is of the Hap Day, Joe P[rimeau] Syl Apps breed and you can only find one of these every five years and it took me ten years to land this kid."

Kennedy, on the other hand, was a seventeen-year-old from Port Colborne about whom Smythe knew little. He'd been invited to Montreal by the Canadiens, but, homesick and unable to speak French, he packed his bags and headed back to Port Colborne, where he played for a local team named the Sailors. The Sailors were coached by the great Nels Stewart, who had scored more goals than anyone in NHL history to that time and happened to be a friend of Hap Day. Impressed with Kennedy's tenacity, he tipped off the Leafs coach and one afternoon shortly afterwards Kennedy was hauled out of a class at high school and instructed to be on a train for Toronto.[6]

Much as he would come to admire Kennedy, Smythe was adamant the trade was a mistake. He fired off orders to reverse it and was even angrier when informed it couldn't be done. Rather than blame Day, whom he considered the best coach in the league, he focused on Selke. "Hap has been a great success and if I could only keep Frank's nose out of the hockey players' end his [Hap's] job would be easier," he wrote Walker. "You know F. is for the experience he's had a very poor judge of hockey player. He has one or two successes but has overlooked or oversold dozens. The latest move in getting rid of Eddolls' contract is a heartbreaker and I'm hoping in some way they can make up for it and get him back."[7]

He convinced himself the trade was a violation of his instructions and a further challenge to his authority. He complained the team was being ruined and he'd have to begin from scratch when he returned, building it back into a winner. His tone toward Selke grew increasingly negative. He accused him of being in league with Bickle and MacBrien to sabotage his position. Unable to contain his rage, he shared his suspicions with Reeve, pulling out a letter of resignation he'd written. Reeve managed to calm him down, and Smythe threw the letter into the English Channel.[8] But the letters from Walker continued, while Smythe grew restless for action, noting that "four years is a long time to march around and only fire shots at the acting manager of the Leafs."[9]

He was getting fed up with the army brass. It is the prerogative of soldiers to question the intelligence of their superiors and Smythe was no exception. He'd battled higher-ranking officers during the first war and did so again in the second. Canadian troops, he told Walker, had been "shadow boxing whilst the other fellows have been slugging it out."[10] He felt the generals suffered a similar affliction to the one he'd identified in his letter to Mackenzie King: rather than asking the troops to trust their leaders, it was the leaders who should be showing faith in their troops.

Just weeks before the orders for D-Day began appearing, he stormed up to London and demanded an end to the constant efforts to oust him. He had honest reason for concern as other officers had been purged since the departure of McNaughton, who'd been hounded into resigning over doubts among Canada's allies about his command abilities. Smythe finally received the reassurances he'd sought and was promised he'd be allowed to lead his battery when it went into battle. The pledge held, and in June, as the successful assault on Normandy took hold and the Allied armies moved inward from the beaches, he received orders to prepare to embark for France.

It was the culmination of all he had been working for, but at the last moment he almost blew it. With the guns and equipment ready to go, the men occupied their time with regular softball games. A few days before they were to leave, Smythe was guarding third base when the ball came to him just as a runner was barrelling from second. He stood his ground and the runner, trying to dislodge him, knocked him right through the coach's box, breaking four ribs. Smythe passed out, then came to long enough to hear the men discussing plans to get him to a hospital. He insisted they find a civilian doctor, knowing if he was taken to a military hospital he'd almost certainly be prevented from going to France.

The men got him to a compliant doctor, but word got around anyway and a colonel turned up at Smythe's bedside warning that he'd have to report the situation.

"My holster was right beside the bed," Smythe recounted. "I reached over and put my hand on the revolver and said, 'Now listen, I've been through a tough two and a half years to get here. If I'm not going, you're not going.'"[11] Remarkably, he was once again allowed to keep his command. His ribs heavily taped, he struggled onto a transport ship on July 7. He lay in sick bay for the crossing and then, unable to climb down a ladder or wade ashore himself, was strapped into the seat of a gun wagon and hoisted ashore at the end of a crane. It was July 9, and they were headed toward Caen, just a few kilometres inland from the channel on the Orne River. There were two bridges in the ruins of what had been the town's suburbs, and the battery was to defend them.

Ralph Allen, the *Globe and Mail* reporter who had signed on with the battery, had been discharged to act as the paper's correspondent. A week after its arrival he visited the battery and sent back a profile of Smythe, recounting the near disaster of the softball game and reporting that just hours after arriving they'd been engaged in a daytime raid by German aircraft.

"The air war has changed a lot," Smythe told him. "Our boys got mixed up in a dogfight the other day. For every Focke-Wulf or Messerschmitt the Jerrys sent over, there must have been a dozen Spits chasing it in the air and 20 or 30 ack-ack guns blazing at it from the ground. It was like a foxhunt. That's the way it was in '17, but it was the Boche who did the chasing and we were the people who ran for our lives."[12]

The dispatch didn't make it to Canadian papers until a week later. Three days after it appeared, Allen filed a second, more chilling story, reporting, "Up near the top of a coming casualty list under the heading 'Wounded in Action' will appear the name of Major C. Smythe, M.C., of Toronto."

The German raids since the battery's arrival had been almost continuous. After several days of action Smythe's men had been visited by Churchill and Montgomery, in advance of an Allied assault on a German position a few kilometres away. On July 18, troops had poured across as the attack began, and soon the sky was filled with German planes trying to halt their progress by destroying the bridges. Allen wrote:

The trouble started about midnight on the night of July 25 while the battery's Bofors guns straddled the jumping-off line for the Canadians' thrust to the south of Caen. Enemy air activity that night was intense. It was a hot night for all the ack-ack guns in the whole beachhead. Through one of those inexplicable coincidences it was hotter for the major's battery than for any other.

At battery headquarters a German plane dropped a flare on an ammunition truck and through its light two other planes paraded back and forth strafing. The burning tarpaulin of an ammunition truck threatened at any moment to blow up the piled boxes of ammunition and battery headquarters and the whole area with it.

The major did exactly what anyone who knows him would have predicted he would do. He was out of his trench and into the middle of it at once, tugging at the flaming tarpaulin of the truck, directing the dispersal of headquarters transport over his shoulder. The other headquarters people were in it too, doing what they could in the red confusion and a few yards away the crew of one of the major's guns was blown right off the gun by a bomb and scrambled right back on and resumed firing.

The transport sergeant was also wounded. When the ammunition truck went up the major caught a piece of shrapnel in the back. When they found him his body was partly paralyzed, but the major's spirit will never be paralyzed by a truckload of ammunition and a few bombs and machine gun bullets.

"I'm all right," he shouted as he lay helpless on the ground, and they came to carry him to shelter. "Get those fires out."[13]

Smythe was far from all right. He couldn't move or feel his legs. A piece of shrapnel was sticking from his back. As he lay on the ground, someone ran by and stole his revolver, guessing he wouldn't need it any more. Allen's story recounted the highlights of his life and spoke of him in the past, a hint to readers that by the time the dispatch passed the censors, Smythe might already be dead. "Today the battery was still nursing the hope that the major would be back before the war ends, but it seemed too much to expect," Allen reported.

Smythe's war was over. It had taken the better part of four years to get to France. He'd been there barely two weeks.

CHAPTER 14

At some point during the six weeks he spent at the Canadian No. 1 Neurological Hospital at Basingstoke, outside London, Smythe realized he was likely to live, though whether he would ever walk again was less certain. He felt a surge of relief and gratitude and quickly determined to treat it as a challenge to be overcome: "I made up my mind that, well, I'm hurt, but if I can even progress to a wheelchair I'll be all right. If Franklin Roosevelt, crippled, can run the United States, I can run Maple Leaf Gardens."[1] *

The transfer from France had been a nightmare. He was one of a planeload of badly wounded men attended by a handful of nurses. He was on a lower pallet, beneath a man from his own unit whose blood dripped on him throughout the crossing. Men with head injuries screamed as the aircraft engines droned. He was almost fifty years old, and six weeks after D-Day here he was with a hole in his back and no feeling where his legs should be. He was at his lowest ebb when Stafford managed to get leave and surprise him by appearing in his room at Basingstoke. His son took one look at the damaged little man with the bandages and tubes, drips and wrappings, and fainted dead away. Some reporters also tracked him down and were allowed in for a peek, during which he managed to wave and whisper, "Things look as if they're going to be okay now, boys."[2]

Irene wrote of her joy that he was alive – surely no one else in his life ever addressed Smythe as "Darling sweetie pie" – and described the scene that unfolded when the news of his injury had arrived. She

* Smythe made this declaration in his memoirs thirty-five years after the event. However, very few people knew of Roosevelt's handicap while he was still alive and it was only later that people came to realize how difficult his last years had been.

had been sitting outside with Miriam and Dorothea. All three had husbands in uniform. When a military man appeared with a telegram, they knew instantly what it meant: one of their husbands was either dead, injured, captured, or missing. They stared in silence, each wondering what to think, since to hope for safety for their man meant wishing the bad news onto one of the others. They watched in horror as the man opened the gate and walked toward them, finally asking, "Mrs. Conn Smythe?"[3]

Smythe's most immediate problem was his inability to relieve himself. The blast had sent a hunk of shrapnel within a hair of his spine, shattering the nerves in his right leg and the nerves controlling his bladder and bowels. Before being evacuated he'd lain in a ward pleading for relief, his bladder swelling ever fatter until a Scottish doctor took pity. He sliced open a section of abdomen and pushed in a tube; Smythe swore the pressure sent forth a geyser that touched the ceiling. But the relief was only temporary and he was still unable to urinate or defecate on his own.

In September he was taken by stretcher to the hospital ship *Lady Nelson* with five hundred others, bound for Halifax. A reporter found him on arrival and sought his reaction to a recent offer from the NHL to make him league president. Frank Calder had died of a heart attack in 1943 and Red Dutton had been filling in. Smythe saw it as the latest twist in the plot to remove him from the Leafs organization, but held his tongue, declaring his only goal was to get home to his family and catch up on events at the Gardens. His injury had been big news. When the *Star* learned of Smythe's injury, it ran his photo on page one, above a report from correspondent Frederick Griffin that read alarmingly like an obituary.

No grander, no nobler soldier left Toronto for this war than Connie Smythe, wearing the pilots' wings and Military Cross he won as a young artilleryman and as a flier in the 1st war. He came because he felt it was his duty, the duty of all men who could run, walk or crawl, to fight the Germans. He enlisted again for war because he felt keenly that sportsmen should show the way and because he sought to give a lead to athletes. . . .

That was Connie Smythe as I have known him and as many others have known him better. He had a sense of duty himself that few men have. Simple, direct, honest, ardent, sentimental, he set his course that led him to France. His duty done, his ambition fulfilled, his splendid service ended as he would have wished, fighting Germans.[4]

It was news again when his train chugged into Toronto two days after leaving Halifax. The papers carried another photo, this time showing an ecstatic-looking Smythe waving and grinning at the camera. He showed reporters his foot-long scar and banged on his leg with his fist. "See that? No life there at all, the nerves are all shot."

The coverage was effusive. "Conn Smythe came home this morning, as peppery and explosive as the day he left Toronto for overseas 23 months ago," began another report. "His blue eyes still breathe fire, his cheeks are so bright they belie a two-months convalescence.

" . . . 'Glad to be back? [said Smythe]. Listen kid, there's only one thing any of us ever dream about when we get over there and that's getting back home. Talk about the romantic cities of Italy and France all you like, they don't even come close to Toronto. That's all I ask.'"[5]

As he had in Halifax, he also hinted at something else, a mission he had in mind "for the lads overseas." He said, "It won't be long before I'm back in more trouble than you can shake a stick at. We've got a great breed of boys fighting for us over there and somebody's got to fight for them over here. They're so used to fighting for somebody else they don't know how to fight for themselves. But they deserve a square deal and we've got to get it for them. I'll have more to say about this."[6]

What he had in mind became quickly apparent. From the train he was taken directly to Chorley Park, a magnificent vice-regal manor built in the northern reaches of Rosedale, which for twenty-two years had served as the official residence of Ontario's Lieutenant-Governors. It had been shut down to save money during the Depression and used as a military hospital since 1940. On the day he arrived, with Irene in attendance, he was visited in his room by George McCullagh, the publisher of the *Globe and Mail*.

McCullagh was a brilliant but erratic man who had bought the *Globe* for $1.3 million and the *Mail and Empire* for $2.5 million and combined them into one. He was a big, outspoken, alpha male who liked to mix things up, which in the newspaper trade was always good for business. At the time he launched the renamed *Globe and Mail* he'd been a big supporter of Ontario's Liberal premier Mitch Hepburn, but – as tended to happen with Hepburn – the two parted ways and McCullagh moved to the Conservative camp. Now he had the passion of the converted and nothing would make him happier than a chance to wage war with Mackenzie King. Smythe, having been back in the city a matter of hours, promptly gave him the opportunity.

Lying in a collection area for casualties the night he was wounded, Smythe had struck up a conversation with a major on the next stretcher. He was from a Quebec unit and had been wounded fighting near Caen. He complained of being chronically short of men, and of sending untrained soldiers into battle under inexperienced officers because reinforcements were scarce and those that arrived had little seasoning. Smythe commiserated with him and wrote down his name. In the ensuing weeks he collected more such stories and wrote down more names. He interviewed each new arrival in his ward and talked to officers and to ministers, who put him in touch with more men with similar stories. Some told him they'd gone into battle with only 60 per cent of their usual strength. Injured men were hustled back into the front lines again and again to plug holes. Soldiers worn down by years in Europe were returned to battle when they should have long since been withdrawn because there was no one to replace them.

"It was pitiful, some things that were happening," Smythe recalled.

"The Army was combing all the lesser trades, trying to make infantry reinforcements out of clerks, switchboard operators, people who had been rejected for frontline duty before. One boy who had been working on telephones for two years, and who talked to me because he was a Leaf fan, was taken that way and wound up paralyzed in the same room with me, only a few weeks later."[7]

Smythe relayed it all to McCullagh,. "If you're sure, that should be published," McCullagh responded. "I'll publish every word you say." Smythe immediately dictated a statement and the next morning it appeared on the front of the *Globe*. The headline read, "UNTRAINED TROOPS HAZARD AT FRONT, SMYTHE COMPLAINS."[8]

It was a no-holds blast at King, charging that brave Canadian men were dying because of his refusal to adopt conscription.

> During my time in France and in the hospitals of France and England, I was able to discuss the reinforcement situation with officers of units representing every section of Canada. They agreed that the reinforcements received now are green, inexperienced and poorly trained.
>
> Besides this general statement, specific charges are that many have never thrown a grenade. Practically all have little or no knowledge of the Bren gun, and, finally, most of them have never seen a PIAT anti-tank gun, let alone fired one. These officers are unanimous in stating that large numbers of unnecessary casualties result from this greenness, both to the rookies and to the older soldiers, who have the added task of trying to look after the newcomers as well as themselves.

He suggested James Ralston, the defence minister, was ill informed, that money was being wasted on troops at home while those overseas went wanting, and that the government was defying a 1942 referendum that had given it the authority to impose conscription. "The relatives of the lads in the fighting zones should ensure no further casualties are caused to their own flesh and blood by the failure to send overseas reinforcements now available in large numbers in Canada."

The statement was just 276 words, but it went to the heart of Ottawa's effort to satisfy English Canada's desire to do its duty while respecting Quebec's ambivalence about the war. If the goal had been to antagonize King and ignite the hostility dividing English and French Canada, he couldn't have done better.

Mackenzie King in late 1944 thought he was doing a magnificent job of shepherding Canada through the war. He was almost seventy years old, had been leader of the Liberal party since 1919 and prime minister for nineteen years, and one of his great achievements as leader had been his ability to hold English and French together in relative harmony, having healed the divide caused by the imposition of conscription during the First World War. To prevent a similar division during the second war he had engineered one of the great compromises of Canadian history, agreeing to conscript soldiers and train them for battle, but with no intention of ever using them.

As a result the army now had sixty thousand trained men in Canada, about 40 per cent of them French-speaking, who were safe from going to war unless Hitler invaded Canada.[9]

They were known as "Zombies" because they were a dead army, still breathing but unavailable to fight. Meanwhile, a separate army of volunteer soldiers was fighting and dying in Europe in large numbers. It was a policy that had proved greatly beneficial to King, whose party had won 64 per cent of the vote in Quebec in 1940, but was rife with danger should English Canada become disgruntled with the situation. And that's exactly what Smythe's plan set out to do. He was implicitly accusing the government of putting the lives of soldiers in danger to satisfy Liberal political interests. Smythe was telling mothers and fathers in English Canada their sons' lives were being risked for want of reinforcements, and all to protect young men in Quebec and ensure they continued to vote for the Liberals in overwhelming numbers.

For King, Smythe couldn't have struck at a worse time. He believed the war was almost over, and was already contemplating his victory election. Just days before, he had informed Churchill at a meeting in

Quebec that he was determined to limit Canada's role in the Pacific once the European war was won, and told Louis St. Laurent, the senior figure in his Quebec caucus, that he would consider resigning if opposed in Cabinet. He was also deep into the strange world of spiritualism that was so much a part of his being, and of which Canadians remained blissfully unaware. He spoke regularly to dead relatives and acquaintances, and was constantly being seized by visions he considered direct communications from the beyond. At the time Smythe launched his conscription crusade, King was beside himself in anticipation of a new portrait of his mother, due to arrive at any time.[10] Thus the initial response to Smythe's accusations was left to Ralston, the senior of the three men who held defence portfolios in King's cabinet. A First World War veteran himself, he had a son fighting in Belgium and shared Smythe's concern over reinforcements, but doubted the situation was as bad as Smythe claimed.

He convened a gathering of military aides to deal with the statement the morning it appeared.[11] They prepared a brief rebuttal, professing bewilderment at the charges, and reassuring Canadians that troops were perfectly well trained. "With regard to overseas, special inquiries are being made, but no complaints whatever have been received from the General Officer Commanding-in-Chief of insufficiently trained reinforcements."

As a slap at Smythe, it added, "It is deeply regretted that stress may have been caused in many thousands of homes in Canada by the suggestion that casualties have been increased on account of insufficiently trained reinforcements. There is nothing whatever which is known which would provide the slightest justification for that conclusion."

Ralston also sent off an urgent message to Gen. Kenneth Stuart, chief of staff at Canada's military headquarters in London, requesting an assessment of the charges. General Stuart replied promptly with the hoped-for assurances that everything was just fine. He included figures indicating recruits were using up plenty of Bren gun bullets in their training and had fired off thousands of PIAT rounds. The Bren was a light machine gun used by Canadian troops, along with the traditional Lee-Enfield rifle. A PIAT gun was a variation on the U.S. bazooka.

The dismissive tone reflected the government's assumption it was dealing with one disgruntled hockey manager. But Smythe had hit a nerve. The press was overwhelmingly on the side of conscription and would spend the next six weeks pounding Ottawa mercilessly on his behalf. On the day his statement appeared, the *Toronto Telegram* produced a stinging editorial arguing that the policy of training men but keeping them in Canada was a giant government sham:

> Major Smythe's statement blasts the argument of those who have loudly asserted that the Home Defense Army was preparing adequate and fully trained reinforcements who could be available at any moment they were needed by the mere stroke of the Government's pen ordering conscription. The actual situation as exposed by Major Smythe shows that the country has been lulled into a sense of false security by propaganda put forward to oppose any pressure upon the government for conscription.[12]

The *Telegram* also reported Ottawa was looking for a way to discipline Smythe. The *Globe* quoted an unnamed government spokesman, warning that "Major Smythe's action was contrary to army regulations, and, in making it, he subjected himself to disciplinary measures."

Unidentified officials suggested Smythe had made his charges for political purposes and planned to run for the Progressive Conservatives in the next election. Although he had considered running for office in the past, and pondered it again when King finally called a general election in June 1945, it seems unlikely political ambition was behind his charge. He couldn't walk, pee, or empty his bowels , and was hardly likely to have spent time contemplating the joys of life in Ottawa while recuperating in his bed in Basingstoke.

He was far more concerned with shoring up his position at the Gardens and fending off a campaign to kick him upstairs into the NHL presidency.

He had been receiving feelers about his interest in replacing Dutton as NHL boss since early in the year. Dutton had replaced Calder on an interim basis after Calder's heart attack, but league governors were divided over his suitability on a permanent basis. Jim Norris may have been the first to formally raise the issue with Smythe, but he already knew it was coming thanks to an alert from Selke, who didn't appreciate the warning bells it would set off.

"There was a move on foot at the last NHL meeting to put Red Dutton in as NHL President for the duration," Selke had written in January. "Patrick, Adams, Tobin and Gorman were for. Toronto and Boston against." The Leafs and Bruins had blocked the move, he said, adding, "I keep rooting for you or Walter Brown [manager of Boston Garden]."[13]

In many ways Smythe made perfect sense as a candidate. He had been telling everyone how to run the league for years anyway, so why not just give him the job? Besides, he was part of an old guard that was starting to disappear. Calder was dead. Lester Patrick had quit coaching in 1939 and handed the job to Frank Boucher. Chicago's Major McLaughlin died in December 1944. Ross was nearing the end of his active days in Boston. The Americans, Maroons, and Senators were all out of business.

Smythe would undoubtedly have attacked the league's problems with relish. The question was whether anyone would have listened. The NHL was replete with big egos, and Smythe wasn't renowned for his diplomatic skills. Even while promoting Smythe's candidacy Selke recognized this, noting that as acting president, Dutton "is in the same unhappy position of having to call on others before being authorized to make a decision. Why he would put himself in that position in spite of the fact he is wealthy enough to be independent is beyond me."[14]

Nonetheless the momentum increased in the wake of his wounding, as news spread of the extent of his injuries. In an August 29 letter addressed to Smythe in Basingstoke, Selke encouraged him to give serious consideration to stepping aside.

The drums are starting to beat for [George Dudley, an amateur hockey executive] as a temporary man – Conny Smythe as a permanent appointee. They meet in Montreal next Friday and if they talk about it again I will ask them to make a definite offer. . . . We are fixing up your office preparatory to your return but if they pay you well enough you might take the other job. Certainly the league could do with a real leader after the beating it has taken from within during the last three or four years.[15]

Although he didn't realize it, there was probably nothing Selke could have done to raise doubts about his loyalty in Smythe's mind more than to write those words. Lying helpless and in pain in a British hospital, the last thing he wanted to hear was a suggestion from his appointed lieutenant that he consider stepping aside. For Selke to note that Bickle and MacBrien favoured his departure only made it worse, as it confirmed – as far as Smythe was concerned – that he now faced a cabal of disloyal interests working against him within the very heart of the Maple Leafs organization.

Reports in the sports pages only added to his alarm. Andy Lytle revealed that Smythe could "write his own salary ticket" if he took the job. League governors were "practically unanimous" in viewing him "not only as the most logical successor . . . but as the standout figure for the position, head and shoulders above the herd."[16]

A few days later he added that "no one except Conn Smythe would be even briefly considered" for the job and that Bickle, Black Hawks director Bill Tobin, and Lester Patrick were all in favour. "If Jim Norris . . . okays that, Smythe is as good as in . . . a nod given from Norris to the NHL is like being given the King's accolade."[17]

Smythe defused the campaign the first chance he got. "That they should offer to pay me a large sum of money annually for service they can get from me for nothing, doesn't make sense," he said after summoning reporters to his hospital bed. He insisted he was "perfectly happy" in his old job as managing director.

"I'm content to take up where I left off, that is if I still have my old

Young Conn at a desk in the dilapidated Scarborough home lent to Albert by a friend in the theosophist society. The house lacked water, power, and indoor plumbing; a stove offered the only heat. (Archives Ontario)

Albert, in his later years. His small apartment in Hamilton contained 35,000 books. (Archives Ontario)

Conn, age 6, with Albert (right) and his grandfather Joseph during a trip to Ireland in 1901. (Courtesy Smythe family)

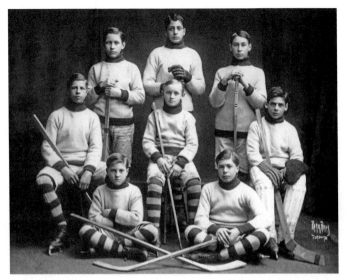

Smythe (centre) hated Upper Canada College, but found solace as captain of the junior hockey team in 1909. The Heintzman brothers, from the wealthy piano manufacturers, are to his right in the front and centre rows. (Archives Ontario)

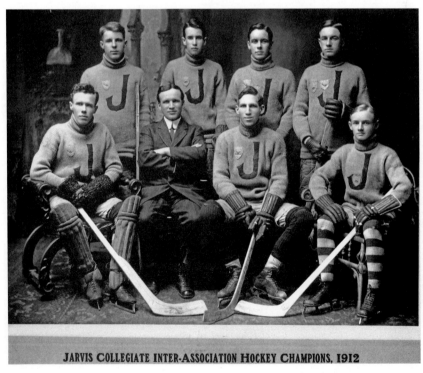

JARVIS COLLEGIATE INTER-ASSOCIATION HOCKEY CHAMPIONS, 1912

Smythe (front row, right) and his friend "Wreck" Aggett (back row, right) on the 1912 Jarvis Collegiate hockey team. Aggett was later killed at Passchendaele. (Archives Ontario)

Lieutenant Conn Smythe in 1915.
(Archives Ontario)

Irene and Conn, after Conn's
return from the war. He once
said of Irene: "It just seemed
that from the moment we met
we talked the same language."
(Archives Ontario)

Smythe (right) in his pilot's uniform during
World War I. (Archives Ontario)

Smythe as "honourary coach" (meaning he wasn't paid) of the Varsity junior team in 1922. At one point, the University of Toronto hockey program consisted largely of teams coached by Conn Smythe. (Archives Ontario)

When Col. John Hammond (centre) showed up at Union Station with Lester Patrick (left) in tow, Smythe knew he was finished with the Rangers. But, he agreed to pretend everyone was parting as friends. (Imperial Oil-Turofsky/ Hockey Hall of Fame)

Smythe in the 1920s was a young man on the rise: he already had a wife, a young family, and a growing business when he turned $10,000 in gambling winnings into a share of the St. Patricks hockey team and re-named it the Maple Leafs. (Hockey Hall of Fame)

It took five months to erect the Gardens in the summer of 1931. "I have always been given the main credit for building Maple Leafs Gardens in the depths of the Depression," Smythe said. "I didn't even know what a Depression was, so I just kept pushing." (Hockey Hall of Fame)

Rare Jewel, who won just a single race before dying from pneumonia, helped supply the money to buy "King" Clancy from Ottawa. (Hockey Hall of Fame)

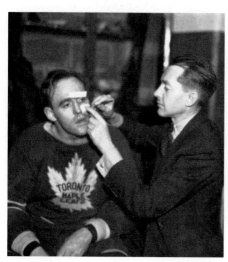

Clancy gets patched up in the dressing room. He rarely won a fight but never let that stop him. (Hockey Hall of Fame)

The cover of the last official program before the Leafs moved to Maple Leaf Gardens shows the team in action against the Montreal Maroons. (City of Toronto Archives)

Charlie Conacher (left), Joe Primeau (centre), and "Busher" Jackson were good-looking local kids who helped fill the Gardens game after game. Foster Hewitt said he often wondered what would have happened to the Gardens if the 1930s team hadn't been so good. (Hockey Hall of Fame)

Dick Irvin and his boss in the Leafs' dressing room. On Irvin's first day as coach, Smythe handled the team until it blew a three-goal lead, then said, "You take over, Dick," and walked away. (Imperial Oil-Turofsky/Hockey Hall of Fame)

"Hap" Day enjoys a taste from the Cup. In thirty years with the Leafs he had his name inscribed on the trophy as captain, coach, and manager. Smythe called him "one of the best men I ever met." (Hockey Hall of Fame)

"The Major." The army embodied everything Smythe valued in life and hockey: teamwork, discipline, loyalty, and clear lines of authority. (Imperial Oil-Turofsky/Hockey Hall of Fame)

While waiting to leave for Normandy, the 30th Battery killed time playing softball. Smythe, rear, next to Ted Reeve, almost missed the boat after breaking four ribs in a collision at third base. (Archives Ontario)

Stafford signed up with the Navy and sent his father this portrait, with the inscription, "From the Navy to the Army." (Archives Ontario)

Syl Apps didn't drink, smoke, swear, or take penalties, but, along with Ted "Teeder" Kennedy, had the "bloodlines" Smythe credited to only the greatest players. (Imperial Oil-Turofsky/Hockey Hall of Fame)

Smythe's arrival on a hospital train from Halifax in September 1944 was big news. He slammed his leg with his fist to show reporters that there was no feeling left. (Archives Ontario)

His war wounds left Smythe intensely sensitive to
cold and forced him to bundle up in heavy, fur-lined
leather coats and pants for practices. In the 1950s,
he and Irene began spending winters in Florida.
(Courtesy Smythe family)

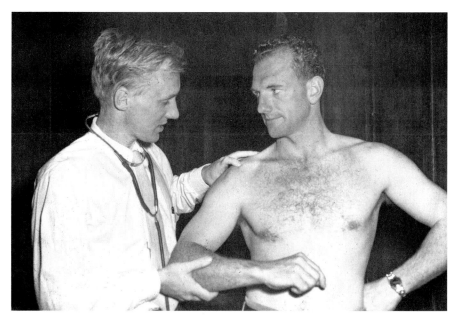

Hugh Smythe with Leafs captain Ted Kennedy. Hugh began as stick boy and went on to serve for many years as the team doctor. (Imperial Oil-Turofsky/ Hockey Hall of Fame)

Walter "Turk" Broda obliges photographers by stripping down for the official weigh-in after Smythe banned him from the net unless he lost seven pounds. (Hockey Hall of Fame)

The ultimate anglophile, Smythe met the Queen in 1951 when she was still Princess Elizabeth. On a later visit, he hosted her at a gathering of children from the Crippled Children's Society. (Archives Ontario)

Smythe, Ted Kennedy, and Hap Day watch Eddie Shore tee one up. Smythe was a keen golfer and, at one time, was a member at four clubs. He never blamed Shore for the check that almost killed Leafs player Ace Bailey. (Imperial Oil-Turofsky/Hockey Hall of Fame)

Conn and Irene at The Breakers, their winter retreat in Florida.
(Imperial Oil-Turofsky/Hockey Hall of Fame)

Conn and Irene with Miriam. Smythe's daughter disapproved of her husband
working at the Gardens, where he came under her father's pervasive control.
(Archives Ontario)

An aerial view of the Smythes' Caledon estate. Conn had a new road built so Irene wouldn't have to pass the unsightly sand and gravel operations nearby. (Archives Ontario)

Horses were a life-long love. Though only moderate in size, Smythe's stables were, for a time, among the most successful in the country. (Bob Olsen /GetStock.com)

job," he said. "You might ask Ed Bickle about that. Right now I don't know where I stand."[18]

The remark produced the expected response. "The job has always been his. You can't make that too strong or too emphatic," Bickle insisted. "I have merely been filling in for him. What's the matter with him, anyway?"

While Smythe was dousing that fire, his conscription crusade was heating up. McCullagh's *Globe* had responded vehemently to the claim Smythe had political ambitions, and was quickly gathering allies, reprinting articles from newspapers across the country that backed his position. The *Ottawa Journal* wrote that Smythe's charge "cannot be dismissed as the complaint of a junior officer, unfamiliar with his subject. It is the considered, written statement of a man who is well known to Canadians, who is a veteran of the last war, and who won the Military Cross for valor. . . . No official brush-off can dispose of these charges by Major Smythe. They are either true or they are not true. If they are not true, the public has a right to expect of the Government that it prove they are not true; to show where, why and how they are false. If they are true, with the Government unable to produce facts to the contrary, then the country has a right to feel that our men overseas and the whole war effort are being betrayed, and to demand that those responsible for the betrayal be punished."[19]

The furor ultimately got through to Ralston in Ottawa. Letters began arriving from the wives, mothers, and fathers of volunteers, worried that the government was taking needless risks with their sons' lives. They were supported by friends, relatives, veterans, and ordinary Canadians, making clear that a significant portion of the country doubted Ottawa's assurances that everything was fine.

"I have no heart to help the war any more in any way," wrote a mother from Smith's Falls whose son received five months' training before being sent to Europe and was killed a month later. "I am a very unimportant person in this world but I am a mother and Major Smythe has put in words the thoughts that have been in my mind.

How could my boy be trained in modern warfare in that time?"[20]

Another woman wrote: "Mr. Ralston says the boys are well trained not only in Canada but also in the United Kingdom. I'd like to ask him how much training our son received . . . He landed in England on July 30, on Aug. 13 he was in France. On the 28th of the same month he was wounded."[21]

Just a few days after Smythe's initial statement he gained a powerful ally when Ontario's premier, George Drew, returned from a trip to Europe and called a press conference. "There is no doubt about the accuracy of [Smythe's] charges," he said. "I know them to be true. Canadians have been sent into action without experience in handling grenades and the Bren and the PIAT anti-tank guns. I know that from my own knowledge gained in contacts with the troops on this trip. I haven't seen Major Smythe's statement but, knowing him I know he would not make a statement that was not right. No man in the services is held in higher regard than Major Smythe."[22]

Drew's intervention in the debate upset Ralston enough that he contacted the government's chief censor to inquire whether the premier had violated any wartime security restrictions. The censor replied that it was not policy to tell provincial premiers what they could say, adding helpfully that he had investigated Smythe's remarks as well, but no rules had been broken.[23]

It was obvious the government was looking for a way to shut Smythe up. Soon after the *Telegram*'s warning, he had been visited at Chorley Park by a staff officer who informed him he was about to be court-martialled. Smythe was delighted, figuring he'd have a chance to make his case in court.

"I said, 'That's the best news I've ever had,'" he related. "I waved the list I had assembled over the last two months. 'You court-martial me and I'll publish every one of these names, the regiments they are with, the number of men they were short when they went into battle, and what it cost in casualties.'

"He just looked at me. I told him to get out."[24]

The court martial didn't happen, though the possibility was revisited again as the crisis grew. Ralston appears to have put it on hold as he prepared for a trip to the battlefield to see for himself. The trip had been long planned and wasn't a reaction to the growing protest, but there were signs he suspected Smythe was closer to the mark than he wanted to admit. At a meeting before his departure he hinted to cabinet colleagues that recent recruitment figures for the infantry were troubling, especially against the sunny predictions he'd been receiving from his generals. He was also wary of the military's tendency to treat civilians like dunderheads, incapable of appreciating the fine art of military planning. But neither Smythe nor any of his allies knew of his misgivings, and when Ralston set off for Europe in the last week of September he could have been forgiven for feeling the pressure. King's government could probably have stared down one angry major, even if he did run the country's favourite hockey team. It might also have managed to dismiss the tandem of Smythe and George McCullagh, since McCullagh's newspaper rarely had anything nice to say about the government anyway. But Smythe, McCullagh, and Drew together, backed by most of the province's biggest newspapers, was something else, an axis of anger with plenty of clout and the resources to implement it, firmly grounded in the solid conservative soil of Tory Toronto, where the organizers of the outcry were all within easy reach of one another.

The three men shared a number of characteristics: they were friends, they were conservatives, they were anglophiles, and they felt the war was a patriotic duty rather than, like King, an unfortunate necessity.

Like Smythe, McCullagh and Drew were both self-made men. At age nine McCullagh was a penniless boy selling newspapers on the streets of London, Ontario. He had just six months of high school, but was a millionaire by age thirty and at thirty-one was named the youngest governor of the University of Toronto. He had initially been an ally of King, but the ardour had cooled over time and by 1939, King was avoiding his calls and accusing him of trying to start a Fascist Party of Canada.[25] In 1942 King had actively encouraged a change of ownership at the paper, indicating he'd be willing to accept ownership by U.S. interests if it would free him from McCullagh's attacks.[26]

Drew shared Smythe's passion for all things military. A year younger than Smythe, he had attended both Upper Canada College and the University of Toronto, and been badly wounded by a piece of shrapnel in 1916.[27]

Drew and King loathed each other. After Canadian troops were routed in Hong Kong in 1939, Drew made similar charges to those now being levelled by Smythe, claiming Ottawa had shipped under-trained men to defend the colony, a hopeless task that ended with half of Canada's 1,975 soldiers being either killed or wounded. Drew was charged under the Defence of Canada Act with making statements likely to prejudice recruiting, but the charges were withdrawn in the face of a public backlash.[28] So Drew had won round one and was now back for round two.

Two weeks after returning from Europe, Drew delivered a fierce speech in support of Smythe, tearing a strip off King and his government. D-Day, he reported, had so depleted Canadian reserves that the army was scouring other services for replacements, seizing men with little or no training and rushing them into action.[29]

He read a number of letters he'd received from Canadian fighting men, decrying the situation and the lack of skilled replacements. In each case, Drew noted, the authors had been killed soon after.

It was a powerful assault, but Smythe wasn't in any condition to appreciate it. After managing a short walk in the hospital garden on the day of the speech, he suffered a relapse and was ordered to bed with no visitors. He was, recalled his son Hugh, in "much worse" shape than was generally known. Part of his treatment in England had been eleven days on a penicillin drip. "These were in the early days of penicillin and it was very crude and he had an allergic reaction to it." He was also given plasma, contracting viral hepatitis from a virus that was in the plasma, "so when he arrived at Chorley Park he was as yellow as a duck's foot."[30]

As some sense of life returned to his limbs he struggled to relearn how to walk. A nerve in his right leg had been cut, causing it to shrink and the toes to curl under. The pain was constant, and he had developed an intense sensitivity to cold. Most frustrating was his continued lack of control over his bowels or bladder, a situation that would never be permanently repaired. He began receiving a daily enema, a routine that would go on the rest of his life. He was told he would also be able to urinate only through a tube, a situation he was determined to avoid. "I . . . could stand at the toilet holding on to support bars, and did that for hours every day, telling the urine to come," he recalled. One day he was distracted by a couple of squirrels having a battle outside the bathroom window. Suddenly the urine began to flow. He yelled for the nurses. "Look at that! Look at that!" he cried, pointing at his penis.

"I've seen better," one of the nurses remarked.[31]

He did short turns around the bed, then across the room, until finally he was able to hobble for short distances. He made progress, though slowly. It would be three months before he could muster enough strength to visit the Gardens for a gathering of players' wives. It would be two more months before he could attend a hockey game. One after another, his battery crew wrote him letters with news from the front. Ted Reeve wrote touchingly: "On guard the other night I was thinking of what a hell of a gap in sport and in the routine of us sports scribes there would be without you around. The Gardens would still be having their 13,742 paid on hand but would nonetheless be rather empty as far as many of us were concerned."[32]

Patricia also wrote, inquiring when he'd be home and wondering, "Do you think you could play marbles with me? I am now in grade four." Patricia was special; in an earlier letter she shared a prayer she'd composed: "Dear heavenly father I thank you for the world so sweet and for the food we eat and for the birds that sing and everything sweet in this world a men."[33] On the back Irene scrawled a note: "Hello Darling Dad. Please come home and see us. We want our Daddie very much and need more affection and love."[34]

Patricia sent him more cards with girlish poems; when Irene brought her to see him for the first time she hurled herself across the room and into his bed, explaining to the alarmed nurses: "I had to kiss my Daddy."

Weakened as he was, Smythe and his allies would have been cheered if they'd known the effect they were having in Ottawa, where Mackenzie King was increasingly disenchanted with his cabinet. Ralston was off in Europe, and King already had intimations he would be returning with bad news. Meanwhile his air minister, Chubby Power, had fallen off the wagon. It was a recurring problem that was becoming difficult to ignore. On October 5, King complained to his diary that Power had gone on a bender, then made himself available to the press, and "obviously went so far that all could see that he was the worst for liquor. Efforts had to be made with the press men to hold back some of the things he had said."[35]

With Ralston gone and Power out of commission, King was stuck with a cabinet he found increasingly irksome. His navy minister, Angus Macdonald, persisted in resisting the prime minister's efforts to minimize Canada's role in the Pacific War. His finance minister, James Lorimer Ilsley, couldn't make up his mind whether a larger navy was a patriotic necessity or an undesirable expense. "He is not a good finance minister," King stated bluntly.[36] King eventually grew so annoyed with their equivocations he abruptly marched from the room partway through a meeting and vowed to quit sharing his thoughts. "I have made up my mind not to discuss policy any further beyond laying it before the Cabinet as a whole as I did before," he fumed. "It is unpardonable for these men to act this way."

On October 8, King directly addressed for the first time the storm that was brewing around conscription, noting that he'd read "with great interest an article by Mrs. Blois" questioning Smythe's charges.

Mrs. Blois was Edna Blois, whose husband, Lt. Kenneth Blois, had been killed in action in France. She had been featured on an October 3 broadcast on CKEY Radio in Toronto, offering "My Opinion of Major Connie Smythe's Charges!" Her views were repeated the next day in the *Toronto Star*, which was doing its best to counter the outpouring of vilification from other less government-friendly publications.

"Frankly, my first reaction to Maj. Smythe's charges was one of momentary alarm," recounted Blois. "He is a Canadian sportsman who has public standing. Then I asked myself, 'Why did Maj. Smythe as an army officer see fit to make these charges public before taking them up with his superior officers? Could it be that the charges flowed from some political motive?"

After suggesting Smythe was just acting as a front for Drew, she complained about the lack of detail to back up his claim. "If a serious man had knowledge of the lives of our soldiers being needlessly thrown away on the field of battle, he would state when, where and how this crime occurred. Major Smythe carefully avoids giving us one single fact to back up his charges. Not one single fact!"

Smythe had, in truth, offered all the details Blois demanded, waving his collection of affidavits at the officer who'd turned up in his hospital room threatening a court martial. The information, he realized, was highly dangerous. Any of the men who had spoken to him could be charged with violating military regulations, and disgraced. The fact they'd provided their names and outfits anyway underlined how seriously they viewed the situation. Smythe wasn't about to make his evidence public unless forced to do so, and thus far the government had proved reluctant to press the issue. Nonetheless, Blois worked herself into a state: "You cannot go about Toronto charging anyone you don't like with vague but horrible crimes," she complained. "Maj. Smythe is doing something much more serious. He is casting suspicion upon our military command; he is undermining public confidence in our military and war leaders by charges unsupported by a single fact that he is prepared to vouch for. And he is doing this from the hospital bed of a wounded officer, thus placing those against whom he makes the charge in a most unfair position."

She was correct in noting the advantage Smythe enjoyed: it was difficult for the government to turn their guns on a wounded war hero.

Nonetheless, when he was up to it Smythe sought to answer the complaints against him, writing letters refuting intimations he was motivated by anything beyond concern for the troops. "Canada never produced and never will produce anything finer than these young men. If the country loses them she's lost everything, and we don't have to get them killed to lose them – get that straight. We can lose them for keeps by forgetting them, or letting them think we have. And that's what we're doing now, letting them think we've forgotten them while we sit here squabbling like a bunch of lousy politicians over whether it will or won't be good for our unity to send them the help they need."[37]

On October 13, the campaign took a crucial turn. King, who had been complaining frequently of fatigue and a need for rest, awoke "burning with fire inside." Just before entering cabinet, he received a cable from Ralston in Europe with clear indications of trouble ahead. He requested an early meeting with the cabinet as soon as he returned, to which he intended to bring General Stuart from London. King immediately guessed what he had in mind. Ralston had gone over to the Smythe gang.

"All of this I can see means that he is coming back prepared to urge that the situation has become so much more serious than contemplated and that drastic steps will have to be taken to secure the necessary number of trained men," he wrote. "All of this of course will be an effort to have the NRMA men serve overseas."

Ralston had indeed gone over. On October 3, from London, he'd accused Smythe of stirring up trouble for political reasons. But even then he'd been halfway into the conscriptionist camp. He no longer had complete faith in his generals. He suspected they were out of touch, too tied to headquarters, and too determined to tell him what they thought he wanted to hear. When Ralston arrived in Europe, General Stuart was still insisting there wasn't the slightest truth in any of Smythe's allegations. He had responded to Drew's October 5 speech with a twenty-four-point memo disputing his claims and

insisting, "The truth is that, up to date, there has been no overall defi-
ciency in reinforcements."[38]

Ralston, however, had discovered that Smythe's claims were accurate. In Italy, where Canadian men were engaged in a fierce effort to
tie up German forces, he was told the situation was dire. The number
of casualties was outpacing replacements by a ratio of two or three to
one. That didn't include the sick and injured, which pushed the
required number of replacements to beyond five hundred a day. If the
fighting continued at the current level of ferocity, the available supply
of men would be exhausted within days.[39] At the same time, he learned
from the commander of the British Eighth Army that the fighting was
expected to go on for weeks, and Canada would play a leading role,
which meant continued casualties at an elevated rate.

Ralston flew to Belgium, where he was met by Col. Richard S.
Malone, a former Winnipeg newspaperman who had served as Ralston's
staff secretary early in the war. Malone had gone on to serve in Sicily,
was assigned as a liaison to Britain's Gen. Bernard Montgomery, and
later still directed Canadian public relations for the landing at Normandy.
Malone hadn't seen Ralston in a year and noticed a stark change. The
minister looked haggard and preoccupied and could think of nothing
but the reinforcement problem. With good reason: the situation, Malone
reported, was "desperate," with many units undermanned and wounded ·
soldiers being sent back repeatedly to the front lines. The trickle of
replacements sent to support them was simply not adequate.

"Many of the men who had recently arrived from Canada were
from the bottom of the barrel and would never be fit for frontline
service," Malone recalled.[40] "The depots at home were scraping the
bottom and had simply shipped many of these chaps over to complete
the quota on a draft." Although wounded men sent back to their units
were counted as available for fighting, "many would never see active
service again." And, as in Italy, it was likely to get worse. At the same
time Ralston was in Belgium Canadian forces were heavily engaged in
clearing German troops from the Scheldt estuary, the approach to the

vital port at Antwerp. On October 13, the day Ralston sent his cable to King, the Canadian 5th Infantry Brigade's Black Watch Battalion had been all but wiped out. Ralston discovered Canadian forces were also slotted to face what was expected to be fierce resistance when the Allied campaign reached the Rhine.

Before he left Brussels, Ralston was invited to dine at headquarters with Gen. Harry Crerar, commander of the 1st Canadian Army. The minister left his food untouched and seemed in a daze. On the way out he invited Malone to his darkened trailer, where he sat on the edge of his bunk, talking despondently until after 3:00 a.m. while Malone huddled in his coat against the cold.

"I am not very popular at home now," he told Malone, recounting the attacks he'd been under. But Ralston sympathized with the troops as much as Smythe did. He saw his first responsibility as ensuring the men were supported to the fullest extent. And it was clear from what he'd seen that the standard wasn't being met.

"His mind was completely made up," Malone recounted. "He would either force the government to bring in full conscription on his return or he would resign."[41]

It was the key moment in the brief but intense contest Smythe had set in motion. As King was aware, Ralston had the sympathy and support of other ministers, considerable clout within the military, and the overwhelming backing of English Canada. When Ralston landed back in Ottawa with Stuart in tow, Mackenzie King had a divided cabinet and a full-fledged crisis on his hands.

He had no intention of flinching. The next two weeks would be a prolonged test of endurance between the prime minister and his defence minister, neither willing to abandon principles each felt were too fundamental to compromise. King was unconvinced the manpower situation was as critical as portrayed, distrusted the military, and was increasingly fed up with his ministers. "Ralston has been a thorn in my flesh right along," he complained after receiving his cable.[42] He began to fill his diary with fevered visions of civil war between French and English. Conscription, he wrote, would be "a criminal thing" that would break up Canada and lead to demands for "complete independence, if not annexation to the U.S." It would doom Britain's empire, which "can only endure by there being complete national unity in Canada," and undermine the war effort by giving aid and comfort to an enemy sure to be cheered by signs of discord. The coming push against Japan, he worried, would be lost before it began.

He insisted conscription couldn't be imposed without recalling Parliament and putting the question to a vote. If the government fell, it would mean a bitter and contentious campaign in the midst of war. He feared he could very well lose the election, which might put the dreaded socialists in charge, since the Co-operative Commonwealth Federation, precursor of the New Democratic Party, was enjoying a surge of support.

Ralston was just as determined not to cede ground. From the time he returned to Canada on October 18 and the peak of the crisis on November 1, he and King faced off in a series of increasingly fraught sessions – at gatherings of the war committee, in meetings of the full cabinet, before the Liberal caucus, and in private talks during which King sought alternately to soothe and bully his unyielding minister. The prime minister wanted to try other alternatives: a new campaign for volunteers, for instance, or a reduction in recruiting standards. Perhaps there should be fewer or smaller units. He snidely asked Ralston if he thought he could form a government if he departed.

The conflict veered from drama to farce on October 25 when the cabinet learned that – in addition to the 60,000 unused Zombies – the military had 120,000 general service troops in Canada and another 90,000 in England, who could have been dispatched to the front without any of the political or national unity implications. The ministers were dumbfounded. "My God," blurted Power, "if that's the case, what are you talking about getting more men under conscription?" But the generals insisted the men were either ill trained or ill suited for infantry duty and would take too long to whip into shape. King found it hard to believe the army couldn't scrape together 15,000 reinforcements out of 210,000 available soldiers.[43]

King began to imagine a conspiracy against him. The same ministers who were demanding conscription had been the most fiercely opposed to many of the social reforms he had championed. He decided they must be in league with one another and with the bankers and other commercial powers who were out to preserve their wealth and stymie his plans. There was no evidence for any of this. The Conservative leader, John Bracken, didn't have a Commons seat and struggled to control his own caucus; he was hardly the man to organize a national conspiracy. And there was no money for the bankers in conscription.

Feeling a boost from Britain's prime minister might help get his cabinet back in line, King cabled Churchill to confirm his claim the war was almost won. Churchill replied that fighting could continue into the summer of 1945, and Canada's forces would certainly be needed. Having got the wrong answer, King kept the information from his cabinet.

He began to consider replacing Ralston and approached General McNaughton, the man Smythe had championed as near-dictator of Canada's war effort. Unbeknownst to Smythe, who had taken for granted the general would support conscription, McNaughton was opposed to forcing the Zombies to serve if they didn't want to. He had been recalled the year before and had been at loose ends for months, supposedly on medical leave as the government looked for something appropriate for him to do. King had decided to make him Governor General – the first Canadian-born appointee to hold that job – and McNaughton had agreed. But before the appointment could be made, King asked whether he would be willing to serve as defence minister in Ralston's place instead.

Replace the man who had humiliated him? You bet he would. McNaughton incorrectly blamed Ralston for his recall. He assured King he could raise all the reinforcements needed without resorting to conscription. He was certain the additional volunteers would be no problem for a man of his prestige.

Thus armed, on November 1 King staged one of the most dramatic moments in Canadian cabinet history. He told McNaughton to be prepared to take Ralston's place immediately. Then he visited the Governor General – who would be required to do the swearing in – and told him to be ready. He contacted a number of key ministers and advised them against acting rashly in response to what was about to happen. Then he entered a planned cabinet meeting, reminded his ministers Ralston had offered to resign over another matter two years earlier, and announced he had now decided to accept it.

King's cabinet was thunderstruck. "This is the most cold-blooded thing I've ever seen," remarked Colin Gibson, the minister of national revenue.[44] King recalled in his diary that there was "intense silence" following his ambush. Finally, Ralston spoke quietly, declared that of course he would stand down if the prime minister required it, and immediately gathered up his papers to leave the room. He shook hands with King, and – as King recalled – thanked him for giving him the opportunity to serve. The other ministers stood and formed a circle to shake his hand. But King, not finished, intercepted him on the way to the door and explained that he'd like to have McNaughton sworn in as soon as possible. "I asked him if it would be possible to let me have his resignation that night." But Ralston wasn't about to be hustled out of town on the first train and told the prime minister he'd have to wait a day. "It was a scene I shall never forget, nor will those who were present," King confided to his diary.

He was correct on that. The newspapers responded with shock. McCullagh's *Globe* noted that Ralston had formed his view on conscription after personally touring the battlefront, while McNaughton had been away from the army for a year. On November 7 it charged: "The government is wickedly sacrificing young men's lives to retain its governing power in Quebec." There was an outpouring of sympathy for Ralston, and something less than an ecstatic welcome for

McNaughton. Smythe gave Ralston his due: "The record shows that he laid it right on the line for the cabinet. But King, to my mind, was the greatest traitor of all time."[45] He now had no time at all for McNaughton, the man he had once considered suitable to serve as virtual czar. "[McNaughton] should have been ashamed of himself for the rest of his life for turning his back on the Army he had helped to form, and taking out his personal dislike of Ralston by siding with King against the best interests of the Canadian army."

Many other veterans agreed. McNaughton's efforts to raise a host of volunteers quickly fizzled. Ralston's allies in cabinet became restless and, seeing another plot, King again threatened to resign. He was saved from carrying out his threat when McNaughton, shaken by events, abruptly declared that conscription would be necessary after all. King convinced himself he was facing a revolt by his generals and, using McNaughton's retreat as cover, reversed his position on the spot. "This really lifts an enormous burden from my mind," he wrote.

It was a momentous victory for Smythe and his supporters, though he felt he never received adequate credit for bringing it about. "I'm sort of the unseen presence," he wrote of the episode. "There is no official record that I can find stating that I was the one who finally blew the lid off of the Army reinforcement scandal."[46] When King's official biographer addressed the situation more than fifteen years later, he couldn't bring himself to even name the men who had besmirched King's legacy, referring to them only as "alarmists and troublemakers who were generally considered to be unreliable," while acknowledging that "events proved, however, that the gloomy prophecies of this group were only too accurate."[47]

Once the conscription order was given, none of the horrific consequences King had foreseen actually occurred. The country endured, the war was won, and the Empire survived. King, in fact, managed to turn his about-face into an enduring victory. By making clear his willingness to go to the wall for Quebec, he had won French support for the Liberal Party that would endure for a generation and more, while dooming the Conservatives to repeated failure. In the 1940 general election, King's Liberals had captured every province in the country. When the 1945 election was held in June, he lost Alberta, Saskatchewan, British Columbia, and Ontario, but was rescued by Quebec, which gave him forty-seven seats, 40 per cent of his total. The Tories won one.

King believed he was under attack by forces hostile to the very soul of the country, motivated by political and material ambitions. But Smythe had never sought anything more than what he urged in the beginning: that Ottawa use its healthy supply of trained men to take the strain off the badly pressed volunteers on the front line. In that he succeeded, though by the time the government got around to sending the conscripts Hitler was in his last days and only about twenty-five hundred men were sent.

Drew and others had been agitating for conscription through much of the war without making a dent in King's resistance. Not until Smythe entered the argument did it make any headway. Drew was premier and head of a minority government. Smythe was a war hero, with an ability to tap into the emotions of average Canadians in a way Drew never could. McNaughton certainly recognized that and continued to press King to court-martial Smythe. King acknowledged the troublesome little major should have been "dealt with" in the early stages, but was too wise a politician to send the boss of the Toronto Maple Leafs limping up to a courthouse to make his case.[48]

CHAPTER 15

In the aftermath of Smythe's victory over Ottawa, the spring of 1945 should have been a time of relative tranquility. Smythe was fifty years old, hardly an old man, and had accomplished a great deal. His hockey team was an enormous success and his arena was almost always filled. People from across the country made their way to Maple Leaf Gardens just to stand and gawk. He had built two profitable businesses, starting with nothing and fuelled by little more than his own fierce determination and willingness to take a risk.

He had a wife who loved him and who attracted admiration for her kindly nature, her devotion to him, and her willingness to tolerate his difficult personality. "God knows what she must put up with," was the kind of remark women made in praising Irene while shaking their heads at her husband. No matter what others thought, the Smythes gave every indication of being a family that enjoyed being together and sharing their good fortune.

He'd come home from his second war in one piece, more or less. The parts were all there, though they didn't all work as well as they once had. By March he was well enough to attend a game at the Gardens, photographed leaning on his cane with a beaming Irene at his side. He had many admirers, not only for his hockey achievements but also for the courage and patriotism that had driven him to endanger all he had to once again defend his country and beliefs. He had challenged the government on a point of principle and won, standing up under immense pressure on behalf of young men fighting overseas.

And, perhaps best of all, the Leafs were champions once again. Against all the odds, after a mediocre season, they surprised everyone by defeating the Montreal Canadiens in a semifinal series they had been universally expected to lose. The Habs were the class of the league that year. They ran away with the regular season, finishing thirteen points ahead of Detroit and twenty-eight ahead of the third-place Leafs. Elmer Lach, Rocket Richard, and Toe Blake finished 1-2-3 in the scoring race, with Richard scoring an inconceivable fifty goals in fifty games. Lach won the Hart Trophy as most valuable player, and Bill Durnan won the Vezina as the best goalie. When the 1945 all-star team was named, Montreal players took five of the six positions, plus Irvin as coach.

The Leafs, in comparison, had one player in the top ten: the young Ted Kennedy, already dubbed "Teeder" at age eighteen and hailed as the obvious successor to the veteran Syl Apps. Neither Apps nor Broda was back from the war, so the team made due in net with the famously nervous Frank McCool, who was photographed during the playoffs gulping milk from a bottle to ease his roiling stomach.

Toronto won just two more games than it lost during the regular season, scoring forty fewer goals than Montreal and allowing forty more to be scored against them. They placed third only because the bottom three teams – Boston, New York, and Chicago – were in terrible shape, stripped of talent and derided as a pack of "palookas" that shouldn't even be in the league. Since there had to be four teams in the playoffs Boston got in by default, despite winning just sixteen games out of fifty. Everyone had great fun repeating a remark by Art Ross, who had let slip that "I am now piloting the worst hockey team at which it was ever my misfortune to look."[1] Earlier that season, Ross had offered one hundred dollars to anyone who could come up with a nickname for his famed "Kraut Line" that didn't include the word *Kraut* in it.[2]

So great was Montreal's advantage that Dick Irvin felt free to take a few jabs at his old team, telling reporters that if Toronto won a game in Montreal he would slit his own throat with a dull knife. Yet the Leafs pulled it off. They won the first two games in Montreal – presenting a serious threat to Irvin's throat – lost two of the next three, including a 10–3 pummelling in Montreal, then shocked just about everyone, including themselves, by wrapping up the series in six games with a victory at home on the last day of March.

They were the underdogs again against Detroit, though on the day the series opened the morning paper carried two pieces of news that would have made Smythe smile. First, the war was going exceedingly well. Canadian tanks had entered Holland and were gobbling up ground quickly against the fleeing Nazis. The Allies were 290 kilometres from Berlin and a Nazi newspaper acknowledged Germany was "perhaps only a few days or weeks" from collapse.[3]

The second bit of news must have made Smythe slap his aching leg with pleasure. Ross, his old nemesis, had announced he was retiring as coach of the Bruins and would henceforth occupy an unspecified "executive position."

Their feud had cooled after Ross visited Smythe in his sick bed and offered his best wishes. He had two sons in the air force, one of whom had been forced to bail out of his burning plane in mid-air. Smythe couldn't continue to hold a grudge against someone with sons like that. Still, it must have pleased him to know he'd outlasted the one man in the league as single-minded, thick-skinned, and unyielding as himself.

Toronto had beaten Detroit just twice in ten chances that season, but nervous little Frank McCool pulled off something akin to a miracle, racking up three straight shutouts. Toronto scored just four goals, but found itself with a three-game lead. They almost let it get away from them, as they lost the next three. McCool's stomach was in such agony during the seventh and deciding game he fled the ice midway through and clomped to the dressing room, where he sat gulping powders for his angry ulcer. Coach Hap Day followed him and pointed out that without him they were finished. There was no backup, the spare goalie having quit in mid-season. McCool steeled himself and returned to the ice, doubling over between whistles, but somehow holding on for a 2–1 win, a victory almost as improbable as the 1942 come-from-behind championship over the same Detroit Red Wings.

All this should have had Smythe wondering what he'd done to be treated so well by The Man Upstairs. And for a time it did, but the summer of 1945 began a period of troubles that started with a tragedy and ended with a broken friendship.

If there was a person in the world who could melt Smythe's heart it was his daughter, Patricia. She was just nine years old that summer, and he'd been away from her for the better part of four years. During the war she sent him letters in her childish printing, relating how "ofly hot" the summer was and that she was saving up money from selling golf balls. When he was released from the hospital she would run home at lunch to play games with him, which he never let her win and which sent her running to Irene or Jessie complaining that Daddy cheated. She held his hand as he took his first few steps around his upstairs bedroom, and then, as he recovered, on short walks around the yard.

Like Stafford, she had health problems. She suffered from food allergies and asthma, and if she accidentally ate a peanut "her eyes would just about pop out of her head."[4] Smythe mourned the fact that her health would make her life difficult. Far less was known about allergies at the time and dealing with them was a much greater burden than it would be in later years. Stafford's asthma was so constricting he spent entire nights in a little room filled with the burning fumes of medication intended to clear his passages.

A few months after the season ended, Irene and Conn were at the cottage for the summer as usual, with Patricia and Jessie. They were awaiting a visit from Dorothea and Stafford, who had only recently returned home after four years in the navy. While they waited, Smythe beat Patricia – again – at a game of croquet. Then he and Irene left to pay a short visit to friends nearby. When they returned, Patricia was lying dead on the veranda.

The cause was never established. There was no autopsy, a fact both Irene and Conn later regretted, when they wondered which of her ailments had killed their daughter. Irene was devastated and sick for months afterwards. Conn, who had watched many men die in battle, was shaken to his core from the loss of the little girl he considered an angel sent to help him. "Irene and I never really got over it," he wrote. "Yet I always felt that there was some kind of fate involved, that she had been sent to look after me, and get me better, hold my hand on our little walks, and then she was needed more elsewhere."[5] He rationalized that she had been saved from a life her health would have made difficult and had "gone to a better place."

Albert Smythe, well into his eighties and in poor health himself, wrote a poem for the theosophist journal, which he still edited. It's not hard to find echoes of her father in the little girl portrayed in its opening lines:

Patricia, darling, your goodbye
Was like your sudden change of moods,
One moment with a laughing eye,
Then all reluctance, coy and shy
As when an enemy stands by
And danger looms

Perhaps to fend off his grief, Smythe buried himself in the business of the new season, warning that no one should take another championship run for granted. He had directed there would be no formal celebration of the Cup triumph while there were still Canadians fighting in the Pacific, but after the Japanese surrender in August he organized a victory dinner at a golf club close to the Smythe home. Invitations went out to an extended list of friends and colleagues representing a cross-section of his life with the Leafs, the league, the business world, and his private friendships.

All the current players were there, as well as sons Hugh and Stafford and a select group from earlier teams that included Primeau, Conacher, Horner, Clancy, and Bailey. George Drew and George McCullagh, his allies in the assault on Ottawa, were invited, as were friends Larkin Maloney and Bob Laidlaw, a lumberman who had been among

Smythe's earliest customers at C. Smythe Ltd. Red Dutton was invited, along with the Black Hawks' Bill Tobin and even Jack Adams, who had replaced Art Ross as Smythe's longest-serving feuding partner. There was a full company of team officials – W.A. Hewitt, Frank Selke, and Harold Ballard, who was now managing the Leafs' Toronto Marlboros organization. Smythe – or more probably Selke, who was den mother to the press pack that covered the team – had even set up a golf tournament for the many reporters who now followed Leafs activities on a year-round basis.

The players' bonus for winning the Cup was the biggest ever awarded at $1,700, about half what many of them were making for a full season. The Depression and the war had combined to push down salaries, so many postwar NHLers toiled for significantly less than Horner or Clancy would have considered acceptable. In April, Smythe had donated the proceeds from a rodeo at the Gardens to help establish a new centre for veterans suffering spinal injuries. Now he announced that proceeds from the annual blue-and-white game – held just before the season opened – would be used to endow three beds at the Hospital for Sick Children in memory of three "Leafs" who had lost their lives in the war. Jack Fox, Dudley Garrett, and Red Tillson had all been somewhere in the Leafs system before the conflict began, though none had ever played an NHL game in a Leafs uniform.[6]

Smythe also wanted to use opening night at the Gardens to honour Canadian troops, and invited all surviving recipients of the Victoria Cross to attend, at the team's expense.[7]

The war had changed him and altered public perceptions of him. He was continually bothered by the cold, even in warm weather, and sat through Leafs practices huddled in a thick fur-lined flight jacket, a blanket on his knees, and warm boots in place of the spats he loved. Less often was he portrayed as madcap Connie Smythe, the galloping general manager who took off like a jackrabbit after fleeing referees. More and more he was referred to as Major Smythe, war veteran and "militant patriot" in the words of Andy Lytle. Selke had worked hard to turn Lytle into a faithful purveyor of the Leafs message, but with mixed results; determinedly irreverent, he had long portrayed Smythe as "the little corporal" in reference to his Napoleonic tendencies. Now he accorded him an unofficial promotion to "the little Major."

At training camp in Owen Sound he sat in the stands accompanied by officials from the Leafs' new Pittsburgh affiliate, a blunt reminder that players who underperformed could be shipped off forthwith. He had promised that every member of the Cup-winning team had an automatic place in the lineup "until he shows he can't hold it." Players returning from active service in the war were guaranteed a job "for at least this year."[8]

At first everything looked promising. The forward positions were expected to remain little changed. The defence was anchored by Babe Pratt and Wally Stanowski, backed by a group of young players that included Bob Goldham, Jim Thomson, Doug Baldwin, and Ernie Dickens.

Pratt was a fun-loving twenty-nine-year-old acquired from New York three years earlier. He'd won the Hart Memorial Trophy in 1944 and was considered one of the best defencemen of the era. At more than six feet and two hundred pounds he was a giant for the time, but could rush the puck or flatten an opponent with equal alacrity. Goldham had played briefly before the war and ranked high on everyone's list of hot prospects, as did eighteen-year-old Thomson, who Smythe predicted was the team's "coming No. 1 star."[9]

Lytle predicted a strong year. Declaring the team a notable improvement over the "wartime lurgons and semi-ossified oafs" of recent campaigns, he advised that "there isn't a body of rival directors in the league who wouldn't settle for that fourteen and go with it on the fair enough assumption that it could make the playoffs."[10]

Almost nothing turned out as anticipated. Frank McCool arrived in Toronto beset by doubts about his stomach and his future. The moment he stepped off the train, he said, his ulcers started kicking up. He visited Smythe at his Gardens office and said he wasn't sure he could carry on.

He didn't like to let down the team, but wasn't looking forward to another season gulping ulcer elixirs between periods. Smythe delivered one of his patented pep talks, and by the time he left the office, McCool recounted he would have entered a den of lions for the team.

His ardour quickly cooled, however, and on October 27 – the day of the opening game – McCool announced his retirement. "Actually I've never liked to play hockey," he told reporters. "I was thrust into goal first against my will when I was a kid by the captain of a team. That's how it's been with me ever since." This time there was more at issue than his stomach problems. He'd agreed to play for $4,500, but now considered the sum inadequate. He wanted $5,000, but neither Day nor Smythe would budge. "Smythe, when I talked with him, said no. He said I'd get $4,500 even if I sat all season on the bench," he said. "It's all over and I'm going home. I don't know what I'm going to do except that I'm through with hockey and it's a personal relief."

He remained retired for the first thirteen games, by which point the Leafs had just three wins. In his first game back, on December 1, Chicago put eight goals past him. But by then it was just one flake in the avalanche that was engulfing the team.

The returning veterans – Apps, Billy Taylor, Bob Goldham – didn't rebound as quickly as hoped. Ted Kennedy was hurt in an early game and never fully recovered, finishing the year with just three goals in twenty-one games. It took seven starts for the Leafs to get their first win, and by Christmas they were deep in the lower reaches, with only seven wins in twenty-three games. When Pratt was hurt in late December they lost five matches in a row. He had been back a few days when Red Dutton announced Pratt had been suspended indefinitely after admitting he'd placed bets on Leafs games.

The ruling attracted widescale mockery. It was no secret that many of the league's brass were gambling men. Jim Norris, Conn Smythe and Frank Selke all owned racehorses. Heavy bettors frequented an area of the Gardens known as as the "bull ring," with Smythe's blessing. Smythe once joked that between his teens and his thirties he'd have bet on anything that moved. Pratt insisted that, while he'd bet on Leafs games, he'd always picked them to win.

"Pratt, in my opinion, is a goof," Dutton declared. He'd been warned several times about gambling but kept at it anyway. Since he lost most of his bets, Dutton feared he might be tempted to bet against the Leafs and play accordingly. "Pratt's expulsion is effected partly to serve as a sharp warning that betting on hockey games and playing in them, do not mix."[11]

The suspension was lifted after just seventeen days when the league governors voted unanimously that Dutton had made the right decision, then unanimously reversed it.[12] Pratt lost nine hundred dollars in salary, which Smythe noted could quickly be recouped if he made the all-star team. (He didn't.) But it was far too late for the Leafs. McCool's play was mediocre and he appeared in just twenty-two games before Turk Broda returned to replace him. Lorne Carr and Sweeney Schriner, both important cogs in previous teams, were on their last legs. Smythe acknowledged neither was playing well, but pledged to keep them in the lineup as a tribute to their past contributions. The promising young defence he'd been counting on proved to need more seasoning. During Pratt's suspension Smythe let it be known that he considered only three players were playing to "big-league" standards: Gaye Stewart, Bob Goldham, and pint-sized Billy "the Kid" Taylor.

By February, Smythe had given up on the season and became increasingly critical in his assessment of the team's woes. His wrath was directed mainly at Selke, who now began to pay the price for the wartime letters Smythe had received from Squib Walker. Although Smythe insisted he hadn't returned home bent on retribution, he had obviously turned against his long-time assistant. Selke had been "disloyal" by getting involved in the trade for Kennedy, which still rankled with Smythe even as Kennedy was establishing himself as a star. He'd failed to abide by the instructions Smythe had left behind, sticking his nose into the hockey operations that were supposed to be Hap Day's bailiwick. He'd proved himself unreliable and vulnerable to ambition.

It was without question an unfair judgment. The team had won two Stanley Cups while Smythe was away. Business at the Gardens was never better. In the twenty years Smythe and Selke had worked together, nobody had worked harder or more diligently on his behalf. Many of the stars of the 1930s had come up through his minor-league operations. The Gardens might not have been built without his intervention. He did much to establish and maintain the Leafs' clean-cut, all-Canadian image and handled the crucial job of press management with great skill, providing the balm to soothe the many cuts inflicted on underpaid reporters by Smythe's sharp-edged style. He was popular around the Gardens and intensely proud of his role in its success.

But Smythe had decided he was unreliable. "I have warned you about him before," he wrote Walker in the months before Normandy. "He has a strange way of taking all credit for anything accomplished and washing his hands completely of anything that goes wrong or undone." He warned Walker not to push his complaints too hard or he could wind up behind the eight ball, "and Frank will say Ed Bickle or Bill MacB or someone wouldn't go for it. And if it goes [well] then of course FJS arranged it all and you owe it all to him."

He assured Walker he'd take care of things after the war. "I expect there will have to be a showdown when I get back, as heads swell easily with success," he wrote, adding, "As you know, I'll either be the boss or not work at the old place."[13]

Selke's misfortune was to get caught in the clash that had been looming since Smythe surrendered his Gardens' responsibilities before the war. His belief that Bickle was trying to get rid of him only grew stronger with each perceived slight. There was little he could do about either Bickle or Bill MacBrien, the Gardens' president, as both held more senior positions than he did. But Selke was vulnerable. Like Smythe he was merely an employee, and Smythe's employee at that.

He had inadvertently hurt his own case in letters he'd written at the same time Smythe was fielding complaints from Walker. Tapped out laboriously on a typewriter at his farm north of Toronto, they were filled with praise for Smythe, news and gossip from the Gardens, and chatter about horses. The consistent message was one of deference. Selke was self-effacing by nature, his in-built inclination being to avoid conflict or confrontation. He portrayed himself to Smythe as a loyal No. 2, who was doing his best to hold the fort in the boss's absence. "Of course I lack the colour and aggressiveness you always showed," he related in a January 1944 letter, adding, "You know I remember every lesson you taught me but have not always had the confidence to put them into practice."

In the same letter he asked for patience and understanding. "Please do not intercede with any bosses here," he pleaded. "Let me stand on my own till you get back the better job I do the better it will be for you when you take over once again and every kick in the pants will make me so much stronger if anyone attempts to horse me around. Good luck Boss, I'm grateful as hell for your kind and encouraging letters and will stick by you come hell or high water in any going." He signed it, "Yours forever and a day, Frank J. Selke."[14]

His biggest mistake may have been in offering regular enthusiastic updates on the Gardens' ongoing financial success, much of which resulted from his own efforts. In Smythe's absence he had worked extensively with a New York agency, filling the Gardens with acts it had never seen before. The Ice Capades, Ice Follies, and other similar spectaculars "have revolutionized the business of arena management in the United States," he enthused, adding that he was keen to get as many of them as he could.

"We have booked Col. Jim Eskews Rodeo, with five special features acts and Roy Rogers, King of the Cowboys with his horse Trigger for a five-day showing," he reported. "We are now selling Ice Follies of 1944. In ten days selling we are four thousand dollars ahead of Ice Capades on 1944 for a similar period. Ice Capades grossed $106,000 . . . in five nights. If we could maintain this slight increase we could sell out for five nights and then be well away. To the best of my recollection the Skating Club carnival top gross was $112,000. We were worried about the shift in dates from March to February . . . Are now hoping that it will make no difference."

Selke was right – people loved the ice shows and rodeos, the clowns and circuses, the Hollywood stars and travelling opera divas, and thanks to the strong wartime economy anyone who wasn't in uniform had money to spend. But his success just aggravated Smythe. He recognized the importance of keeping the Gardens busy between hockey games, but to him the Leafs came first and the rest was just something to keep the lights on and help pay the bills.

No one had ever booked non-hockey events with the enthusiasm Selke showed, and the results were self-evident. Paid attendance grew from 950,000 in 1940 to 1.7 million in 1946. Profits in the years from 1942–1945 were among the best ever. Selke reported on January 14 that a cheque for $80,000 had been sent to Sun Life, wiping out the remaining mortgage on the Gardens. The Leafs organization had also been able to buy $150,000 in war bonds, another show of its support for the boys overseas.

Smythe could hardly complain about the Gardens making money, but he grumbled to Walker that Selke was spending too much time on ice shows and not enough on hockey. The roster he left behind was wearing down, and nothing was being done to rebuild it, he complained. Selke provided fuel for the fire when he observed in mid-1944 that the Leafs were playing "quite bad . . . We have so little experienced first-class material that we sort of fall apart when Babe Pratt plays a bad game, and when he goes bad he is really stinkeroo."

In fact, Day and Selke were keenly aware of the need for fresh prospects. It was concern for the future that had prompted the Kennedy trade. Day wrote Smythe in 1943 that, with so many young men wearing army uniforms, the competition for those that remained was intense. He advocated an intensified scouting program, especially in western Canada. "Ross has scouts out there as have all the teams, including Buffalo and Cleveland."[15] He added that neither he nor Selke had run into any interference from Bickle or MacBrien, and there was plenty of scouting work for Walker if he wanted it.

Smythe showed no particular hostility toward Selke in the months after his return, but a critical moment came in late 1945. The Leafs were fast playing themselves out of contention and Smythe was feeling the effect of his wounds. He'd been in and out of hospital and had recently been ordered by his doctor to take a rest. His mood was dark and aggravated by renewed frustration over his position at the Gardens. He felt that for too long he'd been taking orders from Bickle, MacBrien, and Cottrelle, people who knew far less about the game of hockey than he did, and was determined to force a change. He wanted to be named president.

Success wasn't guaranteed. He owned the shares he'd purchased when the Gardens was launched, plus additional stock he'd bought since then, but remained just one of many small shareholders. While he had supporters on the board, wealthy men don't like to be told what to do, and his habit of barking at people had annoyed any number of potential allies. When he approached directors and outlined his plan, some reacted with surprise and pointed out that MacBrien was expected to succeed Bickle when the time came. Realizing he might have to force a vote on the issue, he stepped up his stock-purchasing efforts, and near the end of the year he called Selke into his office and asked for his support. Selke still held the shares he'd mortgaged his house to buy in 1931. It wasn't much of a holding, but Smythe needed whatever he could get. Selke was reluctant to commit. He'd worked congenially enough with Bickle and MacBrien in Smythe's absence and wasn't interested in getting caught in a civil war between them and Smythe. It was a reasonable enough position – no matter who won the show-down, Selke would have to get along with them, and taking sides wasn't likely to make that any easier. But Smythe didn't approach corporate politics any more gently than he did NHL hockey and warned Selke in blunt language that he was heading for trouble.

"You're making a big mistake, Frankie. I'm going to be president here inside a year or two and if I get it without your help or votes then it would pretty well prove that I don't need you, wouldn't you say?"[16]

But his assistant wouldn't budge, and not long after – with the Leafs floundering toward their first season out of the playoffs in fifteen years – Smythe began giving a series of interviews denigrating the quality of the team. He didn't mention Selke by name, but they were plainly aimed at him and his handling of the club in the war years. He turned to Andy Lytle first, bemoaning that trying to run the Leafs was like trying to drive a five-year-old car that hadn't been properly maintained.

"As the scoring records eloquently show, Leafs no longer possess the necessary class," Lytle noted, choosing words that sounded like they'd come directly from Smythe. "Not since the Gardens was built and Smythe began soaring towards the heights has the quality of material been so low. From the heights to the nadir in one season is a perilously long fall . . . There is much deadwood to be struck from the club strength, and the explorers of this material scarcely know where to search for good replacements."[17]

A month later, with the team officially out of the playoffs, Smythe told reporter Joe Perlove the defence had been "putrid."[18] "To me it looked like some of our veterans had been sucked dry by their efforts during the war years," he said. He noted only eight players on the team had positive plus/minus records, meaning they'd been on the ice for more goals scored by the Leafs than were scored against them. It was a hint of the extensive record-keeping Smythe was already involved in, years before others in the league began obsessively keeping statistics. He could also quote figures for faceoffs won and lost and the "quality" of goals as opposed to the quantity. Thirteen players had negative records, and he didn't see any good young material in the pipeline to replace them. He could name just three players in the minors with real potential – Gus Mortson, Jimmy Thomson, and Joe Klukay, plus junior prospect Tod Sloan on the St. Michael's College junior team.

A week after unloading to Perlove, he told reporter Gordon Walker the team had been allowed to run down during the war. "We had no one feeding 'em in at the bottom for about five years. Our machine was good enough to run on its own power for four years, but it finally ran out of steam." He announced he'd begun putting in place "a perpetual-motion" player machine, which would develop new stars and feed them to the NHL team. It would take time though: he might need five years to right the wrongs that had taken place in his absence.[19]

The reporters weren't blind to Smythe's target, and neither was Selke. The charges against him carried little merit. The notion that he'd somehow ignored a rich crop of promising seventeen- and eighteen-year-old prospects while Smythe was away didn't take much inspection to be found wanting. The army had first call on healthy young men and hadn't missed many. The other teams were all in the same boat, and for the most part were in worse shape than Toronto, which could still boast of winning two Stanley Cups in the years Smythe alleged they were being mishandled. Selke, well aware of the problems the team would have finding young talent, had advocated a plan to begin recruiting prospects at a younger age – before the army could get its hands on them – and had in fact assembled a promising squad of youngsters who would serve the Leafs well in coming years. Smythe could also muster little beyond bluster when he sought to portray Selke as disloyal, his chief evidence being the deal for Ted Kennedy. Kennedy had quickly established his status as the rock on which future Leafs teams would be built, a natural successor to Apps. Eddolls, meanwhile, was on his way to an indifferent career that would end while Kennedy was still starring at the Gardens. Smythe managed somehow to loudly extol the virtues of Kennedy while simultaneously alleging that Selke had betrayed him by bringing the young star into the fold. The fact that Hap Day had been just as intimately involved in the Kennedy transaction was ignored.

Selke's refusal to pledge his shares had been the trigger for Smythe's outburst, but the conflict may have related as much to their very different personalities. Smythe was a straightforward, black-and-white, with-me-or-against-me type of person, who was comfortable dealing with people like Art Ross or Red Dutton or Jack Adams. Ross's way of settling a dispute was to take a swing at somebody and live with the consequences. If Adams thought a player was underperforming, he exiled him to the minors or hustled him out of the league. There was little room for niceties or the finer points of human relations in their approach, and it was an attitude Smythe understood and shared. Selke, on the other hand, sought to avoid confrontation or unnecessary conflict and didn't share Smythe's overwhelming need to issue instructions and have them obeyed. Ted Reeve, like most reporters, found him much easier to deal with than Smythe and called him "the personification of good will." "He just has that knack of making you feel that he is ready to help you and at his busiest seasons he was never too rushed to put his ability and his time at your disposal."[20]

Smythe looked on Selke's efforts at diplomacy with suspicion. He confessed to Walker that he didn't understand how Selke could happily operate as a No. 2, taking orders and carrying them out as commanded. He could never have survived in the kind of atmosphere he imposed on his subordinates.

Selke read his boss's comments in the paper and began making exit plans. He was interested in a hockey development in Cincinnati, where a group of investors was planning an arena modelled on Maple Leaf Gardens. There were other prospects in the United States as well. When he received a note from Smythe in May, demanding to be notified any time he left the building, he decided he'd had enough. He scribbled "Lincoln freed the slaves" on the memo and sent it back to Smythe as his resignation.[21] * He made no public announcement, but word quickly spread. Telephoned at home by reporters, Smythe was evasive. Hap Day conceded he'd heard some rumours, but nothing official. Eventually an enterprising reporter tracked down Selke in Buffalo, where he initially refused to comment, then conceded he'd handed in his resignation and had been persuaded by a remorseful Smythe to spend a week thinking about it.

---

* Smythe's memo wasn't the first or last time he'd insist on being notified when Gardens executives left the building. He had sent Selke a similar notice in 1940 and issued another in the early 1950s.

He did mull it over, but didn't change his mind. On May 31, 1946, a performance took place in Smythe's office that mirrored the one put on by the Rangers when they'd fired Smythe twenty years earlier, only this time it was Selke who had to stand there looking uncomfortable while pretending everyone was parting as friends.

"I would like to say I am leaving here on the best of terms with everybody," Selke insisted, to which Smythe responded, "Your job will be here any time you care to come back."[22]

Later on, Smythe added, "It's upsetting for me and I certainly wish Frank would change his mind." The *Globe*'s Jim Vipond noted that Selke was "a gentleman and a sportsman at all times" and a popular figure around the Gardens. When the *Montreal Star* announced six weeks later that Selke had been hired as general manager of the Canadiens, it assured readers that Smythe, "who is a sentimentalist and a great fellow no matter how you find him, was horrified when Selke resigned, but no amount of persuasion could make him change his mind."[23]

Smythe may indeed have regretted losing his loyal lieutenant. He was well aware that he made life difficult for many of the people who worked for him. The price for driving away a talented and effective ally would be the establishment in Montreal of one of the most potent Cup-winning machines the league would ever see. Many of Selke's ideas were vindicated with the Habs, where he set up a feeder system that would funnel stars to the NHL team while revamping and upgrading the Forum into a profitable, well-run operation that rekindled the city's love affair with the team. He and Smythe would eventually reconcile, but it would take years and saw them competing against each other as the leaders of two powerhouses rather than collaborating in what might have been a single overwhelming juggernaut.

PART FOUR

MOGUL

CHAPTER 16

A lbert Ernest Stafford Smythe died October 2, 1947. He
was eighty-five and had been ill for months. He had been
living in Hamilton in a small apartment with a house-
keeper, who wrote Smythe in July warning that his father was "very
feeble" and had suffered greatly during a recent heat wave:

> He was almost prostrate and I personally began to think it was almost
> more than I could manage. His knees would buckle up, his hands got
> stiff – feet swollen and his eyes running – altogether he was very help-
> less. . . . if the weather gets hot again as it very likely will I hate to think
> of the effect it will have on your father. . . . The doctor said the hand-
> writing is on the wall and it's just a matter of time.[1]

Albert's second wife, Jane, had died in 1940. For a time he'd shared
the apartment with Conn's half-sister Moira and her husband, Thomas
"Doc" Davis, after they married in 1941. Conn sent money every
month – $100 until the fall of 1945, when he raised it to $200. Albert,
Moira recalled, was as indifferent to financial matters as he'd ever
been. He'd add Conn's cheques to the pile of bills and magazines he
kept on a table, foraging for one when he needed it.[2] His estate came
to $1,192.78. He had $742 in one bank account, $193.37 in a second
account, an uncashed dividend cheque for $4 from Goodyear Tire and
Rubber, of which he owned one share, and various worthless shares in
a number of mining firms.

Wherever Conn got his blunt nature and drive for worldly success,
it hadn't come from his gentle, literary, contemplative father. Albert
lived surrounded by the immense library of books that had grown

without interruption throughout his life. There were thirty-five thousand volumes stuffed into the small apartment. In the room he used for an office they were three deep on the shelves lining the walls and piled in neat stacks on the floor, with a narrow path winding through to a "working" area consisting of two overturned orange crates. One held a typewriter, while he sat on the other to work. After the *World* folded in 1920, he'd continued his journalistic career with stints at several other newspapers, primarily in Hamilton. In 1945, when *The Canadian Theosophist* issued a special edition to mark Albert's sixtieth year of service, the *Hamilton Spectator* remarked that he had "established his merits as a journalist of exceptional ability and force" and that his poetry had "won the highest praise from the discerning." He was a recognized authority on the works of Charles Dickens and president of Toronto's Dickens Fellowship for several years.

J.V. McAree, a respected Toronto columnist, wrote: "Like most of us in the newspaper work he had his periods of good and ill fortune. But he never complained. When he told me of some disappointment, some harsh blow of fate, he always smiled. Life, apparently, was turning out much as he had expected; and he had spiritual reserves of strength and buoyancy which made him imperturbable."[3]

After Moira moved out Albert had considered marrying again, if only for the help he needed around the house, but Conn had put a halt to any such thoughts. He considered the woman Albert had in mind wholly unsuitable and wasn't going to stand for it. "Why don't you try living together for a year?' he suggested disingenuously. He hired an agent to go through Albert's belongings after his death and received an awestruck report on the volume of his correspondence: "The letters, of which there are millions, seem to be all personal. I don't think he ever threw anything away, so although we kept a careful eye out for hidden treasure, anything that looked legal or valuable, we junked everything except the enclosed handful."[4]

Conn signed his share of the modest estate over to Moira, except for some bits of furniture for Hugh and Stafford and a few letters. Some of

Albert's books and documents were taken by McMaster University for its archives, others by the Toronto Theosophical Society. Most of the rest were donated to a Hamilton veterans' organization.

Death prevented Albert from seeing his son finally reach the peak of his hockey and business ambitions, which Conn achieved less than two months after his father's cremation. In November, he was named president of Maple Leaf Gardens, with responsibility for overall operations while retaining his titles as managing director of the arena and general manager of the team. Whether Albert would have been impressed is open to question, but for Conn it was a triumphant moment, the victory he'd predicted more than a year earlier when he'd asked Frank Selke to pledge his shares.

It was, said the *Globe*, "a new pinnacle in a storybook hockey career . . . What might be termed 'The Smythe Story' in the nature of a Horatio Alger Jr. sports saga."[5] Smythe downplayed the change, after having manoeuvred for it so fervently. "It's nice, but little will be altered except that as president I will be able to undertake anything that Managing Director Conn wishes to do simply by asking Smythe for the presidential okay."[6]

In truth, a great deal had changed. It had been twenty years since he'd put together the purchase of the St. Patricks and fifteen since he'd built Maple Leaf Gardens, but Smythe was finally his own boss. Ed Bickle had been pushed from the job, Smythe ally George McCullagh had been installed as vice-president, and Bill MacBrien had been kicked upstairs as chairman of the board. Smythe was the power, in reality as well as perception, at last.

His victory had been delivered by two men. J.P. Bickell, whose stature gave him clout beyond his official position as a director, had used it on Smythe's behalf once again. And stockbroker Percy Gardiner had sold him thirty thousand shares at $10 each, enough to exercise control. It was an astonishingly generous act: Gardens shares had risen from 50 cents apiece in the mid 1930s to as high as $100 before splitting four-to-one. At the time of the offer they were around

$20, which meant Smythe was getting them at 50 per cent off. Even at that price he lacked the required $300,000, so Gardiner took a down payment and let him retire the rest of the debt over time. Not surprisingly, Smythe expressed his deep admiration and gratitude to Gardiner, "for quietly and calmly believing in me. He and Jack Bickell were the best friends I ever had."[7]

On the day his elevation was announced, the Gardens reported a profit of $190,000, an increase of $55,000 over the previous year and by far the best year it had ever enjoyed. Net income had doubled in two years and was now four times what it had been a decade earlier. Close to $1 million had been applied to the original mortgage, and Leafs tickets had become such a sought-after commodity not a single seat would go unsold for the next twenty years.

It was the start of a period many considered the greatest in the club's history. It was certainly the most successful of Smythe's career and came closest to producing the type of sports colossus he had hoped to build. From 1947 to 1951, the Leafs would win four Stanley Cups. Although they dominated regular-season play only once during that period, Leaf fans came to take for granted the annual march on the championship and the luxury of knowing that, come April, their heroes were almost certain to find a way to have their names inscribed again on the trophy's silver bands.

They accomplished it, moreover, with teams that more closely reflected Smythe's personal hockey ideals than any previously had. The great Leaf teams of the 1930s – of Conacher, Clancy, and Jackson – had flash and pizzazz. They were young and colourful and carefree. They piled up scoring records and personal awards, but just a single Stanley Cup. The club he would begin assembling in the summer of 1946 had none of the dazzle or daring of the earlier teams. Its biggest stars – Syl Apps and Ted Kennedy – were modest, hardworking team players who led through example. No one would mistake them for Rocket Richard or Gordie Howe, but they had the kind of grit and gristle that Smythe prized and were surrounded by a diligent supporting crew of crashers and bangers, pluggers and checkers, who rarely threatened the upper reaches of the scoring charts, but had a way of besting teams boasting bigger and brighter stars. Montreal had its Punch Line – Richard, Lach, and Blake – and in 1947 Detroit assembled the Production Line of Howe, Sid Abel, and Ted Lindsay, but only once over the next five years was either team able to halt Toronto's annual assault on the Stanley Cup.

Both Apps and Kennedy had the "bloodlines" their boss prized. They were cut from the same mould: honest and upright, with old-fashioned values and unflagging loyalty to the team. Neither touched stimulants of any sort. More than once Smythe would introduce Apps proudly as "our captain, who does not smoke or drink."[8] Kennedy was similarly abstemious, avoiding the get-togethers of younger players where beer or cigarettes were likely to be consumed. It seemed almost fanciful that, later in life when he went into politics, Apps was made minister of corrections. He was put in charge of jails and criminals – a man who simply didn't break rules found himself responsible for dealing with people who broke them regularly and who couldn't imagine the sort of clean-cut existence he personified.

Other players looked up to them for their natural leadership qualities; when Apps decided to retire – despite appeals from Smythe – it was taken for granted Kennedy would succeed him as captain. Teeder didn't have Apps's finesse. He was not a pretty skater – he seemed to struggle up the ice rather than glide the way skilled skaters did. He led the team in scoring just once, got little attention when it came to picking all-stars, and won the Hart Trophy late in his career thanks mainly to Smythe's fervent arm-twisting. The league's chronic refusal to recognize the qualities he saw in Kennedy so annoyed Smythe that he introduced his own trophy, the J.P. Bickell Memorial Award, mainly so he could give it to Kennedy.*

---

* Smythe felt Syl Apps's retirement at age thirty-three cost Kennedy several years off his career. He played twelve full seasons, all with Toronto, but retired at thirty, "worn down" by his responsibilities and the intensity of his work ethic.

With Apps and Kennedy as the foundation – and the ever-reliable Turk Broda in net – what he needed was some bricks to erect around them. A month or so after his blow-up with Selke in 1946, Smythe retreated to his cottage with Hugh to perform his usual autopsy on the season. Hugh Smythe recalls the ensuing weeks as an extended monologue as his father wrestled with himself over the team's future. There was no debating that the season had been a failure. The issue was what to do about it. An argument could be made for standing pat. Half a dozen players on the roster had just returned from war service and needed time to get their edge back. Kennedy had been hurt most of the season. The uncertainty in goal had left them deep in a hole well before the season was two months old. Pratt's suspension had been an unfortunate distraction. All in all, Smythe could have written it off as a sub-par season by an above-par team and satisfied himself with a few tweaks and adjustments.

Hugh listened to his father analyze the situation day after day. "His way of solving problems would be to suggest a solution to himself and then argue with himself and talk himself out of it, and do that over and over and over again."[9]

Nonetheless, the results caught him by surprise. Smythe had decided to dismantle the team and rebuild it with youth. Sweeney Schriner and Lorne Carr had retired, along with Bob Davidson, a defensive-minded forward who had filled in as captain while Apps was in the military. Mel Hill and Ernie Dickens were demoted to Pittsburgh, Billy Taylor shipped to Detroit for Harry Watson, and Babe Pratt exiled to Boston. The decision to dump Pratt was probably the most difficult, as Smythe still considered him a top-quality defenceman. But Pratt enjoyed life far too much for the staid Maple Leafs – Hap Day had concluded the only way to control his nocturnal activities was to room with Pratt himself – and the betting controversy the previous season had been the kiss of death as far as Smythe was concerned. It seemed to take something out of Pratt too. He played just part of one season with Boston before finishing out his career in the minors.

In place of the veterans, Smythe installed a package of eager young players that included Watson, Bill Ezinicki, Howie Meeker, Gus Mortson, Jimmy Thomson, Bill Barilko, Sid Smith, and Joe Klukay. Watson and Klukay were the eldest of the group, at twenty-three. Meeker was twenty-two, Smith and Mortson twenty-one, while Barilko and Thomson were just nineteen. His father, according to Hugh, hadn't talked about any of these moves during his one-man debate.

As he had in 1926, he gathered his rookies from all over Canada. They came mostly from small towns, farms, and northern communities where hockey began with the first freeze and didn't let up until the last, disappointing thaw. Their fathers were mechanics, farmers, gas jockeys, miners. They came from big families – six or seven kids wasn't unusual – and their schooling was limited.

Barilko was born in a mining camp near Timmins, the son of Polish immigrants, and never wanted to be anything but a hockey player. He learned his game at the McIntyre Arena, built by J.P. Bickell, who made much of his fortune from the nearby McIntyre mine and felt the miners deserved an arena as grand as Maple Leaf Gardens was to Toronto.[10] Barilko was such a poor skater as a kid he was forced by the other kids to play goal, just as Charlie Conacher had been as a boy. But he blossomed into both a skilled skater and devastating bodychecker who hammered opponents with enthusiasm.[11]

Ezinicki came from a family of six kids born to a Winnipeg mechanic and his wife. While Barilko threw himself at anything that moved, Ezinicki treated bodychecking like a science, setting up his crushing collisions with careful calculation. Together he and Barilko terrorized the league, joined by Gus Mortson and Jimmy Thomson, who became known as the "Gold Dust Twins" and gave the Leafs the four most fearsome hitters of the era, all together on one team.

Thomson was also from Winnipeg and was just nineteen when he made the Leafs after two years with the St. Michael's Majors and a season in Pittsburgh. Mortson also played at St. Mike's, as did his friend Ted Lindsay. Mortson and Lindsay arrived at the school

together from Kirkland Lake, where a friendly priest had organized a scholarship to the Catholic boys' school so the two could
keep playing hockey after they'd exhausted the best local leagues
could offer.[12]

The son of a railway worker, Mortson would run up 1,380 minutes
in penalties in 797 games over twelve years, 300 more minutes than
"Terrible Ted" would accumulate over seventeen seasons. Although
Mortson and Lindsay were friends off the ice, on skates they gave no
quarter. Once, in a game against Detroit, Lindsay was heading into the
Toronto end with the puck when Mortson clotheslined him. Lindsay
went down, but there was no penalty call, and when a Detroit player
was called for retaliation moments later all hell broke loose, with even
Broda and Detroit goalie Harry Lumley rolling around at centre ice
like two big overstuffed bears. Unable to land a blow, Broda bit Lumley
on the cheek.[13]

In the five years up to 1951, Toronto could claim the most penal-
ized player in the league every season. Twice Mortson led the list,
twice Ezinicki, and once Barilko They were as fearsome a group as
was ever assembled in the NHL, regularly going up against the biggest
and meanest players on the opposing teams. Barilko was once responsible for two opposing players being carted off the ice on stretchers in
a single game.[14] In a match in New York, Meeker and Mortson got
into a punching match with Rangers coach Lynn Patrick in a corridor,
which ended with fans and players alike in the brawl.[15]

Meeker was one of five boys born to Charlie Meeker and his wife,
Kitty, a war bride Charlie met while serving in England. Charlie
owned a truck and sold soda pop and ice cream around the Kitchener
area. Howie, like other boys, played hockey all the time, working
his way through teams in Brantford, Kitchener, and Stratford before
joining the army and almost losing his life when someone tossed a
live grenade between his legs during a training exercise. Not only
did he survive the explosion but he worked his way back into such
excellent shape he was able to return to hockey after the war and

was playing for the Stratford Indians in the senior OHA when the Leafs signed him to a free agent contract in 1946.[16]

Sid Smith was the city boy in the group, raised in Toronto's Christie Pits neighbourhood. NHL teams weren't required to notify players they had placed on their negotiating list, and often didn't bother, so Smith had no idea the Leafs had their eye on him. He rose from the Oshawa Generals to the Hershey Bears in the AHL, and later joined the Quebec Aces, where he got drunk one night with teammate Punch Imlach, stunk the joint out the next night in a 9–0 loss, and was promptly signed by the Leafs.[17] His first two years were divided between Toronto and Pittsburgh. Called up for a couple of games in the playoffs in 1948, he tore his knee ligaments, but returned to the game after Smythe ignored the doctor's protests and ordered the knee frozen. Smythe got his way, but it cost Smith a summer of rehabilitation and a season in the minors before he got another chance with the Leafs.[18]

He didn't protest, of course. The players never protested. They could be benched, traded, released, or sent back to the minors in the blink of an eye, and there was nothing they could do about it. They called their boss "Mr. Smythe" or "the Major" – then and later – and they didn't argue with him. They could be disciplined for so much as a pleasant comment to an opposing player – that would be "fraternizing" and was a mortal sin. They could be sent down if they caught the flu and had a few bad games. They could be disciplined if overheard making snide remarks or failing to accept the Major's criticism in the approved manner, which meant keeping their mouths shut and doing what they were told.

Not only did they not complain, many admired Smythe for his passion and will to win. Kennedy considered Smythe a great Canadian. Ezinicki welcomed the intense discipline of the Leafs, which began in training camp and continued right through the season. To him, it was the mark of a team that took the game seriously. Joe Klukay, who joined the Leafs that year and stayed through all four Stanley Cups, was eventually traded away by Smythe, but wrote him an admiring letter a few years afterwards: "I realize now, looking back over the years, that the decisions you made regarding my hockey future were to my advantage and I am convinced now that on . . . one occasion you were solely responsible for keeping me in the NHL."[19]

Looking over his team of rookies, Smythe calculated they were two to three years from being competitive. He guessed wrong. The Leafs lost just one game in their first eleven, put together a six-game win streak in December, pummelled Chicago 11–0 in one game and 12–4 in another, then survived a mid-season slump to finish the regular season in second place, just six points back of Montreal. Despite Hap Day's defensive focus, they led the league in scoring.

They defeated Detroit handily in the semifinals, advancing to the finals against Montreal, which had won the previous year's Cup and topped the league in the regular season thanks to the miserly goal-tending of Bill Durnan, who allowed thirty-five fewer goals than the next best team. Toronto was blown away 6–0 in the first game, after which someone claimed Durnan had made a slighting remark, wondering what a team as bad as the Leafs was doing in the playoffs. Durnan insisted he never said it, but Smythe didn't care – it was just the ammunition he needed to build a fire under his team.

He was famed for his locker-room tirades, which consisted of furious harangues designed to send the players to the ice determined to prove him wrong. He'd performed his act any number of times – King Clancy and Dick Irvin both had memories of Smythe blasting players mercilessly before games or between periods – and he pulled it out of his repertoire again as his team prepared for Game Two. Meeker recalled him marching in, only the second time that season he'd made a dressing-room appearance. Hands on his hips, eyes burning, he proceeded to dress them down, one at a time. He started with Apps and Kennedy, the men he admired most, tearing a strip off them for their failure to perform as Toronto Maple Leafs were meant to perform. Then he went around the room subjecting each player in turn to a menu of their failures.

As usual, it worked. While a later generation of players might have been texting protests to their agents, the Leafs took it as an assault on their pride and could barely wait to get out the door.[20] They were leading by two goals before the first shift had ended and even a fevered effort by Rocket Richard – he felled two Leafs with sticks to the head, earning himself a one-game suspension and $250 fine – couldn't save Montreal from a 4–0 loss and critical shift in momentum. Toronto won the next two games at home, lost one in Montreal, and then won the sixth and deciding game at home, with Day sending out five of his youngest players in the final moments to face a team of seasoned Montreal sharpshooters.[21] Oddly, there was no Cup to present to the winners. It was still in Montreal, where it had been on hand for the previous game. Smythe had insisted it be left behind for fear that moving it would give the papers an excuse to accuse him of overconfidence and provide a lift to the Habs.[22]

The victory was especially enjoyable, in a vindictive sort of way, because it pitted the Leafs' new management against its old, Smythe and Day emerging triumphant over Selke and Irvin. Selke, as he was the first to admit, had learned a great deal by understudying Smythe for so long, and he had put it into immediate practice after taking over the Canadiens. He made dramatic changes to the Forum, transforming it from a dank, dour, depressing old pit into something resembling a hockey arena. The day he walked in to discuss his contract, he related, the first thing he noticed was the smell of urine. He cleaned up the toilets, ripped out the cheap seats that ensured even a full house barely produced a profit, and expanded and upgraded the seating. "You'd hardly know the Forum today," marvelled one of the Toronto reporters. "Posh box seats done in leather for the nicest people, extra seats hung from the ceiling beams, cheery, polite and efficient ushers; plexiglas back of both goals, no bums biting you in the alleyways . . ."[23] He went on a Smythe-like painting binge, covering up the monotonous brown paint the previous management had slathered on everything. He came up with a novel plan for selling tickets, offering six-game packages that included at least one game against every other team in the league, and, along with Irvin, suggested a plan to introduce a two-referee system that would eventually be adopted . . . about six decades later. He also managed to re-sign all the major players from the previous year's Stanley Cup team with minimal drama, demonstrating a capacity for winning over players that would mark his years with the Habs.

Before the season started he was already being hailed for his innovations. "This city is hockey crazy again," noted a Montreal columnist, adding, "His old Toronto buddies who were prone to discount him have found a foeman worthy of their steel."[24]

Selke had long admired Smythe's capacity for theatrics and had a stab at turning it against the master himself. He started a needling contest before the season even began, accusing his old boss of training his rookies as goons. "Conny Smythe has those young fellows on the Leafs all pepped up to go out and roughhouse," he complained.[25] "They're banging other players into the boards, holding, and charging after play has stopped. They're being turned into 'killers' on order." He threatened to film games to produce evidence of the Leafs' "crude wrestling tactics."

Smythe wasn't about to fall for guff like that from his former assistant. He brushed off Selke's charges as "piffle,"[26] but both Selke and Irvin kept at it. When Elmer Lach suffered a fractured skull after a collision with Don Metz near the end of the season, Irvin sought to turn it into a crusade on behalf of the wounded Hab, claiming on the first night of the playoffs that "the boys were playing this one – and the rest of the series – for Elmer Lach."[27]

The tactic didn't work. Toronto papers dismissed it as "malarkey," and criticized Irvin for running up the score in the first game. "He wasn't satisfied merely to win – he wanted to win by 20," Joe Perlove wrote.[28] Richard's stick attacks on Vic Lynn and Bill Ezinicki only succeeded in forcing his team to play the third game without him. Lynn was especially badly wounded and had been carried off the ice "leaving a trail of blood from the scene of the crime."[29]

Satisfying as the Cup victory had been, Smythe wasn't finished with his reconstruction project. Early the next season, Gaye Stewart, one of the team's best goal scorers, was sitting in his car at Toronto's old Malton airport, waiting for his wife and their ten-week-old son to arrive from Port Arthur. It was a new car, and Stewart was taking his young family to a new apartment, having finally managed to find one in the tough postwar housing market.

Stewart already had his name on the Stanley Cup twice as a Leaf, plus a Calder Trophy as the league's best rookie. In their unhappy 1945 season he had led the team, and the league, in goals with thirty-seven, still the last Toronto Maple Leaf to accomplish that feat. He played on a line with Gus Bodnar and Bud Poile, who, like him, were from Fort William and were therefore known as the "Flying Forts," or, when they were off their game, the "Flying Farts." Listening to the radio as he killed time at the airport, Stewart learned he'd been traded to Chicago. Smythe, in fact, had traded the entire line, plus two defencemen, for Chicago's Max Bentley and one other player. Stewart had spent the afternoon getting the new apartment shipshape, and now he had to explain to his wife that she'd be going back to Port Arthur – which she did the next day – while he tried to get his deposit back from the landlady.[30]

There was some question about the wisdom of trading a thirty-seven-goal scorer, but Smythe pulled out his array of statistics to argue that Stewart's goals weren't the right kind. For some time he had been filming games and compiling the kind of records that wouldn't become commonplace for another generation or more, and he insisted that Stewart scored too many goals against teams that weren't a threat or in games that weren't in doubt. Stewart, of course, didn't argue. He was making $3,500 and the team only paid one fare to Chicago. His family's fare was his problem.

The trade wasn't a surprise to everyone. Just the week before, Smythe and Chicago's Bill Tobin had confirmed they'd been discussing a deal. "I offered Tobin five, not four, players for one of the Bentleys and as I cannot tell the brothers apart I told Hap Day to pick," Smythe had joked.[31] Tobin confirmed Smythe's offer, but wasn't sure whether he was serious – at one point the Leafs boss declared he'd trade Tobin a whole team for Max Bentley.

There was no dispute that Bentley was a prize catch. He'd led the league in scoring two years in a row and Tobin had promised him a new Cadillac if he could make it three (sportingly pledging to keep his promise even if Bentley ended up doing it for the Leafs.) Adding him to Apps and Kennedy gave the Leafs a depth no other team could match. Bentley had won the Hart Trophy the previous season, but Toronto was so strong up the middle he was named to centre the third line. Just five-foot-nine and less than 160 pounds, Bentley was from Delisle, Saskatchewan, and was never really at home anywhere else. The Bentleys had thirteen kids, and Max and his equally talented brother Doug were the youngest.

Bentley didn't look like a star. Even in his official photographs he never looked robust. During a tryout with the Canadiens as a sixteen-year-old he was sent to see a doctor, who told him he was in no condition for a hockey career and should go home if he wanted a long life.[32] In Toronto he was plagued by mysterious ailments and sometimes had to be talked into playing. Though well paid, he lived in a room under a stairway in a nearby hotel, which was owned by a Leafs enthusiast who offered its use for free. "It was a sordid existence, it was awful," said Hugh Smythe. "If you had any tendency toward depression, then this would make it worse."[33] But he was a whirlwind on the ice, and for the next four years Bentley was a reliable offensive force as the Leafs racked up Cup after Cup.

Bentley's addition cemented the lineup, the core of which remained largely the same over the next four years, other than the addition of Cal Gardner when Apps retired and the emergence of Sid Smith and Tod Sloan as solid offensive threats. It wasn't an all-star lineup. In the five years the Leafs dominated the league, only Broda and Mortson were ever named to the first all-star team – once each. Broda and Al Rollins each won a Vezina, but the only other individual award was Meeker's rookie-of-the-year nod in 1947. Only in penalty minutes did the Leafs consistently stand out. The all-star selections in those years were the private domain of Montreal and Detroit, yet it was the Leafs who usually walked away the winners. Twice each they faced Detroit and Montreal in the finals, emerging with the Cup each time. Only once, against Detroit in the semifinals in 1950, did they come up short.

They kept finding different ways to win. In 1947, it had been the Year of the Rookies. In 1948, it was the March of the Champions, as the Leafs placed first in the regular-season standings and lost just one game out of nine as they swept through Boston and Detroit. It was Apps's last season, and with him, Kennedy, and Bentley all enjoying excellent seasons, 1948 may have been the finest Leafs team ever to take the ice.

The next spring they barely made the playoffs, losing more games than they won, giving up more goals than they scored, and finishing fourth, eighteen points behind first-place Detroit. Fortunately something – fear of Smythe, perhaps – woke them up in the playoffs, and once again they polished off Boston and Detroit in efficient order, winning eight out of nine and sweeping the finals in four straight.

The one season they failed to win, in 1949–50, was in many ways the most eventful of all. Over the summer Smythe had all but bludgeoned the other NHL owners into agreeing to add ten games to the sixty-game schedule, facing down protests that the additional workload would be too much of a strain on players, weakening play and adding to injuries.

He had also faced down a complaint by a Toronto city politician who was upset when he shifted the city's supply of free tickets from the expensive red seats to the less expensive blues. "If the controller doesn't appreciate a free blue seat, it's not only possible, it's quite probable, he won't get any free seats at all," Smythe snapped.[34]

In January he was declared the most dominant personality in Canadian sports, a title awarded after a poll of sports editors by Canadian Press. It was the first time the editors had been asked to pick a single person who topped the sports world "in any capacity," and Smythe won handily over Montreal's Grey Cup–winning quarterback Frankie Filchock and third-place Rocket Richard.

But perhaps best of all, Smythe had captivated the city for a week, and provided its sports editors with the kind of fun they rarely enjoyed, when he declared in November he was fed up with running "a fat man's team" and gave a handful of players a week to shed some pounds.

It proved to be one of his most successful publicity stunts ever, simultaneously shaking up the team, delighting headline writers, galvanizing fans, and diverting attention from the team's sorry record. The Gardens sold every seat to every game anyway, but if Smythe could have doubled capacity for that week he would have had little trouble filling them.

The main focus of attention was Turk Broda, the cheerful, easygoing, and chronically chubby goaltender. Broda blithely ignored Smythe's dislike of alcohol and tobacco. He liked to smoke *and* drink, sneaking a smoke before the game and drinking too much after. Once during a night out with Max Bentley he got so drunk he fell down some stairs and spent the next week pretending to have the flu to explain away the aches and pains.[35] Smythe tolerated his lapses because Broda played nerveless goal, always coming up big when the season was on the line.

In late November, however, the Leafs were floundering around aimlessly, and Smythe set out to shake them from their stupor. "SMYTHE READS THE RIOT ACT," the paper said. "BRODA BENCHED IN FAVOR OF MAYER; OTHER OVERWEIGHT PLAYERS WARNED."[36] "The fiery [Smythe], in a history-making action, blasted 'the fat men on the team,' benched goalie Turk Broda, and issued a conditioning ultimatum to four others," the story read. "Besides hockey's fabulous fat man [Broda], Smythe's 'reduce and produce' blast was aimed at Harry Watson, Garth Boesch, Vic Lynn and Sid Smith."

The story was accompanied by a photo of a furtive-looking Broda at a lunch counter, tucking into a sandwich despite the ultimatum.

He was ordered to lose seven of his 197 pounds and told he wouldn't play another game until he did. It was a harsh blow: since taking over from George Hainsworth in 1936, Broda had played every game but one, other than during the war years when he was in uniform. Smythe called up a nineteen-year-old from Pittsburgh, Gil Mayer, to face the Red Wings the next night, and acquired Al Rollins, yet another netminder, from the Cleveland Barons.

Broda's genial nature made him a natural newspaper target: he was more than willing to go along with a gag, even if he was the butt of it. The newspapers didn't spell it out, but Broda wasn't considered the brightest of Leafs. He had no more than a grade school education, and when not playing hockey held down menial jobs, filling his summers labouring at Smythe's sand pit, having bought a house nearby. He often performed poorly in warm-ups and unimportant games, finding it difficult to muster the focus required. Unless the contest meant something he could appear lethargic and uninterested, coming to life when money or a championship was on the line. He was always at his best in the playoffs, no matter how mediocre the season had been. The excitement, Smythe joked, "moves him all the way up to normal."[37]

Reporters took full advantage, treating Broda's humiliation as front page news. The *Star* interviewed his petite, pretty blonde wife, Betty – or "Mrs. Turk," as they identified her – on his eating habits and revealed that he wasn't much of a chowhound to begin with. "He hardly eats a darn thing," she lamented. Seldom ate breakfast, no desserts, not keen on potatoes. "He likes milk, and I guess we'll have to cut that off, or get skim."[38]

Both papers followed him to the gym, the *Star* devoting the better part of a page to a gallery of photos showing "the Turkey" touching his toes, riding a bike, getting a massage, sweating it out in a sauna swathed in towels, and stretching the telltale measuring tape around his middle. Mrs. Turk reported he was surviving on a boiled egg and coffee, no milk. Reporters consulted local experts for dietary advice. Reporter Joe Perlove confessed that after due consideration he'd concluded that Turk's best bet was amputation. The *Globe* approached a "prominent Toronto nutritionist" who disclosed solemnly that "overweight is caused solely by eating more food than is needed." Exercise would be futile, he added, as it only increased the appetite.[39] Shopsy's Deli took out an ad with the tagline "For that 'Old Broda' look, Eat at Shopsy's."

Young Gil Mayer went down to a 2–0 defeat in his single game as fill-in. He played well enough, but got little help as the Leafs directed just eighteen shots at Detroit's Harry Lumley, who newsmen delighted in noting was a fairly chubby fellow himself.

The next day Broda survived an official weigh-in, and the *Star* rushed out an afternoon edition with the headline "Broda Gets Down to 189 Pounds." The story was picked up across the country, the ever-cooperative netminder agreeing to pose, wearing only his white boxer underwear, seated cross-legged on a scale. The *Star* reported that Broda, "proprietor of the most famous fast since Gandhi," would be back for Saturday's game.[40] "Emaciated Broda Returns to Nets Against Rangers," joked the *Globe*.[41]

Smythe's stunt was a spectacular success, no matter how you looked at it. The crowd for the single Broda-less game was 14,015, well over the official capacity, for a mid-week game featuring a team playing mediocre hockey with an unknown goalie. Back on the job, Broda unrolled a four-game winning streak, then eased off again before ending the year with a strong finish.

With their vigour renewed, Leafs players fully expected to add another Cup to the trophy case. They worked their way up to third place in the final standings and faced Detroit in the semifinals, confident they could once again spoil the Red Wings' season for them.

They almost did, and Ted Kennedy remained convinced ever after that they would have succeeded if not for an incident involving him and Gordie Howe that gave the Wings an extra burst of determination.

Labouring up the wing in his usual style in game one, Kennedy spotted Howe barrelling at him with nothing pleasant in mind.

According to Kennedy, the referee already had his hand up to call a penalty, whether for charging or boarding would depend on exactly where Kennedy was located when Howe pulverized him. The Leafs captain managed to pull up short, though, and Howe went headfirst into the boards, fracturing his skull and breaking his nose and cheekbone. Howe lay in hospital in critical condition for days, his life and career both in jeopardy. The Leafs won the game, but Wings manager Jack Adams used Howe's injury just the way Smythe would have, falsely accusing Kennedy of deliberately trying to injure his star.

The next game deteriorated into a three-period brawl that produced a warning from new league president Clarence Campbell to tone things down. Even with the Wings all worked up over the injury, the Leafs almost pulled it off. The series went seven games and Toronto led 3–2 going into the sixth, but lost both that game and the next, surrendering the Cup in a match in which the only goal was scored in overtime.

They made up for the disappointment the next season, the year in which Barilko scored the Cup-winning goal in one of the most storied moments in the team's history.

In terms of team performance it was a better season all-around. Smythe promoted Day to assistant general manager and lured Joe Primeau into replacing him as coach. The team started strong, and by the new year had twenty wins and just nine losses. Tod Sloan, Sid Smith, Ted Kennedy, and Max Bentley all cracked the league's top-ten scorers, with Sloan and Smith both notching more than thirty goals. Only Gordie Howe and Rocket Richard scored more.

The Leafs were a close-knit team, the young players getting together regularly for drinks, dinner, and sometimes dancing with their wives and girlfriends. They favoured the Orchard Park Tavern across from the Greenwood racetrack for drinks[42] or the Old Mill in Etobicoke for more elegant evenings. After one of their Stanley Cup victories, Howie Meeker threw a legendary party at his apartment that ended with police fetching more cases of beer at dawn when the supply had run out.

Barilko was popular, cheerful, good-looking, and outgoing. He had a passion for clothes that his budget couldn't keep up with. In 1949, he and his brother had opened a store on the Danforth, the grand opening thick with fellow Maple Leafs. The Smythe family bought their first television set from Barilko Brothers Appliances.[43] Smythe liked Barilko, even though he constantly broke Primeau's demands that he stay in position. To Smythe he had all the flair and excitement of Busher Jackson, without the personal problems.[44]

He struggled during the early part of the season, though, and Smythe shook up the cozy atmosphere when he sent Ezinicki to Boston in return for Fern Flaman, in a deal that traded one of the league's fiercest checkers for a player who was, if anything, even more violent. For the next two seasons Flaman joined the coterie of the NHL's highest-penalized players, which the Leafs had been dominating for years. Smythe jolted the players further when he demoted utility centre Johnny McCormack to the minors for the crime of getting married in mid-season. McCormack and his bride were wed on a Tuesday morning in January; when McCormack showed up for practice the next day, Primeau told him to be on the next train to Pittsburgh.*

Naturally, he didn't argue. He just phoned his wife at their new apartment and told her to pack. "What could I say but tell John I was going with him?" she said.[45] †

McCormack claimed he didn't know there was a team rule against

---

* Only two players would ever have their numbers "retired" by the Leafs, as opposed to "honoured" – Ace Bailey and Bill Barilko. Significantly, neither was recognized strictly for their hockey performance but for events Smythe viewed as having a larger significance. Bailey almost gave his life on the ice; Barilko lost his after delivering a Stanley Cup to the team.

† Although he had enormous control over the players' lives, Smythe didn't always treat them cavalierly. When he traded Wally Stanowski for Cal Gardner, just weeks after declaring that Stanowski was a fixture with the team, he announced that under the circumstances Stanowski should have the option of rejecting the trade. Stanowski welcomed the opportunity to go to New York, and Smythe let him negotiate his own agreement with the Rangers (*Globe and Mail,* April 27, 1948).

mid-season weddings. Obligingly, the *Star*'s Milt Dunnell laid out the facts of life in Leafland:

> The rules are simple. Aside from what you wear, what you say, what you eat, what you drink, who you're with, where you're going, how much you weigh and what you think, the club has little, if any, interest in the hired help, outside working hours. There's one thing about it: The pay is good, and it's always on time. There's more civil liberty in digging a ditch. But most of these guys are in a rut. They still seem to prefer hockey."[46]

Barilko, who feared he was headed to the minors with McCormack, picked up his play and Toronto finished with forty-one wins in seventy games. Montreal knocked off first place Detroit in the semifinals, while Toronto defeated Boston. The finals pitted the Leafs against the Canadiens in a series Toronto won four games to one, but which was much tighter than the numbers suggest. Every game went to overtime. In the third period of the fifth game, Montreal was leading by a goal when Toronto pulled Al Rollins from the net for an extra attacker and tied the game with thirty-two seconds left. That set up one final overtime, the one in which Barilko – his awed mother watching from the stands – lifted a backhand over a stumbling Gerry McNeil in the Montreal net at 2:53 of the first sudden death period. The moment – flash-frozen in a famous photo of Barilko in mid-air and McNeil falling backwards – won the Leafs one more Stanley Cup.[47]

It was, of course, Barilko's last game. When his plane went down in Ontario's rugged northern bush country that summer a massive search was organized, but it was eleven years before his body was found, and eleven years before the Leafs won another Stanley Cup.

CHAPTER 17

The eminence conveyed by his selection as the country's most dominant sportsman seemed to set off a new phase in Smythe's public persona. The Toronto Maple Leafs were now a legitimate phenomenon: winners of four Stanley Cups in five years, a national passion that kept Canadians glued to their radios every Saturday night, and an overwhelming commercial success that sold out every game and had a lengthening backlog of applicants for its subscribers' list.

The list of season ticket holders had grown to more than ten thousand, meaning 75 per cent of the seats were gone by opening day. The Gardens was the league's most profitable rink, though far from the biggest. It was debt-free, and, from 1950, was in a position to begin paying regular dividends to shareholders, of which Smythe was the biggest.

A profile in *Life* magazine as the Leafs closed out the 1951 season labelled him "Puck's Bad Boy," the "boisterous boss of hockey's Maple Leafs" who overshadowed his players and dominated the league.

> For 23 years, without ever putting on a pair of skates, he has been the Toronto Maple Leafs' star attraction. Certainly no hockey player could begin to compete with him. He is an obstreperous little (5 feet, 7 inches) man whose actions clash violently with his attire. At a hockey game he feels undressed without his spats and pearl grey fedora imported especially from Italy. He wears a toothbrush moustache and sometimes carries a cane. Some critics describe him as 'a conglomeration of opposites, he is more a dead-end kid dressed up as Little Lord Fauntleroy.[1]

Other profilers offered similar glimpses of his many contradictions. He could be the prickliest man in hockey, or the most sentimental. "Conn Smythe never forgets an old friend. His gifts to the underprivileged are his personal affair, but there isn't a day passes by that he doesn't 'dig deep' to help somebody along the road of life," wrote Bunny Morganson at *The Hockey News*. "His outstanding charity is the Ontario Society for Crippled Children, which he serves as Honorary Treasurer. We have seen Smythe carry a crippled child into a banquet hall to receive a cheque for the Society, with tears streaming from his eyes."[2]

Trent Frayne, in a two-part feature in *Maclean's* magazine, dismantled the myth of Smythe as impulsive and impetuous. "Behind everything he does is a meticulous and calculating mind and away from public view, in the confines of his richly, though conservatively, appointed office on the second floor of the Gardens, he becomes as fussily efficient as a bookkeeper."[3]

Fans were told of his painstaking collection of player statistics, his charts and films, and his ability to keep a snapshot in his head of every goal, so he could recount later who was where, how the play had developed, and who had made the mistake. His employees feared but respected him. He liked golf, but didn't like a lot of idle chitchat on the course, and he personally tested the Gardens' hot dogs, even though he hated hot dogs.[4]

He also came in for harsh criticism. *Saturday Night* noted "a duality that no one has explained satisfactorily" in Smythe's attitude. Smythe "does as much as any other individual in Canada for unfortunate children and handicapped adults," it said, yet happily signed naive seventeen-year-olds to professional contracts that made them virtual wards of the Leafs, subject to arbitrary discipline or banishment.

It noted disapprovingly Smythe's pursuit of "monetary gain." Players earned more than they could outside hockey, but not nearly what they were worth. He pushed around the league with the same ease he bossed his players: "If Conn Smythe doesn't want to change the rules, it's a good bet that the rules won't be changed because while he is but one of six owners in the all-powerful NHL, he is certainly the most influential."[5] Ralph Allen, his one-time battery mate, wrote: "Most of Smythe's fellow magnates fear him as a competitor and dislike him personally, but in matters of league policy he is almost invariably able to carry their judgment."[6]

In general his treatment in the press was admiring but wary, noting that he was the kind of boss who could exile a player for getting married while demanding "loyalty" from those who remained. He was cold-hearted and calculating when it came to hockey, but his approach had produced a team that had missed the playoffs just once in eighteen years and was in the midst of an unprecedented run of Stanley Cups.

His work for the Crippled Children Society, as it was then known, began at the end of the 1946 season. He had promised himself, while lying injured in Europe, to do more to benefit the community, and the opportunity arose when an old friend invited him to serve as treasurer of the charity, figuring he could not only raise money but put its finances on a sounder footing. He did both with the usual Smythe fervour. At his first meeting, surveying the free lunch for out-of-town members, he informed them they could pay for their own food in the future.[7] He recruited many of the biggest names in Toronto business circles, organizing fundraising drives that brought in millions of dollars to what had been a fairly sleepy little charity. He posed with many of the children, though he admitted he didn't like the task. Tough in so many ways, he grew queasy in the presence of people, children or adults, with physical afflictions.

In 1948, with the support of Smythe and the Ontario Athletics Commission, the province introduced a 2 per cent charge on professional sports, with the revenue going to agencies "responsible for the care and training of crippled children." The fee would be charged against the gross receipts of any professional event. The bill also provided for a three-week vacation at camps to be set up around the province for "every crippled child in Ontario." An editorial in the

Globe and Mail commended Smythe for pushing through the new plan.

"In a very real sense it is a recognition of the energetic leadership which Mr. Conn Smythe, as financial chairman of the Ontario Society for Crippled Children, has given to the acceleration and expansion of the work among handicapped children," it said. The *Globe*, of course, was owned by Smythe's friend George McCullagh, who was also a Gardens director and owned a big block of shares. The premier was Smythe's other conservative ally, George Drew. And the chairman of the Ontario Athletics Commission happened to be Syl Apps.

Nonetheless, his enthusiasm was authentic and his charitable activities ballooned over the next decade, as he raised large sums of money, and gave away a healthy share of his own, to an expanding list of charities. Thanks to the postwar economic expansion, he had more money than ever to give. When he became president of the Gardens in 1947, his salary was raised to $25,000. His thirty-six thousand Maple Leaf Gardens shares, which grew to about fifty thousand by the decade's end, drew annual dividends that increased through the 1950s from 50 cents a share to $1.50. In 1947, Smythe had a plan drawn up under which he sold his shares to C. Smythe Ltd. in an arrangement that provided him an annual payment, but cut down on taxes. He also continued to receive an annual salary from C. Smythe. Both his major businesses, the Gardens and C. Smythe, increased markedly in value through the decade as both construction and hockey flourished. In November 1950, he announced the Gardens had made the final payment on all its loans, and "for the first time since its inception, the company is clear of debt." From then on, any profits it made, it got to keep, and profits were healthy, rising from $165,000 in 1950 to as high as $289,000 in 1956. Smythe had also been building an investment portfolio for years and had a healthy array of stocks and bonds, as did the Gardens.[8]

In addition to his vow to do good works, his brush with death had convinced him he should enjoy his wealth. The cottage where Patricia died was replaced by a bigger, more comfortable summer home not far away. He began buying up farmland in Caledon, a bucolic rural community in hilly terrain northwest of the city. He had no immediate plans for the land, though it was rich in aggregates and held obvious potential for expansion of his sand and gravel business or replacement of older pits. Through the late 1940s and 1950s he continued to buy, eventually assembling a block of 1,750 acres. It coincided with a renewed interest in horse breeding and racing, which developed through his friendship with Larkin Maloney.

Maloney had continued buying horses when Smythe temporarily shelved his activities during the war, including part ownership of a horse that won the 1955 Queen's Plate. Smythe began investing in horses purchased by Maloney, then branched out and began buying on his own. Together they soon owned more than a dozen horses, including a number bought from James D. Norris, who had inherited part of his father's sports empire when "Big Jim" died in 1952. Smythe set up a stable on some of his land in Caledon, where one of the horses he bought from Norris produced a colt Smythe named Caledon Beau. In 1958, Caledon Beau won Smythe a Queen's Plate of his own. His admiration for horses hadn't diminished. If anything it grew stronger as he wearied of the increasingly complicated world of hockey. Horses, as any number of Smythe critics were willing to point out, didn't argue back and didn't complain at the Olympian standards he set for them.

He loved spending time in the stables and with the working people who ran Woodbine racetrack, though he hated the grand "new" Woodbine built north of Toronto by E.P. Taylor, the emerging giant of Canadian business. He complained frequently – and directly to Taylor – that it had been built to park cars rather than serve horses. He bought a personal box, but complained it was too exposed to wind and cold because Taylor hadn't put in a roof. Sitting outside on cool days aggravated the pain in his leg. Nonetheless, as his equestrian activities increased he built a small but highly successful stable, a fraction of the size of Taylor's, but for a time considered one of the best in the country.

Even Smythe's travel took on a grander air. In 1954, he took Irene on a month-long trip to England, where he revisited wartime haunts and looked up people he had known. Extensive preparations were made by Gardens staff and an array of friends called into service to set up appropriate appointments. They sailed on the *Queen Elizabeth* and spent two weeks at Claridge's, among the toniest of London's tony hotels. Officials at Ontario House, the government office in London, put themselves at his service and arranged a number of business appointments on his behalf. Charlie Conacher, sharing Smythe's affinity for horses, wrote to Frank More O'Ferrall, a friend at the Anglo-Irish Agency Ltd., which exported thoroughbreds. "We will get the red carpet out and give him the full treatment," O'Ferrall promised.[9]

Another friend, John H. Harris, contacted Michael Parker, equerry to the Duke of Edinburgh, angling for a little Royal face time for Smythe, who had met the Duke and then–Princess Elizabeth during their Royal tour in 1951. Smythe remained the ultimate anglophile, praising the "class" and quiet courage of the English, their perseverance, and the beauty of the country. The weather was something else, though, and Smythe's wounds suffered terribly in the cold and damp. Britain was still a country very much in recovery from the war, with meat rationing in place and limits on many important foodstuffs only recently ended. The Smythes were not fancy eaters, but Harris nonetheless arranged for temporary access to two "very good eating clubs."[10]

The expansion of his other activities coincided with a reduction in his workload with the Leafs and a parallel decline in the fortunes of the team. Whether the two were related remains a matter of debate. Many of Smythe's detractors maintained his micromanagement of the team had long been a hindrance. Both Dick Irvin and Hap Day were superlative coaches and would have been even more successful if Smythe had left them alone, they argued. Howie Meeker, who served as a Leafs player, coach, and manager in the 1950s until an unhappy break-up, insisted Day was the chief reason for the team's on-ice success. Smythe "had a fair eye for talent, but, compared to Day, what he knew about playing the game of hockey you could write on the head of a pin."[11]

Whatever the reason, the glory years ended with Barilko's final goal. Smythe said he saw it coming, and his expectations were met in full: the team fell to third place in Primeau's second year and fifth place in his third. Smythe replaced him with King Clancy in 1953 to little effect – they placed fourth, third, and fourth again over the next three years. The slide coincided with the rise of two great dynasties, first Detroit, which won four Cups in five years, then Montreal, which won six in eight years. On February 1, 1955 – his sixtieth birthday – Smythe acknowledged the inevitable and stepped down as general manager, giving the job to Day. In 1956, Clancy was replaced as coach with Meeker, who had retired as a player in 1954 and built a successful coaching record with the Pittsburgh Hornets. In his first year they missed the playoffs, and then, the next year, came the final ignominy: for the first time since 1927, the Leafs placed dead last in the standings.

In two books written years later, Meeker argued that Smythe deliberately let the team deteriorate as a means of easing out Day and paving the way for Stafford to take over the team. As evidence, he pointed to a number of trades that weakened the already aging gang of Cup champions. In 1950, he sent Ezinicki and low-scoring left-winger Vic Lynn to Boston. In 1952, he sent Al Rollins to Chicago, just a year after he'd won the Vezina Trophy, along with Cal Gardner and Gus Mortson, in return for veteran netminder Harry Lumley. He sent Joe Klukay, a steady if unspectacular point-getter, to Boston, where he spent three years before returning to Toronto for two final seasons. "He had to make life so miserable for Hap Day that he would retire," Meeker said. "Look what Conn Smythe gave away for nothing in return."[12]

There's no question it was the Leafs' sorriest decade until the lowest depths of Harold Ballard twenty years later. And Smythe was spending less and less time on the job. He and Irene had begun spending winters in Florida, departing at Christmas and returning around the time of the playoffs. He racked up enormous telephone bills trying to manage from afar, but the results were predictable. He seldom travelled with the team anymore and was less of a presence around the Gardens, where once he had seemed to fill the place.

Unable to walk without pain, he moved his theatre of operations to a small section set aside for him in the front-row greens – well up and behind the expensive red and blue seats – where he could take in the play from a better angle. The sportswriters nicknamed it "Berchtesgaden" after Hitler's mountain lair, and Smythe would sit up there with son Hugh or King Clancy and a changing cast of rookies, injured players, or invited guests, using whomever was available as a runner to speed orders, observations, and other "suggestions" to the coach behind the bench. He was no less intense about the game than he'd ever been. Photographers looking for an angry, red-faced shot of Smythe could readily obtain one by staking out Berchtesgaden and waiting for him to get worked up.

He knew his effectiveness was eroding. He found it harder to freeze a play in his mind and identify the mistakes. When played at its highest level, hockey, like any sport, requires intense focus and constant exposure. Smythe wasn't giving it that any more. In the public mind he was still the all-powerful boss-of-all-bosses, pronouncing opinions from on high, but players knew him more as a distant figure filtering messages through Primeau, Day, or Clancy, often by phone from Florida.

His influence within the league, in contrast, had never been greater. While Montreal, Toronto, and Detroit took turns winning the Stanley Cup, New York, Boston, and Chicago were annual disasters. The Rangers had never recovered from the devastation the war wreaked on their lineup and blundered from one season to the next with a sense of hopelessness that had almost become second nature. Boston endured a decade of similar horrors, though neither team, arguably, reached the levels of ineptitude of the Black Hawks, where nominal owner Bill Tobin, in Smythe's words, "wouldn't pay ten cents to see the Statue of Liberty take a swan dive into New York harbour."[13]

Smythe's regular sparring partners of the pre-war period were gone: Art Ross and Lester Patrick were retired, while Charles Adams,

"Big Jim" Norris, and Frank Calder were all dead. The Red Wings were still run by Jack "Jolly Jawn" Adams – whose nickname was a play on the fact he wasn't jolly at all – but Norris's death had split up his empire and ignited a family feud that served to diminish the clout of any one member. Only Smythe and Selke were around from the old days and still kicking. As the rancour of their split faded and their interests as hockey men merged, the two men found themselves working more often in concert – though with regular flare-ups – to direct the league's activities. When Montreal won the 1953 Stanley Cup, Smythe wired his congratulations. Selke responded with a gracious and typically conciliatory letter, though evidence of their estrangement could be found not far from the surface.

> As you say it has taken a long time for Dick and me to win the Stanley Cup, and I know that Dick sometimes annoys you with his publicity releases, but it should give cause for gratification to know that when we were alone the morning after our victory he said that he felt that we both owed a lot to you; that we learned a lot from you even when you were most severe in your criticisms and that hockey can ill afford the loss of a fellow like yourself.
>
> This sounds like a mutual admiration society and possibly at the next meeting we will be arguing about some fool thing again, but I can only repeat what I have told you on more than one occasion – that our trips to Saratoga, our trip to the Coast and many other individual instances are still the happiest moments of my life.
>
> Undoubtedly you did better after I left your organization and I'm doing allright here, so everybody should be happy.[14]

Smythe never would be able to order around Selke again, but he made up for it by dictating to Clarence Campbell. The league president was a former NHL referee, a Rhodes scholar, and a distinguished lawyer with an impressive war record. Campbell joined the army as a private in 1940 and rose to command the 4th Armoured Division.

After the war he was named prosecutor of the Canadian War Crimes Commission and led the prosecution of a Nazi leader who had executed Canadian prisoners of war. He was awarded the Order of the British Empire, a sign of British favour Smythe must have envied. Despite championing Campbell to replace Dutton, Smythe often treated him with the same offhandedness to which he'd subjected Selke. Campbell, he said, served the owners well "because he would do what he was told. . . . Every time I told him what to do and he did it perfectly he was confirming what I had said when I turned down the job [as NHL president] . . . that I was not good for it, because I would not take orders; and Campbell was the right man, because he would."[15]

In 1951, he set off a lengthy squabble with Campbell over ownership of the Black Hawks, which had become even more opaque since Major McLaughlin's death in 1944. "I do not know who owns the club and I am beginning to think that the lethargic manner in which things are being run in Chicago is part of a plan," he said.[16] "[It] looks as though someone is waiting to step in and buy the club at a bargain."

The Norris family controlled the club, a fact Smythe was likely well aware of. But he professed ignorance and pestered Campbell to clear up the situation. Campbell insisted there was nothing he could do, thanks to the imprecision of league rules. No owner could control more than one club, but an "owner" could be any company or corporation with an independent identity. So by setting up separate companies for each of his franchises, Norris could disguise his ownership. And until Smythe started squawking, the league had been careful not to ask too many questions.

Campbell explained as much in his response to Smythe's queries, which produced a series of acerbic communications between the two. Campbell promised a full investigation, which came to the nebulous conclusion that Bill Tobin appeared to be in charge of the club, as far as anyone could tell. The report was raised at a meeting of NHL governors in April, which Smythe seems not to have attended. Art Ross inquired whether Campbell had the report, producing a response

Smythe would hardly have sat still for if he'd been there: "Yes, and I may add that the information is of such a character that it would allay a lot of unfavourable comment and snide remarks if it was made known generally, because to me the set-up was so generally satisfactory."

The governors decided not to make the report widely known. In fact, they decided not to make it known at all, unless someone asked, at which time the answers would be provided verbally. "If they want to know, they can ask you," Tobin told Campbell.[17] Smythe reacted with a letter so bristling in anger that Campbell responded that "if [the letter] has any sinister implications so far as I am concerned I appreciate the warning."[18]

Smythe's concern was bona fide. He was worried once again about the viability of the league, as he had been before the war when doubts about the future of the Canadiens and New York Americans threatened to leave the NHL with just five teams. Although the Gardens had little trouble selling tickets, the situation could easily change if the three clubs at the bottom of the heap fell too far behind the three at the top, and Tobin's feeble leadership threatened to make that danger a reality. His efforts eventually bore fruit, and the league took two steps to shore up the weaker clubs. An interleague draft was introduced, to ensure that talent-rich teams couldn't bury NHL-calibre players in their minor-league affiliates while weaker teams like Chicago went wanting. And Smythe proposed a plan under which the league would subsidize the less fortunate, guaranteeing a minimum annual return so teams with poor box-office returns could continue to operate nonetheless.

Even after stepping down as general manager, Smythe retained his titles as president and managing director. There was considerable questioning about just how "retired" he would be, but on the appointed day he duly handed over the reins to Day, who had been holidaying with Conn and Irene in Palm Beach.[19]

In preparing for the moment, he had written Day a note with some parting advice. "I know when you first take over a job you want to have it all done at once and this is impossible. Build a good foundation . . . so that the team as a team is a good one, and then try to improve the individuals, without taking away any of the good things which they have."[20]

Neither he nor Day may have realized how bleak the next few years would be. But it was not without hope. The "perpetual" player machine Smythe had promised when he returned from the war was in place and working better than either could then appreciate. In 1949, a pair of nineteen-year-olds, Tim Horton and George Armstrong, were called up briefly from Pittsburgh, Armstrong playing two games and Horton one. It would be a couple more years before they would make the team full-time, but in 1953 they were joined by Ron Stewart, a product of the Barrie Flyers and the Toronto Marlboros. Dick Duff was a regular by 1955, at age nineteen. Billy Harris, twenty, played all seventy games in 1955–56. The next season Bob Baun, nineteen, was brought up for twenty games, the beginning of eighteen years in the NHL. And the season after that a much talked-about young left winger, Frank Mahovlich, was called up for his first three games as a Leaf.

Most were products of the team's two main junior affiliates, the Marlboros, run by Stafford Smythe and Harold Ballard, and the St. Michael's Majors, run by the Basilian Fathers of St. Michael's College.

The Marlies had been assembling and shipping ready-made NHLers since Frank Selke reorganized the team in the 1920s. Its list of NHL alumnae includes more than two hundred players, seven of whom made the Hall of Fame. Toronto was by far the greatest benefactor, scooping up juniors from Marlboros squads and wrapping them in Leafs uniforms throughout the 1930s, 1940s, and 1950s. Conacher, Jackson, and Horner all joined the Leafs via Selke's Marlies. Joe Primeau spent short periods with both St. Michael's and the Marlboros, as did Busher Jackson's brother Art, who played twelve years with the Leafs, Americans, and Bruins. Alex Levinsky, Bob Goldham, Bob Davidson, Gaye Stewart, Ron Stewart, and Bill Thoms were all Leafs with the Marlboros stamp on them, followed by a particularly productive 1950s crop that included Armstrong, Carl Brewer, Billy Harris,

Bob Baun, Ron Ellis, Bob Nevin, Eric Nesterenko, and Bob Pulford. The coaching staff was equally impressive, from Selke, to Bill Thoms, Turk Broda, Jim Gregory, and George Armstrong.

The Marlies ascendancy worked largely to the credit of Stafford Smythe, who began arguing after the war that the Leafs were under-utilizing the Marlboros in spite of the team's productiveness. Toronto by then could draw players from across the country almost at will, easily luring away hotshot young phenoms from small towns and farming communities, eager to do just about anything for the privi-lege of wearing a Maple Leafs uniform. Conn Smythe felt the system, in tandem with farm teams and U.S. affiliates, worked just fine, but Stafford insisted Toronto was rich with players who could be drawn into the Leafs orbit at a younger age. For once, he won an argument with his father and, together with Ballard, began setting up a network of teams that extended the Leafs' grasp to players as young as nine. Kids would join the Marlboros peewee team and work their way up the chain to the junior A club, where they'd jockey for a shot at making the Leafs. Although he struggled with other demons, Stafford proved to have a first-rate hockey mind. While Ballard would take care of the numbers and run the business end of the operation – showing up to have his picture taken when the team began winning Memorial Cups – it was evident even to people who disliked Stafford that he had a talent for spotting and developing players.

In competing for the eye of Leafs management, Marlboros players were up against a similar pool of talent at St. Michael's. Like the Marlies, St. Mike's already had an enviable record of forging NHL talent. According to a history of the school published in 2008, 184 St. Mike's students have played in the NHL, including fourteen Hall of Famers, an astonishing record for a school that supplied its teams entirely from its own the student body.[21]

Few people missed the irony of the outspokenly anti-Catholic Smythe working so closely with the Basilian Fathers. The link was based entirely on mutual self-benefit. Smythe got hockey players, while the school got students and money. When the arrangement was finally put on paper in 1954, Smythe promised Father Ted Flanagan, the school's director of athletics, that the Leafs would pay $10,000 a year, in return for which the priests would keep an eye out for talent. It stipulated that players would be made aware of who was paying their bills and "second to school spirit should be indoctrinated with the Maple Leaf spirit and will sign with us, with your assistance, when requested."[22]

St. Mike's gave the Leafs a unique advantage in recruiting players. It allowed chief scout Bob Davidson to sit down with working-class parents in mining towns and farm communities and offer a first-class education in return for their son's signature. Few prospects realized it, but the negotiations that took place at kitchen tables across the country were their greatest moment of leverage – once a hot teen prospect signed a C form tying him to a team he became, to all intents, an indentured employee subject to the whims of management. Once signed, it was all but impossible to jump teams, and anyone who tried was likely to be labelled a troublemaker and shunned by the other owners. So the quiet talks and promises that Davidson engaged in with wary parents and their excited sons were critical to everything that came after, and no other team had the ability to throw a decent education into the mix.

Dick Duff was spotted on the rinks around Kirkland Lake and invited to a Leafs prospects' camp at age fourteen. A year later he got a telegram inviting him to board at St. Mike's at the team's expense. Duff's father was making $1.08 an hour and had thirteen children,[23] so there wasn't much argument over whether to accept. He gave his son $2 – "I don't know where he got it from," Duff says – and put him on a train to Toronto at age fifteen. It cost Duff $1.75 of his small fortune to get a cab to the school, where he walked in and told the first priest he bumped into that he was there to play hockey.[24]

Davidson spent so much time wooing the Mahovlich family in Schumacher, Ontario, that he and Peter Mahovlich, Frank's father, became friends. Davidson knew he wasn't the first scout in the Mahovlich kitchen – Detroit, Chicago, New York, and Montreal had all been there before him. Young Frank was such a hot prospect that Rudy Pilous, manager of the popular junior A team in St. Catharines, offered to buy his dad a farm if he'd sign to play there.[25] But the Mahovliches were staunch Catholics and Davidson could dangle the prospect of several years at St. Mike's as part of the bargain. After his initial presentation, Davidson returned for another accompanied by Father Flanagan, who extolled the virtues of the school, its high academic standards, and the promise of Catholic discipline.

The Leafs offered to pay tuition, room and board, and provide spending money. It took months of work, but Davidson finally got Mahovlich's signature on a junior B form. (Mahovlich got $1,000 to sign and another $1,000 when he later signed a C form. Leafs lawyers advised Smythe the second bonus was illegal, as rules allowed a maximum $100 for a C form. They got around it by giving the money to Mahovlich's uncle "as scouting expenses.")[26]

The St. Mike's star-making machinery churned out plenty of others – Ted Lindsay, Red Kelly, and Dave Keon among them, though they didn't all end up in Toronto uniforms. It was a lucrative business for Smythe. He paid the juniors on a sliding scale depending on their talent and negotiating skills – Mahovlich made $80 a week as a junior B player and expected a raise to $130 when he jumped to junior A but instead took a $20 cut when junior payments were slashed.[27] But even with a few of the players making substantial amounts, Smythe could fill the Gardens for a junior hockey clash while icing teams that cost him a fraction of the payroll of the Leafs.

His relationship with St. Mike's demonstrated just another of his many contradictions. He was open with his anti-Catholic rhetoric and had made life temporarily miserable for Stafford and Dorothea over their interfaith marriage. Yet for all his harsh verbiage, many of his closest relationships had been with devout Catholics. Joe Primeau and King Clancy were both firm believers who often attended mass together. There were few, if any, people Smythe liked and admired more than Primeau or Clancy. Selke, despite their other quarrels, insisted Smythe never brought his religion into the mix.[28]

Now Smythe found himself in a close alliance with the Basilians and discovered he liked and respected them. He never lost his taste for poking fun at the religion, but his experience with St. Mike's considerably reduced the frequency and ferocity of his assaults. When Father Don Faught, who had managed the school team, left in July 1954, Smythe wrote him a warm letter noting how difficult it was to say goodbye "to someone for whom you have a great deal of respect and confidence," and that he "even enjoyed being taken by you on several deals."[29] When the school eventually elected to drop the hockey program, feeling it was intruding too much on academics, he sent another letter noting that "in my association with your school through your Sports Directors, and knowing the way you have treated the Protestants who have attended your school, [I] have gained a knowledge of your religion which, at least, has made me respect your whole organization very much."[30]

The evidence suggests he was sincere in his appreciation of the professionalism he discovered in the Basilians. His willingness to say so is all the more noteworthy given that it was a St. Michael's graduate – and one of the best players the school ever produced – who created one of the lowest moments in the lowest year of Smythe's career.

Ted Lindsay wasn't aiming specifically at the Toronto Maple Leafs when he announced the formation of an NHL Players' Association in early 1957. And it was Smythe's own bitter reaction that helped turn Lindsay's well-meant foray into a league-wide crisis. But the birth of the Players' Association happened to coincide with an internal bloodletting at the Gardens that would, in itself, have left Smythe with a battered reputation and some seriously damaged relationships. The simultaneous quarrel with the players turned two bad situations into one unholy mess.

CHAPTER 18

Maple Leaf Gardens in 1957 was very much a family business. Hugh Smythe was the team doctor, responsible for keeping the players healthy and occasionally stitching up fans along the sideboards, where the lack of glass made flying pucks a regular hazzard.[1] As a kid Hugh had served as stickboy, as had his older brother Stafford, Stafford's son, Tommy, and Hap Day's son, Kerry. Jack Hoult, who had married Miriam Smythe in 1944, worked in the business office, where he received regular pay rises and generous bonuses. One of his duties was to scout the red seats for patrons who had failed to dress to Smythe's standards and single them out for a polite but firm letter alerting them to their crime.[2]

Apart from family, the building was sprinkled with army buddies from both wars. While a prisoner in the First World War Smythe had met a Russian officer named Logvinoff, who gave him a pair of boots when his own fell apart. Smythe soon realized Logvinoff had given him his best boots; his own were in much worse shape. When Logvinoff moved to Canada years later, Smythe hired him at the Gardens, where he amused people by walking on his hands while smoking a cigarette.[3] He stayed on the Gardens payroll until his death.

Many of the employees had been around forever. Rink manager Henry Bolton was hired soon after the Gardens opened, when Smythe realized W.A. Hewitt was a better newspaperman than he was an attractions manager. Hewitt remained on staff nonetheless, collecting his salary into the 1950s while politely requesting a six-month leave of absence each spring (which was politely granted) "to perform my duties with the Ontario Racing Commission."[4] King Clancy was a permanent fixture, always around in one job or another, though details of his duties were sometimes imprecise. When Smythe inquired one spring what he did from day to day, Clancy replied, "Nothing." When Smythe asked if he was available to keep doing it, Clancy said sure.[5] His salary for doing nothing by the end of the decade was $6,500 plus a "living allowance" of $1,000, and additional bonuses if the team made the playoffs. In all, it meant he made slightly less than he'd earned as a player twenty years earlier.

The whole Leafs system seemed tailored to draw people in and keep them there. Players would be recruited to Shopsy's, the peewee team in the Marlboros network, and work their way up to the Weston Dukes, the Junior B team. From there they'd make the leap to the Junior A Marlies and, if they were lucky, the Leafs. In the summer they got jobs at Smythe's sand and gravel operations. Players didn't make enough to live on their hockey salaries alone, and a parade of Leafs stars had depended on summer jobs at the pit, from Turk Broda to Tim Horton to Bobby Baun. The pit was managed by Hap Day and located near the cement block firm owned by Joe Primeau. Both men, of course, had coached the Leafs, and Primeau continued to help train players at St. Mike's, where Smythe asked him to give special attention to Mahovlich, his rising star. Stafford Smythe, meanwhile, was eyeing Turk Broda as coach of the Marlboros.

Although Smythe was more respected and feared than loved and admired by employees, there were plenty of benefits to be had from working for him. Gardens documents show regular pay increases and Christmas bonuses. There was an annual Christmas party put on for the press, an elaborately planned event that consisted mainly of sketches spoofing the Gardens' all-powerful ruler, which Smythe thoroughly enjoyed. He got on well enough with the press, both sides wary of the other, but locked in mutual need. Like others, reporters had come to respect his accomplishments even if they'd been the target of more than one tongue-lashing. Writer Scott Young, preparing a television profile of him, wrote that Smythe "can treat his assistants so curtly, at a hockey practice or in public, that bystanders wince; yet he never has a loyalty problem." He added, "There are several reasons for this forbearance on the part of men who would punch on the nose unhesitatingly anybody else who spoke to them as Smythe sometimes does. One is that most people who know Smythe admire him and know that his own loyalty to a friend does not require unswerving politeness, so he doesn't feel he has to be unswervingly polite in return."[6]

It was taken for granted that he was preparing the ground to be succeeded by his oldest boy. Stafford would proclaim he didn't want the job, and his brother Hugh still insists Stafford was not burning to follow his father. "He did not want the hockey job. He was trained as an engineer, and liked the sand and gravel business. He had many friends in the sand and gravel business. Both my father and my brother made more money in the sand and gravel business than they ever did in the hockey business. . . . To take over the Gardens with my father still sitting there in the office was a recipe for disaster. My father could run it if he was physically capable. My brother could run it. But there was no way they both could run it."[7]

But to anyone looking on from outside, it had long appeared inevitable that Stafford would replace his father. He had renewed his odd friendship with the much-older Harold Ballard, and together they had built the Marlboros into a champion team. There was obvious friction between the Ballard-Smythe duo and the Leafs' current managers, Hap Day and Howie Meeker. Day stressed an intense, disciplined defensive style that required an all-out team effort. It had produced great success, but Stafford and Ballard muttered loudly that their junior scoring stars were being wasted in Day's defensive approach. When Day and Meeker brought Ted Kennedy out of retirement for a brief comeback, Stafford thought it was a major blunder – arguing the team was falling back on previous heroes rather than trusting in the kids – and let everyone now it. Day wasn't deaf or blind to what was coming. As the 1950s wore on and the Leafs' performance worsened, it appeared the day of reckoning was at hand.

Stafford, like his father, wasn't easy to love, and had the added burden that, while Conn attracted respect for his accomplishments, Stafford was viewed as the snotty kid with the silver spoon in his mouth. It had always been that way. Nothing Stafford did, or could do, would ever be enough to equal his old man. He would always be the man who got to run the hockey team because he inherited it from his father. The knowledge of that made him shy and defensive, which was interpreted as aloof and arrogant. He often gave the impression he wasn't paying attention when someone was speaking to him.[8] He didn't smile easily, was awkward with people, and kept his feelings to himself. He was, like his father, brusque and demanding, but where people would take it from Conn they wouldn't take it from him.

Stafford's life had never been easy. He'd grown up the son of a wealthy and well-known man and subject to all the baiting and taunting that brought with it. He learned to defend himself and won his father's praise for his courage, but might have been happier if he'd never had to. Hugh Smythe came to realize the key to maintaining cordial relations with Conn was to find a career outside his immediate sphere of influence. Hugh became a doctor and noted expert in rheumatology; though a regular presence at the Gardens, he wasn't directly subject to Conn's daily demands and unpredictable temperament. Stafford wasn't so lucky. Although he made an early effort to maintain his independence, resisting Conn's determination to bring him into the hockey business was more than he could manage. "The issue with Stafford was trying to live up to Conn," said Frank Selke's son, Frank Jr., who knew both Conn's sons as boys. "Staff put himself in a position where he was constantly competing with his father or his father's image. That's a tough thing to do."[9]

He didn't handle it particularly well and rarely got credit for his obvious hockey skills. "My father could go on the radio or be on television and be an instant entertainer and hold an audience," said Hugh Smythe. "But my brother did not come across as a likeable person, even though he won as many Stanley Cups as my father did, or almost, certainly in a shorter period of time."

Sportswriters, always quick and merciless in their judgments, were unsympathetic. Columnist Dick Beddoes, an admirer of Conn, wrote: "[Stafford] aped his father, the same raspy voice, the same go-to-hell swagger, a similar arrogance. He exhibited a rudeness which is the weak man's imitation of strength."[10]

The *Star*'s Milt Dunnell, dean of sports reporters, said, "Staff decided to be like his old man. He was going to be a dictatorial little son of a bitch. But he wasn't really like Conn. He couldn't pull it off."[11]

Such harsh opinions weren't universal. Bob Baun admired Stafford and felt he was ill treated. Jim Gregory, whom Stafford hired away from St. Michael's, put a lot of Stafford's problems down to the impact his constant struggles with asthma had on his personality. "He seemed snarly and didn't respond . . . [but] I know that anybody who had time to be with him or get to know him, you very rarely heard them say things that weren't good. Especially hockey people. He treated me unbelievably well, and the people who worked for me he treated the same way."[12]

One person who felt differently was Howie Meeker. The former right winger had been ecstatic when Day called to offer him the Leafs coaching job. He'd coached two years in Pittsburgh and had an attractive offer from the minor-league Hershey Bears, but turned it down to accept the riskier job with the Leafs. "To be selected and given the opportunity to coach your hockey club and to be associated with the many wonderful men that you have in your organization is an honour and a privilege far beyond my wildest dreams of a few years ago," he wrote to Smythe. "It is now my ambition to prove to your associates, the Leaf players and the thousands of Leaf fans that Mr. Smythe and Mr. Day have picked the right man for the job."[13]

But he came to despise Stafford and distrust Conn. "[Conn's] handshake wasn't worth a pinch of coon shit," he says now.[14]

Meeker was in a hopeless position from the start. The Leafs were perilously weak, with few authentic NHL-calibre players. He got off on the wrong foot when he and Day jointly suggested naming veteran defenceman Jimmy Thomson to replace the retiring Sid Smith as captain. Smythe didn't even want to invite Thomson to training camp, but acquiesced and Thomson was made captain. Soon, however, Smythe began to feel he was being ignored and kept a record of ideas he'd put forward that hadn't been acted on.

"Nykoluk joined club. Thought his play an improvement on 2 or 3 centremen. Suggested he be kept and one sent down. SUGGESTION IGNORED," he wrote in a note to himself.

"Suggested that 4 defencemen were better than 5, but if they kept extra one for emergencies he should be understood not to be played unless absolutely necessary. SUGGESTION IGNORED."

"Suggested records show weakness of certain combinations – especially Pulford and Kennedy and if possible these combinations not be used. SUGGESTION IGNORED."[15]

The team started poorly and got worse. By Christmas the Leafs had lost twice as many games as they won. Smythe added to his list of complaints, writing out NO ATTENTION PAID TO THIS or SUGGESTION IGNORED each time his ideas were overlooked.

As the Leafs slid, the internal tensions worsened. The rivalry between his son and Hap Day put Smythe in an excruciating position. The two qualities he admired most, as he had often stated, were "guts and loyalty," and no one had displayed more of both than Day. He'd been the team's captain, its coach, and its general manager. Other than a short period at the end of his playing career, he'd been with the Leafs since before they were Leafs, one of only two players Smythe had kept from the St. Patricks. He'd led them to Stanley Cups in each of his capacities, with victories in each of three decades. He had more victories, by far, than any coach in the team's history, more Cups than any other coach in the league. What's more, he had the enduring respect of his players, and the admiration of the other teams.

If Stafford was going to advance, however, Day would have to retreat. It would require Smythe to find a way to violate his most cherished principles, the very ones he'd been preaching for thirty years. He had heaped praise on Day, sold him a piece of his company, and vowed to keep him forever by his side. But he was also a family man who owned the team and believed in his right to run it as he wanted, and what he wanted was to turn it over to his son. It didn't necessarily have to end with Day's departure, but if Stafford was at odds with Day, a way would have to be found for Day to yield.

Into this troubled cauldron, one cold morning in February, dropped Ted Lindsay. In a letter to Clarence Campbell, signed "Robert B.T. Lindsay, President," the Red Wings star announced formation of the NHL Players' Association, "of which 99% of the players in the National Hockey League are members." It was headed by himself and Canadiens defenceman Doug Harvey, with Chicago's Gus Mortson, Boston's Fern Flaman, Toronto's Jimmy Thomson, and New York's Bill Gadsby serving as officers.

The purpose of the association, he said, was "to promote, foster and protect the best interests of the National Hockey League players." He presented Campbell with a series of questions about the league pension plan, which had been launched ten years earlier and was the subject of regular grumbling among players.

Campbell replied two days later, noting that he had no authority to disclose details of the pension without authorization from directors of the Pension Society and that he would seek that authorization. Then he pointed out that most of the information Lindsay sought was contained in the pension manual supplied to all the players, that players who wanted answers to such questions were free to ask the Pension Society, and that both Lindsay and Harvey had been directors of the society for the previous two years. He also pointed out that the pension plan answered to a large group of retired players as well as those currently active.

It was the opening shot in the fiercest confrontation between players and management since the Hamilton Tigers had been disbanded over pay demands in 1925. It would rumble on for the next year, with Lindsay struggling to hold the association together against the combined opposition of the six team owners, their ally and chief operative, Campbell, and a well-financed legal operation tasked with breaking the back of Lindsay and his crew. The issue wasn't new. Most players had a sense they were being taken advantage of by a league that was controlled by a handful of secretive and self-interested owners. The owners were wealthy men, while players still customarily scratched around for summer jobs to help them get by when the hockey season ended. They were particularly annoyed about the pension plan, which required an annual contribution of $900 from each of the players – a hefty sum when $10,000 was still a good salary – and nothing from the owners.

All that was needed to harness the grumbling was a personality strong enough to take on the task despite the likelihood it would enrage the owners. The job demanded someone respected by the other players, despite the fact they had been conditioned by years of training to avoid and despise members of other teams. It also required someone self-confident enough to defy all the traditions of compliance and unquestioning deference to authority that ruled the NHL. That was Ted Lindsay to a T.

Lindsay was the best left winger in the league and was having his best season. Barely an inch taller than Smythe and 160 pounds, he was tough as a rhino's hide and customarily resided at or near the top of the annual penalty list. At thirty-one he was already in his thirteenth season, all of them with Detroit, and was neck and neck with teammate Gordie Howe in the scoring race. He loved to torment opposing players, the more talented the better. Rocket Richard found him so annoying he identified Lindsay as the only player he honestly hated.[16]

He had been working on the association for months and had signed almost the entire league without a whisper of his activity reaching the owners. His February letter caught the league by surprise, and the ferocity of its reaction reflected that fact. The letter was addressed to Campbell as president of the NHL, and the association viewed the issue as a league matter. Smythe could have left it to Clarence Campbell to deal with, but he took Lindsay's actions as a personal affront and immediately immersed himself in the effort to defeat him.

Histories of the ensuing struggle tend to paint it in black-and-white terms, with the valiant but overmatched players being bested by the greedy, self-interested owners. While elements of that are true, the situation wasn't as simple or straightforward as often presented. The NHL wasn't the billion-dollar juggernaut it is today. It was six teams, three of which were perennial losers struggling to attract fans. New York, Boston, and Chicago only occasionally made the playoffs and were usually eliminated in the first round, precluding them from the additional playoff revenue enjoyed by the other three teams. Detroit and Chicago were hobbies of the Norris family, which drained money away from other Norris enterprises. They needed the Norrises more than the Norrises needed them. Bad management and financial stress had seen four teams disappear over the years, and there was nothing preventing it from happening again.

Toronto's success was more the exception than the rule, and Smythe was never the plutocrat he was sometimes portrayed as. Ticket prices at the Gardens had barely budged in thirty years. When the debt was finally retired in 1950, Smythe calculated the average return to investors since 1932 at 5.4 per cent.[17] For years his own wealth had come more from sand and gravel than from hockey games. He was proud of the fact that the Gardens had been built by union workers and had a memo compiled showing five unions still held shares, while six additional unions represented current Gardens employees.

But he was unquestionably paternalistic. He knew how easy it was to take advantage of hockey players from blue-collar backgrounds with limited education and few interests outside the next game. He did it himself. He felt he was better suited to protect them than a union, which he believed would inevitably become dominated by a handful of disgruntled players and outside advisers with their own agendas to pursue. The association, as he saw it, was an attempt to reverse the balance of power between management and players and transfer to the players the benefits that came from decades of labour in building a successful league and successful business. At some point he had a secretary type up the definition of communism for him and kept it in his files.

He was especially aggravated to find Jimmy Thomson on the association's list of vice-presidents. It convinced him he'd been right to oppose making him captain. If he'd had his way, Thomson wouldn't even be on the team, yet now here he was joining up with that ingrate Lindsay – who had played at St. Michael's and by all rights should have been a Leaf himself – to challenge the authority of the man who'd been signing his paycheques the past ten years.

Smythe knew exactly what that amounted to. With his customary thoroughness he had a report compiled of Thomson's earnings, going back to the laundry and spending money he'd received as a junior at St. Mike's (where he'd played at the same time as Lindsay). It amounted to $127,563 over fourteen years. In addition, Smythe had a second report prepared on the pensions due Lindsay and his five cohorts on the association executive; Thomson topped the list, due $3,415 a year at age sixty-five.

Lindsay and the others weren't communists or anything close to it. They were careful to stipulate that the organization was an association of players, not a union. Many players would have backed away in a hurry if there was any danger of being identified as union members. They were too grounded in the ethos their parents had taught them, of a hard day's work for a fair day's pay. The image of well-paid, privileged hockey players marching out on strike wasn't something they expected the fans to tolerate.

Their demands were moderate. They wanted better compensation for exhibition games, travelling expenses, moving costs and injuries; they wanted the owners to contribute to the pension fund, limits on the owners' ability to transfer contracts, and on the number of exhibitions they were required to play. They also wanted a copy of their own contracts without having to beg the owners to see one.

There was little mention of pay. Players handled that on their own and were regularly outmanoeuvred. No one had agents, and few players had even rudimentary negotiating skills. Lesser players had suffered for years because stars like Howe and Richard allowed themselves to be underpaid by managers skilled at stoking their egos while exploiting their insecurity. If Howe and Richard were satisfied with a measly $1,000 raise every year, who was anyone else to demand more?

The demands weren't very radical, but were too much for Smythe. He had already polled the players individually on their concerns. Not surprisingly, none was willing to complain directly to the man who could end their careers overnight. All the players except Kennedy said they had paid the $100 membership fee and attended one big meeting. A couple mentioned the pension fund, but everyone – including Thomson – insisted they had no specific grievances against the team.

Thomson was already suffering the consequences of Smythe's wrath. For all intents, he'd been kicked off the team. Smythe ordered Day to leave him off the players' list for a late-season trip to New York. Milton Mound, a New York lawyer hired by the association, wrote Smythe – addressing his letter to "Mr. Cornelius Smythe" – inquiring about reports he had called Thomson a traitor and blamed him for the team's mediocre season. He insisted Thomson be reinstated and offered a new contract, warning that if the conditions weren't met, the PA would file charges of unfair labour practices before the U.S. Labor Relations Board.

Smythe ignored the threat and replied briskly to the other accusations: "Any resemblance between the reports you have heard and the truth is only coincidental. However, don't let that stop you."[18]

Over the closing weeks of the season the two crises drifted closer together, like a pair of ships heading for a collision. The festering management situation ate at Smythe as the team sank to the bottom rungs of the standings. Meanwhile, he was being hounded by an organization representing the same players who had dragged his team to fifth place.

In March, the ships finally collided. On March 25, after the Leafs dropped their final game to Detroit, Thomson called a press conference and announced he would never play another game for the Leafs. "There has been a lot said about my loyalty," he complained. "At no time have I been disloyal to the team. I have given them my best for twelve seasons. When I had a good season I asked for a raise; when I had a poor season I expected a cut. One year I took a cut after making the second all-star team because the club as a whole had a mediocre year." Although he wanted to remain in the NHL, he insisted he would never again lace on his skates for the only pro team he'd ever played for. "I would refuse a contract for next season if offered one by the Leafs," he said. "It would be impossible for me to play with a club that questioned my loyalty. After what has happened over the past six weeks, I wouldn't feel right about playing for the Leafs."[19]

Smythe wasn't on hand to respond because he was too busy dealing with the second crisis. After thirty years as player, coach, and manager, Hap Day had chosen the same morning to abruptly end his career as a Toronto Maple Leaf, in a closed-door session with Smythe that reporters clocked at just three minutes. It was the culmination of events set in motion a week earlier in a conference room at the Commodore Hotel in New York, where reporters had been summoned by Smythe. He was on his way back from Florida and it was clear something big was up: the Gardens even offered to arrange train travel for Toronto scribes wishing to attend. Smythe promised there would be "no executions,"[20] but it would take a fine eye to spot the difference. While he didn't exactly fire Day, he left him badly bloodied.

"First of all," he began, "I am making it again doubly clear that what has happened to the team this year, which I consider a year of failure, is my complete responsibility. However there are factors which I would like to discuss with you, and I am not going to debate them." He spelled out five reasons for the team's "failure." First was his own position, as president of the team. Referring to himself in the third person, he suggested reporters evaluate "whether he has contributed too much or too little – make it clear as to whether the team has been run right or not."

Second on the list were Meeker and Day. "They will be able to explain their position as they have the freedom of speech. Thank God we still have it in our country. They will probably give out the right answers and when we get through listening to them the next few weeks, probably we'll have had a successful failure."

Third was the Players' Association and Thomson's alleged treason, especially the decision to launch the PA in the middle of the season. "I find it very difficult to feel that there is time during a hockey season for the Captain of my club to go around and influence young players to join an Association, which has, so far as I can find out, no specific plans or ideas of how they can benefit hockey. I also feel that anything spawned in secrecy, as this Association was, certainly has to have some sort of odour with it. Whoever signs my men next year will have to know whether they are going to understand that they have to give 100% hockey loyalty to the Maple Leaf association and also that they know they are going to have to play when, how and where our organization tells them."

Fourth was the quality of the club's talent. Smythe was optimistic on that front. Despite the poor season, he believed there was plenty of potential in the team's young legs, and on various farm teams and junior affiliates beholden to Toronto, to bode well for the future.

And last was "our system of operation of our club," the first hint at what was to come. "We have a very spartan way of operating our club. Perhaps it is out of date. We prefer the body against the puck. Perhaps that too has gone by the boards. We have stressed at great length the defensive and we have, perhaps, overlooked the offensive. At least the figures show that. I would think that in our practices there might be room for argument as to how we operate that way." It was a convoluted sentence, but the implication was clear to the assembled press. Defence was Hap Day's way of doing business, always had been. Offence was what Staff Smythe wanted to replace it with.

He wrapped up his remarks by suggesting his job as president was "just as vulnerable as anybody else's." Boston had replaced its president, coach, and manager, and "have made great strides," he noted. Then he opened it for questions. Milt Dunnell asked whether "the President has given any thought that there might be a change in President?"

Playing along, President Smythe conceded there had indeed. As to who might replace him, he suggested, "There are, in Toronto, dozens of young men of the ability and liking of hockey that could make a success of Maple Leaf Gardens." After a brief response to the next query, he suggested someone ask him the question he wanted to answer: "Any questions about the manager and coach?"

Dunnell obliged. "Do you want to make a decision as to when they will be rehired?"

Thus prompted, Smythe conspicuously failed to pledge his support to either Day or Meeker. "I think any disposition of these positions would be at the full consent of the Directors," he responded, fooling no one. Everyone knew Smythe called the shots. Similarly, nobody missed the fact Smythe kept referring to the man he'd called the finest coach on earth as "Mr. Day." There was a clear sense of overkill when he insisted, once again, that he took full blame for the team's failure. "These are my appointees. Everything was done with my cognizance, whether I wanted it done that way or not, I could have stopped it if I had wanted to."

Day and Meeker were both on hand to hear their boss's less-than-ringing evaluation, as were Stafford Smythe and Harold Ballard, and King Clancy, dressed "like the top of a pool table" in honour of St. Patrick's Day.[21]

"Not even a fleck of blood soiled the thick carpets as Conn Smythe, the little pistol of Maple Leaf Gardens, fired what sounded like lethal shots into the breasts of his crew-cut lieutenant, Howie Meeker, and the practically thatchless second-in-command, Hap Day, a hockey associate of 30 years," recounted Dunnell the next day.[22] The two had sat through the event grim-faced, he noted, and Smythe made it clear he didn't want them questioned. "Any decision I reach will be given directly to Mr. Smythe," was all Day would say. "The press will not get it first."

But there could be little question, Dunnell wrote, that Smythe wanted to remove Day and clear the way for his son to take over. The dilemma was finding a way to do it without being targeted by accusations of disloyalty like the ones he was flinging at the team's captain. By insisting his own head might be on the chopping block, Dunnell noted, Smythe could absolve himself of blame and pretend it was all a decision for the board. Since Stafford would likely refuse to take on Day's job while his father remained in charge, some tricky footwork remained. But the bottom line was clear: "The fate of Day and Meeker will depend on what Smythe advises the board to do. If you judge by what happened here on the day of St. Patrick you are forced to conclude – no matter how much you like and admire Day and Meeker – that it's the end of the line."

Angry and offended, Day took several days to ponder his situation. He had much at stake. His shares in C. Smythe Ltd. paid him much more than his job as general manger of the Leafs. He ran the pit, rising early to put in hours at the Jane Street site before heading to the Gardens. Including salary, bonus, dividends, and directors' fees he'd earned almost $24,000 from sand and gravel in 1956, compared to $13,600 to manage the Leafs. Disentangling the two would be difficult, if not impossible, so a breach with the Leafs carried heavy financial implications.

While Day thought it over, Smythe, under siege by the press, insisted there'd been no hidden message in any of his remarks. But a week after the New York press conference he agreed to a coast-to-coast radio interview and gave his general manager another nudge. He said he'd named George Armstrong captain in place of Jim Thomson and would "recommend" to the board that both Meeker and Clancy be kept on. As for the status of Hap Day, he was waiting for Day to let him know whether he was "available" for the next season. "I can't do anything until Hap lets me know if he's available. If he tells me he is available, then we'll sit down and talk it over from there." He expected an answer the next day.[23]

As a hint, it was even less subtle than the one he'd offered in New York. Why should Day, after three decades, be required to indicate whether he was "available"? That was certainly the question Day had in mind, and the next morning he put it to Smythe in a brief, heated confrontation in his office. "I asked what he meant by asking me if the job was open would I be available," he told reporters who had huddled outside the office door in anticipation. "I told him I didn't understand that. He told me there was no use discussing next year's plans if I weren't available. I said if that's the case then I'm not available." He said he was pleased Meeker was being kept on, then cut short the questioning and headed to his own office. "In his typical whirlwind 'go-go-go' fashion, Day wrapped up his parting interview, cleared his desk, posed for pictures and was gone, all in about 10 minutes," recounted the *Globe and Mail*.

Smythe appeared at his door and confirmed the outcome: "Mr. Day says he's not available for next season. That's that." The reporters thought he looked crestfallen. "This has put a crimp in my plans," he allowed. "I thought Hap and King and Howie and myself could do a good job next season."[24]

One further surprise was to come. The next morning Day, who usually steered clear of reporters, called his own press conference. "This looks like the dawn of a new Day," joked one scribe.[25] Although Day had hinted at more fireworks, he disappointed the sportswriters. Smythe, he insisted, was "the smartest man in hockey," adding, "at least, he is now that I'm out of it." He had never resented his boss's interference in his coaching or managing. He thought the team had a bright future and plenty of young talent. And he wasn't going home mad.

"I would like to emphasize that I feel no bitterness or rancor to Maple Leaf Gardens. I resigned or became unavailable on my own volition. I might have just beaten the gun, but I beat it." He realized changes were in the offing and he might as well accept it. It had become impossible to ignore after the events in New York. "The inference I took from that press conference was that I had been publicly dismembered . . . that I was walking the plank."[26]

He defended his emphasis on defensive hockey and made a cautionary reference to the hovering shadow of Stafford Smythe: "I understand the new system is to play 100% offensive hockey. All I hope is that players like Gordie Howe will let you do it."

It's possible Smythe was honestly surprised by the turn of events. Much as he was determined to ensure his son succeeded him, he almost certainly hoped to avoid making a man like Hap Day "walk the plank." He was accustomed to people being compliant with his needs. King Clancy was more than willing to stick around and do whatever job was needed. Joe Primeau had come and gone without a fuss, willing to help out when needed and return to his concrete block business when he wasn't. Howie Meeker had agreed to return and had been named general manager. Even at the peak of his conflict with Selke he'd never actually fired the man, he'd just made life unbearable to the point that Selke made the decision for himself.

Given Day's appreciation that Stafford was the heir apparent, Smythe may have assumed he would bow out gracefully with a new title – "vice-president in charge of something." If so, he had badly misjudged Day's temperament. Rather than publicly embarrass him at a press conference in a New York hotel, he could have spoken privately to Day and worked out something they could both live with. But he didn't.

Just weeks before the blow-up, Stafford was still insisting he had no interest in running the Leafs. "I've got too many of my old man's characteristics," he said. "I'd have to fight him."[27] But shortly after Day's departure, Smythe informed Gardens directors he intended to create a "Hockey Committee" headed by Stafford and consisting of his son and six associates "to operate the hockey part of the Maple Leaf Gardens business with respect to personnel, organization, operation and policy." The board would retain authority over financial matters, but otherwise Smythe would hand hockey affairs to the new committee "on or before Sept. 1, 1957."[28]

In his memoirs, Smythe said Stafford had been pushing for more authority for some time. In a heated confrontation, he wrote, Stafford exploded at him: "You're going to have to retire! I should be running this place." He even complained to his mother that he was being taken advantage of, precipitating one of the few serious quarrels between Conn and Irene, which ended when Conn showed her the books indicating Stafford was being amply paid.[29]

The committee was quickly dubbed the "Silver Seven" and became known as much for its late-night partying and generous expense accounts as for its hockey acumen. Ballard wasn't among the initial seven, but soon replaced one of the originals. Among the others were a jewellery manufacturer who owned the cottage next to the Smythes at Lake Simcoe; George Gardiner, son of the stockbroker who had sold Smythe his Gardens shares at half price; a food executive; and George Mara, a UCC graduate and skilled amateur player whose family owned a liquor distribution business.[30] Most notable was John Bassett Jr., owner of the *Toronto Telegram* and Toronto's CFTO television station, who had been looking for a place on the Gardens board for several years.

It didn't take long for the committee to clash with the remnants of the old guard. They felt Day's defensive "system" had run its course, but Meeker was a proponent of a similar approach. Over the summer of 1957, Stafford largely ignored letters, memos, and suggestions from Meeker aimed at preparing the team for the new campaign.[31] Soon after training camp began they got into an argument, Meeker producing documents detailing his efforts to get Stafford's attention and Stafford brushing him off. When Stafford put his hands on Meeker's chest to push him away, Meeker recounted; he slugged the Silver Seven chairman between the eyes and walked out.[32]

Among the powers Stafford still didn't have was the ability to fire Meeker, so he wrote a memo to his father requesting the new general manager be discharged "for obvious reasons of inexperience and incompatibility with the new set-up." Conn met with Meeker the same morning; two days later they signed a document attesting that "the Maple Leaf Gardens and Howie Meeker have agreed to disagree" and that Meeker would give up his duties but receive a full year's salary.[33] There was to be no replacement; new coach Billy Reay would be given added duties and King Clancy would carry on as an "assistant" to the GM, who didn't exist.

As if the situation wasn't sad enough already, in May that summer Dick Irvin succumbed to bone cancer, which had stricken him around the time he left the Canadiens in 1955 to coach the Black Hawks. Smythe arranged for six members of the 1932 Leafs to carry the casket from the hearse to the gravesite. Dick Irvin Jr., who had never met Smythe, was walking from the grave when he heard Smythe call his name. "He said, 'Dick!' And the way he spoke you came to attention. "He said, 'Don't you forget your father saved hockey in Montreal.' And that's the only time the man ever spoke to me."[34] Two nights before Irvin died, his son had asked him who had been the smartest hockey man he ever met.

"Without hesitation, he replied, 'Conn Smythe.'"[35]

In all, the events of that season obviously weren't what Smythe had anticipated. But it was done and Smythe was sticking to it. He was determined to let Stafford run his show and to stay out of his way as much as possible. He would let him succeed or fail on his own.

CHAPTER 19

With the succession settled, happily or otherwise, Smythe was able to concentrate on defeating the upstart new players' organization. He had a number of tools to work with, as there were glaring flaws in Lindsay's project for the owners to exploit.

Support for the association was broad, but shallow. It's one of hockey's oldest clichés, but in this case it happened to be true: most of the players just wanted to play hockey. They had, for generations, accepted the autocratic nature of the NHL and willingly delegated control to the handful of men who owned the teams. They knew careers were short, and once their skills diminished they would be cut loose with little more than a handshake and whatever memories they'd managed to store up. Many – probably most – looked on it as a price worth paying for the privilege they'd been given.

"They were going to make us heroes across Canada," remembers Dick Duff, who carried the Leafs through some of their worst years just to be traded when the rewards started coming in. "They're not going to pay us much, and we're not going to play very long. At thirty we're gone . . . You borrowed some of Canada's kids for a few years to run your business."[1]

The pension plan, focus of most complaints, was only dimly understood. Once a year, Clarence Campbell visited each team to extoll the plan and update players on its activities. Those who asked questions were treated with withering condescension. Frank Mahovlich remembers his first pension meeting as a pro, held at Ted Reeve Arena. "I decided to ask a question. I didn't think our pension was that great. And Campbell says: 'What are you asking questions for, you just got here.' He really put me down. He was serious, he didn't want some young hockey player asking questions."[2]

Bob Baun had a similar experience. "I must have drove Clarence Campbell crazy because I put my hand up all the time. I knew a little bit about the insurance business, but not very much, and I could never figure out how this token of money – and it was all our money to start with – was going to turn into a big amount of money that was going to keep my family and me going until I die. They'd try to explain that to me and I'd say, 'It seems to me the only people who are getting rich are the insurance companies.' I said, 'Actuarially we have to see what's going on.' Well, everybody wondered where I got that word."[3]

But Baun, Mahovlich, and the few others who took an active interest were a small minority, and the owners had plenty of room to work on the others, who were eager to get more benefits but didn't want to endanger their careers. In August, before he got the axe, Meeker had spoken to Tim Horton who, like Baun, was a big proponent of better pensions. But when Meeker filled him in on the details of Milton Mound's demands for Jim Thomson, Horton was offended. "It is Horton's opinion that the two players, Harvey and Lindsay, are the only ones that had any working knowledge of what the Association's lawyers are doing," Meeker informed Smythe. "It is now Horton's opinion that the Association is a bad thing for the Players."[4]

The owners skillfully exploited the players' fear of being labelled a union. Although many were from working-class homes where fathers toiled at low-paying jobs and appreciated the benefits unionization could bring, there was a pride and individuality that came with being a big-league hockey player and a sense that fans wouldn't stick by them if they became the hockey affiliate of organized labour. In a letter to Mound, the players' attorney, Smythe drove home that point:

> I do not believe in threats in a relationship between hockey players and
> their club where the success of all parties depends on mutual loyalties.
> May I, however, be permitted . . . to suggest that if the players are

seriously considering becoming trade unionists, it is a worthy and nowadays often exciting occupation but with little spectator interest. I should consider it impossible to sell tickets to the public to watch players in the same trade union going about their trade with due respect not only to seniority ratings but to officers of the union who happened to be on the opposing club.[5]

Lindsay had also made a tactical error in his choice of vice-president. Montreal's Doug Harvey was the pre-eminent defence-man in the NHL, admired for his skill and popular for his enthusiasm and camaraderie. But he was a kid who couldn't grow up, irresponsible and careless with his money, and already well down the road to the alcoholism that turned his life into a tragedy. The thought of putting Harvey in charge of a pension fund on which hundreds of players were counting made Frank Selke as firm an opponent as Smythe was in Toronto.

Association members were also handicapped by a lack of comparative information. Players on opposing clubs rarely fraternized, and even within teams discussing salaries was taboo. They had no way to judge how they stood versus one another and even less means to assess their income against the profitability of the teams. Year after year the owners insisted they were barely scraping by and that more than a token pay raise could push them into the poorhouse.

In Toronto's case, of course, it was baloney. In the year of the Players' Association appearance, Smythe's salary had been raised to $35,000. His 50,000 Gardens' shares were eligible for a regular dividend of $1.20 each, plus a 30-cent bonus declared in January. Profit was $214,000, not the best year the Gardens ever had, but satisfying nonetheless. Gardens' dividends had tripled since 1950, bringing Smythe an extra $50,000 a year.

The highest-paid Leaf at the time was George Armstrong, whose $1,000 bonus as the new captain put him at $11,500, $500 ahead of Dick Duff. Frank Mahovlich was making $10,000, the same as Ron

Stewart. The league minimum for full-time players was $100 a game, or $7,000 for the season. Toronto had three players at that level, tied with the Rangers for most in the league. In response to a request from Smythe, Clarence Campbell investigated and discovered there were nineteen players on the six teams making less than $8,000.

The players were right to be suspicious of the pension plan. Of the six members of the Players' Association executive, the expected pensions at age sixty ranged from $2,369 for Harvey to $2,669 for Thomson. Harvey's anticipated return after a decade as the league's premier defenceman was approximately double that of Smythe's office secretary. Mahovlich says his pension from the NHL is "embarrassing." Meeker paid $900 a year for five years, which was invested for forty years and pays him less than $200 a month.[6]

The players weren't even allowed to keep the income from their own endorsements. Personal appearances were dictated by the team, with the player getting a flat $10. The 1957–58 contract for Parkhurst Products, which produced bubble gum with hockey cards, was worth $5,000 a year. St. Lawrence Starch paid $4,300 for its Beehive Corn Syrup trading cards and personal endorsements. Of the total, the players were allowed to split $2,000, or about $100 each. Foster Hewitt got $2,433, apparently as negotiating agent, while the Gardens kept $4,866.[7]

When Smythe asked Meeker to estimate the cost of the association's demands, the bill was modest. All told – including improved moving expenses, compensation for income lost due to injuries, higher training allowances, a bigger playoff split, and a $450 per player contribution to the pension fund, it came to less than $20,000 a year for the entire team. Nonetheless, in September Smythe invited four Toronto sportswriters to his office and handed them details of the pension fund. He told them they could do with the information what they wanted, but offered a broad suggestion: "It could be that this whole thing is a smokescreen to enable a small group to get control of the NHL pension fund, which now amounts to about $1,750,000 – and this group might be more interested in its own welfare than that of the players."[8]

In November, Smythe made a special address to Gardens shareholders. When launched, he said, the association had insisted it meant no harm to the game and had no plans to "make trouble" for the owners. "Since that time every Owner, every Club has been sued as a monopoly and has also been charged under the Labour Relations Board of the U.S. with unfair labour practices, and we have been subjected to a certification problem under the Ontario Labour Relations laws," he said.

All this was the doing of Ted Lindsay and Milton Mound, the New York lawyer who "has absolutely no knowledge of hockey" but was smart enough to be making $100,000 a year off clients like the NHL players. Although "a great how-do-you-do" was being made about the pension fund, both Lindsay and Harvey had been on its board for two years without raising a single complaint or opposing a single motion.

"So the record of the Association in nearly a year is that they are causing a good deal of trouble and that no one can point out one thing that has been done which is helpful for hockey or for our team or for our individual players."

Smythe's position got a boost when Syl Apps, who had been instrumental in setting up the pension, announced he and other retirees were "entirely satisfied with the present status and management of this Fund" and expressed "alarm" at reports that current players were trying to seize control. There were as many retirees as there were active players, yet they were unrepresented by the new association. In addition, he said, he had studied the organization's constitution and discovered it put inordinate decision-making power in the hands of members of the executive, as few as four of whom could make binding decisions. In a letter to Clarence Campbell, quickly released to the press, he appealed to the NHL president to block Lindsay.

All this, and similar efforts, enabled Smythe, Campbell, and the other owners to chip away successfully at the commitment of the players. And while Smythe was a leading party to the opposition, he was not the decisive figure, or the most ruthless. For all his efforts, the Leafs players voted overwhelmingly to ratify their support for the association and ignored a fevered locker-room pitch in which Smythe, accompanied by Campbell, spelled out the full horrors of what they were about to do. The events that killed Lindsay's project took place in Detroit, where Jack Adams lied about Lindsay's salary, produced phoney financial records to convince the players the team was in financial peril, and orchestrated a newspaper smear campaign accusing Lindsay of manipulating and duping his team-mates for his own benefit. Lindsay wasn't there to challenge the false-hoods, having been shipped to the Black Hawks, where Smythe had similarly dumped Jimmy Thomson and would send fellow conspirator Tod Sloan. It was crude and effective. Nervous NHLers began to defect and Lindsay was forced to negotiate for what he could get.

The result wasn't a total failure for the players. At a conference with the owners in February 1958 they got most of what they wanted – the clubs would match contributions to the pension and there would be improvements in a range of payments, from moving expenses to exhibition games and the playoff pool. Fines would be deposited in an "emergency fund" for players and former players in need. The association itself, however, was largely neutralized. Henceforth differences with the owners would be thrashed out at an "owner-players council," which quickly became moribund.

The bigger issues would be left for another decade of growing discontent until expansion came along and changed the dynamic – though then again the players would eventually find themselves holding the short straw. Smythe, for one, considered the concessions made by the owners in 1958 a small price to pay and a clear victory over troublesome agitators like Lindsay. A year after his special address to shareholders he was able to attend the NHL's annual meeting and detail the extent to which the threat had been vanquished: "No concessions of any kind were made which would impinge on the right and authority with respect to the conduct of the management of a club, or which acknowledged in any manner a right to share in the revenues of the club except by salary, bonus or incentive money," he stated proudly. "No recognition was given to the NHL Players' Association in any respect."[9]

CHAPTER 20

After his replacement, Hap Day had very little to do with the Maple Leafs. He moved to the small town of St. Thomas, west of Toronto, where he bought a struggling firm that made axe handles. He had offers from other teams, but stayed out of hockey. He had been close to Harold Ballard for years, but Ballard quickly, and characteristically, dropped him once his value waned.

Smythe felt guilty about the end of their thirty-year relationship and tried to ease the guilt with an extravagant parting gift: a fourteen-inch replica of the Stanley Cup in gold, inscribed with the names of "the players and associates in the years of your greatest triumphs." It was delayed when the elderly man hired to do the intricate inscribing fell ill.

Day wouldn't have felt very comfortable with the new atmosphere anyway. Stafford was appointed to head the new committee on May 9, 1957, and immediately disparaged Day's work: "Under the present cut and dried system, you can win a game and they still check how many goals a player had scored against him. It's time we put a little enjoyment back in the game for the players."[1]

Stafford fired Meeker as manager on October 3, a month before he could manage his first game. "He didn't have the kind of experience needed for that kind of job and needs to learn more about it. We don't have the time to let him gain that experience," Stafford said.[2] Meeker, observed the *Star*'s Gordon Campbell, "is probably the only general manager in hockey history who was fired before he could find out whether he could manage."[3]

The first season of the new administration was anything but enjoyable, as the Leafs sank to dead last. But redemption was at hand. In mid-July, a four-paragraph item partway down an inside page announced, "IMLACH APPOINTED LEAFS SECOND AGM." The hiring of the little-known George "Punch" Imlach had been rumoured for some time. He'd spent the previous season as general manager of Eddie Shore's Springfield Indians and would be the first Leafs boss since 1927 – other than Conn Smythe himself – who had never played in the NHL. His hiring would prove the catalyst that reversed the club's slide, as the Leafs went from sixth place to fourth to second in just two years.

As Smythe had promised, he left Stafford to sink or swim on his own, confining himself to financial matters and league-wide affairs. The players who would turn the club into a Stanley Cup winner were mainly in place in any case: the last-place 1957 team included Dick Duff, Billy Harris, George Armstrong, Ron Stewart, Frank Mahovlich, Bob Pulford, Tim Horton, Bob Baun, Carl Brewer, and Bob Nevin, all of whom would feature in Cup winners to come. Imlach rescued Johnny Bower from the minors, traded for Red Kelly and Allan Stanley, and added twenty-year-old centre Dave Keon to complete the transformation.

Smythe busied himself with more prosaic matters. The NHL was growing up, and governors were concerned with an array of vexing bureaucratic preoccupations. They debated an "emergency rehabilitation plan" to take effect should some catastrophe strike them, produced a report on roster sizes and whether they had grown too large, mediated scheduling disputes, plunged into an interminable debate over TV broadcasting policies, and even considered the sliding characteristics of pucks.

He found plenty of opportunities to argue. In 1961, St. Michael's College announced it would withdraw from the Junior A circuit, citing too many games, too much bad publicity over roughness, and too many complaints about the pressure hockey put on academics. The decision set off a chain reaction. If St. Mike's wouldn't play, said Stafford, neither would the Marlboros. Instead, he organized a new Metro League including St. Mike's, the Marlboros, and three former Junior B teams to play a much shorter schedule. Sam Pollock, director of the Montreal farm system, exploded when he heard the news, as the withdrawal of the two talent-heavy Toronto teams would remove a rich crop of future NHLers from the league.

Smythe defended Stafford's action and started a separate battle over formation of the Eastern Professional Hockey League, a semi-pro circuit that had the backing of the other five NHL teams. Toronto was adamant it would not participate.

"We are entirely against this new league," he told Clarence Campbell, predicting it would be a financial disaster. There was a bitter exchange of letters between Toronto and Montreal, as Smythe insisted Metro League teams should be allowed to play interlocking games with OHA teams, but refused to allow EPHL teams anywhere near Toronto. He sent off a series of increasingly irate letters to Selke and Senator Hartland Molson, the Habs' president, accusing them of mistreating the Leafs.

Selke replied wearily that he'd long ago decided not to engage in letter wars with Smythe, and it had been Toronto's own decision to pull out of the OHA. Smythe appealed to Molson, with a thinly veiled threat to make trouble for its beer interests "unless the Canadien organization changes their attitude and acts in a friendly manner towards us." Molson responded that his family had been selling beer in Ontario since 1824, and he could see "no reason these people should have their interests threatened by any difficulties . . . between our two great hockey teams." In the end, neither the Metro League nor EPHL lasted long, and harmony was restored.[4]

Despite that aggravation, Smythe's relations with Selke had steadily improved, largely through co-operation in establishing the Hockey Hall of Fame. Selke had done most of the legwork and had patiently massaged Smythe's ego to get him involved. Smythe remained aloof until a site had been approved at the Canadian National Exhibition, when he agreed to supervise construction. The design contract went to Roper Gouinlock, who had built Smythe's home in Baby Point and been a teammate on the 1915 Varsity team that defeated Selke's Union Jacks.[5] Nonetheless Smythe engaged in a drawn-out dispute over the exact size and location of the lettering for the sign to be placed on top of the CNE building, which he wanted to be visible from a distance, but not unsightly or large enough to overwhelm the Hall itself. When Selke worried that the costs were coming in above estimates, Smythe told him, "Who cares?" and pledged that he and Norris would ensure the money was raised.

The official opening ceremony took place August 26, 1961, with a speech by Prime Minister John Diefenbaker, who, to Smythe's aggravation, included a reference to "my colleague and one of the greatest of Canadian goalkeepers in amateur hockey, Senator Joe Sullivan" – the same Joe Sullivan that Smythe considered a "skunk" for ruining his plans for the 1928 Winter Olympics.

Smythe had been named to the Hall when it existed only on paper. He and King Clancy were approved as members in 1958, along with Dick Irvin, Frank Boucher, and Ching Johnson. Once construction was completed in 1961, he and Selke engaged in friendly back-channel plotting to ensure their favoured candidates were approved by the selection committee, anticipating the demands of the other members and planning tradeoffs they could make in return.

"I know Red Dutton will shill for Harry Oliver. I can name dozens with better records," Selke observed archly one winter from his farm outside Montreal. "Winnipeg will bring up Dick's brother Alex Irvin – a very fine man [but] no better hockey player than a hundred you knew in the senior and Intermediate OHA."[6]

Smythe responded that when a player like Ted Kennedy had to wait his turn after Harry Oliver – who had scored 127 goals in ten years with Boston and New York Americans – "there isn't any sense in having a Hockey Hall of Fame." That brought another burst of flattery from Selke: "It's easy to see why you have been such a success in life as against my near failure. I have always worried about Public opinion – you decide what you want to do and to hell with the fault finders."[7]

Smythe lobbied hard to have Red Horner admitted, even though he was best known for spending time in the penalty box. Horner made it, but Toe Blake missed out on his first attempt when some of the members misunderstood the voting procedure. They demanded a new vote when Blake failed to get the required support, but Selke refused. Blake had to wait another year to gain entry.

Almost from the beginning there was controversy over Busher Jackson, who Smythe was determined to block from entry. Jackson's decline into alcoholism had left him a sad and broken figure, the object of pity and frustration among many who had tried to help him, but failed. "Busher Jackson was a wife beater," said Smythe. "He was thrown in and out of jail a dozen times. He didn't work and he never paid for anything. He had several friends who bailed him out a hundred times."[8]

Smythe, along with Selke, Charlie Conacher, and Joe Primeau, had tried more than once to set him up in business opportunities, but his drinking always got in the way. In 1958, Clarence Campbell had written Smythe a note suggesting the Players' Emergency Fund might also help out. Smythe wrote back that he would support any effort, but contacting Jackson proved difficult. His wife had fled with their seven-year-old son and was working at a garage. She refused to provide an address or any details "on account of her fear that Busher would turn up and do them some violence."

Campbell reported that a job had been arranged for Jackson to act as "front man" for a new gas station, but he had started "hitting the bottle again around Christmas and nobody is interested in assisting him any further." He also discovered his wife's whereabouts and turned up at the garage, almost costing her the job.[9]

Campbell sent Jackson's wife money for clothes and her son's education. He also paid off Jackson's debts and sent an allowance to the elderly aunt with whom he lived. Campbell agreed that he did not deserve membership in the Hall of Fame but Smythe attracted most of the criticism when Toronto papers mounted regular crusades on Jackson's behalf.[10] He sent them a copy of the Hall's selection criteria, which specified that candidates would be evaluated "on the basis of playing ability, integrity, character and their contribution to their Team and the Game of Hockey in general." Jackson, he argued, failed on at least three conditions.

The dispute would run for years. In a characteristic contradiction, Smythe tried to help Jackson quietly while abusing him in public. Jackson was still a familiar figure around the Gardens, a garrulous and sociable man who sometimes cadged broken sticks to sell for drinking money.[11] He was seldom required to pay for anything. Hugh Smythe acted as his personal physician, checking him into hospitals and trying to keep him there after his many alcohol-fuelled accidents, taking away his pyjama bottoms so he couldn't flee.[12]

When he wasn't arguing over league issues or Hall of Fame matters, Smythe pursued his passionate opposition to the federal government's plan to introduce a new Canadian flag. The proposal was a personal priority of Lester Pearson, who became prime minister in 1963. Smythe had known Pearson since his days at the University of Toronto, where Pearson had succeeded him as Varsity coach.

He called the prime minister by his nickname, "Mike," and they exchanged polite but deeply felt arguments over the merits of the Red Ensign versus Pearson's new Maple Leaf flag. The Ensign had represented Canada in both wars in which Smythe fought, but Pearson saw a new flag as a crucial matter of national unity. Quebec was in the early stages of the Quiet Revolution, asserting its individuality as never before, and Pearson considered the flag an essential step toward holding the country together.

Veterans were among his fiercest opponents, arguing that consigning the Ensign to history was a betrayal of the men who had fought for it. The debate was an echo of the conscription crisis Smythe had helped bring about in 1944, with Quebec eager to eliminate symbols that reminded them of English domination. Pearson was accused of aping Mackenzie King in currying favour with Quebec in the face of English opposition. When he appeared at a Royal Canadian Legion convention in Winnipeg in May 1964, he was booed and hissed by two thousand angry members.[13]

But Pearson was adamant, and public opinion was on his side. He assured Smythe Canada could have its own flag while maintaining its links to England. "The official adoption of a national flag for Canada . . . surely need not mean any disrespect to the Mother Country and nothing will be done to show such disrespect while I am the head of the Canadian government," he wrote.[14]

Smythe wasn't mollified and never would be. His hostility to Quebec increased as the debate heated up. "It is hard for me to realize that anybody would consider the pulling down of our flag a means of promoting good will among men," he wrote Pearson in one letter,[15] adding in another: "Do you honestly expect that you will get one more volunteer to fight for our country under a new flag?"[16]

For more than a year he campaigned feverishly. He had a letter printed up and sent out three hundred copies to MPs, senators, cabinet members, and other opinion-makers. Each envelope included a stamp of the Red Ensign and the slogan: "This *is* Canada's Flag. Keep it flying!" He tried buttering up Pearson with flattery at the same time he was regularly sending telegrams to Diefenbaker with messages of support. In March 1964, he wrote Pearson that he appreciated "how lucky we are to have you as our Prime Minister," and that Canadians were "blessed to have you take on this onerous job for us all."[17] But not long after he wrote Diefenbaker urging him to step up the battle, pledging that "you will find that the loyal, solid millions of Canadian citizens will see you re-elected Prime Minister of this country."[18]

His campaign was for naught, however. The country had changed since 1944 and he was on the wrong side of national sentiment. English Canada was no longer the British bastion it had once been, and talk of the glories of Empire had become a relic, like the white-haired men in the Legion halls who spoke of it with such feeling. Unlike King's divided and quarrelsome cabinet, Pearson's supported his plan. Just two days after his legion ordeal, Pearson said his 127 MPs had "almost unanimously" agreed on a new design. Although he promised to hold an open vote in Parliament, he was confident of success: "We're not going to have much trouble in the Liberal party on that vote, I can assure you."[19]

It was no small irony that the symbol he had settled on, the maple leaf, was the same one Smythe had plucked from his wartime experiences to represent his team and the depth of his patriotism. Many times he had spoken of its importance to him, yet now he was denouncing it as an insult to the values he believed in.

As Pearson had predicted, Parliament approved the flag by a wide margin, and the new red and white banner was unfurled in February 1965. Smythe refused to give in. "His" flag was still the Red Ensign and he flew it wherever he had control of the flagpole. He hounded Bassett into agreeing to fly the old flag at the Gardens alongside the new one and was pleased when Ontario adopted the Ensign as its provincial flag soon after. He never changed his mind about the issue, "but I had run out of battlefields," he noted ruefully.[20]

His failure in the flag debate was like a harbinger of a changing tide. His long string of luck suddenly seemed to abandon him, and he was about to experience the better part of a decade in which the tragedies and disappointments seemed to flow ceaselessly from one into the other. While he was sincere in his feelings for the Red Ensign, the debate also served as a diversion, allowing him a respite from the much greater tragedy enveloping him at the same time.

Late in 1963, Irene had begun experiencing lingering pain. Tests found she had cancer. It was terminal and would be painful. Although she might survive a year or more, it would be a time of slowly progressing incapacity, as the cancer spread through her bone marrow. Typically, she did her best to cushion the effect on her husband. "Now, Daddy, don't worry about me," she'd tell him. "It's something we have to put up with."[21]

Her suffering was excruciating, however, and Smythe agonized at his inability to help her. They moved into separate rooms, but he would hear her moaning in the night and lie in his own bed chafing at the injustice. While he had bulldozed his way through life impervious to his effect on others, Irene had charmed the same people who considered her husband a bad-tempered bully. She was kind where he was gruff, friendly where he was cold. Patricia's death had brought them closer together, united in their grief, and Smythe's wounds made him appreciate all the more the care and affection she provided him.

The cancer worsened through 1964 and by year-end Irene was in agony much of the time. Conn, wanting to give her the emotional support she had always given him, concluded it was inhuman to allow people to endure so much. "I can't imagine a good God asking a lovely person like my wife to suffer that much when a doctor could give her something that would end it forever."[22] On a night when she confessed she was near the limit of her endurance, he offered to use his old army revolver to end her suffering.

"If you can't take the pain any more, and want to end it, you tell me. I will stop your suffering myself," he told her.[23] A few nights later she asked if he still had the gun. Taking a deep breath, he said he did and was prepared to use it. But Irene decided that was "a coward's way out" and steeled herself to endure a while longer.

She died early on a Sunday in June 1965. A notice in the paper stipulated: "If you plan to attend the service, please wear cheerful colours, as that is the way she would like it."[24] More than two thousand people attended and paid heed to the request. "Women were in bright dresses and gay colourful hats, men wore summer suits, bright ties and matching socks. All had felt the warmth of this gracious lady's smile and the genuine friendliness in her greeting," the paper reported. Her casket was draped with the Red Ensign.

Her death opened an enormous hole in Smythe's life. He was seventy. He wasn't exactly alone in the world, but he had lost the one woman he had allowed himself to love. His children were long since grown and embarked on their own lives. Hugh, the youngest, was immersed in a career in medicine. Miriam, age forty-two the year her mother died, was married and following a path that bore unnerving reminders of the one that had claimed Smythe's mother at a too-early age. She drank too much and was in the process of ruining her health. There had been car accidents and other mishaps due to alcohol. He tried to help her and ensured her husband was well paid at the Gardens, but father and daughter weren't close.

Which left Stafford, and a relationship that hadn't lost any of its tension after Conn turned over his team and his arena to his son.

In hockey terms, the Silver Seven experiment had been a success. Punch Imlach had proved to be just the tonic to mould and motivate the mix of youth and veterans in the Leaf lineup, and after the first desultory season there had been rapid and regular improvement.

Success only served to exacerbate the friction. It was one thing for Conn to keep Stafford on a short leash when the team was struggling just to make the playoffs, something else altogether when they were challenging for first place and a spot in the Stanley Cup finals. In 1961, the Leafs came within two points of topping the league, and while Detroit kept them from making the finals, they were clearly a team on the rise. Stafford could claim much of the credit: although many of the top players had worked their way through the system while Conn was still titularly in charge, a solid core had been developed by Stafford via the Marlboros network or brought in by Imlach.

It rankled Stafford that his father treated him as no more than a hired employee. If he wanted to spend any money, he had to call someone on the board of directors and get permission. If Imlach bought a player, the cheque had to be approved by Conn. His father kept such tight control that even a new typewriter had to have his okay.

Frustrated, Stafford threatened to quit and go back to the sand and gravel business. He and Conn bickered at board meetings – over hockey, over the antics of the Silver Seven, over Conn's sense that he was being pushed aside. Stafford, Ballard, and John Bassett were all accumulating shares, just as he had done when planning his own take-over after the war. Finally, Conn had had enough and challenged Stafford at a board meeting: "If you think you're so smart why don't you buy my stock?"[25]

He knew Stafford had no way to do so on his own. His son was in the same boat he'd been in when he lacked the money to buy control. Stafford needed a modern version of Percy Gardiner, the broker who'd sold Conn his stock on the installment plan. Stafford's version of Gardiner was Harold Ballard, and Ballard knew that if you wanted money you go to where they keep it – in the bank. After a feverish period of plotting with Stafford, Ballard turned up one morning at his local branch and informed the manager he needed $2 million to buy Maple Leaf Gardens. Within hours the loan was approved. From a drugstore, they called John Bassett, who they agreed to cut in for a third of the deal.

It all happened in a whirlwind. On November 23, 1961, a Thursday, the deal was announced: Smythe would sell all but 5,000 of his 50,000 shares for $40 each, a premium over the previous day's closing price of $34. The trio had hoped to pay just $30, but Smythe was doing them no favours. They would split the shares in three equal divisions, giving them control of about 60 per cent of the stock.

Once again Conn faced the press and pretended everything was fine. "It's a great satisfaction to me that my son, who not so long ago as a stick boy congratulated me on winning the Stanley Cup, now has a chance to do the same thing as president," he said.[26] He almost certainly didn't mean it. He was happy Stafford would succeed him, but he insisted, then and later, that he thought he was selling to Stafford alone and was unaware his son had brought in two partners.

It was, he thought, a stupid thing to do. "That's the worst business mistake you could ever make," he roared at Stafford when he learned the truth. "You have the whole pot, and now you're going to get a third instead, so that every time this place makes a million dollars, you're going to give two-thirds of it away."[27]

It was even worse than that. Unbeknownst to his father, the trio had agreed that if any of them decided to sell, the others would have first claim. In Conn Smythe's mind, the Gardens was a family business he had built for Stafford, to be passed on to Stafford's son,

Tommy, when the time came. But unless both Ballard and Bassett agreed – unlikely as they both had children of their own – that could no longer happen. In one disastrous transaction, Stafford had given away two-thirds of his legacy and all but ensured the eventual loss of the hockey team his father had spent his life assembling. The best Tommy could aspire to would be a fraction of the club he might have owned.

It remains unclear just how much Smythe really knew about the details of Stafford's dealings. He knew Stafford lacked the money to buy him out on his own and was well aware of the close relationship with Ballard, and Ballard's ambitious nature. While he may not have realized Bassett was also involved, he had certainly learned the facts by the time of the public announcement and press conference, but still went ahead with the sale. He never explained why, insisting he'd been caught off guard by the whole thing.

The new owners immediately set about altering much of what he'd done. Stafford was made president and put in charge of the hockey team, Ballard was executive vice-president, in charge of everything else. It was Ballard who came up with most of the money-spinning ideas that turned the Gardens from a profitable but humdrum business into "the Maple Leaf Mint" and "the Cashbox on Carlton Street" as it became known. But Stafford more than went along. On the day of the sale he announced one of the first moves would be to find a way to install more seats. The team had two thousand names on its waiting list for subscribers, and he was eager to accommodate them. Imlach, he said, would be given "more freedom than ever" as he and Ballard concentrated on boosting profits.

They found all sorts of ways to do so. They took down the picture of the Queen that for decades had dominated the end wall and removed the balcony where the military bands had entertained fans between periods. They added seats right away and continued to squeeze in more and more wherever they could find room. When necessary, they made them smaller while simultaneously raising prices. At one point they applied to extend the building over the sidewalk on

Carlton Street for even more seating, but couldn't win approval. Eventually they found ways to pack in thirty-five hundred extra fans for every game.

Both were keen to get moving on a plan for a suitable watering hole for sportsmen-around-town, like them. They calculated the Hot Stove Lounge would cost just $190,000 to build and bring in a profit from food sales alone of $142,000 a year. On top of that they would sell $100 "memberships" to one thousand lucky patrons, then charge them another $50 a year once they were in.[28] (It would, of course, sell alcohol – lots of alcohol, they hoped – which was yet another slight to the thirty-five years of temperance enforced by the previous owner.)

Smythe wasn't pleased. So much of it went against everything he'd represented for so many years. The drive to make money as rapidly as possible, the treatment of customers as just so many rubes to be soaked on a regular basis, the disregard for tradition, and the downgrading of hockey to just another entertainment product among many. One of his reasons for resenting Selke had been the frequency of the ice shows and other attractions he'd booked into the building. Now Ballard put Selke to shame, tracking down and booking every rock 'n' roll group able to fill his seats with screaming teenagers. They sold advertising on everything, including the steps of the escalators.

It was all very profitable. Income tripled, while share prices almost quadrupled. The money they'd borrowed was paid off in four years.[29] When the shares reached a peak and split five-for-one in 1965, the stock Smythe had sold for $2 million was worth close to $6.5 million. Even better, the Leafs were winning: three Stanley Cups in a row, in 1962, 1963, and 1964. Parades to City Hall were becoming so commonplace the fans were growing blasé. Toronto had an entire new pantheon of heroes: Mahovlich, Bower, Kelly, Horton, Keon, and nothing, it appeared, but more good news on the horizon.

But the temperature of Smythe's temper was rising, and less than a year after he'd buried Irene it exploded. The spark was the Gardens' agreement to host a heavyweight fight between champion Muhammad

Ali and challenger Ernie Terrell. The bout had been turned down in several other locations in protest over Ali's conversion to Islam and his controversial statements about race, religion, and the Vietnam War. When he was classified as eligible for the draft he said he would refuse to serve, as war was an offence against the teachings of his religion.

To Major Conn Smythe, wounded veteran of two wars, Ali was no better than a coward and a draft dodger. "A fight that isn't good enough for Chicago or Montreal certainly isn't good enough for Maple Leaf Gardens," he said.[30] But the Ontario government had approved it, and the Gardens was determined to put it on. The top tickets were pegged at $100 each, the first time any event had commanded that much anywhere in the city.

Smythe, who was at his winter home in Palm Beach, telephoned Bassett and resigned from the board. Bassett refused to accept it, but Smythe persisted. "I cannot go along with the policy of present management to put cash ahead of class," he said.[31] "I have no control over the policies of present management so the only alternative is to dissociate myself from it."

Stafford was also vacationing in Florida, but several hours farther south in Delray Beach. He refused to intervene in the quarrel, saying, "Mr. Ballard has complete authority to act on our behalf."

Thus was severed Smythe's last official link to the team and the arena he'd built, named, and turned into a nationally known monument to hockey. The fight went ahead – though Terrell pulled out, complaining Ballard had altered the contract, and Ali was left to pummel Canadian favourite George Chuvalo instead. A few months later Smythe delighted a raucous audience at a Hall of Fame luncheon with a comical rendition of his departure, telling them: "You fellows know what it is to be traded. I was traded for a black Muslim minister and $35,000." Stafford and Ballard, he added, had made Gardens seats "so narrow only thin young men can sit in them and only fat old bankers can afford them."[32]

Smythe retained an office, car, and secretary at the Gardens, but he no longer had an official position and even less clout. For long periods, in fact, he and Stafford were not on speaking terms. When Jammed Lovely, a Smythe horse whose name had been inspired by Irene, won the Queen's Plate in 1967, Stafford didn't turn up at the celebration.[33] At a testimonial dinner for Frank Selke in the mid-sixties, his son delivered an emotional tribute he'd had prepared as a booklet. Afterward, Stafford approached Frank Jr. and told him: "You know, I wish I could write that kind of story about my father, but I can't."[34]

Whether deliberate or not, the timing of his departure was apt. The NHL was going through a period of wrenching change, having determined to double in size in what would prove to be just the beginning of an extended period of growth. Six new teams would be added for the 1967–68 season, the first alteration in the league's makeup since the New York Americans – renamed the Brooklyn Americans in their final season – had disappeared in 1942. Franchises were awarded in Oakland, Los Angeles, Minnesota, Philadelphia, Pittsburgh, and St. Louis. Toronto embraced expansion, not least because the Leafs would receive almost $2.2 million in fees, in return for exposing more than twenty players in the draft organized to stock the new teams. The schedule had also been expanded, adding four more games, which meant two more home games for Staff and Ballard to cash in.

Smythe wanted no part of it. At one time he had backed expansion as a means of keeping the league alive and vibrant, but that was years ago and he'd only figured on adding one or two teams. Six, all at once, was too much, and he predicted a sharp dilution in talent and competition.

"You'd think it was something new," he said at the Hall of Fame gathering. "We expanded forty years ago. And I say this to Clarence Campbell: If you knew what was coming, you'd wipe that grin off your face."[35]

The new, improved NHL would be a much bigger and more complex operation than anything Smythe would have cared for. Salaries exploded, and a wave of lawyers, advisers, and agents arrived to help negotiate and complicate contracts on behalf of both sides. The Players'

Association was re-established and placed under the malevolent leader-ship of Alan Eagleson, a man of voracious ambition and flexible ethics who would spend two decades lying to, cheating, and betraying the players, helping himself to their money while hobnobbing with the owners.

Smythe was better off away from it, and had other things to do. His stables were among the most successful in the country. His charitable operations were extensive and time consuming – in 1962, a decade's worth of fundraising had culminated in construction of the $4 million Ontario Crippled Children's Centre in Toronto, the most modern facility of its kind in the country. The society also operated a network of summer camps, a vocational school for severely disabled children, an educational and rehabilitation centre near London, and a fleet of mobile clinics.[36] As treasurer it was Smythe's task to keep the money flowing in to operate it all.

Irene's death had inevitably drawn his mind to his own mortality, and he began distributing sums of money to friends and relations, writing out notes informing them he saw no reason to wait until he was in the ground.[37] His files began to fill with thank-you notes for surprise gifts and timely cheques, sometimes from acquaintances he had not seen in years, but had heard were going through tough times.

There was still plotting to be done at the Hockey Hall of Fame. In 1966, he and Selke became embroiled in a long-distance snit fit with Ted Lindsay, who had been absolved of the sin of launching the Players' Association and was to be honoured at a luncheon. Strictly speaking, Lindsay should have been ineligible for inclusion, as he had played his last game just a year earlier, but Smythe and Selke had arranged to have the rules changed to ensure his early entry. Lindsay, however, had refused to turn up when he learned the lunch would be men only.

The exclusion of women was a tradition. The get-together was meant as a sentimental affair for former players and their teammates. "It would not be as heart warming if ladies were in attendance," Selke wrote. "They naturally steal the show – common chivalry demands it."

But Lindsay wouldn't budge. He dismissed suggestions there were plenty of diversions for Mrs. Lindsay at the CNE for the hour or two of the lunch and dodged repeated calls from Selke – who, if anything, was angrier than Smythe – imploring him to attend.

"It's just typical of the man that after I spent hours justifying the rule change which makes him eligible he won't come because the CNE will not make a special ruling in his case," he fumed to Smythe.[38]

Smythe continued to veto Busher Jackson from membership, suffering a new round of criticism when Jackson passed away at age fifty-five. The stories were heavy with sentiment, excusing his frailties in a haze of nostalgia: "A weakness for alcohol and the bright lights led to two unsuccessful marriages and a succession of failures in the business world," wrote Red Burnett. "Several times he swore off the grog but always, until his final years, he found his way through the swinging doors to swap yarns with cronies and sample a glass of cheer."[39]

He was, they noted, the only member of the Kid Line not in the Hall. Old-timers called him the greatest left winger of the era. "He was poetry in motion," remembered Alex Levinsky as former stars gathered for his funeral. Smythe and Selke were among the mourners, and between them could have assured his election in a moment, but wouldn't budge. Selke later said he would have approved Jackson if Smythe had agreed, but Smythe was adamant. To anyone who complained he quoted the same paragraph from the Hall's entry rules, requiring candidates be evaluated on "integrity [and] character" as well as hockey skills.

One obituary writer huffed: "If every candidate for the shrine met its demanding moral standards, no human could have qualified."[40]

With all his activities, he barely noticed when federal income tax officials raided the Gardens and seized reams of documents. Stafford was in Vancouver with the team and shrugged it off as a dispute over Toronto's expansion fees: "We got $2 million in fees when the league expanded and we've been negotiating with the tax people ever since. We say it's capital gain, they say it's income."[41] Gardens lawyer Ian

Johnston added, "I don't understand why they'd go after any books, because we made full disclosure about the expansion deal at the time. However, who knows what bureaucrats are up to."

Smythe was ready to believe the worst of the bureaucrats, who had been hounding him personally for much of the decade. After selling the Gardens he had reorganized his finances in a complex scheme designed to minimize taxes and provide an immediate payout for him, Stafford, and Hap Day. Tax authorities ruled it was improper and assessed taxes amounting to more than double the payout, sparking a lengthy legal battle that Smythe lost.

That tussle had barely concluded when Ottawa launched a new one. Smythe's original sand and gravel pit in the city had finally been exhausted, and he had moved operations to the collection of farms he'd bought in Caledon. His extensive breeding and racing operations were located on the same property, as was a large country home he had built for himself and Irene, complete with gardens, fruit trees, pool, and a large artificial pond. One of his largest customers was a firm called Armstrong Holdings in nearby Brampton. In 1967, Smythe agreed to sell Armstrong 1,072 acres containing his gravel operations for $2.5 million, to be paid in installments over ten years. Once again, however, tax officials declared the deal was improper, this time because Smythe wasn't charging Armstrong interest on the delayed payments. They ruled the "fair market value" of the land was just $1.35 million and informed Smythe the rest would be treated as interest, at a hefty tax, plus 12 per cent interest and penalties.*

His lawyers recommended he settle, but Smythe was livid that Ottawa would consider him dishonest and collected a series of bible quotes condemning usury, to fling at his accusers. He rejected his lawyers' advice, "which I think was predicated on my age and the effect this contest would have on my health," and instructed them to

---

* In 1977, Smythe's original sand and gravel pit received a bronze plaque for rehabilitation after being turned into a local park and recreation centre.

prepare for a fight to the finish. It would drag on for several years before Smythe was exonerated, at which point he complained to his victorious lawyers at the size of the bill they sent him.[42]

He became convinced he was being hounded because of his high-profile battles with Ottawa. He claimed the finance minister, John Turner, was hoping to use the much-publicized tax dispute to further his political career. When word trickled out that Stafford's problems were far bigger than just a disagreement over expansion fees, he was more than willing to accept that his son was being persecuted as part of the same conspiracy.

It was much worse than that, though. Once again Stafford had left him in the dark about the truth of his actions, and there was nothing his father could do now to save him. Buoyed by the overwhelming success of the early years of their ownership, Stafford and Ballard had begun pilfering money for personal expenses. At first they stole trivial amounts, submitting personal bills as business expenses and having the Gardens pay for them. For years Stafford had seen his father use staff from the Gardens or the sand pit to shovel his driveway or paint the house, which wasn't strictly legal, but offended nobody. It wasn't hard to justify writing off travel bills or auto costs in the same way. It proved so easy that they took it further and crossed a line into blatant fraud, ordering extensive renovations to their homes and charging it to the Gardens. Stafford bought a company plane and used it regularly to commute to his cottage. They set up a separate account in the name "S.H. Marlie" and transferred almost $150,000 to use for their own expenses, which included chasing women and lots of drinking.[43]

When the truth became known within the company, Bassett moved to distance himself from his two partners, fearful his other business interests at the *Telegram* and CFTO-TV would be harmed. In June 1969, a board meeting was called, to be held at the headquarters of Imperial Oil in the vain hope it would attract less press interest. Stafford and Ballard were fired as president and executive vice-president, though they would remain on the board. The vote against them was tied, until Bassett used his deciding vote as chairman to oust his two friends. A financial controller was hired and an audit committee established to try to clean up the mess.

Conn told reporters he was "absolutely thunderstruck" at his son's firing and had known nothing about the situation. He repeated that he'd never meant to sell his shares to Ballard and Bassett and had thought the Gardens would be Stafford's alone.[44] While Ballard seemed disinclined to fight for his job, Stafford threatened to force a vote of shareholders to overturn the board decision.[45] When he spotted a clutch of reporters waiting for him outside the Gardens after the board session, he drove up over the sidewalk, sending them scattering. Ironically, news of the conflict sent Gardens' shares soaring in the next few days, netting Stafford and Ballard $1 million each.

Stafford did eventually succeed in rallying shareholders behind him and was reinstated as president. Bassett resigned and sold his partners his one-third share, giving them overwhelming control of the company. But it was too late for Stafford: in July 1969, he and Ballard were charged with fraud and income tax evasion – $278,920 for Stafford and $134,685 for Ballard. There were five counts each, and the Crown announced that it would try them by the tougher of two routes available, which meant the possibility of heavier fines and a longer jail term if convicted.

Stafford's drinking increased sharply. "He couldn't sleep. And to help him sleep, he would drink," said his brother, Hugh.[46] His health declined precipitously. Conn spent more time with him, as did Hugh and Tommy, Stafford's son, trying to bolster his spirits, but in November 1971 he collapsed at his office and was rushed to Wellesley Hospital with a bleeding ulcer. The initial operation appeared successful, but four days later he began bleeding internally and a second emergency operation was undertaken to remove part of his stomach. Doctors warned he might not survive the surgery, but Stafford told them to go ahead. He died early on the morning of October 13, at just fifty years of age. The trial had been set to begin twelve days later. "See

Dad," he told Smythe near the end, "I told you they wouldn't put me in jail."[47]

Even in death he elicited little sympathy. An obituary in the *Globe and Mail* noted:

> "Stafford Smythe was called arrogant, autocratic, ruthless, mendacious, domineering and numerous other things by people who didn't know him and by some people who did. He insisted he was immune to what people thought, but this might have been a facade. Those close to him say he was extremely sensitive to public opinion. However, even when he was unjustly maligned he seldom took the trouble to correct the record . . . He was aware that he provoked instant antagonism in many, but he accepted this as inevitable because he was Conn Smythe's son."[48]

He was buried near his cottage on Lake Muskoka, under a plaque – written by Tommy – declaring he'd been "persecuted to death by his enemies."[49] Conn inserted a notice in the papers declaring: "To the friend who wrote that Stafford was brutalized by the press unnecessarily and unfairly, I would like to say those are my sentiments too."[50] *

---

* Tommy Smythe remained angry at his father's treatment until his own death in June 2009, after a lengthy and painful battle with cancer. Just two months before his death he posted a comment on a cottage website in Muskoka, where his father and mother were buried, reading:

> If you read my book you will understand my life of upset that my father is not in the Hockey Hall of Fame. A young owner of the Leafs between the ages of 40 to 47 he won four Stanley Cups. Four years later at 4:44 in the morning he died very unexpectedly and the Leafs have not won since. When Harold Ballard stole the Leafs from the Smythe family he put a curse on the Leafs that will not disappear until his accomplishments are recognized and he is in the hall of fame beside my grandfather where he belongs.
> . . . It is time for the Leaf fans to stand up and correct this curse and have Harold removed and Stafford inducted. I've had a tough life since then and I hope I live to see that day. . . . By the way – I wrote the original headstone with my mother and a few years ago my younger sister changed the stone without consulting me. To this day I still strongly feel what I wrote then. . . ." (www.cottageblog.ca/2008/11/28/conn-stafford-smythe-rip-in-beautiful-muskoka/)

Although Smythe later spoke of the depth of his grief at his son's death, it was often with a sense of conflict. "Poor Stafford, the little guy went wrong. But he should have lived to be treated in the courts like anybody else," he told one interviewer not long afterwards.[51] He told another: "Because of his name, he was cruelly treated by all the publicity. Hundreds of fellows got more out of tax or were caught with more in that position and got off with paying a fine. But they were going to make an example of Stafford and Harold and, well, maybe they should have, because they had positions of trust."[52]

In his memoirs he suggested Stafford "gave up the fight to live because that was the only way he could spare his family, his son and daughters and grandchildren, the stigma of jailbird."

He argued the decision "did not lack courage," but sounded noticeably more impressed with Ballard's very different approach. "Ballard . . . stood his trial, went to the penitentiary, did his time, paid his debt, and joked about it while he was doing it . . . He did good things and bad things, as before. But he went on, faced it all, and Stafford could not."[53]

Stafford's death did not end the turmoil at the Gardens. In the months leading up to the trial, he and Ballard had replaced the rebellious members of the board with allies, including Hugh Smythe as vice-president. The surviving Smythe family members were uncertain whether they could hold on to Stafford's shares. He died with substantial debts, and Ballard was executor of his will, giving him immense power over any purchase offers.

Hugh Smythe quickly concluded there was a limited future for him on a board that included Ballard and his new directors. Friction developed, especially after Hugh began considering a bid to buy out Ballard. Hugh's photo suddenly disappeared from the Gardens program, an early show of the boorishness for which Ballard would become famous. When Tommy Smythe returned to work from the funeral, he found his belongings piled on the sidewalk.[54] Ballard asserted that a sharp drop in the Gardens' share price on the day Stafford died "saved them a million" in estate taxes and bragged that Stafford's widow had been "taken care of."* "Right off the top she got $125,000 in cold cash from the Gardens and a few other frills."[55]

Hugh seriously considered the buyout plan. "I was trying to buy a car at the time and I had to borrow $5,000, and they sent a private detective out to this area to see from the neighbours whether I was good for it. But to borrow $12 million, no question, just a handshake, that would have been easy. I had a lot of people who thought that would be a good idea."[56] His father was not involved and played a large part in scuppering the plan. "He knew it was going to be difficult. They were in the middle of that expansion and overexpansion and the shift in power away from Toronto and Montreal towards the United States." The world, Conn said, would be losing a good doctor if his last remaining son abandoned medicine to take on the headaches of hockey.

"Of course he did me a favour," said Hugh. "I was good at medicine, I would be totally new [in the NHL] and would have to start at the bottom in learning hockey, and the only reason in doing it was to get Tommy to get the Leafs going again."

Instead, Ballard borrowed another $7.5 million from the bank to buy Stafford's shares, and the last Smythe holding a job with the Toronto Maple Leafs walked away from Maple Leaf Gardens.

---

* Hugh Smythe was originally reluctant to challenge Ballard as Leaf boss. He told *The Globe and Mail* shortly after Stafford's death: "I am deeply interested in hockey, but I would have doubts about leaving medicine . . . [All] my long-term goals are in medicine." Though open to the possibility of becoming president, Smythe continued, "There are people more interested than I am . . . I would prefer handing it over to Harold. He has 40 years of effort behind him. He deserves the presidency." He changed his mind as he grew more familiar with Ballard's leadership in ensuing weeks, and as it became evident that Tommy Smythe would not get his chance to head the Gardens as his father and grandfather had.

CHAPTER 21

Busher Jackson finally made it into the Hall of Fame in June 1971, almost five years to the day after he died. Selke, still chairman of the selection committee, fumbled awkwardly in making the announcement, knowing it would cause controversy.[1]

Two days later Smythe quit his position as chairman of the governing committee of the Hall itself, complaining that "standards are going down everywhere today."[2]

He would have less and less to do with hockey as his years dwindled toward a close. He wasn't impressed with the calibre of play, which had suffered with expansion. Just as he'd predicted, there weren't enough players to go around, especially after the NHL added to the first round of new teams with a second, third, and fourth round. Other than the Montreal Canadiens, there wasn't a team he considered worth watching.

He became a convenient curmudgeon, someone that writers could go to when they needed a feature with some salty opinions and a few well-aimed insults. Selling the Gardens had been "a lousy deal," he said, and Ballard was a buccaneer who would storm any boat he thought contained gold. The world was going to hell in a handbasket, filled with fast-buck artists who were in everything for themselves. Bobby Hull was a great player, but a loner and disloyal for turning his back on the NHL for a bigger cheque from the upstart World Hockey Association. He didn't think "contract-breakers" should be allowed on Team Canada.

He was still angry at Pearson over the flag controversy: "It was one of the worst acts that any man ever did in his life. He gave us a label instead of an emblem and divided the country."[3] In any case, he said, democracy needed to be "revamped." There were too many politicians and not enough businessmen running things. Everyone was competing to spend money and not enough to make it. "You should get exactly what you worked for. Take care of the maimed and the sick, those people that need help. The rest, as far as I'm concerned, can have soup kitchens if they want them."[4]

He'd been on an anti-French tear since the rise of Quebec nationalism and the advent of federal bilingualism programs. At a ceremony to award the Hart Trophy to Bobby Orr in May 1971, he began his address, "Gentlemen and Frenchmen . . ."

If French was any good as a language, he argued, it wouldn't need to be protected. "Nobody has a higher respect for Frenchmen than I have, but I will not stand for anyone telling me that I have to listen to something in French or I don't count."[5] While Montreal had some great hockey teams, "they always had to have some English on the team, [Doug] Harvey and Elmer Lach and this Dryden fella today. Know why that is? Because the English may not be able to rise as high as the French, but they never sink as low, either."[6]

He didn't like René Lévesque, the separatist leader who had been involved in a fatal road accident that killed a homeless man. "I don't want to live next door to a province that's got a guy at the head of it who can't drive his own car."[7] Yet he thought Quebec had produced the best prime ministers, and all of them Liberals – Sir Wilfrid Laurier, Louis St. Laurent, and even Pierre Trudeau, who had failed to join the volunteer army when he had the chance in the 1940s but won Smythe's respect with his no-nonsense treatment of separatists. "He's a wily Frenchman and if you get a wily Frenchman there's nothing wilier. We're lucky to have him as the head of our government. He's the best thing that's happened to Canada for a long time."[8]

His relations with Harold Ballard were hard to decipher. He called Ballard an "old friend," but added, "I wouldn't give him a job at 10 cents a week." Ballard was a pirate and a rogue, typical of the money-grubbing attitude of the times, he said, while simultaneously criticizing the newspapers for treating Ballard harshly when he got out of prison.

In 1974, he wrote Ballard a letter suggesting he should be named "president of the year" even though the Leafs had placed fourth in their eight-team division, lost in the quarter finals of the playoffs, and traded the rights to Bernie Parent, the league's best goalie, to Philadelphia. A year later he supported Ballard as a candidate for the Hall of Fame, attesting, "I know of nobody who has done more legwork for hockey." By then Ballard was well into his campaign to drive Tommy Smythe from the Gardens. Ballard sent him his first eviction notice three weeks after Stafford's funeral and a few months later fired him from his job as manager of the Marlboros.[9] But Conn – perhaps to protect Tommy – made a determined effort to coexist peacefully with Ballard, and when he needed a wealthy donor to help achieve one of his last great charitable campaigns, construction of the Ontario Community Centre for the Deaf, he went to Ballard and showed him the floor plan. "Here's a chance for you to do good," Smythe told him. Ballard "just reached for a cheque."

Smythe became involved with the deaf after meeting a charismatic Baptist preacher and former athlete named Rev. Bob Rumball. Smythe arranged a meeting, intent on talking Rumball into joining the Crippled Children's Society and ended up a convert to Rumball's own campaign to build a combination school, residence, and community centre for the deaf. "I came to think of him as about the closest thing I have ever met to a true apostle," Smythe said.[10]

Rumball wanted to buy an estate across the street from the Granite Club, an exclusive haunt for upper-class Torontonians. Smythe, at age eighty-one, threw himself into the effort. The estate could be had for $900,000; transforming it would be another $5 million. Smythe tapped his extensive file of wealthy friends and contacts, approached various foundations, and helped wheedle money out of the provincial government. But Canada's economy had been hit by the twin forces of inflation and stagnation, and individual donors proved hard to come by. In April 1977, he was stewing over the situation while driving with

Margaret Grose, who had been Irene's night nurse and became Smythe's nurse and companion a few years after Irene's death, when he became violently ill. They pulled over to a restaurant, where Grose realized he was suffering a heart attack. She quickly contacted a hospital in nearby Brampton, where he spent most of the next two weeks before being transferred downtown to Wellesley Hospital.

The possibility that the builder of Maple Leaf Gardens might be dying galvanized attention. Cards and letters poured in. He used the attention to plump for the community centre. "We only need $400,000 to meet our goal and we can begin," he said. "There is a lot more Christianity in this world than people think. . . . There are more good people than bad, but the bad ones get all the publicity. It's time the good ones got some attention."[11] It helped, though it would still be two years before ground was broken.

Smythe had been hunting for some time for someone to tell the story of his life. In 1970, he reached a handshake agreement with columnist Dick Beddoes, who shared his enthusiasm for the racetrack. He wanted a book that told "the true story of how a young, poor Canadian kid can make it all the way if he takes advantage of all the good people and all the good teachings of his parents, and the great country we live in."[12]

Beddoes conducted a series of interviews and wrote up some notes in the form of individual features. But the project lagged, and in 1972 Smythe suggested they cancel the plan. He came back to it several years later, telling Beddoes, "Kids are desperately looking for somewhere to get strength from, with the critics so openly castigating everything good, like the worthy teachings of Jesus Christ, and the parables."[13]

But Beddoes declined and Smythe found an alternative, coming to a more formal agreement with Scott Young, the author and sportswriter who had followed his activities since the 1950s. Young suggested the book should be in the form of an autobiography narrated by Smythe. "A man writing his autobiography is entitled to say whatever he thinks is right, whereas in a biography there is an obligation on the author (for instance, me) to broaden the field of fire, even to make judgments."[14] It was a canny suggestion, enabling Smythe to put both his story and his personality into the pages they produced.

Young threw himself into the project with enthusiasm, noting that "time is of the essence." Smythe was eighty-five and ailing; the project would require lengthy sessions in which he relived his life for Young's microphone. Young put other projects on hold and reduced his newspaper workload. His goal was to finish within a year, in time for the fiftieth anniversary of Maple Leaf Gardens in 1981. Smythe would pay him $50,000 plus expenses; all royalties were to go to a personal charitable foundation Smythe had established.

There was less time than either appreciated. Smythe was in near constant pain, his legs aching, his energy slipping away. He weighed less than 130 pounds and railed at the endless supply of pills the doctors insisted he take. Smythe would record his thoughts on tapes and give them to Young, or rise in the night and scribble down episodes from the past. His voice on the tapes was sometimes strong, especially as he rehashed old quarrels or roused himself into indignation at the inequities of the world. He was an old man and he had an old man's complaints: people didn't work hard enough, there was too much concern for the lazy, people didn't appreciate how easy they had it and how hard earlier generations had worked. When he spoke of Irene he could be bombastic – "We didn't argue. I went ahead. We made a deal, I was the boss and she was the wife" – or meek, almost tearful. "She was a lovely little lady. She gave me all the love she could give." There was a time, he confessed, when Irene lost interest in their love life and he had looked elsewhere, though as usual he had standards: no married women, no smokers, no drinkers, no prostitutes. Young asked if he wanted that in the book; Smythe said do whatever you want. He left it out.

He was often harsh, dragging up the old quarrels with Selke and denouncing him anew as disloyal. (In his 1962 memoirs, Selke revealed using a lithograph of King George VI to line one of his chicken pens, an offence Smythe would have considered treasonous.) He treated

Harold Ballard more charitably than he did Clarence Campbell, who had served his interests patiently for two decades. But he was also honest about himself, acknowledging the difficulties he had created for many of the people closest to him. He emphasized how lucky he had been, and how overwhelmed he was at the extent he had benefited from the help and faith of others. He declared himself a committed theosophist, a conclusion he had come to in the latter part of his life. He believed in "The Man Upstairs," "as ye sow, so shall ye reap," and "cast your bread upon the waters." He told Young at one session: "I guess I'm like everybody else, I'm a good guy if I get my own way. The reason I like to get my own way is that I've found I'm right more than the other guy."[15]

Young admired Smythe and wrote to the Governor-General nominating him for the Order of Canada. An aide wrote back enthusiastically, noting that others had also put his name forward. But Smythe, unyielding as ever, wrote Trudeau: "I hear I have been nominated for the Order of Canada. I suppose this letter will blow my chances . . ." and went on to complain about bilingualism. He didn't get the medal.[16]

In late August, he returned to Caledon one day and, despite feeling weak, decided to go for a swim. Jessie Watson, still keeping house and caring for him after fifty years, watched from the house as he splashed toward the deep end, then slowly began to sink. One arm stopped moving, then the other. She managed to reach the pool before he drowned, plunged in, and struggled to haul him to the edge, though she was in her seventies herself and he had all the weight of the inert. His eyes fluttered and he seemed to see her, but he had no strength and once they reached the ladder was unable to climb out. She put her head against his backside and pushed, then dragged him to his feet and to a pole, ordering him to hold on while she got help. As she ran for assistance she heard him yell and looked back to see him vomiting violently while simultaneously losing control of his bowels.[17]

He faded slowly through the fall, spending more and more time in bed. Tommy visited frequently, and one day steeled himself to ask if there were any plans he would like made. "I guess I'm not going to get better this time, am I?" his grandfather responded. They planned his funeral, his pallbearers, and where the memorial service should be held. He felt so good afterwards he asked for champagne.

Young continued to visit and transcribe the results of their talks, hurrying to finish. Sometimes, when he read back what he'd written, Smythe seemed not to hear. On his notes of the sessions, there is a final scribble on a scrap of paper: "Went back in November twice, but he was not well enough to talk, although he listened to last two chapters with enjoyment."

Smythe died at Baby Point on November 18, 1980, just a week after Remembrance Day.*

* Smythe was buried at Park Lawn Cemetery. Also buried at Park Lawn are Busher Jackson, Lou Marsh, Gordon Sinclair, and Harold Ballard, none of whom he liked very much (www.findagrave.com).

NOTES

Foreword

1. Trent Frayne, *The Mad Men of Hockey* (Toronto: McClelland & Stewart, 1974), 150.

2. *Globe and Mail*, October 20, 1980.

3. *Globe and Mail*, July 16, 1944.

4. Scott Young, film proposal, 1957, Conn Smythe fonds, Archives of Ontario.

Chapter 1

1. Dan Diamond, *Total Stanley Cup* (Kingston, New York: Total Sports Publishing, 2000), 5.

2. Andrew Podnieks, *Lord Stanley's Cup* (Toronto: Fenn Publishing, 2004), 4.

3. SS *Sarnia*, manifest, July 1889, www.ancestry.ca.

4. Hugh Smythe, interview by author, February 10, 2010.

5. Frayne, *Mad Men*, 158.

6. Conn Smythe with Scott Young, *If You Can't Beat 'em in the Alley* (Toronto: McClelland & Stewart, 1981), 10.

7. Conn Smythe, interview by Dick Beddoes, undated, Scott Young fonds, #90-003, Trent University Archives.

8. Mike Filey and Victor Russell, *From Horse Power to Horsepower, 1890–1930* (Toronto: Dundurn Press, 1993), 40.

9. Smythe, *If You Can't*, 15.

10. Ibid., 9.

11. June Callwood, *The Naughty Nineties 1890–1900* (Toronto: Natural Science of Canada Ltd., 1977), 44.

12. Conn Smythe speech to St. Michael's College School banquet, April 30, 1946, Conn Smythe fonds, Archives of Ontario.

13. Smythe, *If You Can't*, 11.

14. Toronto Real Estate Board, "Scarborough Village," (www.toronto-realestateboard.com/about_TO/Neighbourhood/regions/scarborough/141.html).

15. Smythe, *If You Can't*, 7.

16. Ibid., 11–13.

17. *Globe and Mail*, December 9, 1929; obituary, *Globe and Mail*, December 7, 1929; William Findlay Maclean, *Dictionary of Canadian Biography Online*, http://www.biographi.ca.

18. Jack Batten, *The Inside Story of Conn Smythe's Hockey Dynasty* (Toronto: Simon & Schuster Canada, 1970), 20.

19. Smythe, *If You Can't*, 13.

20. Ibid., 21–23.

21. Frank Arnoldi, *An Epoch in Canadian History* (Toronto: Upper Canada College Old Boys Association, 1904), 23.

22. Smythe, *If You Can't*, 21.

23. Ibid.

24. Ibid., 13–14.

25. Ibid., 20.

26. Ibid.

27. Michael Barnes, "The Great Clay Belt Hoax," *The Republic of Mining* (blog) June 11, 2008, www.republicofmining.com.

28. Notebook entry, March 1912, Conn Smythe fonds, Archives of Ontario.

Chapter 2

1. Smythe, *If You Can't*, 24.

2. Ibid. 77.

3. Conn Smythe, Beddoes interview, Scott Young fonds, Trent University Archives.

4. Diary entry, winter 1912–13, Conn Smythe's diary, Conn Smythe fonds, Archives of Ontario.

5. Frank J. Selke with Gordon Green, *Behind the Cheering* (Toronto: McClelland & Stewart, 1962), 37; *Canadian Oldtimers Hockey Association Journal*, September–October 1985.

6. Selke, *Behind the Cheering*, 39.

7. Lou Marsh, *Toronto Star*, March 12, 1915.

8. Canadian War Museum, "Canada and the First World War," www.warmuseum.ca/cwm/exhibitions/guerre/canada-at-war-e.aspx.

9. Ibid.

10. Selke, *Behind the Cheering*, 48.

11. J.M.S. Careless, *Toronto to 1918* (Toronto: J. Lorimer, 1984), appendix.

12. Robert Craig Brown, "Sir Robert Borden," *Dictionary of Canadian Biography Online*, www.biographi.ca.

13. Smythe, *If You Can't*, 31.

14. Ibid., 30–40.

15. Selke, *Behind the Cheering*, 82.

16. Albert Smythe letter, Conn Smythe fonds, Archives of Ontario.

17. Brown, "Sir Robert Borden."

18. Smythe, *If You Can't*, 47.

19. Canadian War Museum, "Tanks and Armoured Vehicules," www.warmuseum.ca/cwm/exhibitions/guerre/tanks-vehicles-e.aspx.

20. Smythe, *If You Can't*, 50.

21. Ibid., 51.

22. Veterans Affairs Canada, "The Battle of Vimy Ridge," www.vac-acc.gc.ca/remembers/sub.cfm?source=history/firstwar/vimy/vimy3.

23. Smythe, *If You Can't*, 53.

24. Smythe personal military records, World War One, Library and Archives Canada, CEF Regimental documents, War Service Records, DVA, 9024.

25. Smythe, *If You Can't*, 59.

26. The Vintage Aviator, "RE.8 History," http://thevintageaviator.co.nz/
    projects/re8-reproduction/history

27. Smythe, *If You Can't*, 61.

28. *Toronto World*, November 14, 1917.

29. *Toronto World*, February 24, 1919.

30. Smythe, *If You Can't*, 65.

31. *Toronto World*, February 24, 1919.

32. Smythe, *If You Can't*, 67.

Chapter 3

1. *Toronto Star*, September 29, 1973.

2. Letter to editor, "Not sent on advice of Mr. J. Bassett," September 30,
    1954, Conn Smythe fonds, Archives of Ontario.

3. Smythe, *If You Can't*, 42.

4. Ibid., 42.

5. Ibid., 8.

6. Blavatsky Net – Theosophy, www.blavatsky.net.

7. Smythe, *If You Can't*, 11.

8. Young fonds.

9. Conn Smythe, interview by Ward Cornell, December 1960, Conn
    Smythe fonds, Archives of Ontario.

10. Scott Young, *Hello Canada! The Life and Times of Foster Hewitt*
    (Toronto: Seal Books, 1985), 133–134.

11. Pierre Berton, *The Great Depression, 1929–39* (Toronto: McClelland &
    Stewart, 1990), 58.

12. Smythe personal military records, Library Archives Canada.

13. Smythe, *If You Can't*, 73-74.

14. Hugh Smythe, interview by author, March 30, 2010.

15. Ibid.

16. Smythe, *If You Can't*, 68.

17. Scott Young transcript, Smythe fonds, Archives of Ontario

18. *Globe and Mail*, March 26, 1925.

19. *Globe and Mail*, March 23, 1925.

20. *Toronto Star*, March 24, 1926.

21. *Toronto Star*, March 27, 1926; *Globe and Mail*, March 30, 1926.

22. D'Arcy Jenish, *The Montreal Canadiens: 100 Years of Glory* (Toronto: Doubleday, 2008), 67–68.

23. *Toronto Star*, March 30, 1926.

24. Ibid.

25. Ibid., April 1, 1926.

26. Ibid., April 3, 1926.

Chapter 4

1. Gerald L. Pfeiffer, *The Chicago Blackhawks: A Sixty-Year History* (Chicago: Windy City Publishing, 1986); Brian McFarlane, *Brian McFarlane's Original Six: The Blackhawks* (Toronto: Stoddart, 2001).

2. Frank Boucher with Trent Frayne, *When the Rangers Were Young* (New York: Dodd, Mead, 1973), 75.

3. Eric Whitehead, *The Patricks: Hockey's Royal Family* (Toronto: Doubleday, 1980), 155.

4. Smythe fonds, Archives of Ontario.

5. Smythe, *If You Can't*, 80.

6. Ibid., 80–81.

7. Boucher, *When the Rangers*, 90.

8. Ibid.

9. Ibid., 69.

10. Ibid., 70.

11. Ibid.

12. Ed Fitkin, *Footloose and Fancy Free*, undated, Conn Smythe file, Hockey Hall of Fame and Museum.

13. *Toronto Star*, November 11, 1961.

14. Marsh, *Toronto Star*, October 26, 1926.

Chapter 5

1. Young fonds.

2. Boucher, *When the Rangers*, 73.

3. Whitehead, *The Patricks*, 163.

4. Smythe, *If You Can't*, 84.

5. *Toronto Star*, May 10, 1957.

6. Boucher, *When the Rangers*, 2.

7. Ibid., 6.

8. Ibid., 83–84.

9. Ibid., 10.

10. Ibid.

11. Smythe, *If You Can't*, 85.

12. Ibid.

13. Smythe fonds, Archives of Ontario

14. Marsh, *Toronto Star*, March 12, 1927.

15. W.A. Hewitt, *Down the Stretch: Recollections of a Pioneer Sportsman and Journalist* (Toronto: Ryerson Press, 1958), 46.

16. W.A. Hewitt, *Toronto Star*, April 2, 1927.

17. Smythe, *If You Can't*, 87.

18. Young fonds.

Chapter 6

1. Smythe, *If You Can't*, 86.

2. Jenish, *The Montreal Canadiens*, 54.

3. *Globe and Mail*, *Toronto Star*, February 15, 1927.

4. Morey Holzman and Joseph Nieforth, *Deceptions and Doublecross: How the NHL Conquered Hockey* (Toronto: Dundurn, 2002), 298.

5. Conn Smythe speech, Toronto Maple Leaf club banquet, October 1945, Conn Smythe fonds, Archives of Ontario.

6. Smythe, *If You Can't*, 128.

7. Trent Frayne, "Ice Man," *Collier's*, January 24, 1948.

8. Holzman, *Deceptions*, 300.

9. Bruce Kidd, *The Struggle for Canadian Sport* (Toronto: University of Toronto Press, 1996), 198.

10. Arena Gardens contract, 1927, Conn Smythe fonds, Archives of Ontario.

11. Frayne, *Mad Men*, 127.

12. Ibid., 71.

13. Holzman, *Deceptions*, 204.

14. Foster Hewitt, *Hockey Night in Canada* (Toronto: Ryerson Press, 1958), 75–76.

15. Stan Fischler, *The Greatest Players and Moments of the Boston Bruins* (Champaign, IL: Sports Publishing, 2000), 111–112.

16. *Toronto Star,* April 14, 1927.

17. Smythe, *If You Can't*, 128.

18. Young fonds.

19. Batten, *Hockey Dynasty*, 44.

20. Fischler, *Greatest Players*, 265.

21. Young fonds.

22. Smythe, *If You Can't*, 93.

23. John Chi-Kit Wong, *The Lords of the Rinks: The Emergence of the NHL 1875–1936* (Toronto: University of Toronto Press, 2005), 95.

24. Foster Hewitt, *Down the Ice: Hockey Contacts and Reflections* (Toronto: S. J. R. Saunders, 1934), 8.

25. Selke, *Behind the Cheering*, 77.

26. *Toronto Star,* November 8, 1927.

27. *Toronto Star*, October 27, 1927.

28. Conn Smythe, speech to St. Michael's Majors, April 30, 1946, Conn Smythe fonds, Archives of Ontario.

29. *Toronto Star*, November 2, 1927.

30. *Toronto Star*, November 16, 1927.

31. Ibid.

Chapter 7

1. Smythe, *If You Can't*, 95.

2. *Toronto Star,* January 21, 1928.

3. Smythe, *If You Can't*, 94.

4. *Toronto Star*, October 30, 1947.

5. W. A. Hewitt, *Toronto Star*, February 6, 1928, 10.

6. Ibid.

7. Smythe, *If You Can't*, 93.

8. *Toronto Star*, March 8, 1928.

9. Smythe, *If You Can't*, 94–95.

10. Boucher, *When the Rangers*, 118–121.

11. Red Horner, biography, Hockey Hall of Fame and Museum.

12. Jack Batten, *The Leafs: An Anecdotal History of the Toronto Maple Leafs* (Toronto: Key Porter, 1994), 21.

13. Kidd, *Canadian Sport*, 210-211.

14. Selke, *Behind the Cheering*, 53.

15. Ibid., 45.

16. Ibid., 52.

17. Frank J. Selke tribute booklet, 8. Courtesy of Frank Selke Jr.

18. Selke, *Behind the Cheering*, 55.

19. Scott Young, *Globe and Mail Magazine*, January 29, 1966.

20. Hewitt, *Hockey Night in Canada*, 102.

21. Ibid., 102–103.

22. Frayne, *Mad Men*, 95.

23. Ibid.

24. *Toronto Star*, March 21, 1929.

25. *Gentleman from Toronto* magazine, undated, Conn Smythe fonds, Archives of Ontario.

26. Smythe, *If You Can't*, 99.

27. Selke, *Behind the Cheering*, 82.

28. *Evening Telegram*, September 22, 1930.

29. King Clancy and Brian McFarlane, *Clancy: The King's Story* (Toronto: ECW Press, 1997), 50.

30. Anne M. Logan, *Rare Jewel for a King: A Tribute to King Clancy* (Erin, ON: Boston Mills Press, 1986), 40.

31. Clancy, *Clancy*, 51.

32. Ibid.

33. Wong, *Lords of the Rinks*, 123 and appendices E, F, and G.

34. Logan, *Rare Jewel*, 37.

35. Ibid., 39.

Chapter 8

1. Memorandum of Agreement between Arena Gardens, Ltd. and St. Patricks/TML Hockey Club, July 23, 1927, Conn Smythe fonds, Archives of Ontario.

2. Smythe fonds, Archives of Ontario

3. *Globe and Mail*, November 15, 1930.

4. *Toronto Star*, March 10, 1929.

5. *Toronto Star*, September 11, 1929.

6. *Toronto Star*, November 13, 1929.

7. *Globe and Mail*, November 5, 1929.

8. Michael Benedict and D'Arcy Jenish, eds., *Canada on Ice: 50 Years of Great Hockey from the Archives of Maclean's* (Toronto: Viking, 1998), 59.

9. Scott Young, *The Boys of Saturday Night: Inside Hockey Night in Canada* (Toronto: Macmillan of Canada, 1990), 38.

10. Foster Hewitt, *Foster Hewitt: His Own Story* (Toronto: Ryerson Press, 1967), 36; Young, *Hello Canada!*, 48.

11. *Globe and Mail*, September 3, 1930.

12. *Toronto Star*, October 21, 1930.

13. Official hockey program, Arena Gardens, November 1930, Fonds 70, Series 306, Subseries 1, File 23, City of Toronto Archives.

14. John Clare, "Conn Smythe's Wondrous Pleasure Dome," *Maclean's*, March 1, 1958, 27.

15. *Mail and Empire*, January 9, 1931.

16. *Toronto Star*, January 17, 1931.

17. T. Eaton fonds, *Correspondence of James Elliott*, Archives of Ontario

18. Mark Osbaldeston, *Unbuilt Toronto: A History of the City That Might Have Been* (Toronto: Dundurn, 2008), 160.

19. T. Eaton fonds, Archives of Ontario.

20. Young, *Boys of Saturday* Night, 42.

21. T. Eaton fonds, Archives of Ontario.

22. Marsh, *Toronto Star*, March 2, 1931.

23. Smythe fonds, Archives of Ontario.

24. T. Eaton fonds, Archives of Ontario.

25. Smythe, *If You Can't*, 104.

26. Selke, *Behind the Cheering*, 97.

27. Hewitt, *Toronto Star*, April 18, 1931.

28. T. Eaton fonds, James Elliott memo, May 27, 1931, Archives of Ontario

29. Maple Leaf Sports and Entertainment, *Maple Leaf Gardens Memories and Dreams, 1931–1999* (Toronto: Maple Leaf Sports and Entertainment, 1999), 45.

30. Toronto Maple Leaf program, November 12, 1931, [Fonds 70, Series 306, Subseries 1, File 25], City of Toronto Archives.

31. Selke, *Behind the Cheering*, 88.

32. Ibid.

33. Ibid., 91.

34. Smythe, *If You Can't*, 108.

35. Ibid., 106.

36. *Toronto Star*, June 23, 1931.

37. Selke, *Behind the Cheering*, 88–89.

38. Smythe, *If You Can't*, 106.

Chapter 9

1. *Toronto Star*, November 24, 1961.

2. T. Eaton fonds, Archives of Ontario.

3. Program, Maple Leaf Gardens, November 12, 1931.

4. *Contract Record and Engineering Review*, 45, n0.45 (November 11, 1931).

5. Smythe, *If You Can't*, 108,

6. Hewitt, *Hockey Night in Canada*, 64.

7. Maple Leaf Sports and Entertainment, *Memories and Dreams*, 55.

8. *Globe and Mail*, September 22, 1931.

9. *Globe and Mail*, October 15, 1931.

10. Marsh, *Toronto Star*, October 23, 1931.

11. *Toronto Star*, March 11, 1931.

12. Selke, *Behind the Cheering*, 92.

13. *Toronto Telegram*, November 13, 1931.

14. *Toronto Star*, November 7, 1931.

15. Hewitt, *His Own Story,* 39–40.

16. Hewitt, *Down the Ice*, 131.

17. Young, *Boys of Saturday Night*, 48.

18. Kidd, *Canadian Sport*, 223.

19. Young, *Boys of Saturday Night*, 49.

20. Smythe, *If You Can't*, 113–114.

21. Hewitt, *His Own Story*, 25.

22. Ibid., 34.

23. Smythe, *If You Can't*, 113.

24. Smythe fonds, Archives of Ontario.

25. Selke, *Behind the Cheering*, 93.

26. Dick Irvin, *Now Back to You Dick: Two Lifetimes in Hockey* (Toronto: McClelland & Stewart, 1988), 34.

27. Smythe, *If You Can't*, 110; Irvin, *Back to You*, 37.

28. Smythe, *If You Can't*, 111.

29. *Toronto Star*, April 6, 1931.

30. Ibid.

31. *Toronto Star*, April 8, 1931.

32. Clancy, *Clancy*, 62.

33. *Globe*, April 11, 1932.

Chapter 10

1. Hewitt, *His Own Story*, 70.

2. Clare, "Pleasure Dome."

3. Hewitt, *His Own Story*, 71.

4. Smythe fonds, Archives of Ontario.

5. Selke, *Behind the Cheering*, 100.

6. Ibid., 63

7. Ibid., 174.

8. Frayne, *Mad Men*, 105; Joan Finnegan, *Tallying the Tales of the Old-Timers* (Burnstown, ON: General Store Publishing, 1998).

9. Smythe, *If You Can't*, 109.

10. Smythe speech, June 12, 1947; Smythe fonds, Archives of Ontario.

11. Hockey notes, summarized by Stafford Smythe, 1950, Smythe fonds, Archives of Ontario.

12. Frayne, *Mad Men*, 106.

13. Smythe, *If You Can't*, 94.

14. Young fonds.

15. Hewitt, *Hockey Night in Canada*, 178.

16. Ibid., 101.

17. Selke, *Behind the Cheering*, 68; Hewitt, *Hockey Night in Canada*, 104.

18. Clancy, *Clancy*, 77–78.

19. Selke, *Behind the Cheering*, 67.

20. Ibid., 178–179.

21. Clancy, *Clancy*, 41.

22. *Globe*, April 3, 1933.

23. *Toronto Star*, January 30, 1933.

24. *Detroit News*, April 2, 1945.

25. *Life*, March 5, 1951.

26. Andy Lytle, *Toronto Star*, October 17, 1949.

27. Smythe, *If You Can't*, 137.

28. Bob Baun with Anne Logan, *Lowering the Boom* (Toronto: Stoddart, 2000), 86.

29. Wong, *Lords of the Rinks*, 100.

30. Frayne, *Mad Men*, 158.

31. Smythe, *If You Can't*, 128.

32. Selke, *Behind the Cheering*, 122–123.

33. Frayne, *Mad Men*, 155.

34. Smythe, *If You Can't*, 129.

35. "A Rough Time on the Road," Stan Fischler, *Sports Illustrated*, February 10, 1964.

36. Batten, *The Leafs*, 22.

37. Selke, *Behind the Cheering*, 113.

38. *Toronto Star*, December 13, 1933.

39. *Toronto Star*, December 14, 1933.

40. Selke, *Behind the Cheering*, 116.

41. *Toronto Star*, January 13, 1934.

42. *Toronto Star*, December 14, 1933.

43. Ibid.

44. *Toronto Star*, December 15, 1933.

45. *Toronto Star*, January 9, 1934.

46. Frayne, *Mad Men*, 137.

47. Ibid., 156.

48. *Toronto Star*, February 14, 1934.

49. Smythe fonds, Archives of Ontario.

Chapter 11

1. Young fonds.

2. Smythe, *If You Can't*, 90.

3. Young, *Hello Canada!*, 80.

4. Frank Selke Jr., interview by author, July 26, 2010.

5. David Macfarlane, *Saturday Night*, December 1981, 39.

6. *Toronto Star*, March 14, 1949.

7. Smythe, *If You Can't*, 132.

8. *Toronto Star*, June 13, 1933.

9. *Toronto Star* and *Globe and Mail*, June 20, 1933.

10. *Toronto Star*, June 23, 1933.

11. *Toronto Star*, November 24, 1961.

12. Smythe, *If You Can't*, 119.

13. Selke, *Behind the Cheers*, 98.

14. Smythe, *If You Can't*, 119.

15. Frayne, *Mad Men*, 73.

16. David Cruise and Alison Griffiths, *Net Worth: Exploding the Myth of Professional Hockey* (Toronto: Viking, 1991), 39–40.

17. Ibid., 32.

18. Ibid.

19. Smythe, *If You Can't*, 115–116.

20. *Toronto Star*, November 8, 1947.

21. Hugh Smythe, interview by author, February 20, 2010.

Chapter 12

1. *Toronto Star*, December 11, 1936; *Globe and Mail*, December 17, 1936.

2. *Toronto Star*, November 14, 1936.

3. Lytle, *Toronto Star*, November 24, 1936.

4. *Toronto Star*, November 28, 1936.

5. *Toronto Star*, November 26, 1936.

6. Smythe, *If You Can't*, 138.

7. Ibid.

8. Dick Irvin, *The Habs: An Oral History of the Montreal Canadiens 1940–80* (Toronto: McClelland & Stewart, 1991), 22–23.

9. Smythe fonds, Archives of Ontario.

10. Smythe fonds, Archives of Ontario.

11. Smythe, *If You Can't*, 139.

12. Speech, June 12, 1947, Archives of Ontario.

13. Smythe memo, July 17, 1940, Archives of Ontario.

14. Smythe, *If You Can't*, 143.

15. Jenish, *Montreal Canadiens*, 85.

16. Irvin, *The Habs*, 14.

17. Smythe fonds, Archives of Ontario.

18. Smythe, *If You Can't*, 145.

19. Ibid., 143.

20. Letter October 2, 1940, Smythe fonds, Archives of Ontario.

21. Smythe, *If You Can't*, 141–143.

22. Ibid., 149.

23. Ibid., 146–147.

24. Letter, March 6, 1941, Smythe fonds, Archives of Ontario.

25. Smythe fonds, Archives of Ontario.

26. Canadian Science and Technology Museum, "Andrew McNaughton 1887–1966," www.sciencetech.technomuses.ca.

27. Letter June 1940, Smythe fonds, Archives of Ontario.

28. Ibid.

29. Beddoes, Young fonds.

30. Ibid.

31. Atkinson letter, March 9, 1942, Smythe files, Archives of Ontario.

32. Clark letter, March 26, 1941 Smythe files, Archives of Ontario.

33. *Globe and Mail*, April 13, 1942.

34. Ibid.

35. *Globe and Mail*, April 14, 1942.

36. *Globe and Mail*, April 18, 1942.

37. *Globe and Mail*, April 20, 1942.

38. Ibid.

39. Smythe, *If You Can't*, 146.

40. Ibid, 145.

41. Smythe fonds, Archives of Ontario.

42. Smythe fonds, Archives of Ontario.

43. Smythe fonds, Archives of Ontario.

Chapter 13

1. Brereton Greenhous, "Dieppe Raid," *The Canadian Encyclopedia*, www.thecanadianencyclopedia.com.

2. Smythe, *If You Can't*, 147.

3. *Boston American*, November 11, 1944.

4. Smythe fonds, Archives of Ontario.

5. Ibid.

6. Douglas Hunter, *War Games: The Story of Conn Smythe and Hockey's Fighting Men* (Toronto: Penguin, 1997), 92.

7. Smythe fonds, Archives of Ontario.

8. Young fonds.

9. Walker letter, December 1, 1943/43. Smythe fonds, Archives of Ontario.

10. Ibid, March 24, 1943.

11. Smythe, *If You Can't*, 156.

12. Ralph Allen, *Globe and Mail*, July 25, 1944.

13. Allen, *Globe and Mail*, July 31, 1944.

Chapter 14

1. Smythe, *If You Can't*, 165.

2. *Toronto Star,* July 31, 1944.

3. Smythe, *If You Can't*, 163.

4. Frederick Griffin, *Toronto Star,* July 29, 1944.

5. *Toronto Star*, September 18, 1944.

6. Ibid.

7. Smythe, *If You Can't*, 65.

8. *Globe and Mail*, September 19, 1944.

9. J. L. Granatstein, *Canada's War: The Politics of the Mackenzie King Government, 1939–1945* (Toronto: Oxford University Press, 1975), 336. Note: The figures for Canada's Zombie army varied wildly at the time, and afterward. The 60,000 figure was used by Ralston and is the one most commonly quoted.

10. Diaries of William Lyon Mackenzie King (online), September 19, 1944.

11. Hunter, *War Games*, 138.

12. *Toronto Telegram*, September 19, 1944.

13. Smythe fonds, Archives of Ontario.

14. Smythe fonds, Archives of Ontario.

15. Smythe fonds, Archives of Ontario.

16. Lytle, *Toronto Star*, September 2, 1944.

17. Lytle, *Toronto Star*, September 5, 1944.

18. Lytle, *Toronto Star*, September 20, 1944.

19. Editorial, *Ottawa Journal*, reprinted in *Globe and Mail*, September 23, 1944.

20. Ibid.

21. Ibid.

22. *Globe and Mail*, September 22, 1944.

23. Hunter, *War Games*, 148–149.

24. Smythe, *If You Can't*, 169.

25. King diaries, February, 27, 1939.

26. Ibid., November 11, 1942.

27. Grattan O'Leary, *The George Drew I Knew* (Montreal: Woodward, undated), 2.

28. Pierre Berton, *Marching as to War: Canada's Turbulent Years, 1899–1953* (Toronto: Doubleday Canada, 2001), 334–339; Jonathan Manthorpe, *The Power and the Tories: Ontario Politics, 1943 to the Present* (Toronto: Macmillan of Canada, 1974).

29. George Drew papers, Library Archives Canada, October 5, 1944.

30. Hugh Smythe, interview by author, February 20, 2010.

31. Smythe, *If You Can't*, 172.

32. Smythe fonds, Archives of Ontario.

33. Ibid.

34. Ibid.

35. King diaries, October 5, 1944.

36. Ibid.

37. Smythe, *If You Can't*, 170.

38. Hunter, *War Games*, 175.

39. Ibid., 179.

40. Richard S. Malone, *Missing from the Record* (Toronto: William Collins and Sons, 1946), 150.

41. Ibid., 153.

42. King diaries, October 13, 1944.

43. Ibid., October 25, 1944.

44. Granatstein, *Canada's War*, 357.

45. Smythe, *If You Can't*, 171.

46. Ibid., 168.

47. R. MacGregor Dawson, *The Conscription Crisis of 1944* (Toronto: University of Toronto Press, 1961), 2.

48. King diaries, March 7, 1945.

Chapter 15

1. *Toronto Star*, December 8, 1944.

2. *Toronto Star*, November 12, 1944.

3. *Toronto Star*, April 6, 1944.

4. Smythe, *If You Can't*, 175.

5. Ibid., 176.

6. *Toronto Star,* October 3, 1945.

7. Smythe fonds, Archives of Ontario.

8. *Toronto Star,* October 15, 1945.

9. *Toronto Star,* October 17, 1945.

10. *Toronto Star,* October 18, 1945.

11. Lytle, *Toronto Star,* February 1, 1946.

12. *Toronto Star,* February 15, 1946.

13. Smythe fonds, Archives of Ontario.

14. Ibid.

15. Ibid.

16. Smythe, *If You Can't,* 178.

17. Lytle, *Toronto Star,* February 23, 1946.

18. Joe Perlove, *Toronto Star,* March 23, 1946.

19. Gordon Walker, *Toronto Star,* March 30, 1946.

20. Ted Reeve, undated telegram, Hockey Hall of Fame files, Frank Selke.

21. Frank Selke Jr., interview by author, August 23, 2010.

22. *Globe and Mail,* May 31, 1946.

23. *Montreal Star,* July 10, 1946.

Chapter 16

1. Smythe fonds, Archives of Ontario.

2. Young fonds.

3. J. V. McAree, *Globe and Mail,* October 4, 1947.

4. Smythe fonds, Archives of Ontario.

5. *Globe and Mail,* November 27, 1947.

6. *Toronto Star,* November 21, 1947.

7. Smythe, *If You Can't,* 179.

8. Frayne, "Ice Man."

9. Hugh Smythe, interview by author.

10. Kevin Shea, *Barilko: Without a Trace* (Toronto: Fenn, 2004), 5.

11. Ibid., 22–23.

12. Jack Batten, *The Leafs in Autumn* (Toronto: Macmillan of Canada, 1975), 43.

13. Richard Kincaide, *The Gods of Olympia Stadium: Legends of the Detroit Red Wings* (Champaign, IL: Sports Publishing LLC, 2003), 52.

14. Shea, *Barilko*, 89.

15. Ibid, 100.

16. www.legendsofhockey.net.

17. Batten, *Leafs in Autumn*, 31–32.

18. Ibid., 33.

19. Smythe fonds, Archives of Ontario.

20. Charlie Hodge, *Golly Gee It's Me: The Howie Meeker Story* (Toronto: Stoddart, 1996), 92.

21. Ibid., 94–95.

22. *Globe and Mail*, April 21, 1947.

23. *Toronto Star*, April 19, 1947.

24. Baz O'Meara, *Montreal Star*, October 1946.

25. *Montreal Herald*, October 29, 1946.

26. *Globe and Mail*, October 28, 1946.

27. *Toronto Star*, April 9, 1947.

28. Perlove, *Toronto Star*, April 11, 1947.

29. Ibid.

30. Gaye Stewart, interview by author, July 27, 2010.

31. *Globe and Mail*, October 28, 1947.

32. Max Bentley, www.legendsofhockey.net.

33. Hugh Smythe, interview by author.

34. *Saturday Night*, December 8, 1951.

35. Batten, *Leafs in Autumn*, 109.

36. *Globe and Mail*, November 30, 1949.

37. Frayne, *Mad Men*, 152.

38. *Toronto Star*, November 11, 1949.

39. *Globe and Mail*, December 1, 1949.

40. *Toronto Star*, December 2, 1949.

41. *Globe and Mail*, December 3, 1949.

42. Batten, *Leafs in Autumn*, 87.

43. Hugh Smythe, interview by author.

44. Ibid.

45. Milt Dunnell, *Toronto Star*, February 1, 1951.

46. Ibid.

47. Shea, *Barilko*, 131.

Chapter 17

1. Marshall Smith, *Life*, March 5, 1951, 84.

2. Bunny Morganson, *Hockey News*, January 6, 1949.

3. Trent Frayne, *Maclean's*, January 15, 1952.

4. Ibid.

5. *Saturday Night*, December 8, 1951.

6. Hockey Hall of Fame, Smythe file, undated.

7. Smythe, *If You Can't*, 185.

8. Smythe fonds, Archives of Ontario.

9. Ibid.

10. Ibid.

11. Hodge, *Golly Gee*, 204.

12. Howie Meeker, interview by author, October 7, 2010.

13. Smythe, *If You Can't*, 197.

14. Frank Selke, letter, May 1, 1953, courtesy of Frank Selke Jr.

15. Smythe, *If You Can't*, 191.

16. *Globe and Mail*, February 21, 1951.

17. Smythe fonds, Archives of Ontario.

18. Ibid.

19. *Toronto Star*, February 1, 1955.

20. Smythe fonds, Archives of Ontario.

21. Kevin Shea, *St. Michael's College: 100 Years of Pucks and Prayers* (Toronto: Fenn, 2008), 9.

22. Ibid., 32.

23. Dick Duff, interview by author, July 24, 2010.

24. Ibid.

25. Ted Mahovlich, *The Big M: The Frank Mahovlich Story* (Toronto: HarperCollins, 1999), 16–17.

26. Smythe fonds, Archives of Ontario.

27. Mahovlich, *Big M*, 29.

28. Selke, *Behind the Cheering*, 116.

29. Smythe fonds, Archives of Ontario.

30. Shea, *St. Michael's* College, 33.

Chapter 18

1. Hugh Smythe, interview by author.

2. Batten, *Leafs of Autumn*, 5.

3. Smythe, *If You Can't*, 64.

4. Smythe fonds, Archives of Ontario.

5. *Globe and Mail*, March 25, 1957.

6. Smythe fonds, Archives of Ontario.

7. Hugh Smythe, interview by author.

8. Jim Gregory, interview by author, September 1, 2010.

9. Frank Selke Jr., interview by author, August 23, 2010.

10. Dick Beddoes, *Pal Hal: An Uninhibited, No-Holds Barred Account of the Life and Times of Harold Ballard* (Toronto: Macmillan of Canada, 1989), 83.

11. Ibid.

12. Jim Gregory, interview by author, September 1, 2010.

13. Smythe fonds, Archives of Ontario.

14. Howie Meeker, interview by author, October 7, 2010.

15. Smythe fonds, Archives of Ontario.

16. Irvin, *The Habs,* 107.

17. Smythe fonds, Archives of Ontario.

18. Smythe fonds , Archives of Ontario.

19. *Toronto Star*, March 25, 1957.

20. *Toronto Star*, March 13, 1957.

21. *Toronto Star*, March 18, 1957.

22. Ibid.

23. *Globe and Mail*, March 25, 1957.

24. *Globe and Mail*, March 26, 1957.

25. *Globe and Mail*, March 27, 1957.

26. *Toronto Star* and *Globe and Mail*, March 28, 1957.

27. *Toronto Star*, March 11, 1957.

28. Smythe fonds, Archives of Ontario.

29. Smythe, *If You Can't*, 199–200.

30. Canada's Sports Hall of Fame, www.sporthall.ca.

31. Hodge, *Golly Gee*, 221.

32. Ibid., 224.

33. Smythe fonds, October 3, 1957.

34. Dick Irvin, interview by author, July 31, 2010.

35. Irvin, *Now Back to You Dick*, 39.

Chapter 19

1. Dick Duff, interview by author, July 24, 2010.

2. Frank Mahovlich, interview by author, August 18, 2010.

3. Bob Baun, interview by author, August 16, 2010.

4. Smythe fonds, Archives of Ontario.

5. Ibid.

6. Howie Meeker, interview by author, October 7, 2010.

7. Smythe fonds, Archives of Ontario.

8. Ibid.

9. Ibid.

Chapter 20

1. *Toronto Star*, May 9, 1957.

2. *Toronto Star*, March 10, 1957.

3. Gordon Campbell, *Toronto Star*, April 10, 1957.

4. Smythe fonds, Archives of Ontario.

5. Selke, *Behind the Cheering*, 156.

6. Smythe fonds, Archives of Ontario.

7. Ibid.

8. *Toronto Star*, January 10, 1973.

9. Smythe fonds, Archives of Ontario.

10. Ibid.

11. Bob Baun, interview by author, August 16, 2010.

12. Hugh Smythe, interview by author, October 6, 2010.

13. *Globe and Mail*, May 18, 1964.

14. Lester Pearson papers, Library and Archives Canada.

15. Ibid.

16. Ibid.

17. Smythe fonds, Archives of Ontario.

18. Ibid.

19. *Toronto Star,* May 19, 1964.

20. Smythe, *If You Can't*, 225.

21. Ibid., 222.

22. Ibid., 227.

23. Ibid., 226.

24. *Globe and Mail*, June 21, 1965.

25. Batten, *The Leafs*, 110.

26. *Toronto Star*, November 24, 1961.

27. Smythe, *If You Can't*, 217.

28. Smythe fonds, Archives of Ontario.

29. *Toronto Star*, June 26, 1969.

30. *Toronto Star*, March 9, 1966.

31. Ibid.

32. *Toronto Star*, August 29, 1966.

33. Young fonds.

34. Frank Selke Jr., interview by author, August 23, 2010.

35. *Toronto Star,* August 29, 1966.

36. *Toronto Star,* February 2, 1951.

37. Smythe fonds, Archives of Ontario.

38. Ibid.

39. Red Burnett, *Toronto Star*, August 25, 1966.

40. *Globe and Mail*, June 27, 1966.

41. *Toronto Star* and *Globe and Mail*, October 1, 1968.

42. Smythe fonds, Archives of Ontario.

43. Thomas Stafford Smythe with Kevin Shea, *Centre Ice*, Fenn; Bolton, Ont; 2000, p. 115.

44. *Toronto Star*, June 27, 1969.

45. Ibid.

46. Hugh Smythe, interview by author, October 6, 2010.

47. Smythe, *If You Can't*, 243.

48. *Globe and Mail*, October 14, 1971.

49. www.cottageblog.ca/2008/11/28/conn-stafford-smythe-rip-in-beautiful-muskoka/

50. Smythe, *If You Can't*, 244.

51. Young fonds.

52. *Toronto Star*, January 30, 1975.

53. Smythe, *If You Can't*, 243.

54. www.cottageblog.ca/2008/11/28/conn-stafford-smythe-rip-in-beautiful-muskoka/

55. *Globe and Mail*, January 5, 1972.

56. Hugh Smythe, interview by author.

Chapter 21

1. *Toronto Telegram*, June 12, 1971.

2. *Globe and Mail*, June 12, 1971.

3. *Toronto Star*, September 29 1973, January 10, 1973.

4. Ibid.

5. *Toronto Star*, February 10, 1973.

6. Jack Batten, "King Conn," *The Canadian*, 1978.

7. Ibid.

8. *Toronto Star*, January 30, 1975.

9. Thomas Stafford Smythe with Kevin Shea, *Centre Ice*, Fenn; Bolton, Ont; 2000, p. 127.

10. Smythe, *If You Can't*, 261.

11. *Globe and Mail*, May 14, 1977.

12. Young fonds.

13. Ibid.

14. Ibid.

15. Ibid.

16. Smythe fonds, Archives of Ontario.

17. Young fonds.

INDEX